MW00629791

These Records Are True

A Teaching Commentary on Jacob through Mosiah

Volume 2

by

Monte S. Nyman

Distributed by:

Granite Publishing and Distribution, L.L.C.
868 North 1430 West
Orem, Utah 84057
(801) 229-9023 • Toll Free (800) 574-5779
Fax (801) 229-1924

Page Layout & Design by Myrna Varga, The Office Connection, Inc.
Cover Design by Steve Gray

Cover Art
"King Benjamin Preaches to the Nephites" by Gary L. Kapp
© by Intellectual Reserve, Inc.

ISBN: 1-932280-30-8
Library of Congress Control Number: 2003115488

First Printing, February 2004

Printed in the United States of America

10 9 8 7 6 5 4 3 2 1

Contents

Introduction

Fifty-five years after Lehi and his party left Jerusalem under the direction of the Lord (about 544 B.C.), Nephi, the son of Lehi and keeper of the small plates of Nephi, turned over the responsibility of the sacred record to his younger brother Jacob (see Jacob 1:1).[1] He instructed Jacob on what he should write upon the plates. It is safe to assume that Jacob considered his instructions as commandments from the Lord as Nephi was the prophet, ruler and teacher of his people. Such commandments are important aids to us today in understanding the role of the Book of Mormon in our lives and in determining what emphasis we should place upon our study of it.

Nephi commanded that Jacob "write upon these plates a few of the things which [he] considered to be most precious; that [he] should not touch, save it were lightly, concerning the history of this people which are called the people of Nephi" (Jacob 1:2). This light touch of history is not to be interpreted as a declaration that history is unimportant. The Nephite history was to be kept upon another set of plates. Jacob and his posterity were commanded to keep, upon the small plates, the more precious happenings, or what may be termed

---

[1] Volume One of this work is a commentary on Nephi's writings.

the spiritual history of the people (see Jacob 1:3; 3:13).

Jacob's people had many revelations, and the spirit of much prophecy from which to select the contents of the smaller plates. Because of "faith and great anxiety, it truly had been made manifest" to Jacob and others those things that were to happen to their people (Jacob 1:5). They "knew of Christ and his kingdom, which should come" (Jacob 1:6) and could select those revelations and prophecies that would be most applicable in the day that the Book of Mormon would come forth. Jacob wrote that although it was difficult to engrave upon the plates, he knew his writings would be permanent and he was concerned for his children and his brethren of future generations (see Jacob 4:1–2).

As he was about to die, Jacob turned over the keeping of the records to his son Enos (Jacob 7:27). The records kept by Jacob and Enos make up twenty-one pages in our current edition, covering just four specific incidents. Their writings show that they followed Nephi's admonition not to engrave history upon the small plates. The books of Jarom and Omni cover 290 years in four and a half pages. They both speak to just one central theme, "Inasmuch as ye will not keep [the Lord's] commandments ye shall not prosper in the land" (Omni 1:6). This certainly is not history.

If the Book of Mormon is not a history of people in the Americas, what is it? The Lord calls it "a record of a fallen people, and the fulness of the gospel of Jesus Christ to the Gentiles and to the Jews also" (D&C 20:9). A record is an official written document, not a systematic narrative account or story. So what we have in the small plates of Nephi is an official document from the Lord, a record given to us so we might know how we must live in order to prosper in the land of promise, the Americas.

After Mormon wrote the Words of Mormon to bridge the gap between the smaller plates of Nephi and the large plates that gave "a full account of the history of [Nephi's] people (1 Nephi 9:2), he abridged the book of Mosiah, which is also included in this volume.

The book of Mosiah begins when King Benjamin is an old man, and the first six chapters record his last instructions to his people immediately prior to appointing his son Mosiah to succeed him as king (124 B.C.). It covers about forty years to 90 B.C., including an estimate of the period of King Benjamin's last years.

A more detailed account of Nephite events are given in Mosiah, even though it is an abridgment. This is probably because the time period prior to the birth of Christ (covered in the book of Mosiah) somewhat parallels the time period of the restoration of the gospel prior to the Second Coming of Christ. Mormon stops periodically to write to the modern reader. He addresses them with such phrases as "thus we see" and "I will show unto you" similar to Nephi's style of writing to the reader. A more detailed explanation of these precepts given by the record keepers is given in the introduction of volume one of this work. Also these precepts are identified in the various chapters that follow.

Chapter One

The Sins of Pride and Immorality

Jacob 1–3

*H*istorical Synopsis: Jacob, son of Lehi, begins his record fifty-five years after they left Jerusalem (Jacob 1:1), or 544 B.C. No specific dates are given in his record subsequent to this date. Jacob and Enos, son of Jacob, together cover about one hundred and twenty-four years. Enos turned over his record to his son Jarom in 420 B.C. (Enos 1:23). The actual number of years each was responsible is not given.

These three chapters contain only three incidents: Jacob receiving the records from Nephi (Jacob 1:1–8), Nephi appointing a new king prior to his death (Jacob 1:9–14), and a sermon by Jacob given to the people during the reign of the second king (Jacob 1:15–3:14).

Precepts for this Reading:

Wherefore, we would to God that we could persuade all men not to rebel against God . . . but . . . believe in Christ . . . suffer his cross and bear the shame of the world. [Jacob 1:8]

But before ye seek for riches, seek ye for the kingdom of God. . . . ye shall obtain riches, if ye seek them . . . for the intent to do good. [Jacob 2:18–19]

. . . you that are pure in heart. Look unto God with firmness of

mind, and pray unto him with exceeding faith. . . . receive the
pleasing word of God. [Jacob 3:1–2]

An outline of these chapters to prepare for a deeper study follows.

OUTLINE • JACOB 1–3

Superscription
   a.   The words of his preaching to his brethren.
   b.   He confounded a man seeking to overthrow the doctrine of Christ.
   c.   A few words concerning the history of the people of Nephi.

➤ Jacob 1:1–8 Fifty-five years after Lehi left Jerusalem, Nephi com-
             manded Jacob to write a few things upon these small plates
             that he considered most precious.
   a.   Touch [write] lightly upon the history of this people
        (vv. 2–3).
        1.   The history should be engraven on the other plates
             (large plates).
        2.   These plates were to be handed down from genera-
             tion to generation.
   b.   Engrave as much as possible the heads (most impor-
        tant) of sacred preaching, great revelation, or prophesy-
        ing (v. 4).
        1.   For Christ's sake.
        2.   For the people's sake.
   c.   Because of faith and great anxiety, what would happen
        to this people had been truly manifest (v. 5).
   d.   They had had many revelations and the spirit of proph-
        ecy, and knew of Christ and his kingdom (v. 6).
   e.   They labored diligently to persuade the people to come
        unto Christ, partake of his goodness, and enter into his
        rest; lest they become as the children of Israel in the
        wilderness (vv. 7–8).
        1.   They desired to persuade all men to not rebel
             against God.

    2. To believe in Christ, view his death, suffer his cross, and bear the shame of the world.

    3. Jacob took the responsibility to fulfill the commandment of Nephi.

➤ 1:9–14   Nephi began to be old, and knowing he would soon die, he anointed a man to be a king and a ruler over his people.

    a. The people loved Nephi, and to retain a remembrance of his name, called those who reigned in his stead "second" Nephi, "third" Nephi, etc. (vv. 10–11).

       1. He had been a great protector and wielded the sword of Laban in their defense.

       2. He had labored all his days for their welfare.

    b. Nephi died (v. 12).

    c. The people who were not Lamanites were Nephites (vv. 13–14).

       1. They were called Nephites, Jacobites, Josephites, Zoramites, Lamanites, Lemuelites, and Ishmaelites.

       2. Those who sought to destroy the Nephites were called Lamanites.

       3. Those who were friendly to Nephi were called Nephites.

➤ 1:15–19   The people under the reign of the second king began to grow hard in their hearts and indulged in wicked practices.

    a. They have many wives and concubines like David and Solomon of old (v. 15).

    b. They begin to search for gold and silver and are lifted up in (v. 16).

    c. Jacob taught them in the temple, obtaining his errand [assignment] from the Lord in the temple (v. 17).

    d. Jacob and Joseph were consecrated priests and teachers by Nephi (vv. 18–19).

       1. They magnified their office, taking the sins of the people upon themselves if they did not teach them.

      2.   They labored diligently that the people's blood not come upon them.

➤ 2:1–11   The words that Jacob spoke in the temple were to magnify his office and to declare the word of God.

    a.   He has been diligent in his office, but is weighed down for the welfare of their souls (v. 3).

    b.   So far they had been obedient to the word of the Lord (v. 4).

    c.   With the help of the Creator, Jacob knew their thoughts, and that they were beginning to labor in sin, which was abominable to him and God (v. 5).

    d.   Shamed before his Maker, he grieved to testify of their wickedness (v. 6).

    e.   He grieves to use boldness of speech before their wives and children (vv. 7–9).

        1.   He supposes they have come to hear the pleasing word of God.

        2.   He is burdened by the strict command of God to admonish them of their crimes, to enlarge the wounds of the wounded instead of healing them.

    f.   He tells of their wickedness in the presence of the pure in heart and under the piercing eye of the Almighty God (v. 10).

    g.   Jacob was told by the Lord to go to the temple and declare his word (v. 11).

➤ 2:12–21   Many of them have begun to search for gold, silver, and precious ores that is plentiful in the land of promise.

    a.   Some obtain more riches and are lifted up in pride, supposing they are better than their brethren (vv. 13–16).

        1.   God does not justify them but condemns them.

        2.   God will pierce them and smite them to the dust.

        3.   This pride of their hearts will destroy their souls.

    b.   Think of your brethren like unto yourselves, be familiar with all and free with your substance that they may be rich like unto you (v. 17).

   c.   Before you seek for riches seek the kingdom of God (v. 18).

   d.   After you obtain a hope in Christ ye shall obtain riches (v. 19).

      1.   If ye seek them.

      2.   If ye seek them to do good—clothe the naked, feed the hungry, liberate the captive, and administer relief to the sick and the afflicted.

   e.   Pride is abominable to him who created all flesh (vv. 20–21).

      1.   One being is as precious in his sight as the other.

      2.   All flesh was created to keep his commandments and glorify God.

➤ 2:22–33   Jacob must now speak of a grosser crime. The people begin to wax in iniquity and do not understand the scriptures. They excuse themselves because of what is written concerning David and Solomon.

   a.   David and Solomon did have many wives and concubines which was abominable before the Lord (v. 24).

   b.   The Lord led his people out of Jerusalem to raise up a righteous branch of Joseph (vv. 25–28).

      1.   They are not to do like unto them of old.

      2.   A man shall have only one wife and no concubines.

      3.   The Lord delights in the chastity of women, and whoredoms are an abomination before him.

   c.   They shall keep the commandments of God, or cursed be the land (vv. 29–33).

      1.   If the Lord will raise up seed to himself, he will command his people.

      2.   He had seen the sorrows of his daughters in Jerusalem and other lands because of the wickedness and abominations of their husbands.

           3.   The cries of his fair daughters will cause him to curse the land.

➤ 2:34–35   These commandments were given unto father Lehi, and the people knew them before.

        a.   The people are come under great condemnation for breaking them (v. 34).

        b.   The people have done greater iniquities than the Lamanites (v. 35).

            1.   You have broken the hearts of your tender wives and lost the confidence of your children.

            2.   Because of the strictness of the word of God, many hearts died, pierced with deep wounds.

➤ 3:1–2   Jacob speaks to the pure in heart.

        a.   Look to God with firmness of mind, pray with exceeding faith, and he will console you and send justice upon those who seek your destruction (v. 1).

        b.   Receive the pleasing word of God and feast upon his love (v. 2).

➤ 3:3–11   Jacob spoke to those who were not pure in heart.

        a.   Except ye repent, the land is cursed for your sakes (vv. 3–4).

            1.   The Lamanites, who were not filthy, but were cursed, shall scourge you to destruction.

            2.   They will possess your land, and the righteous will be led from among you.

        b.   The Lamanites, whom you hate because of their filthiness and cursing on their skin, are more righteous than you (vv. 5–8).

            1.   They have not forgotten the commandment given to father Lehi.

            2.   They have one wife and no concubines, and no whoredoms are committed.

            3.   They will not be destroyed, and one day will be-

come a blessed people.

4. Their husbands and their wives love each other and their children.

5. Their hatred of the Nephites is caused by the iniquity of their fathers.

6. Unless the Nephites repent the Lamanites will be purer at the judgment bar.

c. Jacob commanded the Nephites, as the word of God, not to revile against the Lamanites, but to remember their own filthiness (vv. 9–10).

1. Their children are grieved because of their poor example.

2. If they bring their children to destruction, their sins will be on your heads.

d. Jacob invited them to hearken to his words, loose themselves from the pains of hell, that they not become angels to the devil and suffer the second death (v. 11).

➤ 3:12–14   Jacob spoke many more things, warning the Nephites of the awful consequences of fornication and lasciviousness (immorality).

a. A hundredth part of the proceedings of this people can not be written on these plates, but many were written on the other larger plates (v. 13).

b. These plates were called the plates of Jacob, and were made by Nephi.

NOTES AND COMMENTARY

Introduction: What is scripture? This question is often asked in and out of the Church. The Lord answered the question in a revelation to Joseph Smith in November 1831:

> Whatsoever they shall speak when moved upon by the Holy Ghost shall be scripture, shall be the will of the Lord, shall be the mind of the Lord, shall be the word of the Lord, shall be the voice of the Lord, and the power of God unto salvation. [D&C 68:4]

When the Lord's servants speak by the Holy Ghost, there are four categories under which their words may fall, as quoted above and interpreted below:

1. The will of the Lord = the commandments that are to be kept.
2. The mind of the Lord = the mysteries of God that are only understood by the Spirit.
3. The word of the Lord = prophesy of the future that will certainly come to pass.
4. The voice of the Lord = personal revelation to guide the needs of his children.

The receiving and following of scripture will bring salvation through the Lord's power. Jacob's record, kept in accordance with Nephi's instruction, is scripture and will fall into all of these four categories.

Superscription: The Book of Jacob— The Brother of Nephi

> The words of his preaching unto his brethren. He confoundeth a man who seeketh to overthrow the doctrine of Christ. A few words concerning the history of the people of Nephi.

The superscription is a preface or overview of the entire book of Jacob. "The words of his preaching" include the sermon on the sins of pride and immorality (Jacob 2), and his comments introducing the allegory of the house of Israel quoted from the plates of brass, and originally written by an Old Testament prophet named Zenos (Jacob 4–6). His confounding "a man [Sherem] who seeketh to overthrow the doctrine of Christ" is the seventh chapter. "A few words concerning the history" are found in chapter 1 and chapter 7.

Jacob 1:1–3 • A Light Touch of History

> 1 For behold, it came to pass that fifty and five years had passed away from the time that Lehi left Jerusalem; wherefore, Nephi gave

me, Jacob, a commandment concerning the small plates, upon which these things are engraven.

2 And he gave me, Jacob, a commandment that I should write upon these plates a few of the things which I considered to be most precious; that I should not touch, save it were lightly, concerning the history of this people which are called the people of Nephi.

3 For he said that the history of his people should be engraven upon his other plates, and that I should preserve these plates and hand them down unto my seed, from generation to generation.

Jacob certainly followed Nephi's instruction to touch lightly the history of his people. Since Jacob was a younger brother of Nephi, he would have been the record keeper during much of Jacob's life. As mentioned above, only two of the seven chapters of our present text would be considered historical. Those two chapters are less than five of the eighteen and one-half pages written by Jacob. It will be interesting to learn the history that was written on "the other plates" (v. 3).

Jacob 1:4–8 • Persuade Them to Come Unto Christ

4 And if there were preaching which was sacred, or revelation which was great, or prophesying, that I should engraven the heads of them upon these plates, and touch upon them as much as it were possible, for Christ's sake, and for the sake of our people.

5 For because of faith and great anxiety, it truly had been made manifest unto us concerning our people, what things should happen unto them.

6 And we also had many revelations, and the spirit of much prophecy; wherefore, we knew of Christ and his kingdom, which should come.

7 Wherefore we labored diligently among our people, that we might persuade them to come unto Christ, and partake of the goodness of God, that they might enter into his rest, lest by any means he should swear in his wrath they should not enter in, as in the provo-

cation in the days of temptation while the children of Israel were in the wilderness.

> 8 Wherefore, we would to God that we could persuade all men not to rebel against God, to provoke him to anger, but that all men would believe in Christ, and view his death, and suffer his cross and bear the shame of the world; wherefore, I, Jacob, take it upon me to fulfil the commandment of my brother Nephi.

All three of the things Nephi instructed Jacob to record—preaching, revelation, and prophesying—would be scripture. They would have been spoken when "moved upon by the Holy Ghost" (D&C 68:2–4). "Preaching which was sacred" could be "the will of the Lord," or the commandments the people were to keep. "Revelation which was great" could be "the mind of the Lord," or the mysteries of God pertaining to their lives. "Prophesying" could be "the word of the Lord," telling what would come to pass in the future. However, Jacob was instructed to limit his engraving to these three sources of sacred speaking to the "heads of them" or the most significant and precious things. The items that Jacob was inspired to include were probably a part of the restoration of principles and concepts that had been lost or needed clarifying in the Bible (see 1 Nephi 13:24–29). All of what was recorded was to be done "for Christ's sake" (Jacob 1:4), to assist him in his work of bringing "to pass the immortality and eternal life of man" (Moses 1:39); and for "the sake of [Jacob's] people" (Jacob 1:4), to bring them to salvation through the Lord's power.

Jacob acknowledges that there had been more preaching, revelation, and prophesying among his people than he was recording. They were fully aware of the coming of Christ to the earth (vv. 5–6). His objective, as well as the objective of other faithful members, was to bring his people to Christ and prepare them to enter into his rest, "which rest is the fulness of his glory" (D&C 84:24). He desired to help his people avoid what happened to the Israelites when led them in the wilderness (Jacob 1:7). Fully aware of the challenges ahead, Jacob accepted the responsibility of leadership given to him by his brother Nephi (v. 8). His desire to persuade all men to forsake the natural man and take upon them the name of Christ is a great example for us to follow. To view Christ's death is to see and understand that he would come to earth to lay down his life and take it up again to bring about the "resurrection, therefore the grave hath no victory, and the sting of death is swallowed up in Christ" (Mosiah 16:8; see also 1 Corinthians 15:54–55). "For a man to take up his cross, is to deny himself of all ungodliness, and every worldly lust, and keep [Christ's] commandments" (JST, Matthew 16:26). In his denying ungodliness and worldly lusts, it shows he is "not ashamed of [Christ]" (JST, Mark 8:40).

Jacob 1:9–11 • The People Loved Nephi Exceedingly

9 Now Nephi began to be old, and he saw that he must soon die; wherefore, he anointed a man to be a king and a ruler over his people now, according to the reigns of the kings.

10 The people having loved Nephi exceedingly, he having been a great protector for them, having wielded the sword of Laban in their defence, and having labored in all his days for their welfare—

11 Wherefore, the people were desirous to retain in remembrance his name. And whoso should reign in his stead were called by the people, second Nephi, third Nephi, and so forth, according to the reigns of the kings; and thus they were called by the people, let them be of whatever name they would.

It is not clear whether Nephi was a king, or whether the reign of the kings began with his successors. Apparently his successors were a patriarchal or family appointment. Later "all the people of Zara-hemla were numbered with the Nephites, and this because the king-dom had been conferred upon none, but those who were descendants of Nephi" (Mosiah 25:13). However, as indicted by the phrase "let them be of whatever name they would" (Jacob 1:11), this practice could have been initiated at a later time. If it was begun at this time, his successors must have had names different than Nephi. We do know that he had not sought to be their king, and if he had served as king, it was because the Lord had told him he should be "their ruler and their teacher" (2 Nephi 5:19). Note also that the Lord's will that there should be "no kings upon the land," was regarding the time of the Gentiles occupying the land of the Americas in the latter days (2 Nephi 10:10–11). The advantages and disadvantages of having kings are given in Mosiah 29, and will be discussed there.

Nephi died shortly following the fifty-fifth year after their leaving Jerusalem (Jacob 1:12). "Being exceedingly young, nevertheless being large in stature" (1 Nephi 2:16) when they left, it is assumed he lived to be around seventy years of age. Thus, Jacob, the older of the two sons born to Lehi and Sariah in the wilderness, would have been about fifteen years younger than Nephi (see 1 Nephi 17:4; 18:7). Therefore, Jacob would have been somewhere in his early fifties when he began keeping this record.[1]

Jacob 1:13–14 The Nephites and the Lamanites

13 Now the people which were not Lamanites were Nephites; nevertheless, they were called Nephites, Jacobites, Josephites, Zoramites, Lamanites, Lemuelites, and Ishmaelites.

14 But I, Jacob, shall not hereafter distinguish them by these names, but I shall call them Lamanites that seek to destroy the people of Nephi, and those who are friendly to Nephi I shall call Nephites, or the people of Nephi, according to the reigns of the kings.

Jacob designates seven different peoples called by the names of all of Lehi's sons except Sam; plus Ishmael and Zoram, the servant (v. 13). It should be remembered that Sam, as blessed by his father,

---

[1] If Nephi's age at his death is an indication of the Nephite life span, Jacob did not keep the record nearly as long as did his son Enos. Enos turned over the records to his son Jarom in the year 420 B.C. making a total of one hundred and twenty-four years that Jacob and Enos kept them. This time factor indicates both a longer life span for Jacob and Enos than Nephi. Enos must have been one of the younger children of Jacob, since he must have kept the record for many years longer than Jacob.

was to be "numbered with [Nephi's] seed" (2 Nephi 4:11). Sixteenth century native documents, called Quiche-Mayan Guatemala writing, give an interesting corroborative account of the seven peoples:

> The "Totonicapan" record refers to the division into seven tribes. . . . The "Xahila" family, one of the royal lines of the Quiches of the highlands of Guatemala, left an account in the Maya tongue entitled "Annals of Xahila." It states therein: We were brought forth, coming we were begotten by our mothers and our fathers, as they say. . . . They say that the seven tribes arrived first at Tullan, and we the warriors followed, having taken up the tributes of all the seven tribes when the gate of Tullan was opened.[2]

Jacob 1:15–19 • Magnifying our Office Unto the Lord

15 And now it came to pass that the people of Nephi, under the reign of the second king, began to grow hard in their hearts, and indulge themselves somewhat in wicked practices, such as like unto David of old desiring many wives and concubines, and also Solomon, his son.

16 Yea, and they also began to search much gold and silver, and began to be lifted up somewhat in pride.

17 Wherefore I, Jacob, gave unto them these words as I taught them in the temple, having first obtained mine errand from the Lord.

18 For I, Jacob, and my brother Joseph had been consecrated priests and teachers of this people, by the hand of Nephi.

19 And we did magnify our office unto the Lord, taking upon us the responsibility, answering the sins of the people upon our own heads if we did not teach them the word of God with all diligence; wherefore, by laboring with our might their blood might not come upon our garments; otherwise their blood would come upon our garments, and we would not be found spotless at the last day.

The reign of the second king (v. 15) was the first one after Nephi,

---

[2] Milton R. Hunter and Thomas Stuart Ferguson, *Ancient America and the Book of Mormon,* Kolob Book Company, Oakland, California, [1950], 87.

since Jacob's speech in the temple was "after the death of Nephi" (Jacob 2:1). This supports the concept that Nephi was a king. Because of their riches, Jacob warns the people of two sins: immorality and pride. Perhaps the death of Nephi brought a relaxing of their moral standards, but more probably it was the result of prosperity that appears periodically in the Book of Mormon (see Alma 4:6–12; Helaman 3:36; 3 Nephi 6:4–13).

The temple must have been the one built by Nephi (see 2 Nephi 5:16). Although it says that Jacob was teaching them "in the temple," it was probably on the temple grounds, since the "wives and your children" were present (Jacob 2:7). "Having first obtained his errand from the Lord" (Jacob 1:17), he was following the instructions given to him by the Lord. Jacob and Joseph had been consecrated priests and teachers (v. 18) when Nephi had led those who believed in revelation to another land, while the unbelievers remained behind. It was from that time that the two groups become known as Nephites and Lamanites (see 2 Nephi 5:5–26). According to President Joseph Fielding Smith, consecration as priests and teachers does not refer to offices in the Aaronic priesthood.

> The Nephites were descendants of Joseph. Lehi discovered this when reading the brass plates. He was a descendant of Manasseh, and Ishmael, who accompanied him with his family, was of the tribe of Ephraim (Alma 10:3; *Journal of Discourses*, 23:184). Therefore there were no Levites who accompanied Lehi to the Western Hemisphere. Under these conditions the Nephites officiated by virtue of the Melchizedek Priesthood from the days of Lehi to the days of the appearance of our Savior among them. It is true that Nephi "consecrated Jacob and Joseph" that they should be priests and teachers over the land of the Nephites, but the fact that plural terms priests and teachers were used indicated that this was not a reference to the definite office in the priesthood in either case, but it was a general assignment to teach, direct, and admonish the people. Otherwise the

terms priest and teacher would have been given in the singular.[3]

An often used, but often misunderstood principle of the gospel, is the magnifying of one's priesthood or calling. The general definition of magnify is to enlarge or make look bigger. However, Jacob gives us a scriptural definition of magnifying the priesthood (Jacob 1:19). He and Joseph magnified their calling by taking the responsibility of warning the people of their sins. Jacob had taught this principle earlier. Near the conclusion of his great sermon on the Atonement, he said:

> 44 O, my beloved brethren, remember my words. Behold, I take off my garments, and I shake them before you; I pray the God of my salvation that he view me with his all-searching eye; wherefore, ye shall know at the last day, when all men shall be judged of their works, that the God of Israel did witness that I shook your iniquities from my soul, and that I stand with brightness before him, and am rid of your blood. [2 Nephi 9:44]

Failure to do so made them accountable also for the people's sins. The Old Testament prophet Ezekiel taught this plainly:

> When I say unto the wicked, Thou shalt surely die; and thou givest him not warning, nor speakest to warn the wicked from his wicked way, to save his life; the same wicked *man* shall die in his iniquity; but his blood will I require at thine hand. [Ezekiel 3:18]

Thus a bishop is accountable for every sin committed by a member of his ward unless he warns the people. Therefore, leadership is a weighty responsibility.

Why did Jacob select this sermon given in the temple for inclusion on the small plates? Was he magnifying his priesthood? The Lord had shown Moroni the "day when [the Book of Mormon] shall come forth among you" (Mormon 8:34). Jacob had also seen us. An angel spoke

---

[3] *Answers to Gospel Questions* comp. Joseph Fielding Smith Jr., 5 vols. [1957–66], 1:124. See also *Doctrines of Salvation*, comp. Bruce R. McConkie, 3 vols. [1954–56], 3:87.

to him of the coming of Christ in the meridian of time, and of the Gentiles nursing the seed of the Lamanites in the latter days (see 2 Nephi 10:3–9, see also the remainder of the chapter). The Lord named all seven of the groups of descendants among the Nephites and Lamanites mentioned above, as those to whom his work (the Book of Mormon) was to go (see D&C 3:16–20). If Jacob had not seen us, he knew of us, and was inspired to include this warning to our day.

Immorality and pride, the subject of Jacob's sermon that follows, are also sins of our day. President Spencer W. Kimball called immorality "the sins of the day."[4] President Ezra Taft Benson declared: "the sin of this generation is sexual immorality."[5] Pride also came among the Nephites because of riches. The Lord warned this dispensation. "And if ye seek the riches which it is the will of the Father to give unto you, ye shall be the richest of all people, for ye shall have the riches of eternity; and it must needs be that the riches of the earth are mine to give; but beware of pride, lest ye become as the Nephites of old" (D&C 38:39). President Benson also gave the Church a stern warning against pride. "Pride is the great stumbling block to Zion. I repeat: Pride is the great stumbling block to Zion."[6] Thus, Jacob has two presidents of the Church magnifying their priesthood in support of his great sermon.

Jacob 2:1–4 • Much Desire and Anxiety for Your Souls

1 The words which Jacob, the brother of Nephi, spake unto the people of Nephi, after the death of Nephi:

2 Now, my beloved brethren, I, Jacob, according to the responsibility which I am under to God, to magnify mine office with sober-

---

[4] "Love Versus Lust," *Faith Precedes the Miracle*, [1972], 159.

[5] *A Witness And A Warning*, [1988], 74.

[6] "Beware of Pride," in Conference Report, Apr. 7; or *Ensign,* May 1989, 4. This excellent address should be read by all members of the Church periodically, and by any others who would want to learn of the dangers of pride.

ness, and that I might rid my garments of your sins, I come up into the temple this day that I might declare unto you the word of God.

3 And ye yourselves know that I have hitherto been diligent in the office of my calling; but I this day am weighed down with much more desire and anxiety for the welfare of your souls than I have hitherto been.

4 For behold, as yet, ye have been obedient unto the word of the Lord, which I have given unto you.

"I come up into the temple" (v. 2) again suggests it was inside the temple, but it probably refers to the temple complex or grounds as we would identify it today. "As yet ye have been obedient unto the word of the Lord"(v. 4) suggests that those assembled were the more faithful members of the church. Furthermore, the weight and "much more desire and anxiety for the welfare of your souls" (v. 3) reveals the eroding effect of immorality, and the responsibility for Jacob to magnify "the office of my calling" (v. 2).

Jacob 2:5–11 • The Wickedness of Your Hearts

5 But behold, hearken ye unto me, and know that by the help of the all-powerful Creator of heaven and earth I can tell you concerning your thoughts, how that ye are beginning to labor in sin, which sin appeareth very abominable unto me, yea, and abominable unto God.

6 Yea, it grieveth my soul and causeth me to shrink with shame before the presence of my Maker, that I must testify unto you concerning the wickedness of your hearts.

7 And also it grieveth me that I must use so much boldness of speech concerning you, before your wives and your children, many of whose feelings are exceedingly tender and chaste and delicate before God, which thing is pleasing unto God;

8 And it supposeth me that they have come up hither to hear the pleasing word of God, yea, the word which healeth the wounded soul.

9 Wherefore, it burdeneth my soul that I should be constrained, because of the strict commandment which I have received from God,

to admonish you according to your crimes, to enlarge the wounds of those who are already wounded, instead of consoling and healing their wounds; and those who have not been wounded, instead of feasting upon the pleasing word of God have daggers placed to pierce their souls and wound their delicate minds.

10 But, notwithstanding the greatness of the task, I must do according to the strict commands of God, and tell you concerning your wickedness and abominations, in the presence of the pure in heart, and the broken heart, and under the glance of the piercing eye of the Almighty God.

11 Wherefore, I must tell you the truth according to the plainness of the word of God. For behold, as I inquired of the Lord, thus came the word unto me, saying: Jacob, get thou up into the temple on the morrow, and declare the word which I shall give thee unto this people.

Jacob is forthright and yet very tactful in his approach to the people. He illustrates that magnifying of a leader's calling is much more than giving a warning. He also shows the proper use of the priesthood as revealed through the Prophet Joseph Smith: "Reproving betimes with sharpness, when moved upon by the Holy Ghost; and then showing forth afterwards an increase of love toward him whom thou hast reproved, lest he esteem thee to be his enemy" (D&C 121:43). "Reproving" means to rebuke, chastise, reprimand; but it also means a kindly intent to correct. "Betimes" means to do so early, without delay. Jacob knew their thoughts "by the help of the all powerful creator" (Jacob 2:5). God "is a discerner of the thoughts and intents of the heart;" and "there is none else save God that knowest thy thoughts and the intents of thy heart" (D&C 33:1; 6:16). Thus Jacob moved without delay, with a kindly intent to correct. "Sharpness" is defined as clear, well stated, with clarity. Jacob also knew "that [he] must testify unto [them] concerning the wickedness of [their] hearts" (Jacob 2:6).

Again citing his previous sermon recorded by Nephi:

47 But behold, my brethren, is it expedient that I should awake you to an awful reality of these things? Would I harrow up your souls

if your minds were pure? Would I be plain unto you according to the plainness of the truth if ye were freed from sin?

48 Behold, if ye were holy I would speak unto you of holiness; but as ye are not holy, and ye look upon me as a teacher, it must needs be expedient that I teach you the consequences of sin. [2 Nephi 9:47–48]

As will be seen, he clearly and specifically identifies the sins of the Nephite people. "An increase of love" assumes there has been a demonstration of love before. Jacob shows his love for the people by apologizing for the necessity of using boldness in the presence of many "whose feelings are exceedingly tender and chaste and delicate before God."

(Jacob 2:7) His recognition of enlarging "the wounds or those who are already wounded"

(vv. 8–9) further shows his love and concern for those whose hearts were already broken

(v. 10) God also loves these people, but "whom the Lord loveth he chasteneth" (Hebrews 12:6; see also D&C 95:1), and so he sent his servant Jacob to chasten them.

Jacob 2:12–16 • Lifted Up in the Pride of Your Hearts

12 And now behold, my brethren, this is the word which I declare unto you, that many of you have begun to search for gold, and for silver, and for all manner of precious ores, in the which this land, which is a land of promise unto you and to your seed, doth abound most plentifully.

13 And the hand of providence hath smiled upon you most pleasingly, that you have obtained many riches; and because some of you have obtained more abundantly than that of your brethren ye are lifted up in the pride of your hearts, and wear stiff necks and high heads because of the costliness of your apparel, and persecute your brethren because ye suppose that ye are better than they.

14 And now, my brethren, do ye suppose that God justifieth you

in this thing? Behold, I say unto you, Nay. But he condemneth you, and if ye persist in these things his judgments must speedily come unto you.

15 O that he would show you that he can pierce you, and with one glance of his eye he can smite you to the dust!

16 O that he would rid you from this iniquity and abomination. And, O that ye would listen unto the word of his commands, and let not this pride of your hearts destroy your souls!

As directed by the Lord, Jacob commences his chastening the people over their sin of pride. The Lord had led them to this land of promise that had a plentiful and natural supply of precious materials (v. 12). The lands of the Americas, where most of the readers of this work will reside, are the same lands, and the inhabitants today are given the same opportunities for riches. The Father is willing to give his people riches, but gives them the same warning that Jacob gave his people: "And if ye seek the riches which it is the will of the Father to give unto you, ye shall be the richest of all people, for ye shall have the riches of eternity; and it must needs be that the riches of the earth are mine to give; but beware of pride, lest ye become as the Nephites of old" (D&C 38:39).

Jacob identifies the real cause of pride to his people, or any other people, "because some of you have obtained more abundantly than that of your brethren . . . ye suppose that ye are better than they" (Jacob 2:13). Jesus warned the rich young ruler: "With men that trust in riches, it is impossible [to enter the kingdom of God]; but not impossible with men who trust in God and leave all for my sake, for with such all these things are possible" (JST, Mark 10:26). The apostle Paul gave a similar warning to Timothy:

7 For we brought nothing into *this* world, *and it is* certain we can carry nothing out.

8 And having food and raiment let us be therewith content.

9 But they that will be rich fall into temptation and a snare, and *into* many foolish and hurtful lusts, which drown men in destruction and perdition.

10 For the love of money is the root of all evil: which while some coveted after, they have erred from the faith, and pierced themselves through with many sorrows.

11 But thou, O man of God, flee these things; and follow after righteousness, godliness, faith, love, patience, meekness. [1 Timothy 6:7–11]

After warning of God's condemnation and power to smite them, Jacob gives an appropriate admonition to both the latter-day inhabitants of the lands: "let not this pride of your hearts destroy your soul" (Jacob 2:16). How timely for our day of wearing costly apparel, and our concern for what is "politically correct" rather than a desire to follow the will of the Lord. But the poor may also be guilty of pride. The Lord warns both the rich and the poor in this dispensation:

16 Wo unto you rich men, that will not give your substance to the poor, for your riches will canker your souls; and this shall be your lamentation in the day of visitation, and of judgment, and of indignation: The harvest is past, the summer is ended, and my soul is not saved!

17 Wo unto you poor men, whose hearts are not broken, whose spirits are not contrite, and whose bellies are not satisfied, and whose hands are not stayed from laying hold upon other men's goods, whose eyes are full of greediness, and who will not labor with your own hands!

18 But blessed are the poor who are pure in heart, whose hearts are broken, and whose spirits are contrite, for they shall see the kingdom of God coming in power and great glory unto their deliverance; for the fatness of the earth shall be theirs. [D&C 56:16–18]

Jacob 2:17–19 • The Lord's Plan for Riches

17 Think of your brethren like unto yourselves, and be familiar with all and free with your substance, that they may be rich like unto you.

18 But before ye seek for riches, seek ye for the kingdom of God.

19 And after ye have obtained a hope in Christ ye shall obtain riches, if ye seek them; and ye will seek them for the intent to do

good—to clothe the naked, and to feed the hungry, and to liberate the captive, and administer relief to the sick and the afflicted.

The things suggested by Jacob to avoid being prideful is much like the Church Welfare Program. To "think of your brethren like unto yourself" (v. 17) is to live the golden rule: "all things whatsoever ye would that men should do to you, do ye even so to them" (3 Nephi 14:12; Matthew 7:12). To avoid pride, we must have a desire to help those less fortunate than we are.

"Being familiar with all and free with your substance" (Jacob 2:17) is to analyze the assets and liabilities of those in need. While the analysis is being done and further processes to help are being taken, the basic needs of food, clothing and shelter are supplemented according to their needs. The things provided should be of the same quality others around them would eat or wear, and adequate for comfortable living. "That they may be rich like unto you" (v. 17) is to help them help themselves. It is an attempt to raise their standard of living to your standard. This help may be through educating or training for better employment opportunities, teaching them management skills in finances, their time, social relations, or other needed areas. It is not to take from those who have and give to those who haven't, but to help the less fortunate develop their talents and gain other talents (see Matthew 25:14–30). It is to eliminate the dole.

Seek the kingdom of God before seeking for riches (Jacob 2:18) is the setting of priorities. As Jesus taught: "Wherefore, seek not the things of this world but seek ye first to build up the kingdom of God, and to establish his righteousness, and all these things shall be added unto you" (JST, Matthew 6:38). He later taught: "For what is a man profited, if he shall gain the whole world, and lose his soul? Or what shall a man give in exchange for his soul?" (Matthew 16:26). The obtaining of riches after obtaining a hope in Christ is not inevitable. Jacob adds two conditions; the first is to seek them. The talent for obtaining riches must be developed just as do all other talents. Fair and honest procedures must be followed if the soul is to be saved.

The second condition given by Jacob is that riches are to be obtained "for the intent to do good" (Jacob 2:19). Jacob's definition of doing good includes "to clothe the naked, and to feed the hungry." Both of these actions have a temporary and a long range condition. The temporary is to provide the necessities when the person or persons are unable to do so. The long range is to provide the opportunity for them to help themselves as described earlier. Jacob further defines to do good as liberating the captive and administering relief to the sick and the afflicted (v. 19). These two conditions also have a two-fold fulfillment. Temporal help is given to the captives that they may overcome the bondage of debt. Teaching them the gospel will give them an opportunity to overcome the bondage of sin. In Jesus' words, they shall "know the truth, and the truth shall make them free" (John 8:32). The law of the Church was revealed to Joseph Smith regarding administering relief to the sick and the afflicted.

> 43 And whosoever among you are sick, and have not faith to be healed, but believe, shall be nourished with all tenderness, with herbs and mild food, and that not by the hand of an enemy.
>
> 44 And the elders of the church, two or more, shall be called, and shall pray for and lay their hands upon them in my name; and if they die they shall die unto me, and if they live they shall live unto me. [D&C 42:43–44]

Their temporal needs are helped by nourishment and blessing. Spiritually they are forgiven of their sins if they are healed.

> 14 Is any sick among you? let him call for the elders of the church; and let them pray over him, anointing him with oil in the name of the Lord:
>
> 15 And the prayer of faith shall save the sick, and the Lord shall raise him up; and if he have committed sins, they shall be forgiven him. [James 5:14–15]

Failure to do good, as directed by Jacob, may lead to the sin of covetousness. The parable warning the Pharisees of this sin is applicable here. The certain rich man, who tore down his barns and built larger ones to store all his goods, was not prepared when his soul was required of him, and he could not take his goods with him. "He that layeth up treasure for himself, . . . is not rich toward God" (Luke 12:15–21).

The Lord created the earth and commanded men to "subdue it" (Genesis 1:28); or as Nephi said: "Behold, the Lord hath created the earth that it should be inhabited; and he hath created his children that they should possess it" (1 Nephi 17:36). The Lord will provide for his saints and insist that it be done in his way.

> 14 I, the Lord, stretched out the heavens, and built the earth, my very handiwork; and all things therein are mine.
>
> 15 And it is my purpose to provide for my saints, for all things are mine.
>
> 16 But it must needs be done in mine own way; and behold this is the way that I, the Lord, have decreed to provide for my saints, that the poor shall be exalted, in that the rich are made low.
>
> 17 For the earth is full, and there is enough and to spare; yea, I prepared all things, and have given unto the children of men to be agents unto themselves.
>
> 18 Therefore, if any man shall take of the abundance which I have made, and impart not his portion, according to the law of my gospel, unto the poor and the needy, he shall, with the wicked, lift up his eyes in hell, being in torment. [D&C 104:14–18]

Jacob gave the Lord's way to his people. The welfare program to our day is the Lord's way until the law of consecration is to be lived and the saints "impart of their substance as becometh saints, to the poor and afflicted among them" (D&C 105:3).

Jacob 2:20–21 • One Being is as Precious to God as Another

> 20 And now, my brethren, I have spoken unto you concerning pride; and those of you which have afflicted your neighbor, and persecuted him because ye were proud in your hearts, of the things which God hath given you, what say ye of it?

21 Do ye not suppose that such things are abominable unto him who created all flesh? And the one being is as precious in his sight as the other. And all flesh is of the dust; and for the selfsame end hath he created them, that they should keep his commandments and glorify him forever.

Many of those who afflict or persecute their neighbors do so unwittingly. They fail to recognize "the things which God hath given [them]" as coming from him (v. 20). They fail to recognize "his hand in all things" (D&C 59:21). Furthermore, they do not understand that all men were created to keep the commandments of God, which would bring glory to God and to themselves (Jacob 2:21; see also D&C 132:21; Moses 1:39). They also fail to recognize "the worth of souls is great in the sight of God" (D&C 18:10). How much more abominable before God it is for those who know and understand these things and still become lifted up in pride.

Jacob 2:22–26 • I Must Speak Concerning a Grosser Crime

22 And now I make an end of speaking unto you concerning this pride. And were it not that I must speak unto you concerning a grosser crime, my heart would rejoice exceedingly because of you.

23 But the word of God burdens me because of your grosser crimes. For behold, thus saith the Lord: This people begin to wax in iniquity; they understand not the scriptures, for they seek to excuse themselves in committing whoredoms, because of the things which were written concerning David, and Solomon his son.

24 Behold, David and Solomon truly had many wives and concubines, which thing was abominable before me, saith the Lord.

25 Wherefore, thus saith the Lord, I have led this people forth out of the land of Jerusalem, by the power of mine arm, that I might raise up unto me a righteous branch from the fruit of the loins of Joseph.

26 Wherefore, I the Lord God will not suffer that this people shall do like unto them of old.

Jacob switches from the sin of pride to the grosser sin of immorality. Alma later in the Book of Mormon labels immorality as "most abominable above all sins save it be the shedding of innocent blood or denying the Holy Ghost" (Alma 39:5), Jacob here calls it the grosser sin. Grosser means a more serious sin in nature or behavior; unrefined, crudely vulgar. Both pride and immorality are called an abomination before God. In the days prior to Lehi leaving Jerusalem, Jeremiah spoke to the men who had known the way of the Lord, and the judgments of God, but had altogether broken the yoke, he said:

> 7 How shall I pardon thee for this? thy children have forsaken me, and sworn by *them that are* no gods: when I had fed them to the full, they then committed adultery, and assembled themselves by troops in the harlots' houses.
>
> 8 They were *as* fed horses in the morning: every one neighed after his neighbour's wife.
>
> 9 Shall I not visit for these *things*? saith the LORD: and shall not my soul be avenged on such a nation as this? [Jeremiah 5:7–9]

The men in Jacob's day seem to fit the chastisement of Jeremiah, and the sins of pride and immorality can be seen in Jeremiah's prophecy. Our day also fits that description. Jacob said, "they understand not the scriptures," and justified their immorality because of what was written about David and Solomon (Jacob 2:23). Today, for example, we hear the claim that Jesus did not condemn the woman taken in adultery, which supposedly justifies that sin. These people do not understand the scriptures. Jesus told the woman to "go, and sin no more," which acknowledges that adultery was a sin, but did not condemn her because the law of Moses required witnesses and the Pharisees, pricked by their own guilty consciences, would not witness against her (John 8:11).

Jacob records that the many wives of David and Solomon were an abomination to the Lord (Jacob 2:24). Some, in their pride, would say this contradicts what the Lord revealed to Joseph Smith.

> 37 Abraham received concubines, and they bore him children; and it was accounted unto him for righteousness, because they were given unto him, and he abode in my law; as Isaac also and Jacob did none

other things than that which they were commanded; and because they did none other things than that which they were commanded, they have entered into their exaltation, according to the promises, and sit upon thrones, and are not angels but are gods.

38 David also received many wives and concubines, and also Solomon and Moses my servants, as also many others of my servants, from the beginning of creation until this time; and in nothing did they sin save in those things which they received not of me.

39 David's wives and concubines were given unto him of me, by the hand of Nathan, my servant, and others of the prophets who had the keys of this power; and in none of these things did he sin against me save in the case of Uriah and his wife; and, therefore he hath fallen from his exaltation, and received his portion; and he shall not inherit them out of the world, for I gave them unto another, saith the Lord. [D&C 132:37–39]

President Joseph Fielding Smith has responded to these critics:

There is no contradiction between Jacob and the Doctrine and Covenants. Jacob declared that the Lord prevented the Nephites from practicing plural marriage, and called attention to the fact that David and Solomon sinned taking wives that the Lord did not give them, which is true. However, the key to the situation may be found by reading further the account in Jacob. The Lord said: "For if I will, saith the Lord of Hosts, raise up seed unto me, I will command my people; otherwise they shall hearken unto these things." [Jacob 2:30]

It is not strange that the Lord did not condemn Abraham and Jacob (Israel) upon whom he founded the house of Israel; nor did he condemn the parents of Samuel, the great prophet, not others who had plural families. He did not condemn Solomon and David for having wives which the Lord gave them.

Turn to 2 Samuel 12:7–8, and you will find that the Lord gave David wives. In reading the Old Testament you will also find that Solomon was blessed and the Lord appeared to him and gave him visions and great blessings when he had plural wives, but later in life, he took wives that the Lord did not give him. For evidence of this, turn to 1 Kings 11, and read it. You can tell these people that the whole house of Israel was built on the twelve sons of Jacob who had four wives— Mothers of the house of Israel.[7]

Jacob is making a general statement. The Doctrine and Covenants gives specific examples, and is supported by accounts as cited by President Smith.

The Lord knows that immorality destroys a nation. Therefore, the Lord led the people of Lehi out of the immoral nation of Judah by his power, to raise up unto him "a righteous branch from the fruit of the loins of Joseph" (Jacob 2:25). If Jacob's people had become immoral, they would not have accomplished the purpose of their being brought to the promised land. Because they were beginning to become immoral, the Lord commanded Jacob to declare his word to them (v. 26).

Jacob 2:27–30 • The Word of the Lord on Morality

27 Wherefore, my brethren, hear me, and hearken to the word of the Lord: For there shall not any man among you have save it be one wife; and concubines he shall have none;

28 For I, the Lord God, delight in the chastity of women. And whoredoms are an abomination before me; thus saith the Lord of Hosts.

29 Wherefore, this people shall keep my commandments, saith the Lord of Hosts, or cursed be the land for their sakes.

30 For if I will, saith the Lord of Hosts, raise up seed unto me, I will command my people; otherwise they shall hearken unto these things.

There is only one exception to a man's having more than one wife: when the Lord commands otherwise. The plurality of wives was introduced into The Church of Jesus Christ of Latter-day Saints by

---

[7] *Answers to Gospel Questions*, [1957–66], 4:213–14. For more references than cited by President Smith, see 2 Samuel 12:9; 1 Kings 11:1–8; and 15:5. See also JST, 1 Kings reference cited above.

the Prophet Joseph Smith because the Lord commanded it. Although the principle was revealed as early as 1831, it was not practiced until several years later (see D&C 132 section heading). The commandment was under the direction of the Prophet Joseph and limited to those designated by him, as he was inspired of the Lord. In 1843, the same year it was recorded, Joseph said: "I gave instructions to try those persons who were preaching, teaching, or practicing the doctrine of plurality of wives; for, according to the law, I hold the keys of this power in the last days; for there is never but one time on earth at a time on whom the power and its keys are conferred; and I have constantly said no man shall have but one wife at a time, unless the Lord directs otherwise" (*TPJS*, 324). It was also discontinued on the same basis—by revelation. Because of the political circumstances of the day, and probably because its purposes of raising up seed to the Lord was fulfilled, the Lord showed the circumstances to President Wilford Woodruff and then commanded him what to do (see excerpts from "Three Addresses by President Wilford Woodruff Regarding the Manifesto." Doctrine and Covenants, pp. 292–293). Both the beginning and the discontinuance of the plurality of wives in the Church comply with the following teaching of the Prophet Joseph Smith:

> That which is wrong under one circumstance, may be, and often is, right under another . . . that is the principle on which the government of heaven is conducted—by revelation adapted to the circumstances in which the children are placed. Whatever God requires is right, no matter what it is, although we may not see the reason thereof till long after the events transpire. [*TPJS*, 256]

Plural marriage was commanded in the early days of the Church, as it has been periodically throughout the history of the world, "to raise up seed unto [the Lord]" (Jacob 2:30). Although many theories of why plural marriage was commanded have been advanced, the raising up of seed unto the Lord is the only scriptural answer that has been given. Through revelation the Lord discontinued the practice. Therefore, those who enter into plural marriage today do so without the approval of the Church, and are accountable to the Lord for their actions.

The Lord's delight in the chastity of women is echoed in the Old Testament: "Who can find a virtuous woman? for her price *is* far above rubies. The heart of her husband doth safely trust in her, so that he shall have no need of spoil" (Proverbs 31:10–11, see the rest of the chapter for other reasons for chastity).

Jacob 2:31–35 • A Sin Against Your Neighbor

31 For behold, I, the Lord, have seen the sorrow, and heard the mourning of the daughters of my people in the land of Jerusalem, yea, and in all the lands of my people, because of the wickedness and abominations of their husbands.

32 And I will not suffer, saith the Lord of Hosts, that the cries of the fair daughters of this people, which I have led out of the land of Jerusalem, shall come up unto me against the men of my people, saith the Lord of Hosts.

33 For they shall not lead away captive the daughters of my people because of their tenderness, save I shall visit them with a sore curse, even unto destruction; for they shall not commit whoredoms, like unto them of old, saith the Lord of Hosts.

34 And now behold, my brethren, ye know that these commandments were given to our father, Lehi; wherefore, ye have known them before; and ye have come unto great condemnation; for ye have done these things which ye ought not to have done.

35 Behold, ye have done greater iniquities than the Lamanites, our brethren. Ye have broken the hearts of your tender wives, and lost the confidence of your children, because of your bad examples before them; and the sobbings of their hearts ascend up to God against you. And because of the strictness of the word of God, which cometh down against you, many hearts died, pierced with deep wounds.

The hurt and sorrow of the wives of the adulterers bring another warning of "a sore curse, even to destruction" that will follow unless there is repentance (vv. 31–33). Jacob addresses his brethren, probably the priesthood holders, who were responsible not only to set a good example, but to teach the law of chastity to their families and other church members. Lehi had given the same laws of morality to them as cited by Jacob, making them not only accountable for their sins, but more responsible because of their knowing of the seriousness of such sins (v. 34). The adulterers had failed in their stewardship as husbands. Their sins were greater than the Lamanites (v. 35), who, because as Alma later said, "have not kept the commandments of God, they have been cut off from the presence of the Lord . . . Nevertheless I say unto you, that it shall be more tolerable for them in the day of judgment than for you, if ye remain in your sins, yea, and even more tolerable for them in this life than for you, except ye repent" (Alma 9:14–15). In the day of judgement it shall also be more tolerable for those who never embraced the gospel than for an unrepentant member of Christ's Church.

Another sin of these husbands is the loss of their children's confidence. A father should be a good role model, but it seems that their immorality is well known among the Nephite people. The sobbings of the hearts of the children have ascended to God, and because of the embarrassment and shame "many hearts died, pierced with deep wounds" (Jacob 2:35).

The sin of immorality is a sin against the two great commandments:

> 36 Master, which *is* the great commandment in the law?
>
> 37 Jesus said unto him, Thou shalt love the Lord thy God with all thy heart, and with all thy soul, and with all thy mind.
>
> 38 This is the first and great commandment.
>
> 39 And the second *is* like unto it, Thou shalt love thy neighbour as thyself.
>
> 40 On these two commandments hang all the law and the prophets. [Matthew 22:36–40]

When we break the law of chastity we sin against God, as proclaimed by Joseph of Egypt who was tempted by Potiphar's wife: "how then can I do this great wickedness and sin against God" (Genesis 39:9). Immorality breaks the hearts of spouses and wounds the children, who are our closest and dearest neighbors. It also affects our friends and other neighbors in similar ways, thus sinning against them. Furthermore, immorality is a sin against ourselves. As a child of God, we are born with "the true Light, which lighteth every man that cometh into the world" (John 1:8–9); "For behold, the Spirit of Christ is given to every man, that he may know good from evil" (Moroni 7:16). As a member of the Church: "He that is baptized in [Christ's] name, to him will the Father give the Holy Ghost" (2 Nephi 31:12; see also Acts 2:37–39). As Paul taught, "He that committeth fornication sinneth against his own body. What? Know ye not that your body is the temple of the Holy Ghost which is in you, which ye have of God" (1 Corinthians 6:18–19; see also 3:16–17). The Light of Christ nor the Holy Ghost "doth not dwell in unholy temples; neither can filthiness or anything which is unclean be received into the kingdom of God" (Alma 7:21). Therefore we sin against our own bodies when, through immorality, we deprive it of the light of Christ and of the Holy Ghost.

Jacob 3:1–4 • Jacob Speaks to the Pure in Heart

1 But behold, I, Jacob, would speak unto you that are pure in heart. Look unto God with firmness of mind, and pray unto him with exceeding faith, and he will console you in your afflictions, and he will plead your cause, and send down justice upon those who seek your destruction.

2 O all ye that are pure in heart, lift up your heads and receive the pleasing word of God, and feast upon his love; for ye may, if your minds are firm, forever.

3 But, wo, wo, unto you that are not pure in heart, that are filthy this day before God; for except ye repent the land is cursed for your sakes; and the Lamanites, which are not filthy like unto you, never-

theless they are cursed with a sore cursing, shall scourge you even
unto destruction.

4 And the time speedily cometh, that except ye repent they shall
possess the land of your inheritance, and the Lord God will lead away
the righteous out from among you.

Having addressed the sinners, Jacob gives preventive measures
to the pure in heart for maintaining their purity. Alma follows this
pattern when warning his son, Corianton, of the seriousness of
immorality (see Alma 39). The first thing Jacob suggests is prayer.
Alma instructs us to "watch and pray continually that ye may not be
tempted above that ye can bear, and thus be led by the Holy Spirit"
(Alma 13:28). Paul admonished the Corinthians: "There hath no
temptation taken you but such as is common to man: but God *is*
faithful, who will not suffer you to be tempted above that ye are able;
but will with the temptation also make a way to escape, that ye may
be able to bear it" (1 Corinthians 10:13). Combining these admonitions, the Spirit will provide the way of escape. Moral transgressions
are usually made in the dark and in secret. We must avoid enticing
situations by following the directions of the Spirit. However, if we
fail to heed his promptings, the Spirit withdraws, and we are left on
our own. We must do our part. Prayer is also appropriate for parents.
They should pray that their children's purity will be maintained. Likewise, friends may pray for the purity of their friends. Jacob promises
that God will not only comfort those who pray in faith, but will
protect them by sending down justice upon those who seek their
destruction (Jacob 3:1). How God intervenes is not stated, but it is
often unnoticed or unseen. God watches over his children, and knows
how to intervene without revoking their agency. We must listen to the
still small voice.

The second preventive measure, given by Jacob, is "to receive the
pleasing word of God, and feast upon his love" (v. 2). The word of
God plainly tells us what he has commanded concerning chastity and
morality. While the world presents many opposing, and often appeal-
ing points of view, those who study the scriptures and listen to faithful

church leaders and loving parents, will know the Lord's commandments. The Lord's love will be poured out upon those who keep themselves clean. Both preventive measures speak of "firmness of mind," suggesting a commitment to maintain purity, and not waver in any degree in one's thoughts or actions.

The Lord warns of destruction by the Lamanites if those who are immoral do not repent. Immorality will destroy a nation, and although the Lamanites had been cursed they were not immoral (v. 3). Another principle is added by Jacob that had been taught earlier; the Lord will lead the righteous out from among them before a nation is destroyed (v. 4; see also 1 Nephi 17:37–38). That prophecy is fulfilled later (see Omni 1:12–13).

Jacob 3:5–11 • The Lamanites Are More Righteous Than You

5 Behold, the Lamanites your brethren, whom ye hate because of their filthiness and the cursing which hath come upon their skins, are more righteous than you; for they have not forgotten the commandment of the Lord, which was given unto our father—that they should have save it were one wife, and concubines they should have none, and there should not be whoredoms committed among them.

6 And now, this commandment they observe to keep; wherefore, because of this observance, in keeping this commandment, the Lord God will not destroy them, but will be merciful unto them; and one day they shall become a blessed people.

7 Behold, their husbands love their wives, and their wives love their husbands; and their husbands and their wives love their children; and their unbelief and their hatred towards you is because of the iniquity of their fathers; wherefore, how much better are you than they, in the sight of your great Creator?

8 O my brethren, I fear that unless ye shall repent of your sins that their skins will be whiter than yours, when ye shall be brought with them before the throne of God.

9 Wherefore, a commandment I give unto you, which is the word of God, that ye revile no more against them because of the darkness

of their skins; neither shall ye revile against them because of their filthiness; but ye shall remember your own filthiness, and remember that their filthiness came because of their fathers.

10 Wherefore, ye shall remember your children, how that ye have grieved their hearts because of the example that ye have set before them; and also, remember that ye may, because of your filthiness, bring your children unto destruction, and their sins be heaped upon your heads at the last day.

11 O my brethren, hearken unto my words; arouse the faculties of your souls; shake yourselves that ye may awake from the slumber of death; and loose yourselves from the pains of hell that ye may not become angels to the devil, to be cast into that lake of fire and brimstone which is the second death.

As already commented on, the Lamanites were a moral people, which was the reason they were not destroyed (v. 5). Their becoming a blessed people is promised repeatedly in the Book of Mormon (see 1 Nephi 15:14; 2 Nephi 30:4–6; Alma 9:16–17; Helaman 15:10–13; Mormon 5:19–20 and others). Although the Book of Mormon teaches of their being marked with a dark skin, it certainly does not teach any prejudice or inequality because of it. The mark was given "that they might not be enticing unto my people" (2 Nephi 5:21). Association with wickedness affects behavior. As Paul admonished: "Abstain from all appearance of evil" (2 Thessalonians 5:22).

The pains of hell, Alma later said, was: "the memory of my sins ... there could be nothing so exquisite and so bitter as were my pain." They can only be permanently removed by the Atonement of Christ (Alma 36:19–21).

The second death was described by Samuel the Lamanite:

17 But behold, the resurrection of Christ redeemeth mankind, yea, even all mankind, and bringeth them back into the presence of the Lord.

18 Yea, and it bringeth to pass the condition of repentance, that whosoever repenteth the same is not hewn down and cast into the fire; but whosoever repenteth not is hewn down and cast into the fire;

and there cometh upon them again a spiritual death, yea, a second death, for they are cut off again as to things pertaining to righteousness. [Helaman 14:17–18]

Jacob 3:12–14 • Jacob's Final Warning

12 And now I, Jacob, spake many more things unto the people of Nephi, warning them against fornication and lasciviousness [immorality], and every kind of sin, telling them the awful consequences of them.

13 And a hundredth part of the proceedings of this people, which now began to be numerous, cannot be written upon these plates; but many of their proceedings are written upon the larger plates, and their wars, and their contentions, and the reigns of their kings.

14 These plates are called the plates of Jacob, and they were made by the hand of Nephi. And I make an end of speaking these words.

Jacob's having spoken "many more things" to them (v. 12) may refer to other times and occasions, in addition to this speech in the temple. Mormon and Moroni also speak of not writing even a hundredth part of the proceedings of this people (see Words of Mormon 1:5; Helaman 3:14; 3 Nephi 5:8; 26:6; Ether 15:33). Nephi also mentions the brevity of his record (see 1 Nephi 6:9; 19:1–6).

SACRED WRITING

Preaching Which is Sacred:

Jacob 1:2–8	Nephi's instructions to Jacob about what to write on the plates.
Jacob 2:1–3:12	Jacob's sermon in the temple on pride and immorality.

Doctrines Learned:

Jacob 1:19	Magnifying the priesthood is to take upon oneself the responsibility of the sins of the people over whom you have stewardship.
Jacob 2:25	The Nephites were led out of Jerusalem that the Lord

	might raise up a righteous branch unto the tribe of Joseph.
Jacob 2:27	A man shall have no concubines and only one wife, unless commanded otherwise by the Lord.
Jacob 2:28	The Lord delights in the chastity of woman, and whoredoms are an abomination to him.
Jacob 2:30	The purpose of plural marriage, when the Lord commands it, is to raise up seed unto him.
Jacob 3:6	Immorality will cause a nation to be destroyed.
Jacob 3:9	God commands that we do not revile against a people because of their skin color.
Jacob 3:10	If one's example brings destruction upon his or her children, the sins are also heaped upon his or her head.

General Authority Quotations

The First Presidency • Jacob 2:17

Our primary purpose, was to set up, in so far as it might be possible, a system under which the curse of idleness would be done away with, the evils of a dole abolished, and independence, industry, thrift, and self-respect be once more established amongst our people. The aim of the Church is to help the people to help themselves. Work is to be re-enthroned as the ruling principle of the lives of our people. [Heber J. Grant, J. Reuben Clark, Jr., David O. McKay, Conference Report, Oct. 1936, 3]

The First Presidency • Jacob 2:28

To us in this Church, the Lord has declared that adulterers should not be admitted to membership (D&C 42:76); that adulterers in the Church, if unrepentant should be cast out (D&C 42:75) but if repentant should be permitted to remain (D&C 42:74; 42:25) and He said, "By this ye may know if a man repenteth of his sin—behold, he will confess them and forsake them" (D&C 58:43).

In the great revelation on the three heavenly glories, the Lord said, speaking of those who will inherit the lowest of these, or the telestial glory: "These are they who are liars, and sorcerers, and adulterers, and whoremongers, and whosoever loves and makes a lie" (D&C 76:103).

The doctrine of this Church is that sexual sin—the illicit sexual relations of men and women—stands, in its enormity, next to murder (Alma 39:5–6).

The Lord has drawn no essential distinctions between fornication, adultery, and harlotry or prostitution. Each has fallen under His solemn and awful condemnation.

You youth of Zion, you cannot associate in non-marital, illicit sex relationship, which is fornication, and escape the punishments and the judgments which the Lord has declared against this sin. The day of reckoning will come just as certainly as night follows day. They who would palliate this crime and say that such indulgence is but a sinless gratification of a normal desire, like appeasing hunger and thirst, speak filthiness with their lips. Their counsel leads to destruction; their wisdom comes from the Father of Lies.

You husbands and wives who have taken on solemn obligations of chastity in the Holy Temples of the Lord and who violate those sacred vows by illicit sexual relations with others, you not only commit the vile sin of adultery, but you break the oath you yourselves made with the Lord himself before you went to the altar for your sealing. You become subject to the penalties which the Lord has prescribed for those who breach their covenants with him. . . .

But they who sin may repent, and, they repenting, God will forgive them, for the Lord has said, "Behold, he who has repented of his sins, the same is forgiven, and I, the Lord, remember them no more" (D&C 58:42).

By virtue of the authority in us vested as the First Presidency of the Church, we warn our people who are offending of the degradation, the wickedness, the punishment that attend upon unchastity; we urge you to remember the blessings which flow from the living of the clean life; we call upon you to keep, day in and day out, the way of strictest chastity, through which only can God's choice gifts come to you and His Spirit abide with you.

How glorious is he who lives a clean life. He walks unfearful in the full glare of the noon-day sun, for he is without moral infirmity. He can be reached by no shafts of base calumny, for his armor is without flaw. His virtue cannot be challenged by any just accuser, for he lives above reproach. His cheek is never blotched with shame, for he is without hidden shame. He is honored and respected by all mankind, for he is beyond their censure. He is loved by the Lord, for he stands without blemish. The exaltations of eternities await his coming. [Heber J. Grant, J. Reuben Clark' Jr., David O. McKay, CR, Oct., 1942, 11–12]

President Joseph F. Smith • Jacob 2:28

Sexual union is lawful in wedlock, and if participated in with right intent is honorable and sanctifying. But without the bonds of marriage, sexual indulgence is a debasing, abominable in the sight of Deity. [*Gospel Doctrine*, 11th ed. (195?), 309]

Much as all these sins are to be denounced and deplored, we can ourselves see a difference both in intent and consequence between the offence of a young couple who, being betrothed, in an unguarded moment, without premeditation fall into sin, and that of a man, who having entered into holy places and made sacred covenants plots to rob the wife of his neighbor of her virtue either by cunning or force and accomplish his vile intent.

Not only is there a difference in these wrongs, judging from the standpoint of intent, but also from that of the consequences. In the first instance the young couple who have transgressed can make partial amends by sincere repentance and by marrying. One reparation, however, they cannot make. They cannot restore the respect that they previously held for each other; and too often as a consequence of this loss of confidence their married life is clouded or embittered by the fear that each has for the other, having once sinned, may do so again. In the other case, others are most disastrously involved, families are broken up, misery is forced upon innocent parties, society is affected, doubt is thrown upon the paternity of children, and from the standpoint of gospel ordinances, the question of descent is clouded and pedigrees become worthless; altogether, wrongs are committed both to the living and the dead, as well as to the yet unborn, which is out of the power of the offenders to repair or make right. [*Gospel Doctrine*, 11th ed. [195?), 310–11]

Gordon B. Hinckley • Jacob 2:28

. . . there must be cleanliness, for immorality will blight your life and leave a scar that will never entirely leave you. . . .

Let me first assure you that if you have made a mistake, if you have become involved in any immoral behavior, all is not lost. Memory of that mistake will likely linger, but the deed can be forgiven, and you can rise above the past to live a life fully acceptable unto the Lord where there has been repentance. He has promised that He will forgive your sins and remember them no more against you (see D&C 58:42). . . .

But there will be scars that will remain. The best way, the only way for you, is to avoid any entrapment with evil. . . . You have within you instincts, powerful and terribly persuasive, urging you at times to let go and experience a little fling. You must not do it. You cannot do it. You are daughters of God with tremendous potential. He had great expectations concerning you, as do others. You cannot let down for a minute. You cannot give in to an impulse. There must be discipline, strong and unbending. Flee from temptation, as Joseph fled from the wiles of Potiphar's wife.

There is nothing in all this world as magnificent as virtue. It glows without a tarnish. It is precious and beautiful. It is above price. It cannot be bought or sold. It is the fruit of self-mastery.

You young women spend a lot of time thinking about boys. You can have a good time with them, but never overstep the line of virtue. Any young man who invites or encourages you or demands that you indulge in any kind of sexual behavior is unworthy of your company. Get him our of your life before both yours and his are blighted. If you can thus discipline yourselves, you will be grateful as long as you live. Most of you will marry, and your marriage will be much happier for your earlier restraint. You will be worthy to go to the house of the Lord. There is no adequate substitute for this marvelous blessing. The Lord has given a marvelous mandate. He has said, "Let virtue garnish your thoughts unceasingly" (D&C 121:45). This becomes a commandment to be observed with diligence and discipline. And there is attached to it the promise of marvelous and wonderful blessings. He has said to those who live with virtue:

"Then shall thy confidence wax strong in the presence of God. . . .

"The Holy Ghost"—of which we have spoken tonight—"shall be thy constant companion, and thy scepter an unchanging scepter of righteousness and truth; and thy dominion shall be an everlasting dominion, and without compulsory means it shall flow unto thee forever and ever" (D&C 121:45–46).

Could there be a greater or more beautiful promise than this? [General Young Women's Meeting, March 24, 2001 see *Ensign*, May 2001, 93]

Brigham Young • Jacob 2:30

There are multitudes of pure and holy spirits waiting to take tabernacles, now what is our duty?—To prepare tabernacles for them; to take a course that will not tend to drive those spirits into the families of the wicked; where they will be trained in wickedness, debauchery, and every species of crime. It is the duty of every righteous man and woman to prepare tabernacles for all the spirits they can.

This is the reason why the doctrine of plurality of wives was revealed, that the noble spirits which are waiting for tabernacles might be brought forth. [*Discourses of Brigham Young*, sel. John A. Widtsoe (1941), 197]

Elder Boyd K. Packer • Jacob 2:28

"Why Stay Morally Clean?" This sermon, given in the April 1972 General Conference is too long to be included here, but is highly recommended for all to read. It was later published in Elder Packer's book *That All May Be Edified* [1982], 175–85.

Challenges to Eternal Life:

1. Magnify your calling in the Church by taking upon yourself the responsibility of teaching the truth in kindness and love, and as directed by the Spirit (Jacob 1:19).
2. Do not suppose that you are better (or worse) than your neighbor, or associates, but think of them like unto yourself (Jacob 2:17).
3. Before you seek for riches, seek the kingdom of God (Jacob 2:19).
4. Look to the Lord in prayer, and receive his word, that you might always be pure in heart (Jacob 3:1–2).
5. Follow the example of the Lamanites in Jacob's day, and love your spouse and your children (Jacob 3:7).
6. Choose a challenge from the reading, not mentioned above, and apply it to your life.

Chapter Two

The Allegory of the House of Israel

Jacob 4–6

*H*istorical Setting: Sometime after making a record of his speech in the temple, Jacob selected a few other things to record. He limited his selection because of the difficulty of engraving. However, he copied from the plates of brass the longest chapter in the Book of Mormon, the allegory of the house of Israel. He wrote a few things concerning his people before the allegory and a brief, but helpful explanation of the allegory after it. There is no history contained in chapters 5 and 6.

Precepts of this Reading:

Jacob 4:3	Learn with joy and not with sorrow, neither with contempt.
Jacob 4:8	Behold, great and marvelous are the works of the Lord . . . wherefore, brethren, despise not the revelations of God.
Jacob 4:10	Wherefore brethren, seek not to counsel the Lord, but to take counsel from his hand.
Jacob 4:11	Wherefore, beloved brethren, be reconciled unto [God] through the Atonement of Christ.

An outline of the three chapters to prepare for a deeper study follows.

OUTLINE • JACOB 4–6

➤ Jacob 4:1–12   Jacob ministered much to his people in word, but wrote little of it because of the difficulty of engraving.

    a. What is written on plates will remain, but other writing will perish (vv. 1–3).

      1. The few words written will give our children and beloved brethren a small degree of knowledge concerning us and our fathers.

      2. Hopefully they will receive them with thankful hearts, and learn with joy and not with sorrow and contempt concerning their first parents.

    b. The writings were intended to teach that the Nephites knew of Christ and had a hope of his glory many hundred years before his coming (vv. 4–5).

      1. All the holy prophets before them also had a hope of his glory.

      2. All the holy prophets worshipped the Father in his name and so did the Nephites.

      3. The Nephites kept the law of Moses because it pointed their souls to Christ.

      4. Abraham's sacrifice of his son Isaac is in similitude of God and his only Begotten Son.

    c. The Nephites searched the prophets and had many revelations and the spirit of prophecy (vv. 6–7).

      1. They had a hope and a faith so unshaken that they could command in the name of Jesus and the trees, mountains, or waves of the sea obeyed.

      2. The Lord God showed them their weakness that they may know it is through his grace and condescension that they could do these things.

    d. How great and marvelous are the works of the Lord and unsearchable are the depths of the mysteries of him (v. 8).

      1. It is impossible for man to find out all his ways.

      2.   No man knoweth of his ways save it be revealed to him.

      3.   Despise not the revelations of God.

  e.   By the power of the Lord's words the earth was created and man came on the earth (vv. 9–10).

      1.   If man and the earth were created by his word, why can't he command the earth according to his will?

      2.   Seek not to counsel the Lord but to take counsel from his hand.

      3.   He counseleth in wisdom, justice, and mercy over all his works.

  f.   Be reconciled to God through the Atonement of Christ that ye may obtain a resurrection according to his power and be presented as the first-fruits of Christ (vv. 11–12).

➤ 4:13–18   He that prophesieth and does so according to the under-standing of men, speaketh the truth by the Spirit and lieth not.

  a.   The Spirit speaks of things as they really are and really will be (v. 13).

      1.   The things are revealed plainly to the Nephites for their salvation.

      2.   God also spoke these things to the prophets of old.

  b.   The Jews were a stiffnecked people and despised the words of plainness, killed the prophets, and sought for things they could not understand (v. 14).

      1.   Because of their blindness from looking beyond the mark, they must fall.

      2.   God took away his plainness from them and delivered to them things they could not understand.

  c.   Jacob prophesied that the Jews would reject the stone upon which they could build and have safe foundation (vv. 15–18).

      1.   According to the scriptures, this stone will become the great, the last, and the only sure foundation

upon which the Jews could build.

2. Jacob revealed how it is possible for the Jews to reject this sure foundation and yet build upon it that it becomes the head of the corner.

➢ 5:1–2   Jacob read the words of the prophet Zenos concerning the house of Israel.

➢ 5:3–14   The house of Israel is likened unto a tame olive tree that a man nourished in his vineyard; it grew, waxed old, and began to decay.

    a. The master of the vineyard pruned it, digged about it, and nourished it and after many days it put forth little young and tender branches, but the top began to perish (vv. 5–6).

    b. The master's servant plucked off the main branches that were beginning to wither away and cast them into the fire (vv. 7–10).

        1. He took the young and tender branches and grafted them where he willed.

        2. He grafted the branches from a wild olive tree in the tame tree.

    c. The master caused the tree to be digged about, pruned, and nourished that he might preserve the roots (vv. 11–12).

    d. The master took the natural branches and hid them in the nethermost parts of the vineyard, some in one place and some in another (vv. 13–14).

➢ 5:15–28   A long time passed away and the master and his servant went down to the vineyard to labor.

    a. The tree where the branches of the wild branches had been grafted had begun to bear good fruit like unto the natural fruit (vv. 16–18).

        1. The wild branches had taken hold of the moisture and the strength of the root.

        2. If there had been no grafting of the wild branches,

the tree would have perished.

    3.   The master said he would lay up much fruit unto himself.

  b. The master and his servant visited the nethermost part of the vineyard where the natural branches had been hidden (vv. 19–28).

    1.   The first had brought forth much good fruit to be preserved unto the Lord.

       (a) The servant asks why the master had planted this branch in the poorest spot of ground.

       (b) The master admonished the servant to not counsel him. He knew it was a poor spot of ground, but through nourishing it had brought forth much fruit.

    2.   The master showed the servant another branch that was planted in a spot of ground poorer than the first, and it had brought forth much fruit to be gathered and preserved.

    3.   A third branch was shown to the servant that was nourished and also brought forth much fruit.

       (a) This branch was planted in a good spot of ground and part of it had brought forth tame fruit and part of it had brought forth wild fruit.

       (b) The servant was told to pluck off the branches that produced wild fruit and burn them.

       (c) The servant suggested they prune it, and dig about it and nourish it a little longer.

    4.   The Lord and the servant nourished all the fruit of the vineyard.

➤ 5:29–69   The Lord and his servant, after a long time, went down to the vineyard again to labor for the end soon cometh and fruit must be laid up.

  a. On the tree whose natural branches had been broken off and the wild branches grafted in, there was all sorts of fruit cumbering the tree (vv. 31–32).

1. The Lord tasted the fruit and none of it was good.

2. It profited the Lord nothing and he grieved in losing the tree.

b. The Lord asked the servant what to do unto the tree that he may have good fruit again (vv. 33–37).

1. The servant suggested that the wild branches had nourished the roots and they were yet good.

2. The Lord knew the roots were good and he had preserved them for his own purpose.

3. The wild branches would soon ripen and be cast into the fire if something wasn't done.

c. The Lord and the servant visited the natural branches of the tree and all of the fruit had become corrupt; the first, the second and the last (vv. 38–40).

1. The wild fruit of the last had overcome the part that produced good fruit.

2. The branch had withered away and died.

d. The Lord wept and asked, What could I have done more (vv. 41–47)?

1. All the fruit but that of this tree were corrupt. And now this tree, once good, is corrupt.

2. It was planted in a good spot of ground, choice above all other parts of the land.

3. He had cut down that which once cumbered that spot of ground and planted this tree.

4. Because he plucked not the wild fruit branches, they had overcome the good fruit.

5. All the branches had become like the wild branches and were of no worth to the Lord.

6. The Lord reviewed what he had done and asked, Who has corrupted my vineyard?

e. The servant suggested that the loftiness of the branches had overcome the roots, which are good (vv. 48–50).

1. The branches had grown faster than the roots, taking strength unto themselves.

2. The Lord suggested that the trees be cut down and cast into the fire.

3. The servant plead to spare it a little longer.

f. The Lord agreed to spare the vineyard a little longer and presented his plan (vv. 51–56).

1. They grafted the natural branches that had become wild back into the tree from whence they came.

2. The branches whose fruit was most bitter were plucked and the natural branches grafted in.

3. The Lord preserved the roots for his own purpose; they were yet alive.

4. The natural branches grafted into the mother tree would preserve the roots.

5. When the roots were sufficiently strong they would produce good fruit.

g. The Lord instructed the servant to not pluck the wild branches except the most bitter ones (vv. 57–62).

1. They would nourish again the tree, trim the branches, and pluck the ripe branches and burn them.

2. Because of the good branches and the change of branches, the good could overcome the evil.

3. Call servants to labor with their might for the last time, for the end draweth nigh.

h. The natural branches were to be grafted beginning at the last that they may be first, and the first may be last (vv. 63–69).

1. Dig about them, prune, and dung them once more for the last time.

2. Prune the bitter branches according to the strength and size of the good.

3. Do not prune all the bad at once lest the roots be too strong for the graft.

4. The root and the top should be equal in strength.

5. The natural branches were to be grafted into the

natural tree and into the natural branches.

➤ 5:70–75   The Lord sent the servant and the servant gathered other servants. The servants were few, but they obeyed the commandments of the Lord.

   a.   They were to labor with all their might for this the last time. If they labored with their might they would have joy in the fruit (v. 71).

   b.   There began to be natural fruit again in the vineyard (v. 73).

      1.   The branches grew and thrived exceedingly.

      2.   The wild branches began to be plucked off and cast away.

      3.   The root and top were kept equal.

      4.   They became like one body and the fruits were equal.

   c.   He called and blessed his servants. They will have joy with him (v. 75).

➤ 5:76–77   The Lord layed up fruit for a long time.

   a.   When the time comes that evil fruit is again in the vineyard, the Lord will gather the good and the bad.

   b.   The good will be preserved unto the Lord and the bad cast away into its own place (v. 77).

   c.   Then comes the season and the end, and the vineyard will be burned (v. 77).

➤ 6:1–4   Jacob prophesied that the things Zenos spoke concerning the house of Israel which he likened unto an olive tree, must surely come to pass.

   a.   The day the Lord sets his hand to recover his people the second time is the last time the Lord would nourish and prune his vineyard (v. 2).

   b.   How blessed are they who have labored diligently in his vineyard and how cursed are they who shall be cast out. The world shall be burned with fire (v. 3).

    c. God was merciful and remembered Israel, both roots and branches (v. 4).

        1. He stretched forth his hands unto them all day long.

        2. They were a stiffnecked and gainsaying people.

        3. As many as would not harden their hearts will be saved in the kingdom of God.

➤ 6:5–13   Jacob urged his people to repent and come to God while his arm of mercy is extended.

    a. Today, hear his voice, harden not your heart, and be nourished by the word of God (vv. 6–7).

    b. Will ye reject these words, the words of the prophets, and all the words spoken concerning Christ (v. 8)?

    c. Will ye deny the good word of Christ, the power of God, the gift of the Holy Ghost, and quench the Holy Spirit, and make a mock of the great plan of redemption (v. 8–10)?

        1. If ye do these things, the power of the redemption, and the resurrection in Christ, will bring you to stand with shame and awful guilt before the bar of God.

        2. According to the power of justice, which cannot be denied, ye must go away unto endless torment.

    d. Repent and enter the strait gate, continue in the narrow way to eternal life (v. 11).

    e. Be wise, what can Jacob say more (v. 12)?

    f. Jacob bids the reader farewell until he meets them before the pleasing bar of God, which strikes the wicked with awful dread and fear (v. 13).

NOTES AND COMMENTARY

Introduction: Jacob begins this section of his book by apologizing for not being able to write but a little of his words because of the difficulty of engraving on the plates. His entire writing totals about eighteen and one-half pages of our current edition of the Book of

Mormon. However, he took the time and space to engrave the allegory of the house of Israel from the plates of brass which occupies about six and one-half pages of those eighteen and one-half pages, plus he added another page of commentary on the allegory. The allegory and his commentary occupy a good forty percent of his total contribution to the record. What were his reasons for doing this? The answer to this question is given in his comments before he engraves the allegory (chapter 4).

Jacob 4:1–3 • To Learn with Joy

1 Now behold, it came to pass that I, Jacob, having ministered much unto my people in word, (and I cannot write but a little of my words, because of the difficulty of engraving our words upon plates) and we know that the things which we write upon plates must remain;

2 But whatsoever things we write upon anything save it be upon plates must perish and vanish away; but we can write a few words upon plates, which will give our children, and also our beloved brethren, a small degree of knowledge concerning us, or concerning their fathers—

3 Now in this thing we do rejoice; and we labor diligently to engraven these words upon plates, hoping that our beloved brethren and our children will receive them with thankful hearts, and look upon them that they may learn with joy and not with sorrow, neither with contempt, concerning their first parents.

Despite the difficulty of engraving on the plates, the first reason given by Jacob for writing our chapters 4 through 6, was he wanted a permanent record to remain for their beloved brethren and their children to "learn with joy and not with sorrow, neither with contempt, concerning their first parents" (v. 3). The context of "their first parents" is Lehi, Ishmael, and their families who left Jerusalem in 600 B.C. He addresses their beloved brethren and their children throughout chapter 4. To "learn with joy" is to receive the record of Nephi and Jacob with thankful hearts and learn that their first parents, and those accompanying them, were led by the hand of the Lord to "a land which is choice above all other lands" (1 Nephi 2:20). They had great blessings extended to them. As discussed in the previous chapter, these same blessings are extended to their beloved brethren, the Lamanites, in the last days.

To learn "with sorrow" is to reject the record of Nephi, Jacob, and others; to realize that the rejection of that record had cost them the opportunity for their salvation. The Prophet Joseph Smith cautioned the Twelve in his day to beware of pride, and ask them this perplexing question: "Why will not men learn wisdom by precept at this late age of the world, when we have such a cloud of witnesses and examples before us, and not be obliged to learn by sad experience everything we know?" (*TPJS*, 155). Possibly, Joseph had Jacob's admonition in mind when he admonished the Twelve. Regardless, as believers in the Book of Mormon, we should learn with joy from Jacob's admonition and not from the sorrow of our own experiences; or to use a modern expression "learn the hard way."

Jacob was also concerned that the descendants of Lehi and Ishmael not be weighed down with sorrow from being a nation of fallen people, but would rather that they recognize the great blessings extended to them in the latter days. He also seemed concerned that they not react with contempt as did the descendants of the rebellious Laman and Lemuel and the sons of Ishmael. This concern may have been fostered by his knowledge that all of the remnants of Lehi and his party would be designated as Lamanites today; and that while even in his day those who sought "to destroy the people of Nephi" were called Lamanites (Jacob 1:14), he did not want the designation to carry a negative connotation in the last days. He obviously knew, as did Alma, that all those who remained after the downfall of the Nephite nation "shall be numbered among the Lamanites" (Alma 45:14). As the Lord has confirmed by revelation, there are descendants of all the original families of Lehi's party among those called Lamanites today (see D&C 3:16–18). This revelation confirms the teaching that a major purpose for preserving the plates was to make known to all these people the fact that the promises of the Lord would be fulfilled (Jacob 4:19).

Jacob 4:4–5 • We Knew of Christ and Had a Hope

4 For, for this intent have we written these things, that they may know that we knew of Christ, and we had a hope of his glory many hundred years before his coming; and not only we ourselves had a hope of his glory, but also all the holy prophets which were before us.

5 Behold, they believed in Christ and worshiped the Father in his name, and also we worship the Father in his name. And for this intent we keep the law of Moses, it pointing our souls to him; and for this cause it is sanctified unto us for righteousness, even as it was accounted unto Abraham in the wilderness to be obedient unto the commands of God in offering up his son Isaac, which is a similitude of God and his Only Begotten Son.

The second reason for Jacob's engraving a permanent record on plates that would not perish was that their brethren and their children might "know that we knew of Christ, and we had a hope of his glory many hundred years before his coming" as well as all the holy prophets before them (v. 4). The holy prophets must have had reference to the Old Testament prophets whose teachings and prophecies were recorded upon the plates of brass. Although Lehi, Nephi, and Jacob were prophets, Jacob is writing about all who "were before us." Thus, it would extend to before Lehi and Nephi. Even Adam and Eve knew of Christ:

9 And in that day [after being driven out of the garden] the Holy Ghost fell upon Adam, which beareth record of the Father and the Son, saying: I am the Only Begotten of the Father from the beginning, henceforth and forever, that as thou hast fallen thou mayest be redeemed, and all mankind, even as many as will.

12 And Adam and Eve blessed the name of God, and they made all things known unto their sons and their daughters. [Moses 5:9, 12]

Enoch knew of Christ: "Enoch saw the day of the coming of the Son of Man, in the last days, to dwell on the earth in righteousness for the space of a thousand years" (Moses 7:65). Walking with two disciples on the road to Emmaus after his resurrection:

> 25 Then [Jesus] said unto them, O fools, and slow of heart to believe all that the prophets have spoken:
>
> 26 Ought not Christ to have suffered these things, and to enter into his glory?
>
> 27 And beginning at Moses and all the prophets, he expounded unto them in all the scriptures the things concerning himself. [Luke 24:25–27]

Later that evening, after eating with the eleven apostles:

> 44 [Jesus] said unto them, These *are* the words which I spake unto you, while I was yet with you, that all things must be fulfilled, which were written in the law of Moses, and *in* the prophets, and *in* the psalms, concerning me.
>
> 45 Then opened he their understanding, that they might understand the scriptures. [Luke 24:44–45]

Lehi, Nephi, and Jacob quoted freely from the plates of brass. Other prophets worshipped the Father in the name of Christ, i.e. prayed, prophesied, and performed ordinances, but this is a "plain and precious" truth lost from the Bible (1 Nephi 13:28). Jacob's people likewise worshipped. When Jesus ministered in the flesh among the Nephites, he taught them: "ye must always pray unto the Father in my name" (3 Nephi 18:19).

The law of Moses "pointing our souls to [Christ]" (Jacob 4:5) was later taught by Paul, "the law was our schoolmaster to bring us to Christ" (Galatians 3:24). However, Nephi had also labored "to write, to persuade our children, and also our brethren, to believe in Christ, and be reconciled to God" and to know that "the law hath become dead unto us, yet we keep the law because of the commandments" until the law was fulfilled in Christ's coming (2 Nephi 25:23–27). They kept "those outward performances" (Alma 25:15), but not necessarily all the minutia of the law. Nephi's explanation of their keeping the law, but fully believing in Christ, exemplifies what Jacob said, the keeping of the law was "sanctified unto us for righteousness" (Jacob 4:5).

Jacob's reference to Abraham's offering up his son Isaac as an example of sanctification unto righteousness was confirmed in modern revelation: "Abraham was commanded to offer his son Isaac; nevertheless, it was written: Thou shalt not kill. Abraham, however, did not refuse, and it was accounted unto him for righteousness" (D&C 132:36). The sacrifice being in similitude of God and his Only Begotten Son (Jacob 4:5), also teaches a very important, often overlooked concept. A similitude is a similar incident, but, in this case, is much more. It is a pattern, a type and shadow of what Christ was to do. As the Lord told Adam, "All things have their likeness, and all things are created and made to bear record of [Christ]" (Moses 6:63). Isaac was the only covenant son of Abraham, born of Sarah at age ninety through a miraculous conception. This was patterned after Christ being the Only Begotten Son of God, born of the virgin Mary through a miraculous conception (see Genesis 17:15–19; 18:9–15; Luke 1:26–38). Both were taken to Mount Moriah to be sacrificed (see Genesis 22:2; Luke 23:33). Both carried the wood for their sacrifices (see Genesis 22:6; John 19:17). A ram was provided as a vicarious sacrifice for Isaac (see Genesis 22:8, 11–13), and Christ was "the Lamb of God" sacrificed vicariously for "the sin of the world" (John 1:29, 36).[1] The interjection of the example of Abraham and Isaac may appear to be coincidental, but it was undoubtedly inspired of God.

Jacob 4:6–10 • Search the Prophets

> 6 Wherefore, we search the prophets, and we have many revelations and the spirit of prophecy; and having all these witnesses we obtain a hope, and our faith becometh unshaken, insomuch that we truly can command in the name of Jesus and the very trees obey us,

---

[1] The account of Abraham's offering Isaac being literal and not just a symbolic story is verified in D&C 101:4 and 132:6 in addition to the Jacob illustration (see also Helaman 11:17).

or the mountains, or the waves of the sea.

7 Nevertheless, the Lord God showeth us our weakness that we may know that it is by his grace, and his great condescensions unto the children of men, that we have power to do these things.

8 Behold, great and marvelous are the works of the Lord. How unsearchable are the depths of the mysteries of him; and it is impossible that man should find out all his ways. And no man knoweth of his ways save it be revealed unto him; wherefore, brethren, despise not the revelations of God.

9 For behold, by the power of his word man came upon the face of the earth, which earth was created by the power of his word. Wherefore, if God being able to speak and the world was, and to speak and man was created, O then, why not able to command the earth, or the workmanship of his hands upon the face of it, according to his will and pleasure?

10 Wherefore, brethren, seek not to counsel the Lord, but to take counsel from his hand. For behold, ye yourselves know that he counseleth in wisdom, and in justice, and in great mercy, over all his works.

Searching the prophets was a catalyst for receiving revelation and producing miracles among the faithful Nephites. After searching the prophets, even the trees, the mountains, and the waves of the sea obeyed their commands in the name of Jesus (v. 6). They discovered then what Jesus taught and exemplified hundreds of years later: "If ye have faith as a grain of mustard seed, ye shall say unto this mountain, Remove hence to yonder place; and it shall remove" (Matthew 17:20). After he calmed the sea they marveled: "even the winds and the seas obey him" (Matthew 8:27), and the very trees obey him (see Mark 11:12–14). The faithful Jaredites of the Book of Mormon had the same power, "the brother of Jared said unto the mountain Zerin, Remove—and it was removed" (Ether 12:30). The Book of Mormon thus gives us two witnesses of the power of the priesthood. It also gives us two witnesses of why the Lord shows us our weaknesses. We must learn that it is only through "his grace and his great condescension" that men have the power of the priesthood to do these things

(Jacob 4:7). Again from the Jaredite record we get a second witness: "And if men come unto me I will show unto them their weakness. I give unto men weakness that they may be humble; and my grace is sufficient for all men that humble themselves before me; for if they humble themselves before me, and have faith in me, then will I make weak things become strong unto them" (Ether 12:27).

Another lesson taught by Jacob is that we must recognize the greatness of God. In our efforts to teach that man is in the image of God, we sometimes fail to recognize that he and his attributes are beyond our comprehension. Jacob says "it is impossible that man should find out all his ways" (Jacob 4:8). Nor could we understand them if we knew all of them. Our source of knowledge is revelation from him. "Unto him that receiveth I will give more; and from them that shall say, We have enough, from them shall be taken away even that which they have" (2 Nephi 28:30; cp Isaiah 28:13). Therefore, Jacob admonishes, "Despise not the revelation of God" (Jacob 4:8). God's power comes by the power of his word (v. 9). He speaks and the earth or the elements obey. Therefore when he speaks the elements are organized as he directs. "The word create came from the [Hebrew] word *baurau* which does not mean to create out of nothing; it means to organize" (*TPJS*, 350). Thus, God organized and placed man on the earth "by the power of his word" as Jacob teaches. He still governs the earth by the same power. However, man has his agency and does not always obey, therefore he is less than the dust of the earth (see Helaman 12:7–19). Our challenge is to learn the Lord's will and pleasure (Jacob 4:9) and to follow his counsel. Mankind is prone to tell God what ought to be done rather than to seek his direction of perfect wisdom, justice, and mercy (v. 10).

Jacob 4:11–12 • Be Reconciled Through the Atonement

11 Wherefore, beloved brethren, be reconciled unto him through the atonement of Christ, his Only Begotten Son, and ye may obtain a resurrection, according to the power of the resurrection which is in Christ, and be presented as the first-fruits of Christ unto God, having

faith, and obtained a good hope of glory in him before he manifesteth himself in the flesh.

12 And now, beloved, marvel not that I tell you these things; for why not speak of the atonement of Christ, and attain to a perfect knowledge of him, as to attain to the knowledge of a resurrection and the world to come?

To "be reconciled unto [Christ] through the atonement" (v. 11) is to meet the conditions for the Atonement paying for our sins. Paul later taught the same concept:

10 For if, when we were enemies, we were reconciled to God by the death of his Son, much more, being reconciled, we shall be saved by his life.

11 And not only *so,* but we also joy in God through our Lord Jesus Christ, by whom we have now received the atonement. [Romans 5:10–11]

Paul also said Jesus "gave himself a ransom for all" (1 Timothy 2:6), but Jesus said the Son of man came "to minister, and to give his life a ransom for many" (Matthew 20:28). Although his infinite and eternal atonement paid for the sins of all mankind, the condition for it's being efficacious must be met. In a revelation to Martin Harris through Joseph Smith, in 1830, the Lord said:

16 For behold, I, God, have suffered these things for all, that they might not suffer if they would repent;

17 But if they would not repent they must suffer even as I;

18 Which suffering caused myself, even God, the greatest of all, to tremble because of pain, and to bleed at every pore, and to suffer both body and spirit—and would that I might not drink the bitter cup, and shrink. [D&C 19:16–18]

To "obtain a resurrection according to the power of the resurrection which is in Christ, and be presented as the first-fruits of Christ unto God, having faith, and obtained a good hope of glory" (v. 11) is to come forth in the first resurrection and receive a good or a celestial glory (see 1 Corinthians 15:40–42; D&C 88:14–20). Those who do not meet the requirements of a celestial resurrection and glory "will not attain to a perfect knowledge of [Christ]" but will "attain to the knowledge of a resurrection, and the world to come" (Jacob 4:12). Theirs will be a terrestrial or a telestial resurrection, depending on which glory they have prepared themselves to receive.

21 And they who are not sanctified through the law which I have given unto you, even the law of Christ, must inherit another kingdom, even that of a terrestrial kingdom, or that of a telestial kingdom.

22 For he who is not able to abide the law of a celestial kingdom cannot abide a celestial glory.

23 And he who cannot abide the law of a terrestrial kingdom cannot abide a terrestrial glory.

24 And he who cannot abide the law of a telestial kingdom cannot abide a telestial glory; therefore he is not meet for a kingdom of glory. Therefore he must abide a kingdom which is not a kingdom of glory. [D&C 88:21–24]

This brief treatise of the Atonement is an extension of the great sermon given by Jacob earlier and recorded in Second Nephi chapters 9 and 10.

Jacob 4:13–18 • The Sure Foundation to Build Upon

13 Behold, my brethren, he that prophesieth, let him prophesy to the understanding of men; for the Spirit speaketh the truth and lieth not. Wherefore, it speaketh of things as they really are, and of things as they really will be; wherefore, these things are manifested unto us plainly, for the salvation of our souls. But behold, we are not witnesses alone in these things; for God also spake them unto prophets of old.

14 But behold, the Jews were a stiffnecked people; and they despised the words of plainness, and killed the prophets, and sought for things that they could not understand. Wherefore, because of their blindness, which blindness came by looking beyond the mark, they must needs fall; for God hath taken away his plainness from them, and delivered unto them many things which they cannot understand,

because they desired it. And because they desired it God hath done it, that they may stumble.

15 And now I, Jacob, am led on by the Spirit unto prophesying; for I perceive by the workings of the Spirit which is in me, that by the stumbling of the Jews they will reject the stone upon which they might build and have safe foundation.

16 But behold, according to the scriptures, this stone shall become the great, and the last, and the only sure foundation, upon which the Jews can build.

17 And now, my beloved, how is it possible that these, after having rejected the sure foundation, can ever build upon it, that it may become the head of their corner?

18 Behold, my beloved brethren, I will unfold this mystery unto you; if I do not, by any means, get shaken from my firmness in the Spirit, and stumble because of my over anxiety for you.

"Prophesy to the understanding of men" (v. 13) is to speak as the Lord God would. According to Nephi, "the Lord God giveth light unto the understanding; for he speaketh unto men according to their language, unto their understanding" (2 Nephi 31:3; see also D&C 1:24). This is the second time Jacob has defined the truth. The first time he equated "things which are, and things which are to come" with the words of Isaiah (2 Nephi 6:4). On this occasion, he equates it with the Spirit, and gives a fuller definition. The Spirit "speaketh things as they really are, and of things as they really will be" (Jacob 4:13). The Lord has given even a fuller definition: "And truth is knowledge of things as they are, and as they were, and as they are to come" (D&C 93:24). Jacob adds a purpose of prophecy: "the salvation of our souls" (Jacob 4:13). These words of Jacob were apparently written to prepare us for the prophecy he was about to make, but he wanted us to know that the prophets of old had also spoken of what he was about to prophesy (v. 13). He also wants us to have a little background on the previous prophecies and learn why another one is needed.

The Jews, who were a stiffnecked people, killed the prophets and sought for things they could not understand. When it was given to them, it caused them to stumble and fall. They looked beyond the mark (v. 14). Elder Dean L. Larsen commented on these words of Jacob:

> Jacob speaks of people who placed themselves in serious jeopardy in spiritual things because they were unwilling to accept, simple, basic principles of the truth. They entertained and intrigued themselves with "things that they could not understand" (Jacob 4:14). They were apparently afflicted with a pseudo sophistication and a snobbishness that gave them a false sense of superiority over those who came among them with the Lord's words of plainness. They went beyond the mark of wisdom and prudence, and obviously failed to stay within the circle of fundamental gospel truths, which provide a basis for faith. They must have reveled in speculative and theoretical matters that obscured for them the fundamental spiritual truths. As they became infatuated by these "things that they could not understand," their comprehension of and faith in the redeeming role of a true Messiah was lost, and the purpose of life became confused. A study of Israel's history will confirm Jacob's allegations. [Conference Report, Oct. 1987, 12]

Another possible way the Jews looked beyond the mark was to confuse the prophecies of the Second Coming of Christ with the prophecies of his first Coming. Both of these explanations are plausible and caused Jacob to prophesy that because of "the stumbling of the Jews they will reject the stone upon which they might build and have safe foundation" (v. 15). The scriptures to which Jacob refers are in the Psalms: "The stone *which* the builders refused is become the head *stone* of the corner. This is the LORD's doing; it *is* marvellous in our eyes (Psalms 118:22–23). Jesus quoted the same scripture to the chief priests and Pharisees in the last week of his ministry and they perceived that he spoke of them (see Matthew 21:42–46). He also identified himself as "the stone which was set at naught of you builders, which is become the head of the corner" (Acts 4:11). Jacob asks his brethren how it is possible for the Jews to build on this sure foundation and promises to "unfold this mystery unto [them]" (Jacob 4:17–18). He then quotes the allegory of the house of Israel, spoken by Zenos and written upon the plates of brass, to fulfill the promise.

Jacob 5 • The Allegory

The fifth chapter of Jacob is one of the most challenging in the Book of Mormon. Although it is the longest chapter in the book, the analysis and interpretation of the chapter, not its length, present the challenge. The interpretation is difficult because the elements of the story stand for something outside the story. In this way, the allegory and the parable are similar. Both illustrate a principle under the guise of another story, but the allegory is longer and more involved. The apostles asked Jesus why he taught in parables. He answered, "Because it is given unto you to know the mysteries of the kingdom of heaven, but to them it is not given" (Matthew 13:11). According to Joseph Smith: "it is given unto you [the disciples of Jesus], to know the mysteries of the Kingdom of Heaven, but to them [that is, unbelievers] it is not given, for whosoever hath, to him shall be given, and he shall have more abundance; but whosoever hath not, from him shall be taken away even that he hath" (*TPJS*, 95). These unbelievers could be divided into two categories: those who were not yet ready to receive the truth, and those who had hardened their hearts against it. Therefore, a parable rewards the faithful, but is an act of mercy to those who are not yet spiritually attuned, and a condemnation to those who reject the spirit of truth (see Matthew 13:10–17).

The importance and difficulty of the Allegory of the Olive Tree were noted by President Joseph Fielding Smith: "In this chapter we have a parable that nobody could have written unless he had the guidance of the Spirit of the Lord. It would have been impossible. I think that as many as ninety-nine out of every hundred who read the Book of Mormon read this parable through without grasping the fulness and meaning of it. And I think this is one of the greatest passages in the Book of Mormon."[2]

----

[2] *Answers to Gospel Questions,* [1957–66], 4:203.

Imagery of the Allegory

Moses called the promised land; "a land of oil olive" (Deuteronomy 8:8). An understanding of the prevalence and significance of the olive tree to the land of Palestine is helpful in understanding why it is used in the allegory.

In the earliest times the olive was cultivated throughout Palestine (Deuteronomy 28:48); and olive-oil has always been one of the chief products of the country (Deuteronomy 8:8; Joel 1:10; Amos 4:9). . . . Olives were eaten everywhere, either raw or pickled, after the bitter taste had been removed by allowing them to lie in brine. . . .

The wild olive, or oleaster (Romans 11:17 seq.), which is also referred to in the Old Testament, but by a different name (1 Kings 6:23, 31; Nehemiah 8:15), must not be confused with the cultivated olive. This had short, broad leaves and thorny branches, and yielded an inferior quality of oil used only in the preparation of ointment. The wood, on the other hand, furnished good timber. The olive-tree, perennially green and always rejuvenating itself, was a favorite symbol of prosperity (Psalms 52:8; 128:3; Jeremiah 11:16); and the falling off of the leaves after a frost was typical of the early destruction of the wicked (Job 15:33). In case the tree lost its branches, wild olive branches were grafted on the cultivated stock (Romans 11:17). For the Orientals olives and olive-oil are necessities, and the failure of the olive crop is a national calamity (Amos 4:9; Habakkuk 3:17; cf. 2 Kings 4:2 seq.).[3]

Before analyzing the allegory, it is essential to understand its imagery (what each of the figures in the allegory represents). The allegory itself identifies most of the imagery. Those images not identified by the allegory can be identified from other scriptural sources or from latter-day prophets (see table 1).

---

[3] *The New Schaff–Herzog Encyclopedia of Religious Knowledge*, Grand Rapids: Baker House, [1963], 4:403–404.

Table 1

IMAGERY OF THE ALLEGORY

The tame olive tree = the house of Israel.
(Jacob 5:3; 1 Nephi 10:12; 15:12.)

The wild olive tree = the Gentiles. (Romans 11:11–25.)

The roots of the olive tree = the blood
of Israel among the Gentiles. (Joseph Fielding Smith, *Answers
to Gospel Questions* 4:141.)

Grafting = receiving the fulness of the gospel or
coming to a knowledge of the true Messiah.
(1 Nephi 10:14; 15:13–16.)

The vineyard = the world. (Jacob 5:77; 6:2–3.)

Master of the vineyard = Jesus Christ.
(D&C 33; Matthew 23:8–10, 37; 25:1;
Revelation 22:20; 3 Nephi 27:13–21.)

The servant = the prophet or prophets.
(Amos 3:7; Joseph Smith, *Teachings of
the Prophet Joseph Smith* [1976], 157.)

The tame olive tree represents the "house of Israel" (Jacob 5:3). The wild olive tree is identified as the Gentiles by the apostle Paul, in writing to the Romans "and thou, being a wild olive tree, wert grafted in among them, and with them partakest of the root and fatness of the olive tree" (Romans 11:17). From these sources, we can determine that the branches of the tame olive tree are the various tribes of the house of Israel: the lost ten tribes, the nation of Judah, and the Nephite-Lamanite groups of the tribe of Joseph. The branches of the wild olive tree are the various Gentile nations. The roots represent the blood of Israel. This interpretation is based on the following statement of President Joseph Fielding Smith and an overall analysis of the allegory as supported by other scriptures: "In brief, it [the allegory] records the history of Israel down through the ages, the scattering of the tribes to all parts of the earth; *their mingling with, or being grafted in, the wild olive trees, or in other words the mixing of the blood of Israel among the Gentiles* by which the great blessings and promises of the Lord to Abraham are fulfilled" (emphasis added).[4]

As taught by Lehi, grafting refers to the receiving of the fulness of the gospel or "come to the knowledge of the true Messiah, their Lord and their Redeemer" (1 Nephi 10:14; see also 15:13–16).

That the vineyard represents the world is shown by comparing Jacob 5:77 with Jacob's comment that "the world shall be burned with fire" after it is pruned the last time (Jacob 6:2–3).

The master of the vineyard is Jesus Christ. This is shown in the Doctrine and Covenants where the revelator refers to "the last time that I shall call laborers into my vineyard" (D&C 33:3), and then identifies himself in various ways. The revelator refers to "this church have I established, and called forth out of the wilderness" (D&C 33:5). This church is The Church of Jesus Christ of Latter-day Saints. He says further that "so will I gather mine elect" (D&C 33:6). A comparison with "how often would I have gathered thy children together" (Matthew 23:37) also identifies the revelator as Jesus Christ. The revelator next identifies the principles of his gospel (D&C 33:11–12). A comparison with 3 Nephi 27:13–22 again confirms the revelator to be Jesus Christ. Jesus Christ then speaks of the coming of the Bridegroom, saying that he will come quickly (D&C 33:17–18), which, compared with Matthew 25:1 and Revelation 22:20 once more shows the speaker to be the Savior. This is consistent with the Savior's New Testament teaching: "One is your master, even Christ" (Matthew 23:8–10).

The last figure we need to identify is the servant. Servants collectively are identified by Amos as "his servants the prophets" (Amos 3:7). The main servant who comes to the vineyard with the Lord of

---

[4] *Answers to Gospel Questions*, 4:141.

the vineyard could be a specific prophet or a general representation of the prophets. Or, the servant may be the head of each dispensation, such as Joseph Smith, who holds "the keys of the Kingdom" in this dispensation (D&C 90:2–4). However, the interpretation of which prophet is the servant does not affect the message of the allegory, as long as it is kept in mind that the servant of the allegory is a prophet.

Through this imagery, one can see that the allegory teaches the history, scattering, and gathering of the house of Israel. This can be best understood by referring to other related scriptures (see table 2 —end of chapter).

Jacob 5:1–2 • The Words of Zenos, a Prophet of the Lord

1 Behold, my brethren, do ye not remember to have read the words of the prophet Zenos, which he spake unto the house of Israel, saying:

2 Hearken, O ye house of Israel, and hear the words of me, a prophet of the Lord.

Elder Bruce R. McConkie said of the prophet Zenos, whose writings were once in the Old Testament, but have been taken away: "I do not think I overstate the matter when I say that next to Isaiah himself—who is the prototype, pattern, and model for all the prophets—there has not been a greater prophet than Zenos. And our knowledge of his inspired writings is limited to the quotations and paraphrasing summaries found in the Book of Mormon."[5]

Since the allegory outlines the history of the scattering and gathering of the house of Israel, it is only logical that it starts with the beginning. The house of Israel began about 1800 B.C., when the twelve sons of Jacob were living in Canaan. The allegory ends when

---

[5] *The Doctrinal Restoration*, chapter 1, p. 17, The Joseph Smith Translation, Monte S. Nyman and Robert L. Millet, Religious Study Center, Brigham Young University, Provo, Utah, 1985.

the temporal existence of the earth is completed, or, in other words, at the end of the millennium.

A careful analysis of the allegory shows that it refers to seven time periods (see table 3—end of chapter). Two of these time periods are described as merely "a long time passed away" between the visits of the Lord and his servant to the vineyard (Jacob 5:15, 29). These seem easily identified. The first long time period would be about 400 years from the end of the Old Testament prophets to the time of the ministry of Jesus Christ, a period when no revelation was given to Israel. The second would be the great apostasy following the Savior's ministry until the day of the restoration, another period when no revelation was given to Israel. The identification of the other five time periods is made easier by identifying these two. The five are: (1) from Jacob to Malachi, the last of the Old Testament prophets; (2) the ministry of Jesus Christ; (3) the restoration in 1820 to the millennium; (4) the millennium; and (5) the end of the earth.

The first period covers from about 1800–400 B.C. This is the time that Israel was scattered "upon all the face of the earth, and also among all nations" (1 Nephi 22:3). The interpretation of Jacob 5:3–14 is drawn from the scriptures and history of this time.

Jacob 5:3–6 • The Tame Olive Tree

3 For behold, thus saith the Lord, I will liken thee, O house of Israel, like unto a tame olive-tree, which a man took and nourished in his vineyard; and it grew, and waxed old, and began to decay.

4 And it came to pass that the master of the vineyard went forth, and he saw that his olive-tree began to decay; and he said: I will prune it, and dig about it, and nourish it, that perhaps it may shoot forth young and tender branches, and it perish not.

5 And it came to pass that he pruned it, and digged about it, and nourished it according to his word.

6 And it came to pass that after many days it began to put forth somewhat a little, young and tender branches; but behold, the main top thereof began to perish.

After introducing the allegory (vv. 1–2), Jacob begins quoting it. The house of Israel is described as a tame olive tree that is waxing old and beginning to decay (v. 3). Because of this condition, the Lord of the vineyard pruned it, nourished it, and digged about it in an attempt to save it (vv. 4–5). This attempt could be identified as the time when the house of Israel was in Egypt because of the famine in Canaan. We read that: "The famine was over all the face of the earth" (Genesis 41:56–57). The famine is indicative of the decaying of Israel. God does "chasten his people with many afflictions, yea, except he doth visit them with death and with terror, and *with famine*, and with all manner of pestilence, they will not remember him" (Helaman 12:3; emphasis added). He wants them to remember him so that he can bless them for keeping his laws (see D&C 130:20–21). Some may argue that Israel being in Egypt is a transplant rather than a pruning because Jacob (Israel) had left Canaan (the promised land) and sojourned in Egypt. However, it should be remembered that the land covenanted to Abraham, and thus the house of Israel, extended "from the river of Egypt unto the great river, the river Euphrates" (Genesis 15:18). Therefore, the house of Israel is still in the main part of the vineyard. Furthermore, the biblical account of Genesis supports the pruning concept. Joseph tells his brothers that "God sent me before you to preserve you a posterity in the earth, and to save your lives by a great deliverance" and told them to bring their father to Egypt "and there will I *nourish* thee; for there are yet five years of famine" (Genesis 45:5, 7–8, 11; 46:1–7; emphasis added).

The allegory continues with the observation or prophecy "that after many days it began to put forth somewhat a little, young and tender branches; but behold, the main top thereof began to perish" (Jacob 5:6). The phrase "after many days" fits the extended time Israel was in Egypt, from the time of Joseph until their bondage in the days of Moses. The young and tender branches have a double interpretation. First, when Moses led Israel out of Egypt, the Lord became angry with the people because they would not hearken to his voice after having seen his glory and the miracles he did in Egypt. They were therefore detained in the wilderness for forty years until the older generation, except Joshua and Caleb, died (the main top perished). At this time the new faithful generation (the young and tender branches) were allowed to enter Canaan (see Numbers 14:26–38).

Second, Moses sought diligently to prepare his people to behold the face of God through the ordinances and power of the Melchizedek Priesthood, but Israel hardened its heart, and God "took Moses out of their midst, and the Holy [Melchizedek] Priesthood (the main top) out of their midst also; and the lesser [Aaronic] Priesthood (the young and tender branches) continued" (D&C 84:25–26). The Lord had worked with Israel, but Israel had failed to respond to his efforts.

Jacob 5:7–14 • Wild Branches Grafted In

7 And it came to pass that the master of the vineyard saw it, and he said unto his servant: It grieveth me that I should lose this tree; wherefore, go and pluck the branches from a wild olive-tree, and bring them hither unto me; and we will pluck off those main branches which are beginning to wither away, and we will cast them into the fire that they may be burned.

8 And behold, saith the Lord of the vineyard, I take away many of these young and tender branches, and I will graft them whithersoever I will; and it mattereth not that if it so be that the root of this tree will perish, I may preserve the fruit thereof unto myself; wherefore, I will take these young and tender branches, and I will graft them whithersoever I will.

9 Take thou the branches of the wild olive-tree, and graft them in, in the stead thereof; and these which I have plucked off I will cast into the fire and burn them, that they may not cumber the ground of my vineyard.

10 And it came to pass that the servant of the Lord of the vineyard did according to the word of the Lord of the vineyard, and grafted in the branches of the wild olive-tree.

11 And the Lord of the vineyard caused that it should be digged about, and pruned, and nourished, saying unto his servant: It grieveth me that I should lose this tree; wherefore, that perhaps I might preserve the roots thereof that they perish not, that I might preserve

them unto myself, I have done this thing.

12 Wherefore, go thy way; watch the tree, and nourish it, according to my words.

13 And these will I place in the nethermost part of my vineyard, whithersoever I will, it mattereth not unto thee; and I do it that I may preserve unto myself the natural branches of the tree; and also, that I may lay up fruit thereof against the season, unto myself; for it grieveth me that I should lose this tree and the fruit thereof.

14 And it came to pass that the Lord of the vineyard went his way, and hid the natural branches of the tame olive-tree in the nethermost parts of the vineyard, some in one and some in another, according to his will and pleasure.

The next program of the Lord of the vineyard was to graft some wild branches (Gentiles) into the tame olive tree and to graft many of the young and tender branches whithersoever he would (vv. 7–9). The main branches are different from the main top, which had earlier begun to perish. The main branches are possibly the two divisions of the kingdom of Israel—the northern tribes (Ephraim) and the southern tribes (Judah). Both of these branches were plucked off because of their wickedness—Israel in about 721 B.C. by the Assyrians, and Judah about 607 B.C. by the Babylonians. Many people from both branches were destroyed, which is the equivalent of the burning referred to in the allegory (v. 9). Those who destroyed them also took away the young and tender branches to Assyria and Babylon.

One of the grafts of the wild olive-tree into the tame olive-tree can be identified as the Gentiles that Assyria brought to intermarry with the Israelites who had been left behind after the Assyrian conquest. "And the king of Assyria brought *men* from Babylon, and from Cuthah, and from Ava, and from Hamath, and from Sepharvaim, and placed *them* in the cities of Samaria instead of the children of Israel: and they possessed Samaria, and dwelt in the cities thereof" (2 Kings 17:24). The Gentiles' exposure to the roots of the house of Israel is shown by Israelite priests later being sent to teach them how to worship the God of Israel.

26 Wherefore they spake to the king of Assyria, saying, The nations which thou hast removed, and placed in the cities of Samaria, know not the manner of the God of the land: therefore he hath sent lions among them, and, behold, they slay them, because they know not the manner of the God of the land.

27 Then the king of Assyria commanded, saying, Carry thither one of the priests whom ye brought from thence; and let them go and dwell there, and let him teach them the manner of the God of the land.

28 Then one of the priests whom they had carried away from Samaria came and dwelt in Beth-el, and taught them how they should fear the LORD. [2 Kings 17:27–28]

God does work in mysterious ways.

Another Gentile graft into the tame olive tree would be the Babylonian captivity of Judah, in which many of Judeans were carried into Babylon and "served the king of Babylon seventy years" as prophesied (Jeremiah 25:8–11). We also have an account of some of Judah intermarrying with Gentiles at this time (see Ezra 2:61; Nehemiah 7:61–64). The graft's productivity was furthered through the work of the gentile, King Cyrus of Persia, whom the Lord said "is my shepherd, and shall perform all my pleasure, even saying to Jerusalem, Thou shalt be built" and "whose right hand I have holden to subdue nations before him" (Isaiah 44:28–45:1). While Cyrus is mainly known for his work with the return of the Jews, the Lord seems to have used him for the grafting of the wild-olive branch as well. For example, who were the "wise men [who came] from the east to Jerusalem, Saying, Where is he that is born King of the Jews? For we have seen his star in the east, and are come to worship him" (Matthew 2:1–2)? How would they have known of the new born king and of his star? These men may well have been the product of the Gentile graft.

A further grafting may have taken place after the Babylonian captivity when Jeremiah and many of the Jews went down into Egypt (see Jeremiah 43). We have no account of this, but the same pattern probably applies.

While the Gentiles were grafted into Israel, many of the Israelites were also scattered among the Gentiles. This accounts for the roots of Israel being identified as yet alive among the Gentiles (Jacob 5:54). This preservation of the roots is the purpose for the grafting as given in the allegory (v. 11). It also fulfills the prophecy of Amos, that the Lord would "not utterly destroy the house of Jacob" but would sift them "among all nations, like as corn is sifted in a sieve" (Amos 9:8–9). This was also foretold by Nephi, based on Isaiah's prophecies: "It appears that the house of Israel, sooner or later, will be scattered upon all the face of the earth, *and also among all nations* (1 Nephi 22:3; emphasis added).

While Israel was scattered among the nations, three groups (Jacob 5:39), or three branches, were kept intact but planted elsewhere in the vineyard. These can be identified in the order in which they were taken away: the ten tribes in about 721 B.C., the Jews in about 607 B.C., and the Lehi colony in about 600 B.C. (see 2 Kings 17:23; 25:1–11; 1 Nephi 1:1–4). Keeping this order in mind is very important in understanding later parts of the allegory.

Thus, the first period of the allegory is from about 1800–400 B.C., when the house of Israel was "scattered upon all the face of the earth, and also among all nations" (1 Nephi 22:3). The second period is one of apostasy, from 400 B.C. to the ministry of Jesus Christ, which is covered in one verse (29) and needs no further commentary.

Jacob 5:15 • The Earthly
Ministry of Jesus

> 15 And it came to pass that a long time passed away, and the Lord of the vineyard said unto his servant: Come, let us go down into the vineyard, that we may labor in the vineyard.

The third period describes the ministry of Jesus and the apostles in the meridian of time, as is outlined in Jacob 5:16–28. This is the period of which "all the [Old Testament] prophets who have prophesied ever since the world began" had spoken (Mosiah 14:33).

Jacob 5:16–18 • The Wild Branches Produce Fruit

> 16 And it came to pass that the Lord of the vineyard, and also the servant, went down into the vineyard to labor. And it came to pass that the servant said unto his master: Behold, look here; behold the tree.
>
> 17 And it came to pass that the Lord of the vineyard looked and beheld the tree in the which the wild olive branches had been grafted; and it had sprung forth and begun to bear fruit. And he beheld that it was good; and the fruit thereof was like unto the natural fruit.
>
> 18 And he said unto the servant: Behold, the branches of the wild tree have taken hold of the moisture of the root thereof, that the root thereof hath brought forth much strength; and because of the much strength of the root thereof the wild branches have brought forth tame fruit. Now, if we had not grafted in these branches, the tree thereof would have perished. And now, behold, I shall lay up much fruit, which the tree thereof hath brought forth; and the fruit thereof I shall lay up against the season, unto mine own self.

The first observation about this period in the allegory is that the Gentile branches that had been grafted into the tame olive tree were bearing good fruit (vv. 16–18). One place where this part of the allegory was fulfilled is the city of Samaria, where the Savior, at a well originally dug by Jacob, asked a Samaritan woman for a drink of water (John 4). The Samaritans were the product of the intermarriage between the Israelites who remained in the land after the Assyrian conquest of 721 B.C. They married the Babylonians and other Gentiles brought in by the Assyrians (2 Kings 17:24 quoted above). Jesus's disciples' were amazed that he was conversing with the Samaritan woman because it was against the traditional behavior of the Jews. Jesus taught them that the fields of the Samaritans "are white already to harvest" (John 4:35). The graft had taken hold, and the mixture of the Israelites and Gentiles was bearing fruit.

Jacob 5:19–28 • The Three Tame Branches

19 And it came to pass that the Lord of the vineyard said unto the servant: Come, let us go to the nethermost part of the vineyard, and behold if the natural branches of the tree have not brought forth much fruit also, that I may lay up of the fruit thereof against the season, unto mine own self.

20 And it came to pass that they went forth whither the master had hid the natural branches of the tree, and he said unto the servant: Behold these; and he beheld the first that it had brought forth much fruit; and he beheld also that it was good. And he said unto the servant: Take of the fruit thereof, and lay it up against the season, that I may preserve it unto mine own self; for behold, said he, this long time have I nourished it, and it hath brought forth much fruit.

21 And it came to pass that the servant said unto his master: How comest thou hither to plant this tree, or this branch of the tree? For behold, it was the poorest spot in all the land of thy vineyard.

22 And the Lord of the vineyard said unto him: Counsel me not; I knew that it was a poor spot of ground; wherefore, I said unto thee, I have nourished it this long time, and thou beholdest that it hath brought forth much fruit.

23 And it came to pass that the Lord of the vineyard said unto his servant: Look hither; behold I have planted another branch of the tree also; and thou knowest that this spot of ground was poorer than the first. But, behold the tree. I have nourished it this long time, and it hath brought forth much fruit; therefore, gather it, and lay it up against the season, that I may preserve it unto mine own self.

24 And it came to pass that the Lord of the vineyard said again unto his servant: Look hither, and behold another branch also, which I have planted; behold that I have nourished it also, and it hath brought forth fruit.

25 And he said unto the servant: Look hither and behold the last. Behold, this have I planted in a good spot of ground; and I have nourished it this long time, and only a part of the tree hath brought forth tame fruit, and the other part of the tree hath brought forth wild fruit; behold, I have nourished this tree like unto the others.

26 And it came to pass that the Lord of the vineyard said unto the servant: Pluck off the branches that have not brought forth good fruit, and cast them into the fire.

27 But behold, the servant said unto him: Let us prune it, and dig about it, and nourish it a little longer, that perhaps it may bring forth good fruit unto thee, that thou canst lay it up against the season.

28 And it came to pass that the Lord of the vineyard and the servant of the Lord of the vineyard did nourish all the fruit of the vineyard.

The second event of this time period is when the Lord of the vineyard and his servant visited the natural branches that had been grafted into the nethermost parts of the earth (v. 19). Their first visit was to the first branch that had been taken away. This would be the ten and a half tribes that had been taken into Assyria, and then led further into the north (see 2 Kings 18:9–12). While we do not know their location, we do know they were visited by the Savior after his resurrection and his appearance to the Nephites. Near the end of the first day of his three day visit to the Nephites he said: "But now I go unto the Father, and also to show myself unto the lost tribes of Israel, for they are not lost unto the Father, for he knoweth whither he hath taken them" (3 Nephi 17:4). The branch was producing much good fruit. The servant questioned the Lord about his having brought this branch to what was the poorest spot of ground in the vineyard. The Lord responded that the servant should not give counsel, for he (the Lord) knew it was a poor spot, but the branch had produced fruit. The Lord knows all things and guides his children to accomplish his purposes.

As further evidence of his wisdom, the Lord invites the servant to look at a branch that had been planted in an even poorer spot of ground. It too had brought forth much fruit (Jacob 5:23). This undoubtedly refers to the Jews, but whether it is a group in Babylon, Egypt (the Coptics), Palestine, or somewhere else is not clear.

The Lord next invites the servant to behold the third branch that had brought forth fruit (v. 24). Some interpret this branch as different from the one described in verse 25; however, a comparison with verse 39 shows there are only three branches. This is also supported historically, since the Savior mentioned only three groups of Israelites that he had visited or would yet visit. He had visited the Jews and told them of his other sheep (John 10:14–16). He was among the Nephites and identified them as the other sheep he had mentioned to the Jews (see 3 Nephi 15:21–24), and then told the Nephites he was going "to show himself unto the lost tribes of Israel" (3 Nephi 17:4). The following verses are, therefore, an extension of the description of the third group. That the Nephites had been planted in a choice spot of ground (Jacob 5:25) helps to identify them as the people of Lehi in America who were brought to a "choice above all other lands" (1 Nephi 2:20). Further verification of their being the seed of Lehi (and Ishmael) is shown by the allegory's declaration that only a part had brought forth tame fruit while the other part had brought forth wild fruit (Jacob 5:26). This, of course, represents the division of Lehi's people into the Nephites and the Lamanites (see 2 Nephi 5:5–25 or Helaman 15:4–5). The nourishing and pruning (Jacob 5:26–28) must refer to the period between A.D. 34 and 36, when "the people were all converted unto the Lord" (4 Nephi 1:2). Their work was productive for a time.

Jacob 5:29 • The Restoration of the Covenant of Israel

> 29 And it came to pass that a long time had passed away, and the Lord of the vineyard said unto his servant: Come, let us go down into the vineyard, that we may labor again in the vineyard. For behold, the time draweth near, and the end soon cometh; wherefore, I must lay up fruit against the season, unto mine own self.

The fourth period is the apostasy after Jesus' ministry. The fifth period has the longest treatise of any period (Jacob 5:30–75), which is logical since it depicts the latter-day fulfillment of the covenant made to Israel. It was to precede the time when "the end soon cometh," the Second Coming of Christ. This is substantiated by the angel Moroni's visit to Joseph Smith in September 1823. Moroni recited many passages of scripture about the coming of Christ with the admonition that they were "not yet fulfilled, but was soon to be" (Joseph Smith—History 1:36–41).

Jacob 5:30–37 • The Wild Branches All Corrupt

30 And it came to pass that the Lord of the vineyard and the servant went down into the vineyard; and they came to the tree whose natural branches had been broken off, and the wild branches had been grafted in; and behold all sorts of fruit did cumber the tree.

31 And it came to pass that the Lord of the vineyard did taste of the fruit, every sort according to its number. And the Lord of the vineyard said: Behold, this long time have we nourished this tree, and I have laid up unto myself against the season much fruit.

32 But behold, this time it hath brought forth much fruit, and there is none of it which is good. And behold, there are all kinds of bad fruit; and it profiteth me nothing, notwithstanding all our labor; and now it grieveth me that I should lose this tree.

33 And the Lord of the vineyard said unto the servant: What shall we do unto the tree, that I may preserve again good fruit thereof unto mine own self?

34 And the servant said unto his master: Behold, because thou didst graft in the branches of the wild olive-tree they have nourished the roots, that they are alive and they have not perished; wherefore thou beholdest that they are yet good.

35 And it came to pass that the Lord of the vineyard said unto his servant: The tree profiteth me nothing, and the roots thereof profit me nothing so long as it shall bring forth evil fruit.

36 Nevertheless, I know that the roots are good, and for mine own purpose I have preserved them; and because of their much strength they have hitherto brought forth, from the wild branches, good fruit.

37 But behold, the wild branches have grown and have overrun the roots thereof; and because that the wild branches have overcome the roots thereof it hath brought forth much evil fruit; and because that it hath brought forth so much evil fruit thou beholdest that it beginneth to perish; and it will soon become ripened, that it may be

cast into the fire, except we should do something for it to preserve it.

The first eight verses (30–37) of this period of the allegory describe the visit of the Lord of the vineyard and his servant to the Gentiles who had been grafted into the house of Israel. This is easily interpreted by comparing it to Joseph Smith's history as recorded in the Pearl of Great Price. "All sorts of fruit which did cumber the tree" (v. 30) fits the description Joseph Smith gave of the religious revivals that were prevalent in his youth:

> 5 Some time in the second year after our removal to Manchester, there was in the place where we lived an unusual excitement on the subject of religion. It commenced with the Methodists, but soon became general among all the sects in that region of country. Indeed, the whole district of country seemed affected by it, and great mult-itudes united themselves to the different religious parties, which created no small stir and division amongst the people, some crying, "Lo, here!" and others, "Lo, there!" Some were contending for the Methodist faith, some for the Presbyterian, and some for the Baptist.

> 6 For, notwithstanding the great love which the converts to these different faiths expressed at the time of their conversion, and the great zeal manifested by the respective clergy, who were active in getting up and promoting this extraordinary scene of religious feeling, in order to have everybody converted, as they were pleased to call it, let them join what sect they pleased; yet when the converts began to file off, some to one party and some to another, it was seen that the seemingly good feelings of both the priests and the converts were more pretended than real; for a scene of great confusion and bad feeling ensued—priest contending against priest, and convert against convert; so that all their good feelings one for another, if they ever had any, were entirely lost in a strife of words and a contest about opinions. [Joseph Smith— History 1:5–6]

The Lord's tasting of all the fruit with the declaration that none of it was good (Jacob 5:32) corresponds with what we call the First Vision. In response to Joseph's question about "which of all the sects was right," the Savior told him to "join none of them, for they were all wrong" (JS—H 1:18–19). The servant's observation that the wild branches had "nourished the roots, that they are alive" can be understood by referring to the Doctrine and Covenants explanation of the servant of the Lord referred to in Isaiah 11. The servant (Joseph Smith) is identified as "a descendant of Jesse, as well as of Joseph" (D&C 113:3–6). Thus Joseph Smith had the literal blood of Israel in his veins although he was living among the Gentiles and was by culture a Gentile. The blood of Israel had been scattered among the Gentiles and by some genetic process had been preserved. Abraham was promised that the priesthood "shall continue in thee, and in thy seed after thee (that is to say, the literal seed, or the seed of the body)" (Abraham 2:11). Although this may not be proven scientifically, it is a truth fully supported by the Old Testament prophets (see Isaiah 11:11; Amos 9:8–9). This is further verified in the Doctrine and Covenants.

30 Abraham received promises concerning his seed, and of the fruit of his loins—from whose loins ye are, namely, my servant Joseph— which were to continue so long as they were in the world; and as touching Abraham and his seed, out of the world they should continue; both in the world and out of the world should they continue as innumerable as the stars; or, if ye were to count the sand upon the seashore ye could not number them.

31 This promise is yours also, because ye are of Abraham, and the promise was made unto Abraham; and by this law is the continuation of the works of my Father, wherein he glorifieth himself.

32 Go ye, therefore, and do the works of Abraham; enter ye into my law and ye shall be saved. [D&C 132:30–32]

Jacob 5:38–50 • Natural Branches All Corrupt

38 And it came to pass that the Lord of the vineyard said unto his servant: Let us go down into the nethermost parts of the vineyard, and behold if the natural branches have also brought forth evil fruit.

39 And it came to pass that they went down into the nethermost parts of the vineyard. And it came to pass that they beheld that the fruit of the natural branches had become corrupt also; yea, the first and the second and also the last; and they had all become corrupt.

40 And the wild fruit of the last had overcome that part of the tree which brought forth good fruit, even that the branch had withered away and died.

41 And it came to pass that the Lord of the vineyard wept, and said unto the servant: What could I have done more for my vineyard?

42 Behold, I knew that all the fruit of the vineyard, save it were these, had become corrupted. And now these which have once brought forth good fruit have also become corrupted; and now all the trees of my vineyard are good for nothing save it be to be hewn down and cast into the fire.

43 And behold this last, whose branch hath withered away, I did plant in a good spot of ground; yea, even that which was choice unto me above all other parts of the land of my vineyard.

44 And thou beheldest that I also cut down that which cumbered this spot of ground, that I might plant this tree in the stead thereof.

45 And thou beheldest that a part thereof brought forth good fruit, and a part thereof brought forth wild fruit; and because I plucked not the branches thereof and cast them into the fire, behold, they have overcome the good branch that it hath withered away.

46 And now, behold, notwithstanding all the care which we have taken of my vineyard, the trees thereof have become corrupted, that they bring forth no good fruit; and these I had hoped to preserve, to have laid up fruit thereof against the season, unto mine own self. But, behold, they have become like unto the wild olive-tree, and they are of no worth but to be hewn down and cast into the fire; and it grieveth me that I should lose them.

47 But what could I have done more in my vineyard? Have I slackened mine hand, that I have not nourished it? Nay, I have nourished it, and I have digged about it, and I have pruned it, and I have dunged it; and I have stretched forth mine hand almost all the day long, and the end draweth nigh. And it grieveth me that I should hew down all the trees of my vineyard, and cast them into the fire that they should be burned. Who is it that has corrupted my vineyard?

48 And it came to pass that the servant said unto his master: Is it not the loftiness of thy vineyard—have not the branches thereof overcome the roots which are good? And because the branches have overcome the roots thereof, behold they grew faster than the strength

of the roots, taking strength unto themselves. Behold, I say, is not this the cause that the trees of thy vineyard have become corrupted?

49 And it came to pass that the Lord of the vineyard said unto the servant: Let us go to and hew down the trees of the vineyard and cast them into the fire, that they shall not cumber the ground of my vineyard, for I have done all. What could I have done more for my vineyard?

50 But, behold, the servant said unto the Lord of the vineyard: Spare it a little longer.

After the Lord and his servant visited the Gentile grafts, they went to the natural branches that had been planted in the nethermost parts of the vineyard (v. 38). All of these had become corrupt, including the wild fruit (Lamanites) that overcame the tame fruit (Nephites), whose branch withered away and died (vv. 39–40). The fall of the Nephites in the America's is recorded in Mormon 6:10–15. The wild fruit that remained (Lamanites) is described in Mormon 5:15–16.

The Lord lamented over the loss of the natural branch he had planted "in a good spot of the ground." The land was, he emphasized, "choice unto me above all other parts of the land of vineyard" (Jacob 5:43; the Americas, see 1 Nephi 2:20; quoted above). Those he had cut down so that he "might plant this tree" (Jacob 5:44) were the Jaredites. The last survivor of this people, who preceded the people of Lehi's coming to the America's, was Coriantumr. The "account of one Coriantumr, and the slain of his people . . . was discovered by the people of Zarahemla; and he dwelt with them for the space of nine months" (Omni 1:21). That account, the book of Ether, states:

. . . the word of the Lord came to Ether, that he should go and prophesy unto Coriantumr that, if he would repent, and all his household, the Lord would give unto him his kingdom and spare the people—

21 Otherwise they should be destroyed, and all his household save it were himself. And he should only live to see the fulfilling of the prophecies which had been spoken concerning another people receiving the land for their inheritance; and Coriantumr should

receive a burial by them; and every soul should be destroyed save it were Coriantumr. [Ether 13:20–21]

In answer to the Lord's query of what he could have done more, the servant suggested that the branches had overcome the roots and had taken strength unto themselves (Jacob 5:47–48). This probably describes the appointment of officers in the church and kingdom. As apostasy crept in, the apostles and other stalwart officers were killed or imprisoned. Others were given these positions, but their appointments were not by revelation. They were political appointments rather than church or spiritual appointments. This is best exemplified under the rule of Constantine, where Christianity was made the state religion. The offices in the priesthood were appointed by the emperor, instead of by the Lord through his prophets and apostles. The Lord's decision to cut down the vineyard and burn it, and the servant's plea to spare it a little longer (vv. 49–50), display the laws of justice and mercy. Justice would rule that the vineyard be destroyed, but mercy pleads "to appease the demands of justice" (Alma 42:15).

Jacob 5:51–60 • Grafting Into the Mother Trunk

51 And the Lord said: Yea, I will spare it a little longer, for it grieveth me that I should lose the trees of my vineyard.

52 Wherefore, let us take of the branches of these which I have planted in the nethermost parts of my vineyard, and let us graft them into the tree from whence they came; and let us pluck from the tree those branches whose fruit is most bitter, and graft in the natural branches of the tree in the stead thereof.

53 And this will I do that the tree may not perish, that, perhaps, I may preserve unto myself the roots thereof for mine own purpose.

54 And, behold, the roots of the natural branches of the tree which I planted whithersoever I would are yet alive; wherefore, that I may preserve them also for mine own purpose, I will take of the branches of this tree, and I will graft them in unto them. Yea, I will graft in unto them the branches of their mother tree, that I may preserve the roots also unto mine own self, that when they shall be sufficiently

strong perhaps they may bring forth good fruit unto me, and I may yet have glory in the fruit of my vineyard.

55 And it came to pass that they took from the natural tree which had become wild, and grafted in unto the natural trees, which also had become wild.

56 And they also took of the natural trees which had become wild, and grafted into their mother tree.

57 And the Lord of the vineyard said unto the servant: Pluck not the wild branches from the trees, save it be those which are most bitter; and in them ye shall graft according to that which I have said.

58 And we will nourish again the trees of the vineyard, and we will trim up the branches thereof; and we will pluck from the trees those branches which are ripened, that must perish, and cast them into the fire.

59 And this I do that, perhaps, the roots thereof may take strength because of their goodness; and because of the change of the branches, that the good may overcome the evil.

60 And because that I have preserved the natural branches and the roots thereof, and that I have grafted in the natural branches again into their mother tree, and have preserved the roots of their mother tree, that, perhaps, the trees of my vineyard may bring forth again good fruit; and that I may have joy again in the fruit of my vineyard, and, perhaps, that I may rejoice exceedingly that I have preserved the roots and the branches of the first fruit—

Having yielded to mercy, the Lord presents his plan to save his vineyard. It is outlined in verses 52 through 54 and is implemented in verses 55 and 56. These verses must be carefully studied. The Lord's plan is to graft the natural branches of Israel back into the tree from which they had been taken. The mother tree into which the Gentile branches had been grafted was to have these branches (which produce the most bitter fruit) removed so the natural ones could be grafted in their stead. The roots of the natural branches would then be preserved (vv. 52–53). The Israelite roots of the Gentile branches were yet alive; therefore, the Lord would establish these Gentile branches as a mother tree into which the natural branches could be grafted when the mother tree was sufficiently strong to sustain the graft (v. 54). This was done, and then the natural branches were grafted back in (vv. 55–56). This is the overall plan which began with the restoration of the gospel in A.D. 1830.

The first step—the establishment of the mother tree, as father Lehi had explained—was to come "after the Gentiles had received the fullness of the gospel" (1 Nephi 10:14); or "in the latter days, when our seed shall have dwindled in unbelief . . . , then shall the fulness of the gospel of the Messiah come unto the Gentiles, and from the Gentiles unto the remnant of our seed" (1 Nephi 15:13). In other words, the Church would have to be established among the Gentiles before it could bring back the natural branches. The house of Israel had been scattered among the Gentiles, and the roots were still alive (the blood of Israel was still among the Gentiles). The mother tree must be re-established as a tree of Israel, by the gospel being preached to the Gentiles, and by those of the blood of Israel (roots) becoming the tree. It is only logical as well as scriptural that the mother tree be established through the birthright holder of the house of Israel, Ephraim. Jeremiah foresaw this movement.

> 6 For there shall be a day, *that* the watchmen upon the mount Ephraim shall cry, Arise ye, and let us go up to Zion unto the LORD our God.
>
> 7 For thus saith the LORD; Sing with gladness for Jacob, and shout among the chief of the nations: publish ye, praise ye, and say, O LORD, save thy people, the remnant of Israel.
>
> 8 Behold, I will bring them from the north country, and gather them from the coasts of the earth, *and* with them the blind and the lame, the woman with child and her that travaileth with child together: a great company shall return thither.
>
> 9 They shall come with weeping, and with supplications will I lead them: I will cause them to walk by the rivers of waters in a straight way, wherein they shall not stumble: for I am a father to Israel, and Ephraim *is* my firstborn. [Jeremiah 31:6–9]

An explanation of the prophecy will not be given here,[6] but note the role of Ephraim as the administrator of the latter-day gathering because he is the firstborn. Furthermore, the Lord has confirmed by revelation that the early priesthood holders of the Church were "lawful heirs, according to the flesh" (D&C 86:8–9). President Joseph F. Smith made this observation in 1902: "A striking peculiarity of the Saints gathered from all parts of the earth is that they are almost universally of the blood of Ephraim."[7]

The Lord further prescribed that the pruning be light, cutting off only the most bitter wild branches, until the natural branches could derive nourishment from the natural roots or true vine (Jacob 5:57–60; see also 1 Nephi 15:15–16). Jesus Christ told his disciples: "I am the true vine, and my father is the husbandman" (John 15:1). He, of course, is the source of strength to his covenant people who are grafted back or have "come to the knowledge of the true Messiah" (1 Nephi 10:14).

Jacob 5:61–74 • The Order of Grafting

61 Wherefore, go to, and call servants [missionaries], that we may labor diligently with our might in the vineyard [earth], that we may prepare the way, that I may bring forth again the natural fruit [Israel], which natural fruit is good and the most precious above all other fruit.

62 Wherefore, let us go to and labor with our might this last time, for behold the end draweth nigh, and this is for the last time that I shall prune my vineyard.

63 Graft in the branches; begin at the last [Lamanites] that they may be first, and that the first [lost tribes] may be last, and dig about the trees, both old and young, the first and the last; and the last and the first, that all may be nourished once again for the last time.

---

[6] For a detailed explanation of the prophecy see LeGrand Richards, *A Marvelous Work and a Wonder*, [1976], 224–28.

[7] *Gospel Doctrine*, 11th ed. [1959], 115.

64 Wherefore, dig about them, and prune them, and dung them once more, for the last time, for the end [Second Coming] draweth nigh. And if it be so that these last grafts shall grow, and bring forth the natural fruit, then shall ye prepare the way for them, that they may grow.

65 And as they begin to grow ye shall clear away the branches which bring forth bitter fruit [rebellious members], according to the strength of the good and the size thereof; and ye shall not clear away the bad thereof all at once, lest the roots thereof should be too strong for the graft, and the graft thereof shall perish, and I lose the trees of my vineyard.

66 For it grieveth me that I should lose the trees of my vineyard; wherefore ye shall clear away the bad according as the good shall grow, that the root and the top may be equal in strength, until the good shall overcome the bad, and the bad be hewn down and cast into the fire, that they cumber not the ground of my vineyard; and thus will I sweep away the bad out of my vineyard.

67 And the [three branches] branches of the natural tree will I graft in again into the natural tree;

68 And the branches of the natural tree will I graft into the natural branches of the tree; and thus will I bring them together again, that they shall bring forth the natural fruit, and they shall be one.

69 And the bad shall be cast away, yea, even out of all the land of my vineyard; for behold, only this once will I prune my vineyard.

70 And it came to pass that the Lord of the vineyard sent his servant; and the servant went and did as the Lord had commanded him, and brought other servants; and they were few.

71 And the Lord of the vineyard said unto them: Go to, and labor in the vineyard, with your might. For behold, this is the last time that I shall nourish my vineyard; for the end is nigh at hand, and the season speedily cometh; and if ye labor with your might with me ye shall have joy in the fruit which I shall lay up unto myself against the time which will soon come.

72 And it came to pass that the servants did go and labor with their mights; and the Lord of the vineyard labored also with them; and they did obey the commandments of the Lord of the vineyard in all things.

73 And there began to be the natural fruit again in the vineyard; and the natural branches began to grow and thrive exceedingly; and the wild branches began to be plucked off and to be cast away; and they did keep the root and the top thereof equal, according to the strength thereof.

74 And thus they labored, with all diligence, according to the commandments of the Lord of the vineyard, even until the bad had been cast away out of the vineyard, and the Lord had preserved unto himself that the trees had become again the natural fruit; and they became like unto one body; and the fruits were equal; and the Lord of the vineyard had preserved unto himself the natural fruit, which was most precious unto him from the beginning.

Having outlined the program, the Lord instructs his servant to call servants to prune the vineyard for the last time (vv. 61–62). Jacob's interpretation of the allegory was that when the Lord "set his hand again the second time to recover the remnant of his people" (Isaiah 11:11), it would be the last time that he would nourish and prune his vineyard and then the end would soon come (Jacob 6:2). Modern-day revelation confirms that this is the work of the restoration. In July 1830, Oliver Cowdery was "called to prune my vineyard with a mighty pruning, yea, even for the last time; yea, and also all those whom thou hast ordained" (D&C 24:19). Therefore, that nourishing and pruning began over a hundred and seventy years ago and is well under way. Ephraim is firmly established, and the time to begin grafting back the natural branches is near.

The grafting of the natural branches is to be in the reverse order of their dispersion. The last taken away (Lehi's group) is to be grafted back first (Jacob 5:63). The work with the Lamanites has commenced. The second group to be planted in the nethermost part of the vineyard (Judah) is also being prepared. The last branch, the lost tribes, have not yet been positively identified, but will be grafted back in the Lord's own due time.

After these natural branches have been grafted back and begin to grow, the Lord gives further instructions about their pruning. The pruning is to be carefully done according to the strength of the good branches. The roots and the top are to be kept equal in strength (vv. 65–69). These instructions correspond with those given in the Doctrine and Covenants. Just as the vineyard is to be leniently pruned, the Church is to find favor with the people of the world until Israel "become very great, and let it be sanctified" (D&C 105:26–31). Furthermore, before the Lord comes in wrath upon the earth, the Church is to be cleansed or pruned (see D&C 112:23–26). The bad being cast away (Jacob 5:69), was foretold also by the Savior in the parable of the net.

> 47 Again, the kingdom of heaven is like unto a net, that was cast into the sea, and gathered of every kind:
>
> 48 Which, when it was full, they drew to shore, and sat down, and gathered the good into vessels, but cast the bad away.
>
> 49 So shall it be at the end of the world: the angels shall come forth, and sever the wicked from among the just,
>
> 50 And shall cast them into the furnace of fire: there shall be wailing and gnashing of teeth. [Matthew 13:47–50]

The Prophet Joseph said of this parable: "For the work of this pattern, behold the seed of Joseph, spreading forth the Gospel net upon the face of the earth, gathering of every kind, that the good may be saved in vessels prepared for that purpose, and the angels will take care of the bad. So shall it be at the end of the world—the angels shall come forth and sever the wicked from among the just, and cast them into the furnace of fire, and there shall be wailing and gnashing of teeth" (*TPJS*, 102).

The servant of the Lord called other servants, but they were few. These servants were promised joy as they laid up fruit unto the Lord Jacob 5:70–71). The fulfillment of this promise is shown in the Lord's admonition to Oliver Cowdery and David Whitmer to remember the worth of souls and the joy they would receive in bringing one or more souls to Christ.

> 15 And if it so be that you should labor all your days in crying repentance unto this people, and bring, save it be one soul unto me,

how great shall be your joy with him in the kingdom of my Father!

16 And now, if your joy will be great with one soul that you have brought unto me into the kingdom of my Father, how great will be your joy if you should bring many souls unto me! [D&C 18:15–16]

The allegory continues with the work of the servants progressing until the trees become "like unto one body; and the fruits were equal" (Jacob 5:74). This is the same concept taught by Ezekiel in the uniting of the tribes of Israel under one shepherd (see Ezekiel 37:15–23).

Jacob 5:75–77 • The Millennium

75 And it came to pass that when the Lord of the vineyard saw that his fruit was good, and that his vineyard was no more corrupt, he called up his servants, and said unto them: Behold, for this last time have we nourished my vineyard; and thou beholdest that I have done according to my will; and I have preserved the natural fruit, that it is good, even like as it was in the beginning. And blessed art thou; for because ye have been diligent in laboring with me in my vineyard, and have kept my commandments, and have brought unto me again the natural fruit, that my vineyard is no more corrupted, and the bad is cast away, behold ye shall have joy with me because of the fruit of my vineyard.

76 For behold, for a long time will I lay up of the fruit of my vineyard unto mine own self against the season, which speedily cometh; and for the last time have I nourished my vineyard, and pruned it, and dug about it, and dunged it; wherefore I will lay up unto mine own self of the fruit, for a long time, according to that which I have spoken.

77 And when the time cometh that evil fruit shall again come into my vineyard, then will I cause the good and the bad to be gathered; and the good will I preserve unto myself, and the bad will I cast away into its own place. And then cometh the season and the end; and my vineyard will I cause to be burned with fire.

The allegory concludes with three verses covering two periods of time. The first (vv. 75–76) describes the millennium, wherein the Lord will lay up fruit for a long time. Nephi also described this time period apparently commenting upon Isaiah.

> 24 And the time cometh speedily that the righteous must be led up as calves of the stall, and the Holy One of Israel must reign in dominion, and might, and power, and great glory.

> 25 And he gathereth his children from the four quarters of the earth; and he numbereth his sheep, and they know him; and there shall be one fold and one shepherd; and he shall feed his sheep, and in him they shall find pasture.

> 26 And because of the righteousness of his people, Satan has no power; wherefore, he cannot be loosed for the space of many years; for he hath no power over the hearts of the people, for they dwell in righteousness, and the Holy One of Israel reigneth. [1 Nephi 22:24–26]

The millennium is when Christ will "dwell in righteousness with men on earth a thousand years" (D&C 29:11; see also Revelation 20:4).

The second period is the end of the millennium, when evil fruit will again appear and the Lord will again gather both the good and the bad together, preserving the good and casting away the bad.

> 22 And again, verily, verily, I say unto you that when the thousand years are ended, and men again begin to deny their God, then will I spare the earth but for a little season. [D&C 29:22]

Following this, the vineyard will be burned (Jacob 5:77). The temporal existence of the earth will then be completed and the program of the house of Israel finished. The earth will then be celestialized:

> 25 And again, verily I say unto you, the earth abideth the law of a celestial kingdom, for it filleth the measure of its creation, and transgresseth not the law—

> 26 Wherefore, it shall be sanctified; yea, notwithstanding it shall die, it shall be quickened again, and shall abide the power by which it is quickened, and the righteous shall inherit it. [D&C 88:25–26]

Jacob 6:1–4 • Jacob's Interpretation

> 1 And now, behold, my brethren, as I said unto you that I would

prophesy, behold, this is my prophecy—that the things which this prophet Zenos spake, concerning the house of Israel, in the which he likened them unto a tame olive-tree, must surely come to pass.

2 And the day that he shall set his hand again the second time to recover his people, is the day, yea, even the last time, that the servants of the Lord shall go forth in his power, to nourish and prune his vineyard; and after that the end soon cometh.

3 And how blessed are they who have labored diligently in his vineyard; and how cursed are they who shall be cast out into their own place! And the world shall be burned with fire.

4 And how merciful is our God unto us, for he remembereth the house of Israel, both roots and branches; and he stretches forth his hands unto them all the day long; and they are a stiffnecked and a gainsaying people; but as many as will not harden their hearts shall be saved in the kingdom of God.

Jacob's commentary on the allegory (Jacob 6) is brief, but appropriate. After bearing testimony of the surety that the allegory will be fulfilled, he speaks of the blessedness of the servants of the Lord and the mercy of God in remembering the house of Israel, both the roots (those scattered among the Gentiles) and the branches (those planted in the nethermost parts of his vineyard). He concluded with a personal admonition to the reader.

Jacob 6:5–10 • Do Not Reject the Words of Christ

5 Wherefore, my beloved brethren, I beseech of you in words of soberness that ye would repent, and come with full purpose of heart, and cleave unto God as he cleaveth unto you. And while his arm of mercy is extended towards you in the light of the day, harden not your hearts.

6 Yea, today, if ye will hear his voice, harden not your hearts; for why will ye die?

7 For behold, after ye have been nourished by the good word of God all the day long, will ye bring forth evil fruit, that ye must be hewn down and cast into the fire?

8 Behold, will ye reject these words? Will ye reject the words of the prophets; and will ye reject all the words which have been spoken concerning Christ, after so many have spoken concerning him; and deny the good word of Christ, and the power of God, and the gift of the Holy Ghost, and quench the Holy Spirit, and make a mock of the great plan of redemption, which hath been laid for you?

9 Know ye not that if ye will do these things, that the power of the redemption and the resurrection, which is in Christ, will bring you to stand with shame and awful guilt before the bar of God?

10 And according to the power of justice, for justice cannot be denied, ye must go away into that lake of fire and brimstone, whose flames are unquenchable, and whose smoke ascendeth up forever and ever, which lake of fire and brimstone is endless torment.

Following a general plea for repentance (vv. 5–7), Jacob poses some thought-provoking questions. The first question, "Will ye reject these words?" refers to the allegory (v. 8). Remember that this allegory was written probably long before 600 B.C. It has been fulfilled exactly as foretold through the first four periods and it is well into the fifth. That the remainder of it will be fulfilled is certain; therefore, we should not reject the allegory.

The second question is, "Will ye reject the words of the prophets?" Zenos is not the only prophet who has foretold the destiny of Israel. Every aspect of the allegory can be supported or supplemented by other prophets.

The third question, "Will ye reject all the words which have been spoken concerning Christ, after so many have spoken concerning him?" is another affirmation that all the prophets have testified of Christ (see Jacob 4:4–5; 7:11 and comments). Jacob then enumerates other ways we can learn the truth about Christ—by Christ's own word, by receiving the gift of the Holy Ghost, and by the witness of the Holy Spirit. Those who reject these sources mock the great plan of redemption of Israel and will be brought to stand "with shame and awful guilt before the bar of God" (Jacob 6:9).

Jacob 6:11–13 • O Be Wise

11 O then, my beloved brethren, repent ye, and enter in at the strait gate, and continue in the way which is narrow, until ye shall obtain eternal life.

12 O be wise; what can I say more?

13 Finally, I bid you farewell, until I shall meet you before the pleasing bar of God, which bar striketh the wicked with awful dread and fear. Amen.

Jacob returns to his plea to repent and be wise by entering the strait gate (baptism) and continuing in the narrow way until eternal life is obtained. Jacob then bids us farewell until he meets us at the pleasing bar of God, which bar strikes the wicked with awful fear and dread.

The Lord is over all the earth. He is in charge and will bring about his purposes. Our challenge is to be wise and to follow the program as directed by his servants the prophets. We will see Jacob and know his words are true at the bar of God (v. 13). We will also "stand face to face before his bar" with Nephi (2 Nephi 33:11), and meet Moroni "before the pleasing bar of the great Jehovah, the Eternal Judge of both the quick and dead" (Moroni 10:34). Mormon will undoubtedly be there as well. What an incentive to "prepare to stand before the judgment-seat of Christ" (Mormon 3:16–22). Remember what Paul declared: For we must all appear before the judgment seat of Christ, that everyone may receive a reward of the deeds done in the body; things according to what he hath done, whether good or bad (2 Corinthians 5:10).

Table 2

INTERPRETATIONS FROM THE SCRIPTURES

Verses from Jacob 5		Compare
1-2	Introduction	Romans 11:13–26
3-5	Israel decays	Genesis 41:56–57; 45:1–11; 46:1–7
6	Main top	D&C 84:19–26; Numbers 14:26–38
7-11	Wild Branches	2 Kings 17:18–24 (Assyria); 2 Kings 24:14 (Babylon); Isaiah 44:28–45:4 (Cyrus)
8-14	Young, tender branches	2 Kings 18:9–12 (lost tribes); Genesis 49:22–26; Jeremiah 28:8–10 (Judah); 2 Nephi 3:5; 10:20 (Lehi)
16	Jesus' ministry	Mosiah 14:33–34
17-18	Gentile graft	John 4:31–42; Matthew 2:1
19-22	Lost tribes	3 Nephi 16:1–4
23	Jews	Acts 20:21
24-28	People of Nephi	3 Nephi 15:21–24
29	The end soon cometh	JS—H 1:36–41
30-32	All sorts of fruit	JS—H 1:5–9, 19
33-37	Roots are alive	D&C 113:5–6; 86:8–10; 103:17
38-40	All corrupt	Mormon 5:15–16; 6:10–15
41-43	A choice land	Ether 2:12
44-45	Cumbered the land	Omni 1:20–22; Ether 13:20–21
46-48	Roots overcome	Matthew 15:1–9; Isaiah 24:5–6
49-51	Spare the vineyard	Alma 42:15; Exodus 32:7–14
52-56	Mother tree	1 Nephi 10:14; 15:12–14; D&C 86:8–11; Jeremiah 31:1–9
57-60	Trees pruned	John 15:1–8
61-62	The last time	D&C 33:3–4; 39:17; Jacob 6:2
63-64	The last shall be first	Matthew 20:1–6; 3 Nephi 21:22–28
65-69	Branches pruned	D&C 105:26–31; 112:23–26
70-71	The servant's joy	D&C 18:10–16
72-74	One body	Ezekiel 37:15–23
75	Servants called	D&C 116; Daniel 7:13–14, 22
76	A long time	D&C 45:58; Revelation 20:3–6
77	The earth burned	Revelation 20:7–9

Table 3
The Seven Time Periods of the Allegory

Verses 3–14. From Jacob to the end of the prophets. About 1800–400 B.C.	Verse 15. A long time passed away.	Verses 16–28. The Ministry of Jesus Christ. About A.D. 30–34	Verse 29 A long time passed away.	Verses 30–75. The Restoration, about A.D. 1820 to the Millennium.	Verse 76. A long time passed away.	Verse 77. The end of the earth.
A. *Verses 3–5.* The nourishing of the decaying olive tree–the house of Israel (Israel in Egypt). B. *Verse 6.* The main top begins to perish (the wilderness). C. *Verse 7.* The grafting in of the wild olive branches (Gentiles; Assyria, Babylon, etc.). D. *Verses 8, 12–14* The grafting of the natural branches into the nethermost parts of the vineyard (dispersion of Israel). 1. Lost Tribes. 2. Jews. 3. Nephites and Lamanites. 4. People among all nations.	The end of the prophets to the ministry of Jesus Christ, about 400 B.C. to A.D. 30.	A. *Verses 16–18.* The visit to the Gentile grafts–the Samaritans, etc. B. *Verses 19–28.* The visit to the natural branches of Israel. 1. The first (lost tribes) had produced good fruit. 2. The second (Jews) had produced good fruit. 3. The last had produced tame fruit (Nephites) and wild fruit (Lamanites).	From the apostasy following the ministry of Jesus Christ and His apostles to the restoration of the gospel through Joseph Smith, about A.D. 1820.	A. *Verses 30–37.* The visit to the wild branch grafts (the Gentiles). No fruit is good, but the roots are alive. B. *Verses 38–48.* The visit to the natural branches of Israel, all corrupt. C. *Verses 49–75.* The grafting back of Israel into the mother trunk. 1. The roots (blood of Israel among the Gentiles) preserved. 2. The natural branches grafted back—the last to be first. a. Lamanites. b. Jews. c. Lost Tribes.	The Millennium 1,000 years.	A. The good and bad gathered together. The good preserved, the bad cast out. B. The vineyard burned with fire.

SACRED WRITING

Preaching Which is Sacred:

Jacob 4:3–12	Jacob preaches (in writing) and gives a small degree of knowledge concerning the fathers
Jacob 5	Zenos' allegory was spoken to the house of Israel; thus it is considered here to be preaching

Prophesying:

Jacob 4:13–18	Jacob prophesies of the stone rejected by the Jews becoming the head of the corner.
Jacob 6:1–13	Jacob prophesies how the words of Zenos must surely come to pass.

Doctrines Learned:

Jacob 4:4	The Nephites and all the holy prophets before them knew of Christ and had a hope of his glory.
Jacob 4:5	The Nephites and all the prophets before them worshipped the Father in the name of Christ.
Jacob 4:5	Abraham offering Isaac was in similitude of God offering his Only Begotten Son.
Jacob 4:6	The Nephites could command in the name of Jesus and the trees, the mountains and the waves of the sea would obey them (priesthood power).
Jacob 4:8	No man can know of God's ways except by revelation.
Jacob 4:13	Truth is things as they are and as they are to come.
Jacob 6:4	God is merciful remembering both roots (blood of Israel scattered among the Gentiles) and branches (tribes of Israel intact).

General Authority Quotations

Joseph Smith • Jacob 4:5

The sacrifice required of Abraham in the offering up of Isaac, shows that if a man would attain to the keys of the kingdom of an endless life, he must sacrifice all things. When God offers a blessing or knowledge to man, and he refuses to receive it, he will be damned. The Israelites prayed that God would speak to Moses and not to them; in consequence of which he cursed them with a carnal law. [*TPJS*, 322; *DHC*, 5:555]

Joseph Smith • Jacob 4:9

You ask the learned doctors why they say the world was made out of nothing; and they will answer, "Doesn't the Bible say he *created* the world?" And they infer, from the word create, that it must have been made out of nothing. Now, the word create came from the baurau, which does not mean to create out of nothing; it means to organize; the same as a man would organize material and build a ship. Hence we infer that God had material to organize the world out of chaos—chaotic matter, which is element, and in which dwells all his glory. Element had an existence from the time we had. The pure principles of element are principles which can never be destroyed; they may be organized and re-organized, but not destroyed. They had no beginning, and can have no end. . . . [*TPJS*, 350–352]

Joseph Fielding Smith • Jacob 5

I tell you, my brothers and sisters, Joseph Smith did not write it. That was written by the inspiration of the Almighty.

Now there is your answer. That is the answer to those people who approach me with the question, what's the use of going out among the Chinese, the Japanese, the Koreans, and the people of the Far East to preach the gospel to them? The answer: because they are branches of the tree, they are of the house of Israel. The Lord took the branches of the tree, grafted them into the wild olives, the Gentiles, and is bringing the Gentiles into the gospel of Jesus Christ.

When you read that chapter through if you cannot say in your soul, "This is absolutely a revelation from God," then there is something wrong with you. That tells you of history. Are we going to preach the gospel in Korea, in Japan, in China? Yes, we are. Why? Because the blood of Israel is there. And the Lord did just what he said he would do with Abraham and his posterity. He scattered them over the whole face of the earth. So now the Gentiles are sanctified by the blood of Abraham. [*Answers to Gospel*

Questions, comp. Joseph Fielding Smith Jr., 5 vols. (1957–66), 4: 201–207]

Challenges to Eternal Life:

1. When you pray, seek counsel from the Lord rather than counseling him (Jacob 4:10).
2. Be cognizant of not looking beyond the mark by seeking or desiring to know of things which you do not understand (Jacob 4:14).
3. Make a commitment to labor diligently in the vineyard that you may be blessed and not cursed (Jacob 6:3).
4. Choose a challenge or modern message from your reading and apply it to your life.

Chapter Three

Sherem, Jacob and Enos

Jacob 7, Enos

*H*istorical Setting: Sherem the anti-Christ came among the people of Nephi after some years had passed away from the time Jacob recorded Zenos' allegory of the house of Israel (Jacob 7:1). However, it was before Jacob "began to be old" and concluded "this record" (Jacob 7:26). It is not known how old Enos, the son of Jacob, was when he began his recording upon the small plates. Enos began by telling of his conversion as a young man (Enos 1:1–18). It appears, from his record, that he engraved his brief account upon the small plates as a summary of what he and/or others had written upon "the record of this people being kept on the other plates of Nephi" (Jacob 7:26). He ended his record when he "began to be old, and an hundred and seventy and nine years had passed away from the time that our father Lehi left Jerusalem" (Enos 1:25). No more specific dates are given in this reading.

Precepts of this Reading:

And it came to pass that peace and the love of God was restored again among the people; and they searched the scriptures, and hearkened no more to the words of this wicked man. [Jacob 7:23]

Whatsoever thing ye shall ask in faith, believing that ye shall receive in the name of Christ, ye shall receive it. [Enos 1:15]

An outline of Jacob 7 and Enos follows to prepare for a deeper study.

OUTLINE • JACOB 7, ENOS

➤ Jacob 7:1–5 After some years a man named Sherem came among the people of Nephi declaring there should be no Christ.

    a. He preached flattering things trying to overthrow the doctrine of Christ (v. 2).

    b. He labored diligently and led away many hearts (v. 3).

    c. Knowing Jacob had faith in Christ, he sought to come to him (vv. 3–4).

        1. He was learned and had a perfect knowledge of the language.

        2. He could use much flattery, and much power of speech according to the power of the devil.

    d. Sherem had hoped to shake Jacob from the faith in spite of the many revelations and the many things he had seen, but Jacob could not be shaken (v. 5).

        1. Jacob had seen angels and they had ministered to him.

        2. Jacob had heard the voice of the Lord in very word.

➤ 7:6–7 Sherem told Jacob he had heard and also knew that Jacob had been preaching what he called the gospel or the doctrine of Christ.

    a. He said Jacob had led away much people by perverting the law of Moses which was the right way of God (v. 7).

    b. Jacob was accused of converting the law of Moses into the worship of a being who should come many years hence (v. 7).

    c. Sherem said this was blasphemy for no man could tell of things to come (v. 7).

➤ 7:8–22   The Lord poured his Spirit into Jacob's soul and he confounded Sherem.

     a.   Jacob asked Sherem if he denied the coming of Christ (v. 9).

         1.   Sherem said if there should be a Christ, he would not deny him.

         2.   He said that he knew there was no Christ, neither had been nor ever will be.

     b.   Jacob asked Sherem if he believed the scriptures. Sherem said yes (vv. 11–12).

         1.   Jacob: "Then ye do not understand them for they truly testify of Christ."

         2.   None of the prophets had written of prophesied save they spoke of Christ.

         3.   Christ had been manifest to Jacob by sight and sound, and by the power of the Holy Ghost.

         4.   He testified that if there should be no atonement, all mankind must be lost.

     c.   Sherem asked for a sign by the power of the Holy Ghost (vv. 13–14).

         1.   Jacob would not tempt God to show a sign of the truth when Sherem already knew it.

         2.   Jacob knew that Sherem would deny because he was of the devil.

         3.   Jacob declared to him that if God smote him that would be a sign of Christ's power and his coming.

     d.   The power of the Lord came upon Sherem and he fell to the earth. He was nourished many days (v. 15).

     e.   Sherem requested to speak to the people before he died. He spoke plainly (vv. 16–20).

         1.   He denied the things he had taught them.

         2.   He confessed the Christ, the power of the Holy Ghost, and the ministering of angels.

         3.   He admitted that he had been deceived by the power of the devil.

        4. He spoke of hell, eternity, and eternal punishment.

        5. He confessed to God that he feared he had committed the unpardonable sin and lied unto God.

   f. The multitude were astonished and the power of God caused them to fall to the earth (vv. 21–22).

        1. Jacob had requested this of his Father in heaven.

        2. The Father had heard his cry and answered his prayer.

➤ 7:23–25   Peace and the love of God were restored among the people.

   a. They searched the scriptures and hearkened no more to the words of this wicked man (v. 23).

   b. They devised many means to restore the Lamanites to the knowledge of the truth, but it was vain (v. 24).

        1. The Lamanites delighted in war and had an eternal hatred against the Nephites.

        2. They sought to destroy the Nephites continually.

   c. The Nephites fortified and, trusting in God, they conquered their enemies.

➤ 7:26–27   As Jacob grew old he turned the record over to his son Enos.

   a. The record of this people was on the other plates (v. 26).

   b. Their time and their lives passed away as it were a dream (v. 26).

        1. They were a lonesome and solemn people.

        2. They were cast out of Jerusalem, born in tribulation, hated by our brethren which caused wars and contentions.

   c. Enos promised to obey Nephi's instructions for engraving on the plates (v. 27).

   d. Jacob bid the reader farewell, hoping his brethren would read his words (v. 27).

➤ Enos 1:1–18   Enos told of his wrestle before God before he received a remission of sins.

    a. His father was a just man. He had taught Enos in his language and also in the nurture and admonition of the Lord.

    b. While hunting, the words of his father concerning eternal life and the joy of the saints had sunk deep into his heart (v. 3).

    c. With hungry soul he knelt in mighty prayer and supplication for his soul (v. 4).

        1. All day long he cried to him.

        2. When the night came he still raised his voice that it reached the heavens.

    d. He heard a voice say his sins were forgiven (vv. 5–6).

        1. He knew God could not lie.

        2. His guilt was swept away.

    e. Enos asks in prayer how this was done, and is told it is because of his faith in Christ whom he has never seen nor heard (vv. 7–8).

        1. Many years would pass before Christ would manifest himself in the flesh.

        2. Enos is told to go forth, his faith had made him whole.

    f. After hearing these words, Enos felt a desire for the welfare of his brethren the Nephites, and poured out his soul to God for them. The voice of the Lord came into his mind again saying (vv. 9–10):

        1. I will visit thy brethren according to their diligence in keeping the commandments.

        2. They have been given this holy land and it would only be cursed for the cause of iniquity.

        3. Their transgressions will bring down sorrow upon their own heads.

    g. His faith unshaken, Enos prayed long for his brethren

the Lamanites and is granted his desires because of his faith (vv. 11–17).

1. If the Nephites are destroyed for their transgressions may the record of the Nephites be preserved and come to the Lamanites at some future day and bring them salvation.

2. The Lamanites of Enos' day sought to destroy the Nephite records and their traditions.

3. The Lord told Enos that whatever he asked in faith in the name of Christ, believing he would receive, would be given to him.

4. The Lord covenanted to preserve the records and to bring them forth in his own due time.

5. Because of the covenant, Enos' soul did rest.

h. The Lord told Enos that his fathers had also required this of the Lord because of their faith (v. 18).

➤ 1:19–24   Enos went among the people of Nephi, prophesying of things to come, and testifying of what he had seen and heard.

a. The people of Nephi sought diligently to restore the Lamanites unto the true faith of God, but their labors were in vain (v. 20).

1. The Lamanites were led by an evil nature. They became a wild and blood-thirsty people, full of idolatry and filthiness, feeding on beasts of prey.

2. They dwelt in tents, wandered in the wilderness wearing a short skin girdle, and heads shaven.

3. Their skill was in the bow, the cimeter, and the ax and many ate nothing but raw meat.

4. They sought continually to destroy the Nephites.

b. The people of Nephi did till the land and raised all manner of grain and animals (v. 21).

c. There were many prophets among the stiffnecked Nephites, but it was hard to make them understand (vv. 22–23).

1. Nothing short of harshness, preaching, and prophesying of wars and destructions could keep them in the fear of the Lord.

2. Nothing but exceeding great plainness of speech kept them from destruction.

d. Enos saw wars and contentions all his days (v. 24).

➤ 1:25–27 One hundred and seventy-nine years had passed away since Lehi had left Jerusalem and Enos had begun to be old.

a. He had been wrought upon by the power of God to preach and prophesy, and declare the word of Christ all of his days, and he rejoiced in it (v. 26).

b. He would soon go to his place of rest with his Redeemer (v. 27).

1. He rejoiced in the day when his mortal should put on immortality and he will stand before him.

2. He will hear his voice and be invited to the place prepared for him in the mansions of his Father.

NOTES AND COMMENTARY

Introduction: There are three main characters in this section of the Book of Mormon:

• Sherem, an anti-Christ (preached there should be no Christ)

• Jacob, a prophet of the Lord (brother and successor to Nephi)

• Enos, a natural man (son of the prophet Jacob; conversion experience related)

The above definitions will be enlarged upon as we study these chapters.

Jacob 7:1–5 • Flattery to Overthrow the Doctrine of Christ

1 And now it came to pass after some years had passed away, there came a man among the people of Nephi, whose name was Sherem.

2 And it came to pass that he began to preach among the people, and to declare unto them that there should be no Christ. And he preached many things which were flattering unto the people; and this he did that he might overthrow the doctrine of Christ.

3 And he labored diligently that he might lead away the hearts of the people, insomuch that he did lead away many hearts; and he knowing that I, Jacob, had faith in Christ who should come, he sought much opportunity that he might come unto me.

4 And he was learned, that he had a perfect knowledge of the language of the people; wherefore, he could use much flattery, and much power of speech, according to the power of the devil.

5 And he had hope to shake me from the faith, notwithstanding the many revelations and the many things which I had seen concerning these things; for I truly had seen angels, and they had ministered unto me. And also, I had heard the voice of the Lord speaking unto me in very word, from time to time; wherefore, I could not be shaken.

These verses give three characteristics of an anti-Christ and two characteristics of a prophet. Other characteristics will be added in subsequent verses. An account of another anti-Christ named Korihor, who lived about four hundred years later, is also recorded in the Book of Mormon (see Alma 30). Korihor is described in greater detail, but the characteristic of an anti-Christ are basically the same. Only Sherem will be considered here.

➤ *The Anti-Christ: Sherem; "there should be no Christ"* (v. 2).

1.   He designs and attempts to overthrow the doctrine of Christ (v. 2). The doctrine of Christ is the plan of salvation for all mankind:

> 32 And this is my doctrine, and it is the doctrine which the Father hath given unto me; and I bear record of the Father, and the Father beareth record of me, and the Holy Ghost beareth record of the Father and me; and I bear record that the Father commandeth all men, everywhere, to repent and believe in me.
>
> 33 And whoso believeth in me, and is baptized, the same shall be saved; and they are they who shall inherit the kingdom of God.

Wrong – Right & Right- Wrong

34 And whoso believeth not in me, and is not baptized, shall be damned. [3 Nephi 11:32–34]

Therefore, Sherem was attempting to damn or stop the eternal progression of man. This is the work of the devil: "an angel of God, according to that which is written, had fallen from heaven; wherefore, he became a devil, having sought that which was evil before God. And because he had fallen from heaven, and had become miserable forever, he sought also the misery of all mankind" (2 Nephi 2:17–18).

2. Sherem challenges the brethren or the leaders of the Church ("he sought much opportunity that he might come unto [Jacob]" (v. 3). Jesus told the Nephite multitude they "must watch and pray always lest ye enter into temptation; for Satan desireth to have you, that he may sift you as wheat" (3 Nephi 18:18). Wheat is sifted to eliminate the chaff and broken kernels. In the Church, Satan will sift out those who do not follow the doctrines of Christ. Not only will they be damned, but their examples will lead others astray. The more important the position that one holds, the more effect it will have on others. For example, Jesus warned Peter, the chief apostle: "Satan hath desired to have you, that he may sift you as wheat" (Luke 12:31; see also D&C 52:12).

3. Sherem is learned and has "a perfect knowledge of the language of the people;" wherefore, he can "use much flattery, and much power of speech, according to the power of the devil," and he hopes to shake people "from the faith" (Jacob 7:4–5).

Remember Jacob's previous warning:

28 O that cunning plan of the evil one! O the vainness, and the frailties, and the foolishness of men! When they are learned they think they are wise, and they hearken not unto the counsel of God, for they set it aside, supposing they know of themselves, wherefore, their wisdom is foolishness and it profiteth them not. And they shall perish.

29 But to be learned is good if they hearken unto the counsels of God. [2 Nephi 9:28–29]

➤ *The Prophet: Jacob; "had faith in Christ"* (v. 3)

1. He had "many revelations," and had "heard the voice of the Lord speaking unto [him] in very word, from time to time" (v. 5). We have no specific record, but we do have another general statement of Jacob and others having "many revelations" (Jacob 4:6). They were possibly recorded on the other plates of Nephi.

2. He had "seen angels, and they [had] ministered unto him" (v. 5). The speeches of Jacob recorded by Nephi refer to "the words of an angel that spake [of Christ] unto me" (2 Nephi 6:9), and "that Christ—for in the last night the angel spake unto me that this should be his name" (2 Nephi 10:3). There were undoubtedly other appearances.

Jacob 7:6–14 • The Conversation Between Jacob and Sherem

6 And it came to pass that he came unto me, and on this wise did he speak unto me, saying: Brother Jacob, I have sought much opportunity that I might speak unto you; for I have heard and also know that thou goest about much, preaching that which ye call the gospel, or the doctrine of Christ.

7 And ye have led away much of this people that they pervert the right way of God, and keep not the law of Moses which is the right way; and convert the law of Moses into the worship of a being which ye say shall come many hundred years hence. And now behold, I, Sherem, declare unto you that this is blasphemy; for no man knoweth of such things; for he cannot tell of things to come. And after this manner did Sherem contend against me.

8 But behold, the Lord God poured in his Spirit into my soul, insomuch that I did confound him in all his words.

9 And I said unto him: Deniest thou the Christ who shall come? And he said: If there should be a Christ, I would not deny him; but I know that there is no Christ, neither has been, nor ever will be.

10 And I said unto him: Believest thou the scriptures? And he said, Yea.

11 And I said unto him: Then ye do not understand them; for they truly testify of Christ. Behold, I say unto you that none of the proph-

What are attributes/prophet? of Anti Christ

ets have written, nor prophesied, save they have spoken concerning this Christ.

12 And this is not all—it has been made manifest unto me, for I have heard and seen; and it also has been made manifest unto me by the power of the Holy Ghost; wherefore, I know if there should be no atonement made all mankind must be lost.

13 And it came to pass that he said unto me: Show me a sign by this power of the Holy Ghost, in the which ye know so much.

14 And I said unto him: What am I that I should tempt God to show unto thee a sign in the thing which thou knowest to be true? Yet thou wilt deny it, because thou art of the devil. Nevertheless, not my will be done; but if God shall smite thee, let that be a sign unto thee that he has power, both in heaven and in earth; and also, that Christ shall come. And thy will, O Lord, be done, and not mine.

➤ *The Anti-Christ (continued): Sherem; "I know that there is no Christ, neither has been nor ever will be" (v. 9).*

3.   Sherem accuses the Church leaders of deceiving and misleading the people, i.e. "preaching that which ye call the gospel, or the doctrine of Christ," perverting "the right way of God, and keep not the law of Moses" [Mormons are not Christians] (vv. 6–7). Sherem's words "that which ye call" implies Jacob is introducing his own ideas for doctrine. He is rejecting the principle of ongoing revelation. Sherem's reliance on the law of Moses shows his rejection of the higher law of Christ, the purpose for which the law of Moses had been given and the Nephites had attained (see 2 Nephi 25:23–30). He is relying on the dead prophets and rejecting the living ones.

4.   An anti-Christ denies the omniscience of God; no man can "tell of things to come" (Jacob 7:7). If Sherem believed the scriptures, as he later claimed, he would have believed "I am God, and there is none like me, Declaring the end from the beginning, and from ancient times the things that are not yet done" (Isaiah 46:9–10); and also believed what he told Abraham: "My name is Jehovah, and I know the end from the beginning; therefore my hand shall be over thee" (Abraham 2:8).

5.   Sherem professes to believe in the scriptures but does "not under-

stand them" (Jacob 7:10–11). Moroni later testifies:

7 And again I speak unto you who deny the revelations of God, and say that they are done away, that there are no revelations, nor prophecies, nor gifts, nor healing, nor speaking with tongues, and the interpretation of tongues;

8 Behold I say unto you, he that denieth these things knoweth not the gospel of Christ; yea, he has not read the scriptures; if so, he does not understand them.

9 For do we not read that God is the same yesterday, today, and forever, and in him there is no variableness neither shadow of changing? [Mormon 9:7–9]

6. Sherem seeks for a sign (Jacob 7:13). Jesus said: "An evil and adulterous generation seeketh after a sign" (Matthew 12:39; 16:4). This declaration tells us something about Sherem. The Prophet Joseph Smith said the saying of Jesus "that he who seeketh a sign is an adulterous person, and that principle is eternal, undeviating, and firm as the pillars of heaven, for whenever you see a man seeking after a sign, you may set it down that he is an adulterous man" (*TPJS*, 157). "He that seeketh signs shall see signs, but not unto salvation" (D&C 63:7).

➤ *The Prophet (continued): Jacob; I have heard and seen; and it has also been made manifest unto me by the power of the Holy Ghost" that there is a Christ. He knew if there was "no atonement made all mankind must be lost"* (Jacob 7:12).

7. The Lord God pours out "his Spirit into [Jacob's] soul" (v. 8). A prophet waits for the Spirit to direct him. Nephi "was led by the Spirit, not knowing beforehand the things which [Nephi] should do" (1 Nephi 4:6). Amulek would "say nothing which is contrary to the Spirit of the Lord" (Alma 11:22).

8. Jacob knows that all the scriptures, and all the prophets, testify and speak of Christ (Jacob 7:11). Jesus said: "Search the scriptures; for in them ye think ye have eternal life [without searching]: and they are they that testify of me" (John 5:39). Jacob had testified earlier that all the holy prophets knew of Christ (see Jacob 4:4).

9. Jacob knows the thoughts and intents of his associates; he knew that Sherem knew of Christ and was led about by the devil (Jacob 7:14). "There is none else save God that knowest thy thoughts and the intents of thy heart" (D&C 6:16); but he reveals those thoughts to his prophets. Amulek "perceived [the people of Ammonihah's] thoughts" (Alma 10:17). Ammon, being filled with the Spirit of God, therefore he perceived the thoughts of the king" (Alma 18:17).

10. Jacob leaves the manifestation of signs and witnesses up to the will of God, not his own will (Jacob 7:14). "Signs follow those that believe. Yea, signs come by faith, not by the will of men, nor as they please, but by the will of God" (D&C 63:9–10; see also Mark 16:17–18).

Not all of the characteristics mentioned above are necessary to qualify or mark someone as an anti-Christ, or a prophet; but one of them could qualify him (or her) as either one. Every characteristic of an anti-Christ should be avoided lest we are guilty by association, or become led astray by the devil as was Sherem. Likewise, in a general sense, "the testimony of Jesus is the spirit of prophecy" (Revelation 19:10; *TPJS*, 119); therefore, although we are not "the Prophet," or one of "the prophets" of the Church, we should seek the characteristics of a prophet outlined above as guidelines for our lives.

Jacob 7:15–22 • The Confession of Sherem

15 And it came to pass that when I, Jacob, had spoken these words, the power of the Lord came upon him, insomuch that he fell to the earth. And it came to pass that he was nourished for the space of many days.

16 And it came to pass that he said unto the people: Gather together on the morrow, for I shall die; wherefore, I desire to speak unto the people before I shall die.

17 And it came to pass that on the morrow the multitude were gathered together; and he spake plainly unto them and denied the things which he had taught them, and confessed the Christ, and the power of the Holy Ghost, and the ministering of angels.

18 And he spake plainly unto them, that he had been deceived by the power of the devil. And he spake of hell, and of eternity, and of eternal punishment.

19 And he said: I fear lest I have committed the unpardonable sin, for I have lied unto God; for I denied the Christ, and said that I believed the scriptures; and they truly testify of him. And because I have thus lied unto God I greatly fear lest my case shall be awful; but I confess unto God.

20 And it came to pass that when he had said these words he could say no more, and he gave up the ghost.

21 And when the multitude had witnessed that he spake these things as he was about to give up the ghost, they were astonished exceedingly; insomuch that the power of God came down upon them, and they were overcome that they fell to the earth.

22 Now, this thing was pleasing unto me, Jacob, for I had requested it of my Father who was in heaven; for he had heard my cry and answered my prayer.

Sherem was smitten as a sign of the power of God and of the coming of Christ. The text does not say who nourished Sherem for many days, but from the context, we assume it was those who believed Jacob. Neither does the text tell us how Sherem knew he was going to die. Apparently it had been made known to him while he was being nourished. It appears that he was going through much tribulation during those many days. His confession confirmed what Jacob had told Sherem before he was smitten, he did know the things he had been denying were true. Whether he had committed the unpardonable sin is not known. The unpardonable sin is to "deny the Holy Ghost when it once has had place in you, and ye know that ye deny it: (Alma 39:6). The text only says he feared that he had. However, his possible fate is a warning to us to beware of what can happen when we choose to follow Satan. His confession was not a death-bed forgiveness. He was repentant, but was beginning to suffer for sins he had knowingly committed.

16 For behold, I, God, have suffered these things for all, that they might not suffer if they would repent;

17 But if they would not repent they must suffer even as I;

18 Which suffering caused myself, even God, the greatest of all, to tremble because of pain, and to bleed at every pore, and to suffer both body and spirit—and would that I might not drink the bitter cup, and shrink— [D&C 19:16–18]

Another request of God by Jacob was honored when the multitude was overcome (Jacob 7:21). As always, the Lord sustained his prophet in the eyes of the people.

Jacob 7:23–25 • The Love of God Restored

23 And it came to pass that peace and the love of God was restored again among the people; and they searched the scriptures, and hearkened no more to the words of this wicked man.

24 And it came to pass that many means were devised to reclaim and restore the Lamanites to the knowledge of the truth; but it all was vain, for they delighted in wars and bloodshed, and they had an eternal hatred against us, their brethren. And they sought by the power of their arms to destroy us continually.

25 Wherefore, the people of Nephi did fortify against them with their arms, and with all their might, trusting in the God and rock of their salvation; wherefore, they became as yet, conquerors of their enemies.

The restoration of peace and the love of God shows two things: one, the people of Nephi had those desired qualities before the coming of Sherem; and two, the teaching of an anti-Christ had temporarily caused the loss of both. This loss apparently came upon enough people individually that it had a collective effect as well. Another observation; to maintain peace and the love of God, the scriptures must be searched and the teachings of wicked men must be rejected or ignored. The apostle John wrote: "If a man say, I love God, and hateth his brother, he is a liar: for he that loveth not his brother whom he hath seen, how can he love God whom he hath not seen? And this commandment have we from him, That he who loveth God love his brother also" (1 John 4:20–21).

The Nephites love was evident by their attempts to reclaim and restore the Lamanites to the truth. However, the Lamanites continual aggression (Jacob 7:24) made it expedient for the Nephites to prepare to defend themselves, although their primary defense was to trust in God (v. 25).

Jacob 7:26–27 • Our Lives Passed as a Dream

> 26 And it came to pass that I, Jacob, began to be old; and the record of this people being kept on the other plates of Nephi, wherefore, I conclude this record, declaring that I have written according to the best of my knowledge, by saying that the time passed away with us, and also our lives passed away like as it were unto us a dream, we being a lonesome and a solemn people, wanderers, cast out from Jerusalem, born in tribulation, in a wilderness, and hated of our brethren, which caused wars and contentions; wherefore, we did mourn out our days.

> 27 And I, Jacob, saw that I must soon go down to my grave; wherefore, I said unto my son Enos: Take these plates. And I told him the things which my brother Nephi had commanded me, and he promised obedience unto the commands. And I make an end of my writing upon these plates, which writing has been small; and to the reader I bid farewell, hoping that many of my brethren may read my words. Brethren, adieu.

These parting words of Jacob, "I began to be old . . . and also our lives passed like as it were unto us a dream" implies he is describing a fairly long time period that followed the Sherem experience as "we did mourn out our days" (v. 26). Although Jacob had not lived in Jerusalem, he had heard the experiences of the older family members. "A lonesome and solemn people" reflects their sadness in not being able to bring the peace of the gospel to their Lamanite brothers and sisters.

The farewell, "Brethren, adieu," after turning over the plates to his son Enos (v. 27), has drawn some criticism. Dr. Daniel H. Ludlow has answered these critics:

Some anti-LDS critics of the Book of Mormon have raised the question as to how Jacob could possibly have used such a word as *adieu* when this word clearly comes from the French language, which was not developed until hundreds of years after the time of Jacob. Such critics evidently overlook the fact that the Book of Mormon is translation literature, and Joseph Smith felt free in his translation to use any words familiar to himself and his readers that would best convey the meaning of the original author. It is interesting to note that there is a Hebrew word *Lehitra'ot*, which has essentially the same meaning in Hebrew as the word *adieu* has in French. Both of these words are much more than a simple farewell; they include the idea of a blessing. Would it be unreasonable to remind these critics that *none of the words* contained in the English translation of the book of Jacob were used by Jacob himself? These words all come from the English language, which did not come into existence until long after Jacob's time![1]

Even if Joseph Smith was not familiar with the French word, although he probably was, it could certainly have been given him by the Lord. The Lord knew the closest word in common use to the word used by Jacob. Nephi earlier said, quoting from Isaiah, "thou shalt read the words which I shall give unto thee" (2 Nephi 27:20).

Enos 1:1–4 • The Natural Man is Converted

1 Behold, it came to pass that I, Enos, knowing my father that he was a just man—for he taught me in his language, and also in the nurture and admonition of the Lord—and blessed be the name of my God for it—

Enos begins his record by acknowledging the goodness of Jacob, his father (v. 1). It reminds us of Nephi's beginning, " . . . having been born of goodly parents" (1 Nephi 1:1). Enos says his father "was a just man" (Enos 1:1). The Bible calls Joseph, espoused to Mary, the mother to be of Jesus, "a just man." A just man is a man whom the

---

[1] Daniel H. Ludlow, *A Companion To Your Study of the Book Of Mormon,* [1977], 163.

Savior will "hold guiltless before my Father at that day when I shall stand to judge the world" (3 Nephi 27:16). He is justified because he has kept the commandments given unto him. "For not the hearers of the law *are* just before God, but the doers of the law shall be justified" (Romans 2:13). The recognition of his father as a just man (Enos 1:1) is a confirmation that the writings of his father, Jacob, were true and in accordance with the commandments of God.

The first experience of Enos, apparently written many years after, was the account of his conversion through "the wrestle which [Enos] had before God" (v. 2). This was, of course, a spiritual wrestle similar to Jacob's wrestle by the brook Jabbok (see Genesis 32:22–30), or Jonah (see Jonah 1:17–2:10) or Alma's (see Alma 36:5–34). What took place within Enos was eloquently described by Elder Spencer W. Kimball to the Brigham Young University student body. We will follow his format, quoting the verses of Enos within.

To those of us who would pay pennies toward our unfathomable debt, there is no better example than Enos. Like many sons of good families he strayed; his sins weighed heavily upon him. He wrote:

And I will tell you of the wrestle which I had before God, before I received a remission of my sins. [Enos 1:2]

He speaks graphically. He speaks not of a trite prayer but of an intense striving, a vigorous wrestling and almost interminable struggling.

Behold, I went to hunt beasts in the forests;

But no animal did he shoot nor capture. He was traveling a path he had never walked before. He was reaching, knocking, asking, pleading; he was being born again. He was seeing the pleasant valleys across the barren wastes. He was searching his soul. He might have lived all his life in a weed patch, but now he envisioned a watered garden. He continues:

and the words which I had often heard my father speak concerning eternal life, and the joy of the saints, sunk deep into my heart. [Enos 1:3]

Memory was both cruel and kind. The pictures his father had painted in sermon and admonition now stirred his soul. He was warmed and inspired. He hungered for the good. Then memory opened the doors to his ugly past. His soul revolted at the reliving of the baser things but yearned now for the better. A rebirth was in process. It was painful but rewarding.

And my soul hungered

The spirit of repentance was taking hold. He was self-convicted. He was remorseful for his transgression, eager to bury the old man of sin, to resurrect the new man of faith, godliness.

and I kneeled down before my Maker, and I cried unto him in mighty prayer and supplication for mine own soul;

This was no silent, unexpressed wish or hope, but a heart-wrenching, imploring, begging, and pleading. It was vocal and powerful prayer.

He had now come to realize that no one can be saved in his sins, that no unclean thing can enter into the kingdom of God, that there must be a cleansing, that stains must be eliminated, new flesh over wounds. He came to realize that there must be a purging, a new heart in a new man. He knew it was not a small thing to change hearts and minds. He writes:

and all the day long did I cry unto him;

Here is no causal prayer; no worn phrases; no momentary appeal by silent lips. All the day long, with seconds turning into minutes, and minutes turning into hours and hours. But when the sun had set, relief had still not come, for repentance is not a single act nor forgiveness an unearned gift. So precious to him was communication with and approval of his Redeemer that his determined soul pressed on without ceasing.

yea, and when the night came I did still raise my voice high that it reached the heavens. [Enos 1:4]

Could the Redeemer resist such determined imploring? How many have thus resisted? How many with or without serious transgression, have ever prayed all day and into the night? How many have ever wept and prayed for ten hours? for five hours? for one? for thirty minutes? for ten? Our praying is usually measured in seconds and yet with a heavy debt to pay we still expect forgiveness of our sins. We offer pennies to pay the debt of thousands of dollars.

How much do you pray, my friends? How often? How earnestly? If you have errors in your life, have you really wrestled before the Lord? Have you yet found your deep forest of solitude? How much has your soul hungered? How deeply have your needs impressed your heart? When did you kneel before your Maker in total quiet? For what did you pray—your own soul? How long did you thus plead for recognition—all day long? And when the shadows fell, did you still raise your voice in mighty prayer, or did you satisfy yourself with some hackneyed word and phrase?

If you have not, I sincerely hope that the time will come when, as others before you have, you will struggle in the spirit and cry mightily and covenant sincerely, so that the voice of the Lord God will come into your mind, as it did to Enos, saying:

> *. . . thy sins are forgiven thee, and thou shalt be blessed. Because of thy faith in Christ . . . I will grant unto thee according to thy desires. . . .* [Enos 1:5, 8, 12)]

For this is the ultimate object of all prayer, to bring men closer to God, to give them a new birth, to make them heirs of his kingdom."[2]

Enos 1:5–8 • Thy Faith Hath Made Thee Whole

5 And there came a voice unto me, saying: Enos, thy sins are forgiven thee, and thou shalt be blessed.

6 And I, Enos, knew that God could not lie; wherefore, my guilt was swept away.

7 And I said: Lord, how is it done?

8 And he said unto me: Because of thy faith in Christ, whom thou hast never before heard nor seen. And many years pass away before he shall manifest himself in the flesh; wherefore, go to, thy faith hath made thee whole.

---

[2] Spencer W. Kimball, *Faith Precedes the Miracle*, [1973], 209–12. The speech was originally given at a Brigham Young University devotional, October 11, 1961.

Enos was promised to be blessed (v. 5, also partially quoted above by Elder Kimball). His brief record that follows enumerates only some of the blessings. Enos' knowledge that God could not lie (v. 6) probably came to him with the experience he was having. When the Lord asked the brother of Jared if he would believe the things he was about to tell him, he responded: "Yea, Lord, I know that thou speakest the truth, for thou art a God of truth, and canst not lie" (Ether 3:11–12). Another possibility is that his father, Jacob, had taught him this concept from the scriptures. In the book of Numbers, which would have been on the plates of brass, the Lord told Balaam to tell Balak: "God is not a man that he should lie" (Numbers 23:19; see also 1 Samuel 15:28–29). Satan is "the father of all lies" (Moses 4:4), and only man will be enticed by him.

Enos had his guilt taken away (v. 6) as well as having his sins forgiven (v. 5). Some people remove their guilt without being forgiven. They harden their hearts. "But behold, there are many that harden their hearts against the Holy Spirit, that it hath no place in them; wherefore, they cast many things away which are written and esteem them as things of naught" (2 Nephi 33:2). Others are forgiven, but will not rid themselves of the guilt. They cannot forgive themselves. While the Lord leaves the memory of the sin in our mind as a preventive against future sins, we must forgive ourselves after going through the repentance process.

The guilt will be taken away when the Lord sees fit. Both the forgiveness and the guilt removal come because of faith in Christ. For Enos it was faith in His coming in the flesh (Enos 1:8). For us it is that he has come in the flesh.

Enos 1:9–18 • Whatsoever ye Shall Ask in Faith

9 Now, it came to pass that when I had heard these words I began to feel a desire for the welfare of my brethren, the Nephites; wherefore, I did pour out my whole soul unto God for them.

10 And while I was thus struggling in the spirit, behold, the voice of the Lord came into my mind again, saying: I will visit thy brethren

according to their diligence in keeping my commandments. I have given unto them this land, and it is a holy land; and I curse it not save it be for the cause of iniquity; wherefore, I will visit thy brethren according as I have said; and their transgressions will I bring down with sorrow upon their own heads.

11 And after I, Enos, had heard these words, my faith began to be unshaken in the Lord; and I prayed unto him with many long strugglings for my brethren, the Lamanites.

12 And it came to pass that after I had prayed and labored with all diligence, the Lord said unto me: I will grant unto thee according to thy desires, because of thy faith.

13 And now behold, this was the desire which I desired of him— that if it should so be, that my people, the Nephites, should fall into transgression, and by any means be destroyed, and the Lamanites should not be destroyed, that the Lord God would preserve a record of my people, the Nephites; even if it so be by the power of his holy arm, that it might be brought forth at some future day unto the Lamanites, that, perhaps, they might be brought unto salvation—

14 For at the present our strugglings were vain in restoring them to the true faith. And they swore in their wrath that, if it were possible, they would destroy our records and us, and also all the traditions of our fathers.

15 Wherefore, I knowing that the Lord God was able to preserve our records, I cried unto him continually, for he had said unto me: Whatsoever thing ye shall ask in faith, believing that ye shall receive in the name of Christ, ye shall receive it.

16 And I had faith, and I did cry unto God that he would preserve the records; and he covenanted with me that he would bring them forth unto the Lamanites in his own due time.

17 And I, Enos, knew it would be according to the covenant which he had made; wherefore my soul did rest.

18 And the Lord said unto me: Thy fathers have also required of me this thing; and it shall be done unto them according to their faith; for their faith was like unto thine.

Revelation comes in various ways. The Lord defined the spirit of revelation: "Yea, behold, I will tell you in your mind and in your heart, by the Holy Ghost, which shall come upon you and which shall dwell in your heart" (D&C 8:2).

Elder Marion G. Romney cited this kind of revelation as an example of what he called the unspoken word: "'While I was thus struggling in the spirit, behold the voice of the lord came into my mind again, saying . . .' (Enos 1:10). Then he tells what the voice of the Lord put in his mind. This is a very common means of revelation. It comes into one's mind in words and sentences. With this means of revelation I am personally well acquainted" (CR, April 1964, 124).

The answer to Enos' prayer was conditional upon the actions of his brethren. They would be visited "according to their diligence in keeping [the Lord's] commandments" (v. 10). Elder Harold B. Lee, after quoting this verse, said: "There you have in simple language, a great principle: It isn't the Lord who withholds himself from us. It is we who withhold ourselves from him because of our failure to keep his commandments" (CR, Oct. 1966, 116). Parents may pray for their children, or children may pray for other family members, or friends may pray for friends with diligence and faith, and the Lord will provide opportunities for those prayed for to receive the desired blessings, but he always respects their agency. They must meet the law upon which the blessing is predicated.

> 20 There is a law, irrevocably decreed in heaven before the foundations of this world, upon which all blessings are predicated—
>
> 21 And when we obtain any blessing from God, it is by obedience to that law upon which it is predicated [D&C 130:20–21].

We must be careful in judging why a blessing is given or not given, for only the Lord knows all of the conditions upon which the blessing may be given or withheld.

Enos' experience illustrates the working of the Spirit of the Lord upon him. He began the day "in mighty prayer and supplication for mine [his] own soul" (Enos 1: 4). After knowing his sins were forgiven and his guilt was swept away (vv. 5–6), he "began to feel a desire for the welfare of my brethren, the Nephites" (v. 9). After consoling words from the Lord regarding the Nephites (v. 10), he prayed "with many long strugglings for my brethren, the Lamanites" (v. 11). He loved "his [Nephite] neighbor as himself," the second great commandment (see Matthew 22:36–40), and did "pray for them who despitefully use you and persecute you [his enemies]" (3 Nephi 12:44; Matthew 5:44).

The Lord has fulfilled his promise to preserve a record of the Nephites (Enos 1:13). In a revelation to Joseph Smith, concerning the loss of the 116 pages of manuscript, the Lord said:

> 46 And, behold, all the remainder of this work does contain all those parts of my gospel which my holy prophets, yea, and also my disciples, desired in their prayers should come forth unto this people.
>
> 47 And I said unto them, that it should be granted unto them according to their faith in their prayers;
>
> 48 Yea, and this was their faith—that my gospel, which I gave unto them that they might preach in their days, might come unto their brethren the Lamanites, and also all that had become Lamanites because of their dissensions.
>
> 49 Now, this is not all—their faith in their prayers was that this gospel should be made known also, if it were possible that other nations should possess this land;
>
> 50 And thus they did leave a blessing upon this land in their prayers, that whosoever should believe in this gospel in this land might have eternal life;
>
> 51 Yea, that it might be free unto all of whatsoever nation, kindred, tongue, or people they may be.
>
> 52 And now, behold, according to their faith in their prayers will I bring this part of my gospel to the knowledge of my people. Behold, I do not bring it to destroy that which they have received, but to build it up. [D&C 10:46–52]

Note that many others besides Enos had requested that the records be preserved. Enos was told that his fathers "also required of me this thing; and it shall be done unto them according to their faith; for their faith was like unto thine" (Enos 1:18). His fathers would be Jacob, and Lehi (and probably also Nephi) of which requirement the record is silent. The revelation cited above states that the "holy prophets, yea, and also my disciples [the twelve] desired in their prayers" for the records to come forth (D&C 10:46). The records have come forth and the time has come for the Lamanites to individually accept or reject them according to their agency. They must also be diligent in keeping the Lord's commandments to receive the promised blessings.

Enos 1:19–24 • The Nephites Seek to Restore the Lamanites

19 And now it came to pass that I, Enos, went about among the people of Nephi, prophesying of things to come, and testifying of the things which I had heard and seen.

20 And I bear record that the people of Nephi did seek diligently to restore the Lamanites unto the true faith in God. But our labors were vain; their hatred was fixed, and they were led by their evil nature that they became wild, and ferocious, and a blood-thirsty people, full of idolatry and filthiness; feeding upon beasts of prey; dwelling in tents, and wandering about in the wilderness with a short skin girdle about their loins and their heads shaven; and their skill was in the bow, and in the cimeter, and the ax. And many of them did eat nothing save it was raw meat; and they were continually seeking to destroy us.

21 And it came to pass that the people of Nephi did till the land, and raise all manner of grain, and of fruit, and flocks of herds, and flocks of all manner of cattle of every kind, and goats, and wild goats, and also many horses.

22 And there were exceedingly many prophets among us. And the people were a stiffnecked people, hard to understand.

23 And there was nothing save it was exceeding harshness, preaching and prophesying of wars, and contentions, and destructions, and continually reminding them of death, and the duration of eternity, and the judgments and the power of God, and all these things—stirring them up continually to keep them in the fear of the Lord. I say there was nothing short of these things, and exceedingly great plainness of speech, would keep them from going down

speedily to destruction. And after this manner do I write concerning them.

24 And I saw wars between the Nephites and Lamanites in the course of my days.

The contrast between the Nephites and the Lamanites is not unique. The pattern described here continues throughout the record. However, the Nephite society was stiffnecked and needed constant warning by the prophets to keep them from "going down speedily to destruction" (v. 23). We may conclude that the wars in Enos' day were not all the fault of the Lamanites. We may ask ourselves how the record of our day would be summarized.

Enos 1:25–27 • I Soon Go to my Rest with My Redeemer

25 And it came to pass that I began to be old, and an hundred and seventy and nine years had passed away from the time that our father Lehi left Jerusalem.

26 And I saw that I must soon go down to my grave, having been wrought upon by the power of God that I must preach and prophesy unto this people, and declare the word according to the truth which is in Christ. And I have declared it in all my days, and have rejoiced in it above that of the world.

27 And I soon go to the place of my rest, which is with my Redeemer; for I know that in him I shall rest. And I rejoice in the day when my mortal shall put on immortality, and shall stand before him; then shall I see his face with pleasure, and he will say unto me: Come unto me, ye blessed, there is a place prepared for you in the mansions of my Father. Amen.

It was one hundred and eighty years since Lehi and his people left Jerusalem. Three generations of Lehi's family were now history: Lehi, Nephi and Jacob, and Enos. All of these great men were stalwart leaders for Christ. Each seems to have received the Second Comforter or made their calling and election sure. The Prophet Joseph described the Second Comforter:

The other Comforter spoken of is a subject of great interest, and perhaps understood by few of this generation. After a person has faith in Christ, repents of his sins, and is baptized for the remission of his sins and receives the Holy Ghost, (by the laying on of hands), which is the first Comforter, then let him continue to humble himself before God, hungering and thirsting after righteousness, and living by every word of God, and the Lord will soon say unto him, Son, thou shalt be exalted. When the Lord has thoroughly proved him, and finds that the man is determined to serve him at all hazards, then the man will find his calling and his election made sure, then it will be his privilege to receive the other Comforter, which the Lord has promised his Saints, as is recorded in the testimony of St. John, in the 14th chapter, from the 12th to the 27th verses.

Note verses 16, 17, 18, 21 and 23:

16 And I will pray the Father, and he shall give you another Comforter, that he may abide with you for ever;

17 *Even* the Spirit of truth; whom the world cannot receive, because it seeth him not, neither knoweth him: but ye know him; for he dwelleth with you, and shall be in you.

18 I will not leave you comfortless: I will come to you.

21 He that hath my commandments, and keepeth them, he it is that loveth me: and he that loveth me shall be loved of my Father, and I will love him, and will manifest myself to him.

22 Judas saith unto him, not Iscariot, Lord, how is it that thou wilt manifest thyself unto us, and not unto the world?

23 Jesus answered and said unto him, If a man love me, he will keep my words: and my Father will love him, and we will come unto him, and make our abode with him.[3]

Now what is this other Comforter? It is no more nor less than the Lord Jesus Christ himself; and this is the sum and substance of the whole matter, that when any man obtains this last Comforter, he will have the personage of Jesus Christ to attend him, or appear unto him

---

[3] For a clarification of which verses refer to the first Comforter, and which ones refer to the second Comforter, see General Authority Quotes, Joseph Fielding Smith, the Second Comforter.

from time to time, and even he will manifest the Father unto him, and they will take up their abode with him, and the visions of the heavens will be opened unto him, and the Lord will teach him face to face, and he may have a perfect knowledge of the mysteries of the kingdom of God; and this is the state and place the ancient Saints arrived at when they had such glorious visions—Isaiah, Ezekiel, John on the Isle of Patmos, St. Paul in the three heavens, and all the Saints who held communion with the general assembly and Church of the First born. [*TPJS*, 150–51]

Lehi recorded: "But behold, the Lord hath redeemed my soul from hell; I have beheld his glory, and I am encircled about eternally in the arms of his love" (2 Nephi 1:15). Nephi said: "my brother, Jacob, also has seen [Christ] as I have seen him" (2 Nephi 11:3). He also said: "I glory in my Jesus, for he hath redeemed my soul from hell" (2 Nephi 33:6). Lehi told Jacob: "I know that thou art redeemed, because of the righteousness of thy Redeemer; for thou hast beheld that in the fullness of time he cometh to bring salvation unto men. And thou hast beheld in thy youth his glory" (2 Nephi 2:3–4). Now Enos declares that he will soon "go to the place of my rest, which is with my Redeemer" (Enos 1:27). They each served as examples for their brethren, the Nephites, and for the readers of their records as well. May we learn from them as well.

SACRED WRITING

Revelation Which is Great:

Enos 1:3–18   Enos has his sins forgiven and is promised that a record of the Nephites would be preserved for the Lamanites in the Lord's own due time.

Prophesying:

Jacob 7:3–19   Jacob's debate with Sherem. Sherem is smitten.

Enos 1:26–27   Enos goes to his Redeemer.

Doctrines Learned:

Jacob 7:12	If no atonement had been made all mankind must be lost.
Enos 1:6	God cannot lie.
Enos 1:8	Sins are forgiven through faith in Christ.
Enos 1:10	Revelation comes through the voice of the Lord into one's mind.
Enos 1:10	Blessings are conditional according to diligence in keeping the Lord's commandments.
Enos 1:15	Prayers are answered according to one's faith in Christ.

General Authority Quotations:

Joseph Smith • Jacob 7:13

When I was preaching in Philadelphia, a quaker called out for a sign. I told him to be still. After the sermon, he again asked for a sign. I told the congregation the man was an adulterer; that a wicked and adulterous generation seeketh after a sign; and that the Lord had said to me in a revelation, that any man who wanted a sign was an adulterous person. "It is true" cried one, "for I caught him in the very act," which the man afterwards confessed when he was baptized. [*TPJS*, 278]

The Prophet Joseph Smith • Jacob 7:19

The unpardonable sin is to shed innocent blood, or be accessory thereto. All other sins will be visited with judgment in the flesh, and the spirit being delivered to the buffetings of Satan until the day of the Lord Jesus Christ. [*TPJS*, 301]

What has Jesus said? All sins, and all blasphemies, and every transgression, except one, that man can be guilty of, may be forgiven; and there is salvation for all men, either in this world or in the world to come, who have not committed the unpardonable sin, there being a provision either in this world or the world of spirits. Hence God hath made a provision that every spirit in the eternal world can be ferreted out and saved unless he has committed the unpardonable sin which cannot be remitted to him either in this world or the world of spirits. God has wrought out a salvation for all men, unless they have committed a certain sin; and every man who has a friend in the eternal world can save him, unless he has committed the unpardonable sin. And so you can see how far you can be savior.

A man cannot commit the unpardonable sin after the dissolution of the body, and there is a way possible for escape. Knowledge saves a man; and in the world of spirits no man can be exalted but by knowledge. . . . no man can commit the unpardonable sin after the dissolution of the body, nor in this life, until he receives the Holy Ghost; but they must do it in this world.

All sins shall be forgiven, except the sin against the Holy Ghost; for Jesus will save all except the sons of perdition. What must a man do to commit the unpardonable sin? He must receive the Holy Ghost, have the heavens opened unto him, and know God, and sin against Him. After a man has sinned against the Holy Ghost, there is no repentance for him. He has got to say the sun does not shine while he sees it; he has got to deny Jesus Christ when the heavens have been opened unto him, and to deny the plan of salvation with his eyes open to the truth of it; and from that time he begins to be an enemy. This is the case with many apostates of the Church of Jesus Christ of Latter-day Saints.

When a man begins to be an enemy to this work, he hunts me, he seeks to kill me, and never ceases to thirst for my blood. He gets the spirit of the devil—the same spirit that they had who crucified the Lord of Life—the same spirit that sins against the Holy Ghost. You cannot save such persons; you cannot bring them to repentance; they make open war, like the devil, and awful is the consequence. [*TPJS*, 356–358]

Spencer W. Kimball • Enos 1:10

When you received your confirmation, you were commanded to receive the Holy Ghost. He was not obligated to seek you out. The Lord says, "I will visit thy brethren according to their diligence in keeping my command-ments" (Enos 1:10). If our lives are responsive and clean, if we are reaching and cultivating, the Holy Ghost will come, and we may retain him and have the peace his presence thus affords. [*Speeches of the Year,* "Prayer," Discourses at BYU, October 11, (1961), 7]

Harold B. Lee • Enos 1:10

A way by which we receive revelation is the way that the Prophet Enos spoke of. After he'd gone up and received the great commission to carry on the work and to write the record, he pens this very significant statement in his record in the Book of Mormon; "And while I was thus struggling in the spirit, the voice of the Lord came into my mind saying . . ." (Enos 1:10). In other words, sometimes we hear the voice of the Lord coming into our minds and when it comes the impressions are just as strong as though he were talking as with a trumpet into our ear. Jeremiah says something like that in the first chapter of the book of Jeremiah: "Then the word of the Lord came unto me saying . . ." In the story of the Book of Mormon we have Nephi upbraiding his brothers, calling them to repentance, and in his statement to them he gives voice to same thought when he says, "And he hath spoken unto you in a still, small voice, but ye were past feeling, so that ye could not feel his words" (1 Nephi 17:45). Thus the Lord, by revelations, brings into our minds as though a voice were speaking. May I bear humble testimony, if I may be pardoned, to that fact? I was once in a situation where I needed help. The Lord knew I needed help and I was on an important mission. I was awakened in the hours of the morning as though someone had wakened me to straighten me out on something that I had planned to do in a contrary course, and there was clearly mapped out before me as I lay there that morning what I should do and what I should say the following morning, just as surely as though someone had sat on the edge of my bed and told me just what to do. Yes, the voice of the Lord comes into our minds and we are directed thereby. [Brigham Young University Speeches of the Year, October 14, 1962]

President Joseph Fielding Smith • The Second Comforter

Joseph Smith speaks of two Comforters: the first is the Holy Ghost, the second is the Son of God himself. He uses the 14th chapter of John as the basis of his discourse. Verses 16, 17, and 26, definitely refer to the Holy Ghost. They speak of the Spirit of Truth which "dwelleth with you, and shall be in you." Verses 18, 21, and 23 clearly refer to the Lord himself and his coming to man. [*Doctrines of Salvation*, comp. Bruce R. McConkie, 3 vols. (1954–56), 1:55]

Challenges to Eternal Life:

1. As you hear or read statements of prominent people in the world, compare their teachings to those of Sherem. Do they support the teachings of Christ or go against them?
2. Choose a problem in your life and follow the formula of Enos for its solution. Soul hunger (desire)—struggle or wrestle—mighty prayer and supplication (plea)—answer (Enos 1:4–5).
3. Analyze your feelings toward your associates and determine the degree of the Love of God you have with you (Enos 1:9–12).
4. Select a challenge or a modern message from the reading and incorporate it into your life.

Chapter Four

A Very Light Touch of History

Jarom; Omni;
Words of Mormon 1:1–11

*H*istorical Setting: The two little books of Jarom and Omni cover from 420 B.C. (see Enos 1:25) until sometime between 279 and about 130 B.C., or about two hundred and ninety years. There are six engravers upon the plates, five of them on the book of Omni.

Engraver	Years after Lehi left		Years kept	References
Jarom	180 through 238		59—420 to 361 B.C.	Enos 1:25; Jarom 1:13
Omni	239 through 282		44—361 to 317 B.C.	Jarom 1:15; Omni 1:3
Amaron	283 through 320[1]		38—317 to 279 B.C.	Omni 1:3–5
Chemish	321 through ?			
Abinadom	?	?		
Amaleki	? about 470		150—280 to 130 B.C.	Omni 1:6; Moses 6:4

Only the first two of the five writers in the book of Omni give any dates. The next three writers, Chemish, a brother of Amaron, Abinadom, and Amaleki, covered from Chemish (279 B.C.) to the reign of Mosiah, son of Benjamin (124 B.C.), or one hundred and fifty-five

---

[1] Amaron does not give a date for beginning or ending his record. It is assumed he began in the 283rd year after Lehi left Jerusalem and ended in the year that he recorded.

years. The dates listed in the Book of Mormon text in the lower left hand corners of the page estimate the beginning of the book of Mosiah at "about 130 B.C." (p. 145). Therefore, from the book of Jarom to the end of Omni is about two hundred and ninety years. Mormon does add a few verses about King Benjamin as he bridges the gap between the small plates of Nephi and his abridgment of the large plates (Words of Mormon 1:12–18), but the length of time Mormon covers of King Benjamin's life is not given.[2]

The years covered in the two books, Jarom and Omni, are given in just four and one-half pages of the present Book of Mormon text (pages 138–143), and as Nephi instructed, do "not touch, save it were lightly, concerning the history of this people" (Jacob 1:2). Mormon obviously drew upon the larger record of the Nephites to supplement the reign of King Benjamin (Words of Mormon 1:12–18) that had already been briefly summarized by Amaleki (Omni 1:23–24). However, both books have the same message given much earlier to Nephi, son of Lehi, and reiterated by Lehi: "Inasmuch as you will keep my commandments ye shall prosper in the land" (1 Nephi 2:19–24; 2 Nephi 1:20). This repeated statement throughout the Book of Mormon is a vital message to our day. Jarom bears witness of the Lord's promise being verified (Jarom 1:9). Amaron bears witness that they did not prosper because they did not keep the commandments.

Precepts of This Reading:

> And thus being prepared to meet the Lamanites, they did not prosper against us. But the word of the Lord was verified, which he spake unto our fathers, saying that: Inasmuch as ye will keep my commandments ye shall prosper in the land. [Jarom 1:9]

> And now, my beloved brethren, I would that ye should come unto

---

[2] The three generations from Chemish to Mosiah, son of Benjamin (Chemish, Abinadom, and Amaleki) were responsible for 155 years of the Nephite record (279–124 B.C.). Chemish was probably responsible for only a few years since his brother Amoran, of the same generation, had covered thirty-eight years of that generation. Therefore Abinadom and Amaleki were probably responsible for over sixty years each.

Christ, who is the Holy One of Israel, and partake of his salvation, and the power of his redemption. Yea, come unto him, and offer your whole souls as an offering unto him, and continue in fasting and praying, and endure to the end; and as the Lord liveth ye will be saved. [Omni 1:26]

And I do this for a wise purpose; for thus it whispereth me, according to the workings of the Spirit of the Lord which is in me. And now, I do not know all things; but the Lord knoweth all things which are to come; wherefore, he worketh in me to do according to his will.

8 And my prayer to God is concerning my brethren, that they may once again come to the knowledge of God, yea, the redemption of Christ; that they may once again be a delightsome people. [Words of Mormon 1:7–8]

An outline of the two books will further verify the witness of both Jarom and Amoran and prepare the reader for a deeper study.

OUTLINE • JAROM; OMNI;
WORDS OF MORMON 1:1–11

➤ Jarom 1:1–4   Jarom wrote a few things by commandment of Enos, his father, that their genealogy may be kept.

    a. Because the plates were small, he wrote only a few things with the intent to benefit the Lamanites.

    b. He did not write his prophecies or his revelations for the plan of salvation was revealed to his fathers (v. 2).

    c. There was much to do among his people because of their wickedness. God was merciful and had not yet swept them off the land (v. 3).

    d. Many had revelations and faith and communed with the Holy Spirit (v. 4).

➤ 1:5–12   Two hundred years passed away, the Nephites waxed strong in the land.

    a. They kept the law of Moses and the Sabbath Day holy (v. 5).

    b.   They did not profane or blaspheme and strictly kept the laws of the land (v. 5).

    c.   The Lamanites were exceedingly more numerous than the Nephites, and both were scattered upon all the land (v. 6).

    d.   The Lamanites loved murder, drank the blood of beasts and came to battle many times against the Nephites (vv. 5–7).

    e.   The kings and leaders of the Nephites were mighty men in the faith of the Lord and taught their people his ways (v. 7).

        1.   They withstood the Lamanites and swept them out of the Nephite lands.

        2.   They fortified their cities and places of inheritance.

    f.   The Nephites multiplied and spread over the land (v. 8).

        1.   They became rich in gold, silver, and precious things.

        2.   They were fine workmen in wood, buildings, and machinery.

        3.   They made all manner of tools to till the ground.

        4.   They made all manner of weapons of war in preparation for war.

    g.   The Lamanites did not prosper against the Nephites, verifying the Lord's promise that if you keep the commandments ye shall prosper in the land (v. 9).

    h.   The prophets threatened the Nephites to keep the commandments, or they should be destroyed (vv. 10–11).

        1.   They taught the law of Moses and its purpose of looking forward to the Messiah, and to believe in him as though he had already come.

        2.   They kept them from being destroyed by stirring them up to repentance.

➤ 1:13–15   Two hundred and thirty-eight years had passed away having wars, contentions, and dissensions.

    a. Not much was written because the plates were small, but the records of their wars were engraved on the other plates (v. 14).

    b. Jarom delivered the plates to his son Omni to keep, as commanded of the fathers (v. 15).

➤ Omni 1:1–3 Being commanded by his father Jarom, Omni wrote to preserve their genealogy.

    a. He fought with the sword to keep them from falling to the Lamanites (v. 1).

    b. He was a wicked man and had not kept the commandments as he should (v. 2).

    c. Two hundred and seventy-six years passed. They had many seasons of peace and many seasons of serious war and bloodshed (v. 3).

    d. When two hundred and eighty-two years were passed, he conferred the plates on Amaron, his son (v. 3).

➤ 1:4–8 Amaron wrote a few things in the book of his father.

    a. Three hundred and twenty years passed and the more wicked part of the Nephites were destroyed (v. 5).

      1. The Lord's words were verified, if you don't keep the commandments, ye shall not prosper.

      2. The Lord did visit them with great judgment, but did deliver the righteous from their enemies.

    b. He delivered the plates to his brother Chemish (v. 8).

➤ 1:9 Chemish wrote a few things in the same book with his brother.

    a. He saw him write in the same day he delivered them to him.

    b. They kept the record because it was a commandment of our fathers.

➤ 1:10–11 Abinadom son of Chemish kept the record.

    a. He had seen much war and contention between the

Nephites and Lamanites (v. 10).

    b. He had taken the lives of many Lamanites with his own sword in defense of his brethren (v. 10).

    c. The record of this people is engraven on plates had by the kings (v. 11).

    d. He knew of no revelation or prophecy save what had been written (v. 11).

➤ 1:12–13   Amaleki, the son of Abinadom, speaks of Mosiah, king over the land of Zarahemla.

    a. Mosiah was warned of the Lord to flee out of the land of Nephi, with as many as would depart out of the land, into the wilderness (vv. 12–13).

        1. They were led by preachings and prophesying, and admonished continually by the word of God.

        2. They were led by the power of God's arm through the wilderness to Zarahemla.

➤ 1:14–19   They discovered the people of Zarahemla.

    a. Zarahemla and his people rejoiced because Mosiah brought the plates of brass containing the record of the Jews (v. 14).

    b. The people of Zarahemla came out of Jerusalem when King Zedekiah was carried captive to Babylon (v. 15).

    c. They journeyed in the wilderness and were led by the Lord across the great waters into the land where Mosiah discovered them (v. 16).

    d. They had become exceedingly numerous, but had had wars and contentions (v. 17).

        1. Their language had become corrupted.

        2. They had brought no records with them.

        3. They denied the being of their creator.

        4. Mosiah and his people could not understand them.

    e. They were taught the language of Mosiah (v. 18).

        1. Zarahemla gave a genealogy of his fathers according to his memory.

2. They were written but not in these plates.

f. The people of Zarahemla and the people of Mosiah united and Mosiah was appointed their king (v. 19).

➤ 1:20–22   A large stone was brought to Mosiah, and he interpreted it by the gift and power of God.

a. It gave an account of one Coriantumr and his people who were slain (v. 21).

1. He was discovered by the people of Zarahemla.

2. He dwelt with them for nine moons.

b. It also gave an account of Coriantumr's fathers (v. 22).

1. Their first parents came from the tower at the time the Lord confounded the language of the people.

2. The Lord's judgments fell upon them and their bones lay scattered in the land northward.

➤ 1:23–26   Amaleki was born in the days of Mosiah. Mosiah died and Benjamin his son reigned in his stead.

a. There was a serious war in the days of King Benjamin between the Nephites and the Lamanites (v. 24).

1. The Nephites gained advantage over the Lamanites.

2. King Benjamin drove them out of the land of Zarahemla.

b. Amaleki was old and had no seed. He delivered the plates to King Benjamin, a just man.

1. He exhorted all men to come to God and believe in the various spiritual gifts and all good things (v. 25).

2. He exhorted his brethren to come unto Christ and partake of his salvation and redemption (v. 26).

➤ 1:27–30   Amaleki spoke of a number who desired to return and possess the land of Nephi.

a. There was contention among them in the wilderness and all but fifty were slain. They returned to Zarahemla.

        b. A considerable number left again and have not been heard of since.

➢ Words of Mormon 1:1–2

        Mormon delivered his record to his son Moroni.

        a. He had witnessed almost all the destruction of his people, the Nephites (v. 1).

           1. It was many hundred years after the coming of Christ.

           2. He supposed Moroni would witness the entire destruction of the Nephites.

        b. He prayed that Moroni would survive that he may write somewhat concerning the Nephites, and of Christ, that it may profit them someday (v. 2).

➢ 1:3–9   After making an abridgment of the (large) plates of Nephi down to the reign of King Benjamin, Mormon found these records of Jacob to King Benjamin and many of the words of Nephi.

        a. Mormon was pleased with these plates because of the prophecies of the coming of Christ (v. 4).

           1. There were many prophecies of the Nephite fathers that have been fulfilled.

           2. Those that had not been fulfilled must surely be.

        b. Mormon finished his record upon these plates (v. 5).

           1. The things he wrote were taken from the (large) plates of Nephi.

           2. He could not write a hundredth part of the things of the Nephites.

        c. Mormon put these plates with the remainder of his record (vv. 6–7, 9).

           1. They were choice to him and will be to his brethren.

           2. The Spirit of the Lord said to do so, and he did it by the knowledge and understanding God gave him.

3. The Lord knows all things to come and worked in Mormon to do His will.

d. Mormon prayed to God that his brethren would come to the knowledge of God and Christ and again become a delightsome people (v. 8).

➤ 1:10–11   Amaleki delivered these plates to King Benjamin who handed them down (along with the large plates) from generation to generation until Mormon received them.

a. Mormon prayed for and knew they would be preserved (v. 10).

b. There were great things written upon them and Mormon's people will be judged by the things written on them (v. 10).

NOTES AND COMMENTARY

Introduction: One of the desires expressed by Job was "that mine adversary had written a book" (Job 31:35). Why would he express such an unusual desire? A probable answer is that once something is written it is open to criticism, and in Job's case, the accusations against him would have been easily refuted. With this in mind, let us look at an accusation sometimes used against the Book of Mormon:

> *it is not an account of the ancient inhabitants of America,*
> *but was imagined and written by Joseph Smith Jr.*

There are eleven different authors who engraved their writings upon the plates from which the Book of Mormon was translated. In the words of one modern-day professional writer:

> Every writer has a style of writing just as he has his own finger-prints. Style differs from fingerprints, though, in that it grows, develops, changes. At the beginning of a writer's career his style may be partially borrowed from other writers. As he learns to know

himself and have confidence in himself, his style becomes something that is really his own.[3]

Does each one of these eleven authors have a different style of writing? If they do, it would seem impossible for the unlearned Joseph to have duplicated eleven different styles of writing. Three of the eleven authors, Nephi, Jacob, and Enos, made their contributions to the record prior to the books of Jarom and Omni. Mormon and Moroni's writings upon the plates follow these two books. In answering the question of differing styles of writing we will consider the style of Enos, Jarom, and the five authors who wrote in the book of Omni. Our source is Dr. Robert K. Thomas, now deceased but former professor of English and Academic Vice-President of Brigham Young University:

> But perhaps the most remarkable demonstration of literary sensitivity in the entire Book of Mormon can be enjoyed in the seven pages which comprise the books of Enos, Jarom, and Omni. Though these books at first glance seem too short to be very significant, they are actually a tour de force without parallel in Hebraic scripture, illustrating that style is the man.
>
> The headlong impetuosity of Enos is suggested by his rather imprecise, fragmentary opening sentence. You know, as an English teacher this always makes me shiver a little as I read it. "Behold, it came to pass that I, Enos, knowing my father that he was a just man—for he taught me in his language, and also in the nurture and admonition of the Lord—and blessed be the name of my God for it."
>
> The vitality of this man fairly crackles on the page. Note especially his use of verbs and verb forms: wrestled, sunk, hungered, kneeled, cried, raised, poured out, struggling, swept. Enos simply can't wait for logic to catch up with him. His words roll forth in an irresistible flood. In describing the Lamanites he pours attitudes on top of environment, adds physical description, then skills, shifts to diet and back to attitudes again. His sentences all have a spoken quality, and their length seems determined only by a need for breath.

---

[3] Helen Hinckley Jones, "A Writer Looks at the Book of Mormon," *Improvement Era,* Nov. 1960.

Listen as you read the following description of his own people: "And there was nothing save it was exceeding harshness, preaching and prophesying of wars, and contentions, and destructions, and continually reminding them of death, and the duration of eternity, and the judgments and the power of God, and all these things—stirring them up continually to keep them in the fear of the Lord." Just one magnificent sentence—about a deep breath long.

This man wrings meaning from every moment. His concluding words are beautiful in character: "And I rejoice in the day when my mortal shall put on immortality, and shall stand before him; then shall I see his face with pleasure." It had been suggested in all Western literature there is a singular lack of friendship toward God. Reverence, awe, wonder, transport, even ecstacy we know; but all these have overtures of the supernal. Enos, in the company of the English poet George Herbert, might well make an affectionate call on the Lord.

From Enos to his son Jarom is the shortest of genealogical steps but a gigantic shift in style. Except for the expected, conventional beginning, note the difference: "Now behold, I, Jarom, write a few words according to the commandment of my father, Enos, that our genealogy may be kept." You are suddenly aware that nothing in the whole book of Enos came to bear on a problem with such crispness. The succeeding verses develop the reasons for the length of his account and the special problems of his day in coherent, beautifully modulated sentences. His diction too is precise. In discussing his people he lets us see their total strength in saying that, "They profaned not, neither did they blaspheme." This is not merely synonymous parallelism, that standard device of Hebraic positive. This is an incremental repetition in which additional meanings are added within a parallel framework. . . .

From calm, exacting Jarom we come to Omni. At once we are struck by a focus on the first person. There are seven "I"s in two verses. Omni is a soldier, dutifully carrying out the command of his father but not a bit averse to identifying himself as a wicked man. We soon see what really interests him. He not only lets us know of his valor in battle but describes his times solely in terms of war and peace. "We had many seasons of peace, we had many seasons of serious war and bloodshed."

That reference to "serious war" gives him away. It suggests the concern of a man to whom war is neither inconsequential nor detestable. It's simply a vocation. Omni is forthright, not very reflective, and his sentences march briskly but to no great end.

Amaron, Omni's son, is more like his grandfather, Jarom. He is careful, organized, and in a few verses manages to turn our attention from personalities to issues. Yet Amaron lack's Jarom's linguistic sensitivity. His sentences, unlike Omni's, are neatly balanced, but it is a mechanical neatness. Here is a style which tries to synthesize the no-nonsense approach of his father with the carefully controlled cadence of his grandfather.

If Amaron is not quite successful, what shall we say of Chemish? Poor, dear Chemish! Possibly he didn't expect to have to take his turn at the records, since they usually went from father to son, but overwhelmed by the responsibility that is suddenly his, he can only belabor the obvious: "They all write in the same book, and they all write with their own hands." You can just see the half-hopeful, half-relieved smile with which he turns the records over to his son. . . .

I know of no more revealing verse in all scripture. How clearly Chemish is given to us. Not in what is said about him, but in what he says about himself

Through his style. Just one verse, but in it the whole history of inadequacy. . . .

It's a relief to pass on to Abinadom. But in reading his account I seem to detect a bit of insecurity. I suspect he's looked back to see what others have written. There are echoes of Omni and Jarom, but nothing else. At this point we have had four men write in a total of eleven verses. This is all we know of them, yet I feel I might recognize them on the street.

The final nineteen, rather long verses are the breezy contribution of Amaleki. He just loves to write. He mixes exhortation with history in about equal amounts and stops only when he's used up all the space that remained on the plates.

Joseph Smith's translation of the small plates concludes here. Not only have we encountered typically Hebraic figures, but they have been presented with undeniable skill. Styles which should have been distinctive have been consistently so. Yet there's an overall tone which bespeaks a single translator.

We have only to check the markedly different versions of the Bible in English to recognize how much a translator can provide in achieving that integration of nuance and emphasis that turns words into life. . . .[4]

The record speaks for itself. Joseph Smith could not possibly have written the book. Having determined the authenticity of the record, let us examine the message of the books of Jarom and Omni and also the brief account given us in the first part of the Words of Mormon as he bridges the gap between the two sets of Nephi's plates.

Jarom 1:1–4 • The Plan of Salvation Has Been Revealed

1 Now behold, I, Jarom, write a few words according to the commandment of my father, Enos, that our genealogy may be kept.

2 And as these plates are small, and as these things are written for the intent of the benefit of our brethren the Lamanites, wherefore, it must needs be that I write a little; but I shall not write the things of my prophesying, nor of my revelations. For what could I write more than my fathers have written? For have not they revealed the plan of salvation? I say unto you, Yea; and this sufficeth me.

3 Behold, it is expedient that much should be done among this people, because of the hardness of their hearts, and the deafness of their ears, and the blindness of their minds, and the stiffness of their necks; nevertheless, God is exceedingly merciful unto them, and has not as yet swept them off from the face of the land.

4 And there are many among us who have many revelations, for they are not all stiffnecked. And as many as are not stiffnecked and have faith, have communion with the Holy Spirit, which maketh manifest unto the children of men, according to their faith.

---

[4] Robert K. Thomas, A Literary Critic Looks At The Book Of Mormon, 8th of 12 essays published in TO THE GLORY OF GOD, Dedicated to the life and memory of B. West Belnap, [1972], 156–159. Originally published in The Joseph Smith Memorial Sermons, Twenty-Second Annual, December 6, 1964, LDS Institute of Religion, Logan, Utah.

These four verses apparently cover a twenty-one year period, assuming Enos died one hundred and eighty years (420 B.C.) after Lehi left Jerusalem. Although Jarom had prophesied and received revelation, he did not include their content on the plates because the revelations and prophecies of his fathers had been recorded, and thus had given his people the plan of salvation (v. 2). Jarom's statement answers an often asked question today. Since the Church believes in continuous revelation, and the Church leaders do receive revelations constantly, why are these revelations not added to the Doctrine and Covenants? The revelations given to Joseph Smith likewise revealed the plan of salvation and succeeding prophets of the Church have received revelations that clarified or added to our knowledge of the plan of salvation. These revelations were periodically added (i.e. sections 137 and 138 were added to the Pearl of Great Price in 1976 and later to the Doctrine and Covenants in 1980). However, most of the revelations received today are instructions on how to administer the Church in its expanding growth and development toward a Zion society. Nephi admonished Jacob to include "preaching which was sacred, or revelation which was great, or prophesying" (Jacob 1:4), but, although those received by Jarom were important for the Church in his day, they were not significant enough to benefit his Lamanite brethren in the future. As the Lamanites have and will come back into the Church restored by the Prophet Joseph, new revelation was and will be given to administer the latter-day Church.

59 Thou shalt take the things which thou hast received, which have been given unto thee in my scriptures for a law, to be my law to govern my church;

60 And he that doeth according to these things shall be saved, and he that doeth them not shall be damned if he so continue.

61 If thou shalt ask, thou shalt receive revelation upon revelation, knowledge upon knowledge, that thou mayest know the mysteries and peaceable things—that which bringeth joy, that which bringeth life eternal.

62 Thou shalt ask, and it shall be revealed unto you in mine own due time where the New Jerusalem shall be built. [D&C 42:59–62]

Jarom and his brethren received revelations and had communion with the Holy Spirit (Jarom 1:4). At least some of these revelations were probably on how to govern the Church.

Jarom 1:5–12 • The Law of Moses and the Sabbath Observed

5 And now, behold, two hundred years had passed away, and the people of Nephi had waxed strong in the land. They observed to keep the law of Moses and the sabbath day holy unto the Lord. And they profaned not; neither did they blaspheme. And the laws of the land were exceedingly strict.

6 And they were scattered upon much of the face of the land, and the Lamanites also. And they were exceedingly more numerous than were they of the Nephites; and they loved murder and would drink the blood of beasts.

7 And it came to pass that they came many times against us, the Nephites, to battle. But our kings and our leaders were mighty men in the faith of the Lord; and they taught the people the ways of the Lord; wherefore, we withstood the Lamanites and swept them away out of our lands, and began to fortify our cities, or whatsoever place of our inheritance.

8 And we multiplied exceedingly, and spread upon the face of the land, and became exceedingly rich in gold, and in silver, and in precious things, and in fine workmanship of wood, in buildings, and in machinery, and also in iron and copper, and brass and steel, making all manner of tools of every kind to till the ground, and weapons of war—yea, the sharp pointed arrow, and the quiver, and the dart, and the javelin, and all preparations for war.

9 And thus being prepared to meet the Lamanites, they did not prosper against us. But the word of the Lord was verified, which he spake unto our fathers, saying that: Inasmuch as ye will keep my commandments ye shall prosper in the land.

10 And it came to pass that the prophets of the Lord did threaten the people of Nephi, according to the word of God, that if they did not keep the commandments, but should fall into transgression, they should be destroyed from off the face of the land.

11 Wherefore, the prophets, and the priests, and the teachers, did labor diligently, exhorting with all long-suffering the people to diligence; teaching the law of Moses, and the intent for which it was given; persuading them to look forward unto the Messiah, and believe in him to come as though he already was. And after this manner did they teach them.

12 And it came to pass that by so doing they kept them from being destroyed upon the face of the land; for they did prick their hearts with the word, continually stirring them up unto repentance.

These eight verses describe thirty-eight years, from two hundred years to two hundred thirty-eight years after Lehi left Jerusalem (399–361 B.C.) (vv. 5, 13). The contrast between the Nephites and the Lamanites is very similar to what was described by Jarom's father (see Enos 1:19–24).

The Lord's promise, "Inasmuch as ye will keep my commandments ye shall prosper in the land," was fulfilled among the Nephites (Jarom 1:9), but it was not without effort. Although the Nephites prospered (v. 8), it was the political and priesthood leaders who kept the prosperity going (vv. 7, 11–12). The formula that maintained their prosperous conditions was keeping the sabbath day holy, keeping the law of Moses for the intended purpose, looking forward to and believing in the Messiah to come, refraining from profanity and blasphemy, and having very strict laws of the land (vv. 5, 11). Our society should collectively learn and observe the same formula. The Nephites were warned conditionally of being destroyed from off the face of the land (vv. 10, 12). Our society is warned to defend the constitutional laws of the land to maintain our freedom.

6 Therefore, I, the Lord, justify you, and your brethren of my church, in befriending that law which is the constitutional law of the land;

7 And as pertaining to law of man, whatsoever is more or less than this, cometh of evil.

8 I, the Lord God, make you free, therefore ye are free indeed; and the law also maketh you free. [D&C 98:6–8]

The description of their prosperity including machinery (v. 8) may raise some question. Machinery is something that has moving parts. What were these machines? How were they powered or operated? We will probably have to wait for the larger records of Nephi for our answers (Jarom 1:14). These answers will be restored after our faith in the present text of the Book of Mormon is tested (see 3 Nephi 26:8–11).

The weapons of war mentioned by Jarom and Enos suggest that the machinery was not too far advanced (Jarom 1:8 and Enos 1:20). However, an open mind as to the possibilities of what the Nephites had developed should be kept.

Jarom 1:13–15 • The Record of the Kings

13 And it came to pass that two hundred and thirty and eight years had passed away—after the manner of wars, and contentions, and dissensions, for the space of much of the time.

14 And I, Jarom, do not write more, for the plates are small. But behold, my brethren, ye can go to the other plates of Nephi; for behold, upon them the records of our wars are engraven, according to the writings of the kings, or those which they caused to be written.

15 And I deliver these plates into the hands of my son Omni, that they may be kept according to the commandments of my fathers.

Jarom kept the record for probably fifty-nine years. His comments are general on each of the two time periods into which he divides his record, as noted above. He records only about one and two-thirds pages, a total of fifteen verses as divided in our present-day text. To reflect upon the last fifty-nine years of the events in our day and age will emphasize the brevity of his record. To summarize that number of years in such a short space would depend upon your objective. Jarom chose to emphasize the promises of the Lord regarding the keeping of his commandments. There will be much historical information gained from the record kept by the kings, or their appointed scribes (v. 14), when they are made available through the work of the Lord.

Omni 1:1–3 • The Record of Omni

1 Behold, it came to pass that I, Omni, being commanded by my father, Jarom, that I should write somewhat upon these plates, to preserve our genealogy—

2 Wherefore, in my days, I would that ye should know that I fought much with the sword to preserve my people, the Nephites, from falling into the hands of their enemies, the Lamanites. But behold, I of myself am a wicked man, and I have not kept the statutes and the commandments of the Lord as I ought to have done.

3 And it came to pass that two hundred and seventy and six years had passed away, and we had many seasons of peace; and we had many seasons of serious war and bloodshed. Yea, and in fine, two hundred and eighty and two years had passed away, and I had kept these plates according to the commandments of my fathers; and I conferred them upon my son Amaron. And I make an end.

Omni kept the record for forty-four years breaking it into two time periods; from 239 B.C. to 276 B.C. (38 years), and 276 B.C. to 282 B.C. (6 years). As noted in the introduction, he writes in the first person. He used the word "I" ten times in the three verses of his writing. He acknowledges his own wickedness in not keeping "the statutes and commandments of the Lord" (v. 2), and his personal involvement in defending his people from the Lamanites. His general description of the forty-four years, as also noted in the introduction, was "we had many seasons of peace; and we had many seasons of serious war and bloodshed" (v. 3). He makes no contribution to principles or doctrines of the gospel.

Omni 1:4–8 • The Record of Amaron

4 And now I, Amaron, write the things whatsoever I write, which are few, in the book of my father.

5 Behold, it came to pass that three hundred and twenty years had passed away, and the more wicked part of the Nephites were destroyed.

6 For the Lord would not suffer, after he had led them out of the

land of Jerusalem and kept and preserved them from falling into the hands of their enemies, yea, he would not suffer that the words should not be verified, which he spake unto our fathers, saying that: Inasmuch as ye will not keep my commandments ye shall not prosper in the land.

7 Wherefore, the Lord did visit them in great judgment; nevertheless, he did spare the righteous that they should not perish, but did deliver them out of the hands of their enemies.

8 And it came to pass that I did deliver the plates unto my brother Chemish.

Amaron kept the record for thirty-eight years, from the 283rd (317 B.C.) through the 320th (279 B.C.) since Lehi left Jerusalem. He follows the theme of his grandfather, but in the negative aspect, bearing witness of the more wicked Nephites being destroyed. This verified the Lord's word to his fathers: "Inasmuch as ye will not keep my commandments ye shall not prosper in the land" (v. 6). However, the righteous were spared and delivered "out of the hands of their enemies" (v. 7).

Omni 1:9 • The Record of Chemish

Now I, Chemish, write what few things I write, in the same book with my brother; for behold, I saw the last which he wrote, that he wrote it with his own hand; and he wrote it in the day that he delivered them unto me. And after this manner we keep the records, for it is according to the commandments of our fathers. And I make an end.

How long Chemish kept the record is not given. Since he was a brother of Amaron, and of the same generation, the time period he covered was probably quite short. He didn't really contribute anything to the record. His record is the shortest of the eleven engravers on the plates. The inclusion of these three sentences is indicative that Joseph Smith did not write the book. If he was the author, he would not have included such details.

Omni 1:10–11 • The Record of Abinadom

10 Behold, I, Abinadom, am the son of Chemish. Behold, it came to pass that I saw much war and contention between my people, the Nephites, and the Lamanites; and I, with my own sword, have taken the lives of many of the Lamanites in the defence of my brethren.

11 And behold, the record of this people is engraven upon plates which is had by the kings, according to the generations; and I know of no revelation save that which has been written, neither prophecy; wherefore, that which is sufficient is written. And I make an end.

There are no dates given in Chemish's, Abinadom's, or Amaleki's record. However, Chemish's note that his brother, Amaron, made his engravings on the plates on the same day he delivered them to him indirectly affirmed that the three men kept the record for about one hundred and fifty years (see footnote #1). Because Chemish was a brother of Amaron, it is assumed that Abinadom and Amaleki kept the record longer than he did. Therefore, Abinadom's recording of wars with the Lamanites is certainly a brief account of more than a fifty-year time period. His having defended his brethren with his own sword reflects his grandfather Omni's contribution, suggesting he had read what was written. His knowing of "no revelation save that which has been written, neither prophecy" (v. 11) shows that he was aware of what was to be written on the plates (see Jacob 1:4). He was also aware of the more complete record kept by the kings (Omni 1:11).

Omni 1:12–13 • The Record of Amaleki

12 Behold, I am Amaleki, the son of Abinadom. Behold, I will speak unto you somewhat concerning Mosiah, who was made king over the land of Zarahemla; for behold, he being warned of the Lord that he should flee out of the land of Nephi, and as many as would hearken unto the voice of the Lord should also depart out of the land with him, into the wilderness—

13 And it came to pass that he did according as the Lord had commanded him. And they departed out of the land into the wilderness, as many as would hearken unto the voice of the Lord; and they were led by many preachings and prophesyings. And they were

admonished continually by the word of God; and they were led by
the power of his arm, through the wilderness until they came down
into the land which is called the land of Zarahemla.

Amaleki makes the greatest contribution of any of the five writers
in the book of Omni. His nineteen verses occupy almost twice as
much space as the other four writers combined. These four writers
gave general summaries of their time period, but Amaleki gives
specific yet brief incidents. Amaleki records the departure of the
righteous Nephites under the leadership of Mosiah the first, and their
discovery of the people of Zarahemla. These people had left Jerusalem prior to its destruction in about 589 B.C. The people of Zarahemla
had previously discovered Coriantumr, a survivor of the Jaredites.
Amaleki also told of King Benjamin who had succeeded his father
Mosiah as the king of the people of Zarahemla. Without the information given by Amaleki, the Book of Mormon record would have been
incomplete. For those who claim that Joseph Smith made up and
wrote the Book of Mormon, we ask: Would he have complicated the
storyline with three separate peoples coming at three different times
to the land of promise? Such detail does not seem reasonable, especially as supporting evidence about these groups has come forth.

The departure out of the land of Nephi under Mosiah was a
fulfillment of a prophecy made by Jacob: "And the time speedily
cometh, that except ye repent [the Lamanites] shall possess the land
of your inheritance, and the Lord God will lead away the righteous
out from among you" (Jacob 3:4). It was the second time since Lehi
and his people had left Jerusalem for the same reason that a righteous
group had been led away, exemplifying the same principle that was
taught by Nephi: The Lord "leadeth away the righteous into precious
lands, and the wicked he destroyeth, and curseth the land unto them
for their sakes" (1 Nephi 17:38). Nephi had been warned of the Lord
to take "those who believed in the warnings and the revelations of
God" to the land they called Nephi (2 Nephi 5:5–8). Mosiah was
similarly warned. Those who followed him were likewise those who
would hearken to the voice of the Lord (Omni 1:12). Both the

journeys of the people of Nephi and the people of Mosiah were lengthy. Amaleki mentions that Mosiah's people were led continually by the power of God (v. 13), and Nephi's people "did travel for the space of many days" (2 Nephi 5:7).

Omni 1:14–19 • The People of Zarahemla

14 And they discovered a people, who were called the people of Zarahemla. Now, there was great rejoicing among the people of Zarahemla; and also Zarahemla did rejoice exceedingly, because the Lord had sent the people of Mosiah with the plates of brass which contained the record of the Jews.

15 Behold, it came to pass that Mosiah discovered that the people of Zarahemla came out from Jerusalem at the time that Zedekiah, king of Judah, was carried away captive into Babylon.

16 And they journeyed in the wilderness, and were brought by the hand of the Lord across the great waters, into the land where Mosiah discovered them; and they had dwelt there from that time forth.

17 And at the time that Mosiah discovered them, they had become exceedingly numerous. Nevertheless, they had had many wars and serious contentions, and had fallen by the sword from time to time; and their language had become corrupted; and they had brought no records with them; and they denied the being of their Creator; and Mosiah, nor the people of Mosiah, could understand them.

18 But it came to pass that Mosiah caused that they should be taught in his language. And it came to pass that after they were taught in the language of Mosiah, Zarahemla gave a genealogy of his fathers, according to his memory; and they are written, but not in these plates.

19 And it came to pass that the people of Zarahemla, and of Mosiah, did unite together; and Mosiah was appointed to be their king.

The people of Zarahemla are known as the "people of Mulek" in later Book of Mormon passages because Mulek, a son of Zedekiah, was among them (see Mosiah 25:2; Helaman 6:10). They are also commonly referred to as Mulekites in Church literature, although the name is never used in the Book of Mormon. They had left Jerusalem at the time "Zedekiah, king of Judah, was carried captive into Babylon" (Omni 1:15). The Bible records that the army of the Chaldees "slew the sons of Zedekiah before his eyes" (2 Kings 24:7). The Book of Mormon tells us that his sons were slain "all except it was Mulek" (Helaman 8:21). Josephus wrote that Zedekiah took his wives and his children, and his captains and friends, and with them fled out of the city. The Babylonians "overtook him not far from Jericho" and the friends and captains "dispersed themselves; some one way and some another, and every one resolved to save himself; so the enemy took Zedekiah alive, when he was deserted by all but a few, with his children and his wives, and brought him to the king [Nebuchadnezzar]."[5]

Since Zedekiah was made the puppet king of Judah at age twenty-one, and reigned eleven years, he would have been thirty-one or thirty-two at the time of his capture by the Babylonians. Thus his children would not have been very old at the time (see 2 Kings 24:7). Based on these facts, some postulations have been made:

> According to Jewish tradition, the number of his sons who were slain by the order of Nebuchadnezzar was ten.
>
> Assuming that Zedekiah was married at the early age of eighteen, his oldest child could not have exceeded twelve or thirteen years of age at the time of his death (sic-captivity). If ten of his sons were slain, and in the meantime he had a family of daughters, as is well attested, then there is a high probability that Mulek was a mere infant at the time he escaped . . . male babies were not counted among the sons or men of Israel as such and were the subjects of a special immunity, along with women and girls. . . .
>
> It is at once apparent that where the word all is not used . . . the narrative is even weaker, and it is perfectly proper to reach the true

---

[5] *Josephus' Complete Works*, translated by William Whiston, A. M. Kregel Publications, Grand Rapids, Michigan 49503, 1960, book X, chapter VIII, 2:220.

sense by inferring "they slew the sons of Zedekiah who did not escape.[6]

> That one escaped is not too surprising after all. Remember, Zedekiah was only thirty-two at his capture. All his children must have been pre-adolescent. Mulek might very well have been a disguised infant whom devoted servants spirited out of the Babylonian grasp. Possibly he was in the company of the "king's daughters" when they finally reached Egypt along with Jeremiah (see Jeremiah 41:10; 43:6).[7]

While these postulations of why Mulek was not killed with Zedekiah's other sons are very probably true, we do know what the Book of Mormon tells us is true. Mulek was not slain. The voice of the Lord told the three special witnesses of the Book of Mormon that the plates "have been translated by the gift and power of God, . . . wherefore, we know of a surety that the work is true" (The Testimony of the Three Witnesses, in the front of the Book of Mormon. See also D&C 6:17; 17:6; 18:2–3).

The importance of the Lord sending Lehi's sons to obtain the plates of brass (1 Nephi 3:2–4) is shown by the Mulekites having "brought no records with them." The first effect of having no records was "their language had become corrupted." The second effect was more serious: "they denied the being of their Creator" (Omni 1:17). Amaleki records that "the Lord had sent the people of Mosiah with the plates of brass which contained the record of the Jews" (v. 14). The plates were apparently a major factor in teaching the people of Mulek the Nephite language, about the Creator, and the uniting of the two people under Mosiah (vv. 18–19).

Whether they journeyed into the wilderness (v. 16) from the area

---

[6] Ariel L. Crowley, About the Book of Mormon, The Escape of Mulek, pp. 86–90, copyright 1961 Idaho City, Idaho, originally printed in *The Improvement Era*, May 1955, 324–25.

[7] A Book of Mormon Treasury: selections from the pages of the *Improvement Era*, [1959]. Bible Prophecies of the Mulekites, 229–237. John L. Sorenson, "The Twig of the Cedar." *The Improvement Era*, May [1957], 330.

of Jericho where Josephus tells us they scattered, or whether they went into Egypt with Jeremiah, as suggested above, is not known. However, that they were "brought by the hand of the Lord across the great waters, into the land where Mosiah discovered them; and they had dwelt there from that time forth" (v. 16), was in fulfillment of biblical prophecies.

Ezekiel was given a parable and its interpretation of the downfall of King Zedekiah and his being taken captive into Babylon (see Ezekiel 17:1–21). An addendum to that parable stated:

> 22 Thus saith the Lord GOD; I will also take of the highest branch of the high cedar, and will set *it*; I will crop off from the top of his young twigs a tender one, and will plant *it* upon an high mountain and eminent:
>
> 23 In the mountain of the height of Israel will I plant it: and it shall bring forth boughs, and bear fruit, and be a goodly cedar: and under it shall dwell all fowl of every wing; in the shadow of the branches thereof shall they dwell.
>
> 24 And all the trees of the field shall know that I the LORD have brought down the high tree, have exalted the low tree, have dried up the green tree, and have made the dry tree to flourish: I the LORD have spoken and have done *it*. [Ezekiel 17:22–24]

The highest branch of the high cedar [king of Judah] was to have a young twig [son of the king] taken off and planted in a high mountain of Israel (Omni 1:22 above). There it was to bear fruit and be a goodly cedar and dwell in the shadow of the branch of Israel (v. 23 above). The high mountain of Israel is the land of America. It was given to "a remnant of the house of Joseph" by the Father, as stated by Jesus when he came to visit the Nephites in America (3 Nephi 15:12–13). The planting of the young twig was to dwell in the "shadow of the branches" (Omni 1:23 above). The branches would be the two branches of Joseph: Manasseh (Lehi; see Alma 10:3) and Ephraim (Ishmael; see *JD*, 23:184), who came to America in fulfillment of father Jacob's prophecy of Joseph "whose branches [would] run over the wall" (Genesis 49:22). The merging of the people of Mulek with the Nephites (Mosiah's people), under the leadership of Mosiah as their king, placed them under the shadow of their branches. In a later merger, the Nephites and the Mulekites combined were not as numerous as the Lamanites. Thus they dwelt in the shadows of both the Nephites and the Lamanites (see Mosiah 25:1–4). The Lord "brought down the high tree [the nation of Judah], (and) have exalted the low tree [the young twig of the king, Mulek]" as Ezekiel prophesied (v. 24 above). The rest of the verse (24) "have dried up the green tree [the nation of Judah], and have made the dry tree to flourish [the young twig of the king, Mulek]" are examples of Hebrew parallelism, repeating the same message as the previous verses.

Elder Orson Pratt gave a similar interpretation of Ezekiel 17:22–23:

> When Zedekiah, king of Judah was carried away captive into Babylon, the Lord took one of his sons, whose name was Mulek, with a company of those who would hearken unto His words, and brought them over the ocean, and planted them in America. This was done in fulfillment of the 22nd and 23rd verses of the seventeenth chapter of Ezekiel . . . By reading this chapter, it will be seen that the Jews were the "high cedar," that Zedekiah the king was the "highest branch," that the "tender one" cropped off from the top of his young twigs, was one of his sons, whom the Lord brought out and planted him and his company upon the choice land of America, which He had given unto a remnant of the tribe of Joseph for an inheritance, in fulfillment of the blessing of Jacob and Moses upon the head of that tribe.[8]

Father Bernardino Sahagun, a catholic priest who spent his life among the Central American people in the sixteenth century A.D., gives the following account:

> Concerning the origin of this people the account which the old people [ancient inhabitants] give is that they came by sea from toward the north . . . and they came along the coast and disembarked at the port of Panuco, which they call Panco, which means "place

---

[8] Orson Pratt, Orson Pratt's Works, *The Deseret News*, 280–81.

where those who crossed the waters arrived."... These people came looking for an earthly paradise . . . and they settled near the high mountains they found.[9]

Note that Sahagun says they crossed the waters and settled near the high mountains, which correlates with the Ezekiel prophecy.

The escape of the party that included Mulek also fulfilled a prophecy of Isaiah: "And the remnant that is escaped of the house of Judah shall again take root downward, and bear fruit upward: For out of Jerusalem shall go forth a remnant, and they that escape out of Jerusalem shall come up upon mount Zion: the zeal of the Lord of hosts shall do this" (JST, Isaiah 37:31–32). The prophecy of Ezekiel concerning the Mulekites is supported by the prophecy of Isaiah, the Book of Mormon, the record of Josephus, and sixteenth-century accounts of the ancient inhabitants of Central America. "At the mouth of two witnesses, or at the mouth of three witnesses, shall the matter be established" (Deuteronomy 19:15).

Omni 1:20–22 • An Account of One Coriantumr

20 And it came to pass in the days of Mosiah, there was a large stone brought unto him with engravings on it; and he did interpret the engravings by the gift and power of God.

21 And they gave an account of one Coriantumr, and the slain of his people. And Coriantumr was discovered by the people of Zarahemla; and he dwelt with them for the space of nine moons.

22 It also spake a few words concerning his fathers. And his first parents came out from the tower, at the time the Lord confounded the language of the people; and the severity of the Lord fell upon them

---

[9] John L. Sorenson, "Bible Prophesies of the Mulekites," [1976], 229–237, published in *Book of Mormon Treasury*, Significant articles from the pages of the Book of Mormon. See also "The Twig of the Cedar," *The Improvement Era,* May 1957, 330–38; "The Mulekites," BYU Studies 30/3 (1960): 6–22; and Joseph L. Allen, *Exploring the Land of the Book of Mormon.* S A Publishers, Inc. Orem, Utah. Dec. 1989, 260.

according to his judgments, which are just; and their bones lay scattered in the land northward.

Mosiah I translated the engravings on the large stone discovered by the people of Zarahemla (the Mulekites) through the Urim and Thummim, or by the Liahona, "the miraculous directors which were given to Lehi" (D&C 17:6). It was done "by the gift and power of God" (v. 20), the power by which both instruments worked. His grandson, Mosiah son of Benjamin, had possession of "two stones which were fastened into the two rims of a bow. Now these things were prepared from the beginning, and were handed down from generation to generation, for the purpose of interpreting languages" (Mosiah 28:13–14). The description of this instrument is basically the same as the one described by Moroni to Joseph Smith and which he later used to translate the Book of Mormon.

> 34 He said there was a book deposited, written upon gold plates, giving an account of the former inhabitants of this continent, and the source from whence they sprang. He also said that the fulness of the everlasting Gospel was contained in it, as delivered by the Savior to the ancient inhabitants;
>
> 35 Also, that there were two stones in silver bows—and these stones, fastened to a breastplate, constituted what is called the Urim and Thummim—deposited with the plates; and the possession and use of these stones were what constituted "seers" in ancient or former times; and that God had prepared them for the purpose of translating the book. [Joseph Smith—History 1:34–35]

While there is no record given of where Mosiah I had obtained the Urim and Thummim, it is not mentioned as being with the records found by Limhi's people in searching for the land of Zarahemla (Mosiah 21:25–27). Nor was it with the large stone brought to Mosiah I. We do know that Joseph Smith used the one "given to the brother of Jared on the mount" (D&C 17:1). We will have to wait for the larger plates of Nephi to come forth to know where Mosiah I obtained them.

Coriantumr was the lone survivor of the royal family and of the nation of the Jaredites, fulfilling the prophecy of the prophet Ether, who called him to repentance.

> 20 And in the second year the word of the Lord came to Ether, that he should go and prophesy unto Coriantumr that, if he would repent, and all his household, the Lord would give unto him his kingdom and spare the people—
>
> 21 Otherwise they should be destroyed, and all his household save it were himself. And he should only live to see the fulfilling of the prophecies which had been spoken concerning another people receiving the land for their inheritance; and Coriantumr should receive a burial by them; and every soul should be destroyed save it were Coriantumr. [Ether 13:20–21]

How long he lived before he was found by the people of Zarahemla is not known, but the Jaredites, as a nation, were destroyed before Mosiah led his people out of the land of Nephi (after 279 B.C.).

Coriantumr's "first parents came out from the tower at the time the Lord confounded the language of the people" (Omni 1:22). The book of Ether, a book in the Book of Mormon, is a second witness to the biblical account of the building of the tower of Babel:

> 6 And the LORD said, Behold, the people *is* one, and they have all one language; and this they begin to do: and now nothing will be restrained from them, which they have imagined to do.
>
> 7 Go to, let us go down, and there confound their language, that they may not understand one another's speech.
>
> 8 So the LORD scattered them abroad from thence upon the face of all the earth: and they left off to build the city.
>
> 9 Therefore is the name of it called Babel; because the LORD did there confound the language of all the earth: and from thence did the LORD scatter them abroad upon the face of all the earth. [Genesis 11:6–9]

The book of Ether states: "Jared came forth with his brother and their families, with some others and their families, from the great tower, at the time the Lord confounded the language of the people, and

swore in his wrath that they should be scattered upon all the face of
the earth; and according to the word of the Lord the people were
scattered" (Ether 1:33). Both accounts are verified in The Works of
Ixtlilxochitl, an ancient Mexican history written by the "grandson of
the last king of Texcuco, from whom he inherited all that were saved
of the records in the public archives." It was written in Mexico at
about the close of the sixteenth century and published in England in
1848 in the Spanish language.

> And [the Tulteca history tells] how afterwards men, multiplying
> made a very tall and strong Zacualli (tower), in order to shelter them-
> selves in it when the second world should be destroyed.
>
> When things were at their best, their languages were changed and,
> not understanding each other, they went to different parts of the
> world; and the Tultecas, who were as many as seven companions and
> their wives, who understood their language among themselves, came
> to these parts, having first crossed large lands and seas, living in
> caves and undergoing great hardships, until they came to this land,
> which they found good and fertile for their habitation. . . .
>
> As we study the *Works of Ixtlilxochitl*, we find that he gives an
> account of three separate groups of people who came from across the
> ocean to colonize America. The first of these, he claims, migrated to
> the New World from "*the very high tower*" at the time of the confu-
> sion of tongues. He calls this group by several different names. First
> he calls them "Tultecas" and he distinguishes them from the later
> Tultecas by calling them "*the Ancient Ones*." He also refers to them
> as "*the Giants*."
>
> Later in his book he speaks of another group of advanced who
> came to Middle America by sea. These he also calls *Tultecas*. . . .
>
> *Ixtlilxochitl* speaks of a third group of people who came across
> the ocean to settle America. These he calls the *Ulmecs*. The spelling
> that is usually given for the name is *Olmecs*.[10]

Thus the three peoples coming to the promised land as recorded

---

[10] Milton R. Hunter and Thomas Stuart Ferguson. *Ancient America and the Book of Mormon.* [1950], 6–7, 15, 24–25.

in the Book of Mormon (Omni 1:12–21) are supported by the Bible and external sources. The Lord does establish his word "in the mouth of two or three witnesses" (Matthew 18:16).

Omni 1:23–26 • The Reign of King Benjamin

> 23 Behold, I, Amaleki, was born in the days of Mosiah; and I have lived to see his death; and Benjamin, his son, reigneth in his stead.
>
> 24 And behold, I have seen, in the days of king Benjamin, a serious war and much bloodshed between the Nephites and the Lamanites. But behold, the Nephites did obtain much advantage over them; yea, insomuch that king Benjamin did drive them out of the land of Zarahemla.
>
> 25 And it came to pass that I began to be old; and, having no seed, and knowing king Benjamin to be a just man before the Lord, wherefore, I shall deliver up these plates unto him, exhorting all men to come unto God, the Holy One of Israel, and believe in prophesying, and in revelations, and in the ministering of angels, and in the gift of speaking with tongues, and in the gift of interpreting languages, and in all things which are good; for there is nothing which is good save it comes from the Lord; and that which is evil cometh from the devil.
>
> 26 And now, my beloved brethren, I would that ye should come unto Christ, who is the Holy One of Israel, and partake of his salvation, and the power of his redemption. Yea, come unto him, and offer your whole souls as an offering unto him, and continue in fasting and praying, and endure to the end; and as the Lord liveth ye will be saved.

Amaleki, prior to his turning the records to King Benjamin, gives us a brief summary of the king's reign. More concerning his reign is given in the Words of Mormon that follows (1:12–18), and discussed in chapter 5 of this work. The book of Mosiah begins with the final speeches of King Benjamin. Thus we have only a brief sketch of the life of this great king who was "a just man before the Lord" (Omni 1:25).

Amaleki's exhortation to all men once more reminds us of the brevity of the record. Little has been recorded about the gifts mentioned by him, especially "the gift of speaking with tongues," but it does verify that the gifts of the Spirit were had among the Nephites. His final admonition to "come unto Christ" is another of several testaments of Jesus Christ that are contained in the Book of Mormon.

Omni 1:27–30 • Return Trips to the Land of Nephi

27 And now I would speak somewhat concerning a certain number who went up into the wilderness to return to the land of Nephi; for there was a large number who were desirous to possess the land of their inheritance.

28 Wherefore, they went up into the wilderness. And their leader being a strong and mighty man, and a stiffnecked man, wherefore he caused a contention among them; and they were all slain, save fifty, in the wilderness, and they returned again to the land of Zarahemla.

29 And it came to pass that they also took others to a considerable number, and took their journey again into the wilderness.

30 And I, Amaleki, had a brother, who also went with them; and I have not since known concerning them. And I am about to lie down in my grave; and these plates are full. And I make an end of my speaking.

Amaleki tells of two different attempts of a certain number, who went up into the wilderness to return to the land of Nephi, in much detail beginning in the ninth chapter of Mosiah. We will leave a discussion of these men for later.

Amaleki quits recording because the plates are full, but he has certainly added to our knowledge of the entire Book of Mormon. Without his contribution we would only have a very brief summation of the history and one principle: "Inasmuch as ye will not keep my commandments ye shall not prosper in the land" (v. 6).

Words of Mormon 1:1–2 • Mormon Delivers the Record to His Son

1 And now I, Mormon, being about to deliver up the record which I have been making into the hands of my son Moroni, behold I have witnessed almost all the destruction of my people, the Nephites.

2 And it is many hundred years after the coming of Christ that I deliver these records into the hands of my son; and it supposeth me that he will witness the entire destruction of my people. But may God grant that he may survive them, that he may write somewhat concerning them, and somewhat concerning Christ, that perhaps some day it may profit them.

The Words of Mormon jumps ahead to about A.D. 385. He writes to bridge the gap between the ending of the smaller plates of Nephi and the book of Mosiah that he has abridged from the larger plates of Nephi, as he now explains.

Words of Mormon 1:3–8 • A Wise Purpose

3 And now, I speak somewhat concerning that which I have written; for after I had made an abridgment from the plates of Nephi, down to the reign of this king Benjamin, of whom Amaleki spake, I searched among the records which had been delivered into my hands, and I found these plates, which contained this small account of the prophets, from Jacob down to the reign of this king Benjamin, and also many of the words of Nephi.

4 And the things which are upon these plates pleasing me, because of the prophecies of the coming of Christ; and my fathers knowing that many of them have been fulfilled; yea, and I also know that as many things as have been prophesied concerning us down to this day have been fulfilled, and as many as go beyond this day must surely come to pass—

5 Wherefore, I chose these things, to finish my record upon them, which remainder of my record I shall take from the plates of Nephi; and I cannot write the hundredth part of the things of my people.

6 But behold, I shall take these plates, which contain these prophesyings and revelations, and put them with the remainder of my

record, for they are choice unto me; and I know they will be choice unto my brethren.

7 And I do this for a wise purpose; for thus it whispereth me, according to the workings of the Spirit of the Lord which is in me. And now, I do not know all things; but the Lord knoweth all things which are to come; wherefore, he worketh in me to do according to his will.

8 And my prayer to God is concerning my brethren, that they may once again come to the knowledge of God, yea, the redemption of Christ; that they may once again be a delightsome people.

The abridgment of the plates of Nephi down to the reign of King Benjamin would be the book of Lehi that was translated by Joseph Smith with Martin Harris as his scribe or the one hundred and sixteen pages that were lost by Martin Harris (see *HC*, 1:18–21). The plates that were found by Mormon were, of course, the smaller plates of Nephi and were translated into what is now the first one hundred and forty-three pages of today's edition (1981) of the Book of Mormon (1 Nephi through Omni).

A brief review of the major prophecies of Christ in the first book of Nephi illustrates why Mormon would be pleased with them. Lehi prophesied of his coming (1 Nephi 10). Nephi was shown his divine birth and ministry (1 Nephi 11). He saw Christ's visit to his seed and the seed of his brethren (1 Nephi 12). Nephi prophesied of his coming; foretold the signs of his coming; and quoted Isaiah to more fully persuade his brethren to believe in their Redeemer (1 Nephi 19–21). The second book of Nephi and the following books are just as impressive. Certainly they are another testament of Jesus Christ as stated in the subtitle (1982).

Mormon chose to finish his record upon "these things," implying he would write upon the smaller plates of Nephi (Words of Mormon 1:5). However, Amaleki said, "these plates are full" (Omni 1:30). Therefore, Mormon may be saying he will finish his record by adding the smaller plates to the end of his abridged plates. This is the most probable place for the smaller plates, not inserted between Mormon's abridgment of the book of Lehi (116 lost pages) and the "remainder of my record," that which he abridged "from the plates of Nephi, and I cannot write the hundredth part of the things of my people" (v. 5). The plates being placed at the end of his record is supported by Mormon's next statement: "I shall take these plates, . . . and put them with the remainder of my record" (v. 6). A further implication that the plates were added to the end of Mormon's work is in the Prophet's history: "In the course of the work of translation we ascertained that three special witnesses were to be provided by the Lord . . . as will be found recorded, Book of Mormon, page 581 [book of Ether, chapter 5, verses 2, 3, and 4], also page 86 [2 Nephi, chapter 11, verse 3]"[11] (*HC*, 1:52). Why would Joseph make reference to the book of Ether before the reference to the second book of Nephi? Why did he not include 2 Nephi 27:12 which is a direct reference to the three witnesses while 2 Nephi 11:3 is only a reference to three other witnesses and supports the principle of the Lord establishing his word by three witnesses? The answers to these questions seem to be in the sequence of the translation. The revelation that follows there, having attention drawn to the promised witnesses, confirms who the three witnesses were to be (D&C 17). This revelation was given in June, 1829 (no specific day in June was recorded). The work of translation had been completed (D&C 17:6). Therefore, they were near the end of the translation when they "ascertained that three witnesses were to be provided by the Lord" (*HC*, 1:52). They had obviously translated the book of Ether and part of the second book of Nephi, but not the part now designated as 2 Nephi 27:12. This sequence further supports the theory of the smaller plates being placed at the end of Mormon's work. However, later verses in the Words of Mormon does support the fact that Mormon actually engraved his words upon the smaller plates of Nephi. This fact will be considered after the "wise purpose" (Words of Mormon 1:7) for Mormon's including the unabridged record of Nephi's smaller plates is discussed.

---

[11] The brackets identifying the books and chapters and verses were added by later editors.

Over fourteen hundred years before Joseph would translate the plates (A.D. 385–1829), the Spirit whispered to Mormon to include the smaller plates of Nephi with his abridgment of the larger plates. Acknowledging that "the Lord knoweth all things that are to come," Mormon did "according to [God's] will" (v. 7). The Lord knew that Mormon's abridgment of the book of Lehi on the larger plates of Nephi (116 pages) would be lost. Therefore, about nine hundred years earlier (570 B.C.), he commanded Nephi to keep a second record, which was a more spiritual account to "persuade men to come unto the God of Abraham, and the God of Isaac, and the God of Jacob, and be saved" (1 Nephi 6:4). Nephi knew it was "for a wise purpose in [the Lord]" and acknowledged that "the Lord knoweth all things from the beginning; wherefore, he prepareth a way to accomplish all his works" (1 Nephi 9:5–6). Mormon also had the same desire as Nephi, for his brethren to "once again come to the knowledge of God, yea, the redemption of Christ, that they may once again be a delightsome people" (Words of Mormon 1:8). Someday the contents of Mormon's abridged book of Lehi will be restored along with the unabridged record of Nephi's larger plates, but for now, we have the essential record of Nephi to bring us to Christ and be saved.

Words of Mormon 1:9–11 • These Plates and Those Handed Down by the Kings

9 And now I, Mormon, proceed to finish out my record, which I take from the plates of Nephi; and I make it according to the knowledge and the understanding which God has given me.

10 Wherefore, it came to pass that after Amaleki had delivered up these plates into the hands of king Benjamin, he took them and put them with the other plates, which contained records which had been handed down by the kings, from generation to generation until the days of king Benjamin.

11 And they were handed down from king Benjamin, from generation to generation until they have fallen into my hands. And I, Mormon, pray to God that they may be preserved from this time henceforth. And I know that they will be preserved; for there are great things written upon them, out of which my people and their

brethren shall be judged at the great and last day, according to the word of God which is written.

Although Amaleki said "these plates are full" (Omni 1:30), he apparently knew he was to leave some room for a future writer. Mormon's statement that "after Amaleki had delivered up *these plates* into the hands of King Benjamin" (Words of Mormon 1:10; emphasis added) strongly suggests that Mormon was engraving upon the same plates that Amaleki had engraven his record. The other alternative is that Mormon had attached a plate or two to the smaller plates of Nephi. Regardless, Mormon again traces the passing down of both plates to his time. The smaller set of plates ended at the time of Amaleki, but they were still passed on with the larger set of plates until the time of Mormon. The importance of the plates to God to Mormon's people is once more emphasized. The remaining verses of the Words of Mormon, concerning Benjamin (vv. 12–18), will be included in the following chapter of this work.

SACRED WRITING

Preaching Which is Sacred:
Omni 1:25–26   Amaleki teaches of Christ, and the good things that come from him.

Revelation Which is Great:
Omni 1:12–13   Mosiah leads his people to the land of Zarahemla being led by the power of the Lord.

Words of Mormon 1:6–8   Mormon includes the unabridged small plates of Nephi with his abridgment for a wise purpose.

Doctrines Learned:
Jarom 1:9   Inasmuch as ye keep the commandments of the Lord in the land of America, ye shall prosper.

Omni 1:17   Without records, language becomes corrupted and a knowledge of the Creator is lost.

Omni 1:21	The Jaredites came out of the land at the time of the confounding of the languages of the people.
Omni 1:25	The Nephites had the gifts of revelation, speaking in tongues, interpreting languages and all good things.
Omni 1:26	All that is good comes from God and evil comes from the devil.
Words of Mormon 1:7	The Lord knows all things and works through men to do his will.

General Authority Quotations

Joseph Smith • Omni 1:12

It is certainly a good thing for the excellency and the veracity of the divine authority of the Book of Mormon, that the ruins of Zarahemla have been found where the Nephites left them; and that a large stone with engravings upon it, as Mosiah said; and a "large stone" with the sides sculptured in hieroglyphics, as Mr. Stevens has published, is also among the remembrances of the (to him) lost and unknown.

We are not going to declare positively that the ruins of Quirigua are those of Zarahemla, but when the land and the stones and the books tell so plain, we are of the opinion that it would require more proof than the Jews could bring to prove the disciples stole the body of Jesus Christ from the tomb, to prove the ruins of the city in question, are not one of those referred to in the Book of Mormon. . . .

It will not be a bad plan to compare Mr. Stephens' ruined cities with those of the Book of Mormon; light cleaves to light, and the facts are supported by facts. [*Times and Seasons,* vol. 3, 927]

Challenges to Eternal Life:

1. Although we have access to the records that God has preserved or revealed unto us, if we do not use them we are subject to the same degeneracy as the Mulekites experienced (Omni 1:17). Make a resolution to systematically study the scriptures.

2. Record your spiritual experiences in a journal for the benefit of posterity

lest you be as Omni, Chemish, and Abinadom in recording your life's activities.

3.   Seek to follow the example of Mormon by following the Spirit although you do not understand the reason why (Words of Mormon 1:7).

4.   Choose a challenge of your own from this reading and apply it to your life.

Chapter Five

King Benjamin's Sermon

Words of Mormon 1:12
through Mosiah 2:41

*H*istorical Setting: King Benjamin succeeded his father Mosiah I as the king of the land of Zarahemla as discussed in the previous chapter (see Omni 1:12–19). His reign began at least two generations after the last recorded date in the small plates.[1] How long he reigned is not stated, but it was a considerable time. All we know of his people is recorded in the Words of Mormon 1:12–18 and the first six chapters of Mosiah. These chapters record his final instructions to his people before he turns his reign to his son Mosiah II (Mosiah 6:4). The last year of King Benjamin's reign is accurately estimated in the footnotes as 130 B.C.

Dating in the Book of Mosiah:

There are only three definite dates given in this book: the beginning of King Mosiah II's reign (124 B.C., 476 years from the time

---

[1] Amaron's record stated that "three hundred and twenty years had passed away [since Lehi left Jerusalem]," making it 279 B.C. He passed the record to his brother Chemish who was succeeded by his son Abinadom and grandson Amaleki. Since we do not know the age difference between Amaron and his brother Chemish, we state at least two generations, but have the possibility of a third. Amaleki lived to see Benjamin succeed Mosiah as king (Omni 1:23).

Lehi left Jerusalem), King Benjamin's death three years later (121 B.C.), and the death of Alma the elder and Mosiah son of Benjamin (91 B.C., 509 years from the time Lehi left Jerusalem). The other dates in the footnotes are approximate, based upon the premise of Zeniff's leaving being somewhere around 200 B.C.

Thirty years previous to 121 B.C., Ammon and fifteen others left Zarahemla and found Limhi. Alma had left long before this and must have spent several years in the Land of Helam.

Alma's death in 91 B.C. at the age of 82 (Mosiah 29:44–45) would place his birth date at 173 B.C. He was one of the priests appointed by Noah when Noah became king, and was a young man when he wrote the words of the prophet Abinadi (Alma 17:1–2). This would place the date of Abinadi around 150 B.C., which is the date given in the Book of Mormon (page 169). Alma copied Abinadi's words when Abinadi reentered the city after a two-year absence, which the Book of Mormon dates about 148 B.C. (page 171). Alma would be around 25 years old at this time.

Zeniff and his people had dwelt in the land of Lehi-Nephi for twelve years (Mosiah 9:11) before having trouble with the Lamanites in the thirteenth year (Mosiah 9:14). This is followed by twenty-two years of continual peace in the land (Mosiah 10:3–5). The two combined periods equal thirty-five years. A war with the Lamanites follows this period of peace, but its length is not given. Noah succeeds his father as king following this war, but the length of his reign is not given. The Book of Mormon's footnotes date King Noah's appointment as approximately 160 B.C. (page 167).

The approximate dates given in the Book of Mormon footnotes appear to be accurate and will be used in this work.

Precepts of this Reading:

O my sons, I would that ye should remember that these sayings are true, and also that these records are true. And behold, also the plates of Nephi, which contain the records and the sayings of our fathers from the time they left Jerusalem until now, and they are true;

and we can know of their surety because we have them before our eyes. [Mosiah 1:6]

And behold, I tell you these things that ye may learn wisdom; that ye may learn that when ye are in the service of your fellow beings ye are only in the service of your God. [Mosiah 2:17]

An outline of his reign and the first instructions he gave, as a preparation for deeper study, follows.

OUTLINE • WORDS OF MORMON 1:12
THROUGH MOSIAH 2:41

➤ Words of Mormon 1:12–14

Concerning this King Benjamin

a. There were contentions among his own people (v. 12).

b. The Lamanite armies come out of the land of Nephi to battle (vv. 13–14).

1. King Benjamin gathered his armies to fight against them.

2. He himself fought with the sword of Laban.

3. They fought with the strength of the Lord, slaying thousands of the Lamanites and driving them out of the land.

➤ 1:15–18   With the help of the holy prophets, peace was established in the land.

a. False Christs had their mouths shut and were punished according to their crime (v. 15).

b. False prophets, preachers, and teachers were punished according to their crimes (v. 16).

c. King Benjamin reigned over his people in righteousness (v. 17).

1. Many holy men in the land spoke the word of God with authority.

2. They used much sharpness because of the stiffneckedness of the people.

➣ Mosiah 1:1   King Benjamin had continual peace all the remainder of his days.

➣ 1:2–8   King Benjamin had three sons: Mosiah, Helorum, and Helaman.

    a.   He caused them to be taught in all the language of his fathers that they might become men of understanding and know concerning the prophecies of the Lord (v. 2).

    b.   He also taught them concerning the plates of brass (vv. 3–6).

        1.   If not for these plates they would have suffered in ignorance not knowing the mysteries of God.

        2.   Lehi could not have remembered all these things to teach his children.

        3.   Lehi could read the Egyptian engravings and teach them to his children so they could teach their children as God had commanded.

        4.   They had been kept and preserved by the hand of God to understand his mysteries and always have his commandments before their eyes, lest they dwindle in unbelief as had the Lamanites.

        5.   These sayings were true and also the plates of brass were true.

    c.   The plates of Nephi were also true, therefore search them diligently (v. 6).

    d.   Keep the commandments that ye may prosper in the land (v. 7).

    e.   He taught many more things which were not written in this book (v. 8).

➣ 1:9–14   King Benjamin waxed old and it was expedient to confer the kingdom upon one of his sons.

    a.   He had his son Mosiah send a proclamation for all the people to gather together that he may appoint Mosiah as king and ruler (v. 10).

    b.   He gave his people a name to distinguish them above

all the people the Lord had brought out of Jerusalem
(vv. 11–14).

   1. They had been a diligent people in keeping the
commandments of God.

   2. The name would never be blotted out except by
transgression.

   3. If this people fell into transgression they would
become weak like their brethren and not be preserved any longer by the Lord.

   4. If the Lord had not extended his arm, they would
have fallen into the hands of the Lamanites.

➢ 1:15–18   King Benjamin gave his son charge concerning all the
affairs of the kingdom.

   a. He gave him charge of the plates of brass and the plates
of Nephi (v. 16).

   b. He gave him charge of the sword of Laban, and the ball
or director that led their fathers through the wilderness
(vv. 16–17).

      1. When they were unfaithful they did not prosper,
but were driven back.

      2. They were smitten and afflicted to stir them up to
remember their duty.

   c. Mosiah proclaimed that the people gather to hear his
father speak (v. 18).

➢ 2:1–8   The people gathered to the temple to hear the words of
King Benjamin.

   a. There was such a great number that they did not number them (v. 2).

   b. They took the firstlings of their flock to offer sacrifice
and burnt offerings according to the law of Moses, and
to give thanks to God (vv. 3–4).

      1. He had delivered them from Jerusalem, and from
their enemies.

      2. He had appointed just men as teachers, and a king
to establish peace and to keep the commandments.

c. They came up to the temple and pitched their tents round about (vv. 5–6).

   1. Every man according to his family, the eldest to the youngest.

   2. Every tent had the door of the tent towards the temple in order to remain in their tent and hear King Benjamin.

d. King Benjamin caused a tower to be built because the multitude was too great for all to hear (v. 7).

e. His words were written because all the people could still not hear (v. 8).

➤ 2:9–41   The words which King Benjamin spoke and caused to be written.

a. He had not commanded them to trifle with his words, but to open their ears that they may hear, their hearts that they may understand, and their minds that the mysteries of God may be unfolded (v. 9).

b. They should not fear or think of him as more than a mortal man (vv. 10–11).

   1. He was subject to all manner of infirmities in body and mind.

   2. He was chosen by the people, consecrated by his father, and suffered by the hand of the Lord to be a ruler and king.

   3. He had been kept and preserved by the Lord to serve with all his might, mind, and strength.

c. He had spent his days in service to his people but had not sought for any manner of riches (v. 12).

d. He had not confined them in dungeons, to be enslaved, or allowed murder, plunder, stealing, committing adultery, or any manner of wickedness, but had taught them to keep the commandments (v. 13).

e. He had labored with his own hands to serve them, and they were not laden with taxes or other grievous burdens (v. 14).

f.   He did not boast or accuse them, but told them of these things to answer with a clear conscience before God (v. 15).

g.   He had been in the service of God even as he served his people, for when we serve our fellow beings we are only in the service of God (vv. 16–17).

h.   If the king labored to serve them, they should serve one another (vv. 18–21).

    1.   If the king merited any thanks from them, how much more they ought to thank their heavenly king.

    2.   If they rendered all their thanks and praise to that God who created and had preserved them and served him with their whole souls, they would yet be unprofitable servants.

i.   All that God required of them was to keep his commandments and if so he would bless and prosper them (vv. 22–25).

    1.   He created them and granted unto them their lives, for which they are indebted.

    2.   If they do as commanded, he will immediately bless them and thus they will be forever indebted to him.

    3.   They cannot say they are even as much as the dust of the earth, for they were created of the dust, and it belonged to him.

j.   King Benjamin is also of the dust of the earth, and is about to yield his mortal frame to mother earth (vv. 26–28).

    1.   He assembled them that he might be found blameless before God when he is judged.

    2.   He wants to rid himself of their blood that he might die in peace and his immortal spirit join the choirs above in singing praises to God.

k.   King Benjamin could no longer be their teacher nor their king (vv. 29–30).

    1. His whole frame trembles while attempting to speak to them.

    2. The Lord supported him and commanded him to tell them that Mosiah, his son, was now their king and ruler.

l. If they will keep the commandments of God as declared by his son, they will prosper and their enemies will have no power over them (vv. 31–33).

    1. Beware lest there be contentions among them and they obey the evil spirit.

    2. Those who obey that evil spirit and remained in sin will drink damnation to their soul.

    3. Their wages will be an everlasting punishment since they have transgressed the law of God according to their own knowledge.

m. There are none among them, except their little children, who had not been taught that they are eternally indebted to their Heavenly Father and that they must render to him all that they have and are (vv. 34–35).

    1. They had been taught the prophecies of the holy prophets.

    2. They had been taught by their fathers as the Lord commanded.

n. After being taught these things, if they transgressed the Spirit of the Lord would withdraw, and they would have no guidance in wisdom's paths (vv. 36–37).

    1. They would come out in open rebellion against God, and because they want to obey the evil spirit, they will become an enemy to all righteousness.

    2. The Lord would have no place in them for he dwelleth not in unholy temples.

o. If that man repent not and dies an enemy to God, the demands of divine justice will awaken his immortal soul to his own guilt, causing him to withdraw from the presence of the Lord and filling his breast with guilt, pain, and anguish which is like an unquenchable fire (vv. 38–40).

1. Mercy has no claim and he will endure a never-ending torment.
2. Old men, young men, and little children who understand should awake to their awful situation.

p. King Benjamin desired they consider the blessed and happy state of those who keep the commandments of God (v. 41).

1. They are blessed in all things, both temporal and spiritual.
2. If they hold out faithful to the end, they may dwell with God in a state of never-ending happiness.

NOTES AND COMMENTARY

Introduction: As the people gathered "to the temple to hear the words which King Benjamin should speak unto them" (Mosiah 2:1), the multitude was so great that the king "caused a tower to be erected, that thereby his people might hear the words which he should speak unto them" (Mosiah 2:7). What are some towers that have been built today to expedite the hearing of the word of God? Radio and television towers have enabled the gospel message of the restoration to be broadcast to the world. The written word is also sent throughout the Church and the world just as "the words which [King Benjamin] spake and caused to be written" (Mosiah 2:9) were made available to his people. Of course, the missionaries, as "the voice of warning [are sent] unto all people, by the mouth of [the Lord's] disciples" (D&C 1:4), will eventually take his word unto all the inhabitants of the earth.

Words of Mormon 1:12–14 • Concerning This King Benjamin

12 And now, concerning this king Benjamin—he had somewhat of contentions among his own people.

13 And it came to pass also that the armies of the Lamanites came down out of the land of Nephi, to battle against his people. But

behold, king Benjamin gathered together his armies, and he did stand against them; and he did fight with the strength of his own arm, with the sword of Laban.

14 And in the strength of the Lord they did contend against their enemies, until they had slain many thousands of the Lamanites. And it came to pass that they did contend against the Lamanites until they had driven them out of all the lands of their inheritance.

The brief overview of the people of King Benjamin's battle with the Lamanites shows the secret of their success: to contend "in the strength of the Lord" (v. 14). Confirmation of this concept will be given repeatedly throughout the remainder of the Book of Mormon (see for examples Mosiah 9:17; 10:10). King Benjamin's personal use of the sword of Laban illustrates its durability with a hilt "of pure gold" and a blade of "the most precious steel" (1 Nephi 4:9). By this time it would be over four hundred years old, Nephi having obtained it about 600 B.C. and King Benjamin using it several years before 130 B.C. Of course it had been given special care as a sacred keepsake among the Nephites (see Mosiah 1:16).

Words of Mormon 1:15–18 • King Benjamin and the Prophets Establish Peace

15 And it came to pass that after there had been false Christs, and their mouths had been shut, and they punished according to their crimes;

16 And after there had been false prophets, and false preachers and teachers among the people, and all these having been punished according to their crimes; and after there having been much contention and many dissensions away unto the Lamanites, behold, it came to pass that king Benjamin, with the assistance of the holy prophets who were among his people—

17 For behold, king Benjamin was a holy man, and he did reign over his people in righteousness; and there were many holy men in the land, and they did speak the word of God with power and with authority; and they did use much sharpness because of the stiff-neckedness of the people—

18 Wherefore, with the help of these, king Benjamin, by laboring with all the might of his body and the faculty of his whole soul, and also the prophets, did once more establish peace in the land.

The false Christs, false prophets, false preachers, and false teachers were all influenced by Satan; but what were their crimes and punishments? Among the Nephites "there was no law against a man's belief" (Alma 30:11), but there were laws against "murder, or plunder, or steal[ing], or commit[ting] adultery" (Mosiah 2:13). The punishments were apparently based upon some form of crime related and advocated by these men's falsehoods. They had caused "contentions among [Benjamin's] own people" (Words of Mormon 1:12, 16), which may have resulted in civil disturbances among the people. Whatever the crimes, they were punished for them and peace was established. The combination of holy men and political leaders shows a separation of church and state responsibilities, but co-operation among them for attaining moral and ethical goals. The king "did reign over his people in righteousness," and the holy men "did speak the word of God with power [by the Spirit] and with authority [the priesthood]." Their use of "much sharpness [clear, concise, clarity]" (vv. 16–18) was certainly as "moved upon by the Holy Spirit" (D&C 121:43). This should be the goal of every society.

Mosiah 1:1–2 • The Three Sons of King Benjamin

1 And now there was no more contention in all the land of Zarahemla, among all the people who belonged to king Benjamin, so that king Benjamin had continual peace all the remainder of his days.

2 And it came to pass that he had three sons; and he called their names Mosiah, and Helorum, and Helaman. And he caused that they should be taught in all the language of his fathers, that thereby they might become men of understanding; and that they might know concerning the prophecies which had been spoken by the mouths of their fathers, which were delivered them by the hand of the Lord.

During this period of continual peace, King Benjamin has two objectives for his three sons: first to educate them in the language of their fathers that "they might become men of understanding;" and secondly, that they might know of the prophecies of the Lord (v. 2). The Lord revealed similar objectives as a commandment for Hyrum Smith in this dispensation.

15 Behold, I command you that you need not suppose that you are called to preach until you are called.

16 Wait a little longer, until you shall have my word, my rock, my church, and my gospel, that you may know of a surety my doctrine.

17 And then, behold, according to your desires, yea, even according to your faith shall it be done unto you.

18 Keep my commandments; hold your peace; appeal unto my Spirit;

19 Yea, cleave unto me with all your heart, that you may assist in bringing to light those things of which has been spoken—yea, the translation of my work; be patient until you shall accomplish it.

20 Behold, this is your work, to keep my commandments, yea, with all your might, mind and strength.

21 Seek not to declare my word, but first seek to obtain my word, and then shall your tongue be loosed; then, if you desire, you shall have my Spirit and my word, yea, the power of God unto the convincing of men.

22 But now hold your peace; study my word which hath gone forth among the children of men, and also study my word which shall come forth among the children of men, or that which is now translating, yea, until you have obtained all which I shall grant unto the children of men in this generation, and then shall all things be added thereto. [D&C 11:15–22]

Later, the Lord gave these instructions as a commandment to a conference of high priests in their preparation to minister in their callings.

77 And I give unto you a commandment that you shall teach one another the doctrine of the kingdom.

78 Teach ye diligently and my grace shall attend you, that you may be instructed more perfectly in theory, in principle, in doctrine, in the law of the gospel, in all things that pertain unto the kingdom of God, that are expedient for you to understand;

79 Of things both in heaven and in the earth, and under the earth; things which have been, things which are, things which must shortly come to pass; things which are at home, things which are abroad; the wars and the perplexities of the nations, and the judgments which are on the land; and a knowledge also of countries and of kingdoms—

80 That ye may be prepared in all things when I shall send you again to magnify the calling whereunto I have called you, and the mission with which I have commissioned you.

81 Behold, I sent you out to testify and warn the people, and it becometh every man who hath been warned to warn his neighbor.

82 Therefore, they are left without excuse, and their sins are upon their own heads. [D&C 88:77–82]

The last two verses of this commandment make it applicable to every member of the Church.

To know of the language of their fathers was to enable them to read the scriptures as will be discussed in following verses. However, it reminds us of President Spencer W. Kimball's calling for every worthy young man to serve a mission:

When I ask for more missionaries, I am not asking for more testimony-barren or unworthy missionaries. I am asking that we start earlier and train our missionaries better in every branch and every ward in the world. That is another challenge—that the young people will understand that it is a great privilege to go on a mission and that they must be physically well, mentally well, spiritually well, and that "the Lord cannot look upon sin with the least degree of allowance." [D&C 1:31]

I am asking for missionaries who have been carefully indoctrinated and trained through the family and the organizations of the Church, and who come to the mission with a great desire. I am asking for better interviews, more searching interviews, more sympathetic and understanding interviews, but especially that we train prospective missionaries much better, much earlier, much longer, so that each anticipates his mission with great joy.[2]

President Gordon B. Hinckley also encouraged the young men of the Church to prepare themselves for missions and emphasized the study of languages:

> To our young men I would like to say, prepare yourselves, not only financially as you have been urged to do, but also intellectually and morally and spiritually. Study languages. This gospel is not for the American people only. This gospel is for the people of the earth, and we have incumbent upon us the obligation to learn to speak their tongues. If you be called to a foreign language mission, you will be better equipped if you have studied the language. If you be called to an English-speaking mission, you will understand your own language better.[3]

Knowing the prophecies of the Lord "spoken by the mouths of their fathers" had reference to the Nephite prophets from Lehi to King Mosiah. In over four hundred years, the language must have changed somewhat, and their merging with the people of Zarahemla (see Omni 1:14–19) would also have had its effect. This objective further confirms that the Nephites had kept records of the prophecies of their fathers and these were in King Benjamin's possession (see Omni 1:25). Knowing the future would prepare the sons to live righteously and also to teach others to do likewise.

Mosiah 1:3–8 • Know the Mysteries of God

> 3 And he also taught them concerning the records which were engraven on the plates of brass, saying: My sons, I would that ye should remember that were it not for these plates, which contain these records and these commandments, we must have suffered in ignorance, even at this present time, not knowing the mysteries of God.

> 4 For it were not possible that our father, Lehi, could have

---

[2] *The Teachings of Spencer W. Kimball,* [1982], 561–62.

[3] *Teachings of Gordon B. Hinckley,* [1997], 344.

remembered all these things, to have taught them to his children, except it were for the help of these plates; for he having been taught in the language of the Egyptians therefore he could read these engravings, and teach them to his children, that thereby they could teach them to their children, and so fulfilling the commandments of God, even down to this present time.

5 I say unto you, my sons, were it not for these things, which have been kept and preserved by the hand of God, that we might read and understand of his mysteries, and have his commandments always before our eyes, that even our fathers would have dwindled in unbelief, and we should have been like unto our brethren, the Lamanites, who know nothing concerning these things, or even do not believe them when they are taught them, because of the traditions of their fathers, which are not correct.

6 O my sons, I would that ye should remember that these sayings are true, and also that these records are true. And behold, also the plates of Nephi, which contain the records and the sayings of our fathers from the time they left Jerusalem until now, and they are true; and we can know of their surety because we have them before our eyes.

7 And now, my sons, I would that ye should remember to search them diligently, that ye may profit thereby; and I would that ye should keep the commandments of God, that ye may prosper in the land according to the promises which the Lord made unto our fathers.

8 And many more things did king Benjamin teach his sons, which are not written in this book.

King Benjamin's recognition of the importance of the plates of brass was based upon the degenerate condition of the Mulekites when his father discovered them. "They [the Mulekites] had brought no records with them, and they denied the being of their Creator" (Omni 1:17). The positive influence of the plates of brass was taught by Nephi, son of Lehi. Although "the mysteries of God shall be unfolded unto [you], by the power of the Holy Ghost" (1 Nephi 10:19), if one will "feast upon the words of Christ [the scriptures] . . . the words of Christ will tell you all things what ye should do" (2 Nephi 32:3).

Dr. Daniel H. Ludlow, to whom I owe much for planting a desire in me to study the Book of Mormon, has written regarding the language of the plates of brass.

> The statement that "Lehi . . . having been taught in the language of the Egyptians therefore he could read" the engravings on the plates of Laban quite clearly indicates these plates were written in the Egyptian language. Thus they were almost certainly not started until after the flood and the tower of Babel, as there was no Egyptian language before these events. The brass plates were probably not started until after the Israelites went down into Egypt in the days of Joseph, although the writers may have had access to records that had been written earlier.[4]

Lehi's ability to read Egyptian had enabled several generations to know the scriptures and understand the mysteries of God. Such knowledge and understanding came from having "his commandments always before [their] eyes" (Mosiah 1:4–5). The king's testimony of the truth of his sayings, the plates of Nephi, and the plates of brass (v. 6) are elements which led Joseph Smith to proclaim: "a man would get nearer to God by abiding by its precepts, than by any other book" (Introduction to the Book of Mormon). The title of this volume, *These Records are True,* was also chosen from verse 6 of Mosiah chapter one.

As implied by King Benjamin, the scriptures must be searched diligently in order to be profited therefrom (v. 7). Casual or occasional reading of scriptures does not bring their full benefit. The promise of prospering in the land when the commandments of God are kept (v. 7) is one of the most prevalent teachings running throughout the Book of Mormon. It began with the Lord's promise to Nephi: "inasmuch as ye shall keep my commandments, ye shall prosper, and shall be led to a land of promise" (1 Nephi 2:20). This promise is mentioned periodically throughout the Nephite record ending with the downfall of the Nephites because they "rejected that Jesus who stood with open arms to receive [them]" (Mormon 6:17) and did not

---

[4] David H. Ludlow, *A Companion to Your Study of the Book of Mormon*, [1977], 173.

keep his commandments. It really began with the Jaredites and was extended to all who occupy the lands of America (see Ether 2:9–12). The Americas are a promised land forever. We should look forward to reading the "many more things [that] King Benjamin [did] teach his sons" (Mosiah 1:8) when the fuller records of the Nephites are brought forth (see 3 Nephi 26:6–9).

Mosiah 1:9–14 • The Kingdom to be Conferred upon Mosiah II

9 And it came to pass that after king Benjamin had made an end of teaching his sons, that he waxed old, and he saw that he must very soon go the way of all the earth; therefore, he thought it expedient that he should confer the kingdom upon one of his sons.

10 Therefore, he had Mosiah brought before him; and these are the words which he spake unto him, saying: My son, I would that ye should make a proclamation throughout all this land among all this people, or the people of Zarahemla, and the people of Mosiah who dwell in the land, that thereby they may be gathered together; for on the morrow I shall proclaim unto this my people out of mine own mouth that thou art a king and a ruler over this people, whom the Lord our God hath given us.

11 And moreover, I shall give this people a name, that thereby they may be distinguished above all the people which the Lord God hath brought out of the land of Jerusalem; and this I do because they have been a diligent people in keeping the commandments of the Lord.

12 And I give unto them a name that never shall be blotted out, except it be through transgression.

13 Yea, and moreover I say unto you, that if this highly favored people of the Lord should fall into transgression, and become a wicked and an adulterous people, that the Lord will deliver them up, that thereby they become weak like unto their brethren; and he will no more preserve them by his matchless and marvelous power, as he has hitherto preserved our fathers.

14 For I say unto you, that if he had not extended his arm in the preservation of our fathers they must have fallen into the hands of the Lamanites, and become victims to their hatred.

Mosiah, son of Benjamin, was apparently the oldest son, his being named first of the king's three sons (see v. 2 above). His selection as king suggests the kingship followed a patriarchal order. However, at the end of Mosiah's reign, he asked the people for "their will concerning who should be king" and they desired Aaron, Mosiah's son (Mosiah 29:1–2). Four of Mosiah's sons were named in Mosiah 27:34, and Aaron is named second, but their order of birth is not mentioned. Nor does the context limit Mosiah's sons to these four. After Aaron refuses to be king, Mosiah son of Benjamin informs the people "that he to whom the kingdom doth rightly belong has declined" (Mosiah 29:3, 6). The text suggests it was rightfully Aaron's because of "the voice of the people" (Mosiah 29:2). However, it may have been because of his being the first born and the sons were not listed according to age. Therefore, we cannot definitely say it was a patriarchal kingship.

The name King Mosiah informs the people he would give unto them (Mosiah 1:11) was "the name of Christ" (Mosiah 5:8), and will be commented upon further in chapter 7. The conditions placed upon their name by Mosiah son of Benjamin are both mortal and eternal promises. The "name shall never be blotted out, except it be through transgression" (Mosiah 1:12); and if any "highly favored people of the Lord should fall into transgression, and become a wicked and adulterous people" they will become weak and no more preserved by the Lord" (v. 13). The example of their fathers falling "into the hands of the Lamanites" because of their wickedness will be verified time and time again with other peoples when the true history of the world is made known.

Mosiah 1:15–18 • The Charge to King Mosiah II

15 And it came to pass that after king Benjamin had made an end of these sayings to his son, that he gave him charge concerning all the affairs of the kingdom.

16 And moreover, he also gave him charge concerning the records

which were engraven on the plates of brass; and also the plates of Nephi; and also, the sword of Laban, and the ball or director, which led our fathers through the wilderness, which was prepared by the hand of the Lord that thereby they might be led, every one according to the heed and diligence which they gave unto him.

17 Therefore, as they were unfaithful they did not prosper nor progress in their journey, but were driven back, and incurred the displeasure of God upon them; and therefore they were smitten with famine and sore afflictions, to stir them up in remembrance of their duty.

18 And now, it came to pass that Mosiah went and did as his father had commanded him, and proclaimed unto all the people who were in the land of Zarahemla that thereby they might gather themselves together, to go up to the temple to hear the words which his father should speak unto them.

Mosiah, son of Benjamin, having charge of the records and the sacred instruments (v. 16) continues the line of responsibility as stated by Mormon: "they were handed down . . . from generation to generation until they have fallen into my hands" (Words of Mormon 1:11). The ball or director working according to the heed and diligence given to the Lord (Mosiah 1:16) was also noted in 1 Nephi 16:28. The Nephites being unfaithful and not prospering (Mosiah 1:17) confirms the consequences of those who take the name of Christ and then fall into transgression. They will not be preserved by the Lord (v. 13). Mosiah son of Benjamin proclaiming to all the people to gather to the temple to hear his father's words (v. 18) prepares us for what is recorded in Mosiah chapter 2. Therefore, these verses (15–18) are a brief summary of what happened between the time King Benjamin instructed his sons (v. 3–14) and the time he instructed the people at the temple in the land of Zarahemla.

Mosiah 2:1–8 • The People Gather Around the Temple

1 And it came to pass that after Mosiah had done as his father had commanded him, and had made a proclamation throughout all the land, that the people gathered themselves together throughout all the

land, that they might go up to the temple to hear the words which king Benjamin should speak unto them.

2 And there were a great number, even so many that they did not number them; for they had multiplied exceedingly and waxed great in the land.

3 And they also took of the firstlings of their flocks, that they might offer sacrifice and burnt offerings according to the law of Moses;

4 And also that they might give thanks to the Lord their God, who had brought them out of the land of Jerusalem, and who had delivered them out of the hands of their enemies, and had appointed just men to be their teachers, and also a just man to be their king, who had established peace in the land of Zarahemla, and who had taught them to keep the commandments of God, that they might rejoice and be filled with love towards God and all men.

5 And it came to pass that when they came up to the temple, they pitched their tents round about, every man according to his family, consisting of his wife, and his sons, and his daughters, and their sons, and their daughters, from the eldest down to the youngest, every family being separate one from another.

6 And they pitched their tents round about the temple, every man having his tent with the door thereof towards the temple, that thereby they might remain in their tents and hear the words which king Benjamin should speak unto them;

7 For the multitude being so great that king Benjamin could not teach them all within the walls of the temple, therefore he caused a tower to be erected, that thereby his people might hear the words which he should speak unto them.

8 And it came to pass that he began to speak to his people from the tower; and they could not all hear his words because of the greatness of the multitude; therefore he caused that the words which he spake should be written and sent forth among those that were not under the sound of his voice, that they might also receive his words.

This is the second Nephite temple mentioned in the Book of Mormon. "Nephi, did build a temple . . . after the manner of the temple of Solomon save it were not built of so many precious things;

for they were not to be found upon the land" (2 Nephi 5:16). We assume the temple in Zarahemla was built after the same manner, but we have no record of it's being built.

The gathering to the temple in Zarahemla was literally to the temple grounds as indicated by their pitching "their tents round about the temple" (Mosiah 2:6). Jacob's coming "up into the temple" in the land of Nephi to "declare unto you the word of God" (Jacob 2:2), was also suggested to be the temple grounds, but King Benjamin "could not teach them all within the walls of the temple" (Mosiah 2:7). It was a special gathering, not a regularly scheduled event, to which they had been summoned. It would be similar to a solemn assembly, one of the purposes of temples given in modern revelation (see D&C 124:39). As with Jacob in the land of Nephi, the families assembled, but with King Benjamin it was the extended family suggesting again a patriarchal order (Mosiah 2:5). Jacob mentions "your wives and your children" (Jacob 2:7), but says nothing of the family unit. In this writer's opinion, to attempt to associate it with a specific Jewish festival, as some writers do, is without sufficient foundation. If it had been a regular festival, it seems it would have been mentioned. While "sacrifices and burnt offerings according to the law of Moses" were made (Mosiah 2:3), they were made on a daily basis (Mosiah 13:30, discussed later). They were "a type and a shadow of things [of Christ] which are to come" (Mosiah 13:10, also discussed later), and also of thanksgiving for their blessings (Mosiah 2:4, compare Leviticus 7:12). It should also be mentioned that the Nephites operated under the Melchizedek priesthood for "the law hath become dead" unto them. Nevertheless, they kept it until Christ had fulfilled the law (2 Nephi 25:24–25 and discussed more fully in chapter 10). The building of the tower and the writing of the king's words (Mosiah 2:7–8) were previously commented on in the "Introduction" of the "Notes and Commentary."

Mosiah 2:9–11 • Do Not Trifle with my Words

> 9 And these are the words which he spake and caused to be written, saying: My brethren, all ye that have assembled yourselves together, you that can hear my words which I shall speak unto you this day; for I have not commanded you to come up hither to trifle with the words which I shall speak, but that you should hearken unto me, and open your ears that ye may hear, and your hearts that ye may understand, and your minds that the mysteries of God may be unfolded to your view.

> 10 I have not commanded you to come up hither that ye should fear me, or that ye should think that I of myself am more than a mortal man.

> 11 But I am like as yourselves, subject to all manner of infirmities in body and mind; yet I have been chosen by this people, and consecrated by my father, and was suffered by the hand of the Lord that I should be a ruler and a king over this people; and have been kept and preserved by his matchless power, to serve you with all the might, mind and strength which the Lord hath granted unto me.

Just as a radio or television set must be tuned properly to get good reception, King Benjamin invites his people to be tuned in (v. 9). It is possible to be in hearing distance of what is said, but to let your mind wander and not hear what is said. Thus our ears must be open to hear. As Nephi said, "When a man speaketh by the power of the Holy Ghost the power of the Holy Ghost carries it unto the hearts of the children of men." Those who "harden their hearts against the Holy Spirit" will not receive the message being delivered (2 Nephi 33:1–2). Thus our hearts must be open to understand. To have the mysteries of God unfolded, our minds must also comprehend and make connection to what is already understood. The Lord gives revelation "in your mind, and in your heart, by the power of the Holy Ghost" (D&C 8:2–3). Those who trifle with the words spoken by the servants of God are making intellectual judgments rather than receiving spiritual insights. The desire of King Benjamin was for his people to know and understand the mysteries of God; those things only revealed to the faithful.

King Benjamin's life was also a sermon. As a mortal man (Mosiah 2:10), he had not "exalt[ed] himself" (Luke 14:11), but as "chief among [them]" had been their servant (Matthew 20:27). He "was suffered [allowed] by the hand of the Lord that [he] should be a ruler and a king "over his people, and he recognized the Lord in all his accomplishments. Furthermore, he had given "all the might, mind, and strength which the Lord had granted unto [him]" (Mosiah 2:11) into his service as king. The political leaders of our day would do well to follow his example.

Mosiah 2:12–17 • In the Service of Your God

12 I say unto you that as I have been suffered to spend my days in your service, even up to this time, and have not sought gold nor silver nor any manner of riches of you;

13 Neither have I suffered that ye should be confined in dungeons, nor that ye should make slaves one of another, nor that ye should murder, or plunder, or steal, or commit adultery; nor even have I suffered that ye should commit any manner of wickedness, and have taught you that ye should keep the commandments of the Lord, in all things which he hath commanded you—

14 And even I, myself, have labored with mine own hands that I might serve you, and that ye should not be laden with taxes, and that there should nothing come upon you which was grievous to be borne—and of all these things which I have spoken, ye yourselves are witnesses this day.

15 Yet, my brethren, I have not done these things that I might boast, neither do I tell these things that thereby I might accuse you; but I tell you these things that ye may know that I can answer a clear conscience before God this day.

16 Behold, I say unto you that because I said unto you that I had spent my days in your service, I do not desire to boast, for I have only been in the service of God.

17 And behold, I tell you these things that ye may learn wisdom; that ye may learn that when ye are in the service of your fellow beings ye are only in the service of your God.

King Benjamin had not sought for monetary gain, a comfort usually afforded by kings (v. 12). He had protected the individual rights of his people, and sought for high moral and ethical standards among them (v. 13). He labored with his own hands so that taxes could be kept low (v. 14). Whether he had worked at other professions for his own support, or done menial tasks within the kingdom to keep down expenses of government is not stated, but the latter seems more probable.

He sought neither self-acclaim nor guilt complexes for others. His concern was to have God's approval upon his efforts (v. 15). He looked upon his service to the people as a service to God (v. 16). He was joining in the work of God, "to bring to pass the immortality and eternal life of man" (Moses 1:39). Thus he gives us another precept to bring us nearer to God if obeyed: "When ye are in the service of your fellow beings ye are only in the service of your God" (Mosiah 2:17). This precept is one of the most widely known in the Book of Mormon. Jesus taught the same precept: "Inasmuch as ye have done it unto one of the least of these my brethren, ye have done it unto me" (Matthew 25:40).

Mosiah 2:18–21 • How You Ought to Thank Your Heavenly King

18 Behold, ye have called me your king; and if I, whom ye call your king, do labor to serve you, then ought not ye to labor to serve one another?

19 And behold also, if I, whom ye call your king, who has spent his days in your service, and yet has been in the service of God, do merit any thanks from you, O how you ought to thank your heavenly King!

20 I say unto you, my brethren, that if you should render all the thanks and praise which your whole soul has power to possess, to that

God who has created you, and has kept and preserved you, and has caused that ye should rejoice, and has granted that ye should live in peace one with another—

21 I say unto you that if ye should serve him who has created you from the beginning, and is preserving you from day to day, by lending you breath, that ye may live and move and do according to your own will, and even supporting you from one moment to another—I say, if ye should serve him with all your whole souls yet ye would be unprofitable servants.

The first lesson taught in these verses, if the king labors to serve you, you ought to labor to serve one another (v. 18), is a part of the second great commandment: "Thou shalt love thy neighbor as thyself" (Matthew 22:39). As Jesus taught in the parable of the Good Samaritan, the neighbor of "him that fell among thieves" is, "He that shewed mercy on him." Wherefore, Jesus said, "Go, and do thou likewise" (Luke 10:37).

The second lesson, if the king does "merit any thanks from you, O how you ought to thank your heavenly King" (Mosiah 2:19), is an acknowledgment that "all things which are good cometh of God" (Moroni 7:12). The Bible also gives a second witness of this doctrine: "Every good gift and every perfect gift is from above, and cometh down from the Father of lights, with whom is no variableness, neither shadow of turning" (James 1:17). King Benjamin expounds upon this doctrine. God "created you and has kept and preserved you" and enabled you to "live in peace one with another" (Mosiah 2:20). That God is lending us breath to live and move according to our own will (v. 21) was echoed by Paul: "For in him we live, and move, and have our being; as certain also as your own poets have said, For we are also his offspring" (Acts 17:28). King Benjamin's declaration that if they served him with all their souls they "would be unprofitable servants" (Mosiah 2:21) is in keeping with the Savior's teachings: "So likewise ye, when ye shall have done all those things which are commanded you, say, We are unprofitable servants: we have done that which was our duty to do" (Luke 17:10). "The doctrine of Christ, and the only and true doctrine of the Father, and of the Son, and of the Holy Ghost, which is one God, without end" (2 Nephi 31:21) is the same whether spoken to the Nephites, or to the Jews, or to any other people.

Mosiah 2:22–25 • Eternal Indebtedness

22 And behold, all that he requires of you is to keep his commandments; and he has promised you that if ye would keep his commandments ye should prosper in the land; and he never doth vary from that which he hath said; therefore, if ye do keep his commandments he doth bless you and prosper you.

23 And now, in the first place, he hath created you, and granted unto you your lives, for which ye are indebted unto him.

24 And secondly, he doth require that ye should do as he hath commanded you; for which if ye do, he doth immediately bless you; and therefore he hath paid you. And ye are still indebted unto him, and are, and will be, forever and ever; therefore, of what have ye to boast?

25 And now I ask, can ye say aught of yourselves? I answer you, Nay. Ye cannot say that ye are even as much as the dust of the earth; yet ye were created of the dust of the earth; but behold, it belongeth to him who created you.

Here, King Benjamin introduces us to a doctrine we shall call divine indebtedness (v. 34). If the commandments of God are kept, we will prosper, which is a blessing from God (v. 22), as he had previously said. He then explains the doctrine. God "created [us], and granted [us our] lives, for which [we] are indebted unto him" (v. 23). All he requires of us is to keep his commandments, and if we do "he doth immediately bless you, and therefore he hath paid you." Therefore, you are still indebted to him and will be forever, because he blesses us for every commandment that is kept (v. 24). Even the dust of the earth from which we are created belongs to God (v. 25). Mormon, in one of his editorial inserts, gives an extension of this doctrine. He gives many examples of the earth and its many components always obeying the commands of God, but the children of men do not always obey him and therefore are "less than the dust of the earth" (see Helaman 12:7–21).

Some may question whether or not "the Lord doth immediately bless [us]." The Prophet Joseph Smith gave an explanation that answers that question.

> The inhabitants of this continent anciently were so constituted, and were so determined and persevering, either in righteousness or wickedness, that God visited them immediately with great judgments of blessings. But the present generation, if they were going to battle, if they got any assistance from God, they would have to obtain it by faith. [*TPJS*, 299]

Mosiah 2:26–31 • Rid My Garments of Your Blood

> 26 And I, even I, whom ye call your king, am no better than ye yourselves are; for I am also of the dust. And ye behold that I am old, and am about to yield up this mortal frame to its mother earth.
>
> 27 Therefore, as I said unto you that I had served you, walking with a clear conscience before God, even so I at this time have caused that ye should assemble yourselves together, that I might be found blameless, and that your blood should not come upon me, when I shall stand to be judged of God of the things whereof he hath commanded me concerning you.
>
> 28 I say unto you that I have caused that ye should assemble yourselves together that I might rid my garments of your blood, at this period of time when I am about to go down to my grave, that I might go down in peace, and my immortal spirit may join the choirs above in singing the praises of a just God.
>
> 29 And moreover, I say unto you that I have caused that ye should assemble yourselves together, that I might declare unto you that I can no longer be your teacher, nor your king;
>
> 30 For even at this time, my whole frame doth tremble exceedingly while attempting to speak unto you; but the Lord God doth support me, and hath suffered me that I should speak unto you, and hath commanded me that I should declare unto you this day, that my son Mosiah is a king and a ruler over you.
>
> 31 And now, my brethren, I would that ye should do as ye have hitherto done. As ye have kept my commandments, and also the commandments of my father, and have prospered, and have been kept

from falling into the hands of your enemies, even so if ye shall keep the commandments of my son, or the commandments of God which shall be delivered unto you by him, ye shall prosper in the land, and your enemies shall have no power over you.

King Benjamin knows he will soon die. He desires to finalize the magnifying of his stewardship as king. He did not want the responsibility of his subject's sins upon his own head if he did not teach them the word of God (see Jacob 1:19). Therefore, he once more admonishes them to keep the commandments of God under their new king, his son Mosiah (Mosiah 2:30). The general results of keeping the commandments would be the same as under his reign: they would prosper in the land, and their enemies would have no power over them (v. 31). He then gives some warnings and admonitions.

Mosiah 2:32–35 • Do Not Obey the Evil Spirit

32 But, O my people, beware lest there shall arise contentions among you, and ye list to obey the evil spirit, which was spoken of by my father Mosiah.

33 For behold, there is a wo pronounced upon him who listeth to obey that spirit; for if he listeth to obey him, and remaineth and dieth in his sins, the same drinketh damnation to his own soul; for he receiveth for his wages an everlasting punishment, having transgressed the law of God contrary to his own knowledge.

34 I say unto you, that there are not any among you, except it be your little children that have not been taught concerning these things, but what knoweth that ye are eternally indebted to your heavenly Father, to render to him all that you have and are; and also have been taught concerning the records which contain the prophecies which have been spoken by the holy prophets, even down to the time our father, Lehi, left Jerusalem;

35 And also, all that has been spoken by our fathers until now. And behold, also, they spake that which was commanded them of the Lord; therefore, they are just and true.

Contentions come from the evil spirit (v. 32). The Savior said the devil is "the father of contention" (3 Nephi 11:29). Those who obey the evil spirit and die in their sins will receive an everlasting punishment (Mosiah 2:33). The reason for such punishment gives us an excellent definition of sin: "having transgressed the law of God contrary to his own knowledge" (v. 33). The apostle John wrote, "Whosoever committeth sin transgresseth the law: for sin is the transgression of the law" (1 John 3:4). However, a broken law without knowledge may not always be a sin. The natural effects of the broken law will still follow, but the punishment of God may be withheld and the Atonement will pay for the demands of justice through the mercy of Christ. The Prophet Ezekiel said: "Again, when the wicked *man* turneth away from his wickedness that he hath committed, and doeth that which is lawful and right, he shall save his soul alive. Because he considereth, and turneth away from all his transgressions that he hath committed, he shall surely live, he shall not die" (Ezekiel 18:27–28).

The children of Israel, under the law of Moses, differed in their sacrifices brought unto the Lord for a person with knowledge who sinned (see Leviticus 5:1–6), and for those who did "sin through ignorance, in the holy things of the Lord" (Leviticus 5:15; see also 4:2). While the difference is sometimes hard to determine, the Lord knows who sins and who transgresses, and judges accordingly.

King Benjamin warns that all of his people who break the commandments of God will be sinning because they have all been taught from the records brought out of Jerusalem and by the Nephite prophets. The only exception is the little children (Mosiah 2:34–35). As stated before, the blessings the people receive from God for keeping the commandments leaves them "eternally indebted to [their] heavenly Father" (v. 34).

Mosiah 2:36–40 • A Never-Ending Torment

36 And now, I say unto you, my brethren, that after ye have known and have been taught all these things, if ye should transgress and go contrary to that which has been spoken, that ye do withdraw yourselves from the Spirit of the Lord, that it may have no place in

you to guide you in wisdom's paths that ye may be blessed, prospered, and preserved—

37 I say unto you, that the man that doeth this, the same cometh out in open rebellion against God; therefore he listeth to obey the evil spirit, and becometh an enemy to all righteousness; therefore, the Lord has no place in him, for he dwelleth not in unholy temples.

38 Therefore if that man repenteth not, and remaineth and dieth an enemy to God, the demands of divine justice do awaken his immortal soul to a lively sense of his own guilt, which doth cause him to shrink from the presence of the Lord, and doth fill his breast with guilt, and pain, and anguish, which is like an unquenchable fire, whose flame ascendeth up forever and ever.

39 And now I say unto you, that mercy hath no claim on that man; therefore his final doom is to endure a never-ending torment.

40 O, all ye old men, and also ye young men, and you little children who can understand my words, for I have spoken plainly unto you that ye might understand, I pray that ye should awake to a remembrance of the awful situation of those that have fallen into transgression.

King Benjamin further warns his subjects that breaking the commandments will result in the withdrawing of themselves from the Spirit of the Lord and coming out in open rebellion against God; for the Lord will not dwell in an unholy temple (vv. 36–37). Unless that person repents before he dies, the demands of divine justice will cause him to shrink from the presence of the Lord (v. 38). This is not a plea for death-bed repentance, for without time to meet the conditions of repentance, as Jacob says, "they who are filthy shall be filthy still" (2 Nephi 9:16). The breast being filled with guilt, pain, and anguish (Mosiah 2:38) is symbolic of the soul or the spirit of the sinner. King Benjamin says this will be "*like* an unquenchable fire" (v. 38; emphasis added). Jacob's testimony is the same. These conditions will be "*as* a lake of fire and brimstone whose flame ascendeth up forever and ever and has no end" (2 Nephi 9:16; emphasis added). Thus we have two witnesses in the Book of Mormon of this symbolism.

Mercy exercises no claim on the unrepentant man and his final doom is "a never-ending torment" (Mosiah 2:39). This verse is describing the fate of the sons of perdition, one of the few such descriptions in the Book of Mormon (see 2 Nephi 9:38; and Mosiah 16:5 to be discussed in a later chapter). Because God is Endless and Eternal, "Eternal punishment is God's punishment. Endless punishment is God's punishment" (D&C 19:10–12), a punishment when satisfied would be ended. Alma the elder experienced everlasting burning and eternal torment, but was pained no more (see Mosiah 27:28–29 discussed in a later chapter). Never-ending punishment is the punishment of the damned who receive no glory. Thus, it is the suffering of the sons of perdition. The Prophet Joseph Smith's description of sons of perdition, included in the General Authority quotes of the previous chapter, confirms the conditions set forth by King Benjamin. Jesus also warned of speaking against the Holy Ghost:

> 31 Wherefore I say unto you, All manner of sin and blasphemy shall be forgiven unto men: but the blasphemy *against* the *Holy* Ghost shall not be forgiven unto men.
>
> 32 And whosoever speaketh a word against the Son of man, it shall be forgiven him: but whosoever speaketh against the Holy Ghost, it shall not be forgiven him, neither in this world, neither in the *world* to come. [Matthew 12:31–32]

Paul taught the same doctrine to the Hebrews:

> 4 For *it is* impossible for those who were once enlightened, and have tasted of the heavenly gift, and were made partakers of the Holy Ghost,
>
> 5 And have tasted the good word of God, and the powers of the world to come,
>
> 6 If they shall fall away, to renew them again unto repentance; seeing they crucify to themselves the Son of God afresh, and put *him* to an open shame. [Hebrews 6:4–6]

As quoted in the previous chapter, Joseph also taught that "no man can commit the unpardonable sin after the dissolution of the body, nor in this life, unless he receives the Holy Ghost, but they must do it in this world" (*TPJS*, 357). His teaching is consistent with the context of King Benjamin's warning. The awful situation of those who fall into transgression (Mosiah 2:40), who have yielded to the evil spirit, could be on the road to becoming a son of perdition. Although there will be few by percentages, the Prophet Joseph said, "This is the case with many apostates of the Church of Jesus Christ of Latter-day Saints" (*TPJS*, 358). The warning of the king including "old men" to awake to the remembrance of these conditions shows that it is always possible while in this world.

Mosiah 2:41 • A Never-Ending Happiness

41 And moreover, I would desire that ye should consider on the blessed and happy state of those that keep the commandments of God. For behold, they are blessed in all things, both temporal and spiritual; and if they hold out faithful to the end they are received into heaven, that thereby they may dwell with God in a state of never-ending happiness. O remember, remember that these things are true; for the Lord God hath spoken it.

The comparison with those who keep the commandments should be sufficient to bring about a total commitment to serve God and keep his commandments. However, the spiritual blessings are often unnoticed, and often some of the physical blessings are taken for granted. Therefore, we must confess his hand in all things and keep the commandments (see D&C 59:21). We live in a world of sin, and temptations are continually around us, thus we too must "remember, remember that these things are true; for the Lord God hath spoken it."

Although King Benjamin's speech is not ended, the remainder of it is the words of an angel. Because of the length and importance of the angel's words, we will discuss them in the following chapter.

SACRED WRITING

Preaching Which is Sacred:

Mosiah 1:3–14   King Benjamin to his sons.

Mosiah 2:9–41   King Benjamin to his people.

Doctrines Learned:

Mosiah 2:21   God created man and preserves him by lending him breath from day to day.

Mosiah 2:24, 34   When we keep the commandments we are blessed and so we are eternally indebted to God.

Mosiah 2:33   Sin is a transgression of the law of God contrary to knowledge.

Mosiah 2:37   The Lord dwells not in unholy temples.

Mosiah 2:39   Those who die an enemy to God (sons of perdition) endure a never-ending punishment.

Mosiah 2:41   Those who keep the commandments and hold out faithful to the end are received into heaven and dwell in a state of never-ending happiness.

General Authority Quotations

Elder Marion D. Hanks • Mosiah 1:6–7

As members of the Church in this day and age, we too have been blessed with a great treasury of scriptures. Like the sons of Benjamin, we are continually being encouraged by our leaders to study the scriptures that we may profit from them and receive inspiration to keep the commandments of God. The Lord has repeatedly counseled us to "search the scriptures." Notwithstanding this, many of us do not take time to read and ponder them. Some have thought that the scriptures hold no meaning in modern times, but in fact the people whose lives are written in the sacred records were in many ways like us. Their lives were crowded with decisions to be made, with temptations and problems and opportunities and uncertainties. Their responses and their experiences can be very helpful to us in our time. But someone has said that a person who *will* not read is not better off than one who *cannot*.

A study of the scriptures can be a fascinating adventure. Often we hear of young people in their teen years who read the Book of Mormon and join the Church with a personal testimony that it is true and of God. Nothing in this world could be more precious than to have such an assurance and know for ourselves that the Church is of God and has been re-established upon the earth in our time by divine revelation, and the witness is available to all who really desire it. *[The Instructor*, March 1959, 93]

President Spencer W. Kimball • Mosiah 2:7

I believe that the Lord is anxious to put into our hands inventions of which we laymen have hardly had a glimpse. . . .

A significant revelation states: "For, verily, the sound must go forth from this place into all the world, and unto the uttermost parts of the earth—the gospel must be preached unto every creature." [D&C 58:64]

I am confident that the only way we can reach most of these millions of our Father's children is through the spoken word over the airwaves, since so many are illiterate. We have proved the ability of our young men to learn other languages. . . .

King Benjamin, that humble but mighty servant of the Lord, called together all the people in the land of Zarahemla, and the multitude was so great that King Benjamin "caused a tower to be erected, that thereby his people might hear the words which he should speak unto them." [Mosiah 2:7]

Our Father in Heaven has now provided us mighty towers—radio and television towers with possibilities beyond comprehension—to help fulfill the words of the Lord that "the sound must go forth from this place unto all the world." *[The Teachings of Spencer W. Kimball* (1982), 587–88]

President Joseph Fielding Smith • Mosiah 2:17

Service in behalf of others is one thing required of every soul. He who is able but will not serve his fellows in some way is not fit to have place among them. Serving others is its own reward. When we receive the priesthood, we do so with the understanding that it will be used for the benefit of others. This is an obligation we take upon us. In fact, priesthood blesses us in two ways: First, it is the means through which exaltation comes to those who hold it; second, it is to be used in behalf of others that they also may be blessed. No man is independent. Put a man off by himself, where he could communicate with none of his fellow beings or receive aid from them, and he would perish miserably. It is a mistake for us to draw within ourselves as does a snail into its shell. No man has been given the priesthood as an ornament only. He is expected to use it in behalf of the salvation of others.

Not only is he expected, but he is commanded to do so, for the Lord said, after pointing out the various offices in the priesthood and the duties assigned to each: "Wherefore, now let every man learn his duty, and to act in the office in which he is appointed, in all diligence.

He that is slothful shall not be counted worthy to stand, and he that learns not his duty and shows himself not approved shall not be counted worthy to stand. Even so , Amen" (D&C 107:99–100) [CR, April 1966, 101–102]

Elder Marion D. Hanks • Mosiah 2:20–21

In a day when many are inactive and indifferent, when others feel they have served enough, given enough, worshipped enough, these words are as pertinent as if they were specifically directed to each of us by name. All over the Church there are wonderful opportunities for service as teachers, scout workers, youth leaders and in many other capacities. There can never be a time when we have given enough or served enough to justify our ceasing to serve and to give. Many recall the moving statement of President David O. McKay as he was about to dedicate one of our temples, having heard an account of the devotion of the people in contributing to the building of the sacred edifice, and how they had increased in faithfulness as they did so. The living prophet touched all in attendance when he said with feeling, "We can never give too much to the Lord." [*The Instructor*, March 1959, 93–94]

Challenges to Eternal Life:

1. As you study the Book of Mormon, pray for understanding and learning of the mysteries of God (Mosiah 2:9).

2. Endeavor to serve more fully your fellow men, and thank those who serve in your behalf, especially your heavenly King (Mosiah 2:17–19).

3. Commit yourself to more faithfully keep the commandments of God that your enemies shall have no power over you (Mosiah 2:31).

4. Choose a challenge or modern message of your own from this reading and apply it unto life.

Chapter Six

The Words of an Angel

Mosiah 3

Historical Setting: King Benjamin continues his sermon by relating to his people the words which an angel spoke to him after awakening him from his sleep (v. 2). The king does not tell us when this experience took place, but it appears to have been very recent since he was commanded to tell the words to his people (v. 3).

Precepts of this Reading:

> And moreover, I say unto you, that there shall be no other name given nor any other way nor means whereby salvation can come unto the children of men, only in and through the name of Christ, the Lord Omnipotent. [Mosiah 3:17]

> For the natural man is an enemy to God, and has been from the fall of Adam, and will be, forever and ever, unless he yields to the enticings of the Holy Spirit, and putteth off the natural man and becometh a saint through the atonement of Christ the Lord, and becometh as a child, submissive, meek, humble, patient, full of love, willing to submit to all things which the Lord seeth fit to inflict upon him, even as a child doth submit to his father. [Mosiah 3:19]

Although this reading is short, it is one of the most complete descriptions of the mission of the Lord God Omnipotent, or Jesus Christ, in coming to the earth in the meridian of time. An outline of the reading follows in preparation for a deeper study of this great theological prophecy.

Outline • Mosiah 3

➤ Mosiah 3:1–23 The words of an angel concerning things which are to come.

    a. He came to King Benjamin to declare glad tidings of great joy (vv. 3–4).

        1. The Lord had heard Benjamin's prayers and judged his righteousness.

        2. He sent the angel that Benjamin might rejoice and his people be filled with joy.

    b. The time is not far distant when the Lord Omnipotent will come down from heaven and dwell in a tabernacle of clay (vv. 5–7).

        1. He shall go among men working mighty miracles.

        2. He shall cast out evil spirits.

        3. He shall suffer temptation, pain of body, hunger, thirst, and fatigue more than man can suffer except unto death.

        4. Blood cometh from every pore so great shall be his anguish for the wickedness and abominations of his people.

    c. He shall be called Jesus Christ, the Son of God, the Father of heaven and earth, the Creator of all things, and his mother shall be called Mary (v. 8).

    d. He shall come to his own that salvation may come through faith on his name (v. 9).

        1. They shall consider him a man and say he hath a devil.

        2. They shall scourge him and crucify him.

    e. He shall rise the third day from the dead, ready to bring a righteous judgment upon the world and men (vv. 10–12).

        1. His blood will atone for those who died not know-

ing the will of God or who ignorantly sinned.

2. Wo unto those who know the laws and yet sin against God, for salvation comes to them only through repentance and faith on the Lord Jesus Christ.

f. God sent his holy prophets to declare to all that whosoever believes that Christ should come may receive salvation on the same principles as if he had come already (v. 13).

g. Because the people were stiffnecked, the Lord God appointed the law of Moses to them (vv. 14–16).

1. Many signs, wonders, types and shadows of his coming were given.

2. Many holy prophets spoke concerning his coming.

3. They hardened their hearts and understood not that the law of Moses availed them nothing except through the Atonement.

4. Little children are blessed only through the Atonement.

5. As in Adam, or by nature, men fall, and the blood of Christ atoned for their sins.

h. There is only one name or means whereby salvation comes, only in and through the name of Christ, the Lord Omnipotent (vv. 17–18).

1. He judges and his judgment is just.

2. The infant perishes not that dies in his infancy.

3. Men drink damnation to their souls except they humble themselves and become as little children and believe in the atoning blood of Christ.

i. The natural man is an enemy to God and has been from the fall of Adam, and will be forever and unless he yields to the Spirit and becomes a saint through the Atonement (v. 19).

1. He must become as a child, submissive, meek, humble, patient, full of love.

2. He must be willing to submit to all things that the

Lord sees fit to inflict, even as a child to his father.

j.   The knowledge of the Savior shall soon come to all people (vv. 21–22).

1.   Except little children, none will be blameless before God, only through repentance and faith.

2.   After being taught, they are blameless only according to the words I have spoken.

➤ 3:24–27   The Lord declares that the words of the angel shall stand as a bright testimony against this people at the judgment day.

a.   Every man will be judged by his works, whether good or evil (v. 24).

b.   If their works are evil, their own guilt will cause them to shrink from the Lord to a state of misery and endless torment (vv. 25–27).

1.   They have drunk of the wrath of God which justice could not deny.

2.   The same justice caused Adam to fall because he partook of the forbidden fruit.

3.   Mercy could have claim on them no more forever.

4.   Their torment is as a lake of unquenchable fire and brimstone.

NOTES AND COMMENTARY

Introduction: The importance of a message is often determined by the source from which it originated. When the primary source is an angel of God sent to deliver a message for a people on the earth, it would have to be given a label of "top priority."

Mosiah 3:1–4 • Glad Tidings of Great Joy

1 And again my brethren, I would call your attention, for I have somewhat more to speak unto you; for behold, I have things to tell you concerning that which is to come.

2 And the things which I shall tell you are made known unto me

by an angel from God. And he said unto me: Awake; and I awoke, and behold he stood before me.

3 And he said unto me: Awake, and hear the words which I shall tell thee; for behold, I am come to declare unto you the glad tidings of great joy.

4 For the Lord hath heard thy prayers, and hath judged of thy righteousness, and hath sent me to declare unto thee that thou mayest rejoice; and that thou mayest declare unto thy people, that they may also be filled with joy.

The angel's appearance was in answer to the prayers of King Benjamin because of his righteousness (v. 4). The Nephites "believed in Christ and worshipped [and thus prayed to] the Father in his name" (Jacob 4:5; see also 3 Nephi 18:19). It was the Lord Omnipotent who sent the angel to answer the prayer. The Lord Omnipotent, who is Christ (Mosiah 3:17), was to come to the earth (v. 5). Jesus said "the Father and I are one (3 Nephi 28:10), and thus may speak for each other.

"Glad tidings of great joy" (Mosiah 3:3) is the English translation of the Hebrew word for gospel. The declaration the angel was about to give would cause King Benjamin and his people to rejoice, and be filled with Joy (v. 4). The angel's knowing that his message would bring the people joy is an indicator of their present righteousness. As we review that message, we can appreciate why the angel said they would rejoice and be filled with joy.

Mosiah 3:5–8 • He Shall be Called Jesus Christ

5 For behold, the time cometh, and is not far distant, that with power, the Lord Omnipotent who reigneth, who was, and is from all eternity to all eternity, shall come down from heaven among the children of men, and shall dwell in a tabernacle of clay, and shall go forth amongst men, working mighty miracles, such as healing the sick, raising the dead, causing the lame to walk, the blind to receive their sight, and the deaf to hear, and curing all manner of diseases.

6 And he shall cast out devils, or the evil spirits which dwell in

the hearts of the children of men.

7 And lo, he shall suffer temptations, and pain of body, hunger, thirst, and fatigue, even more than man can suffer, except it be unto death; for behold, blood cometh from every pore, so great shall be his anguish for the wickedness and the abominations of his people.

8 And he shall be called Jesus Christ, the Son of God, the Father of heaven and earth, the Creator of all things from the beginning; and his mother shall be called Mary.

The time of the Lord Omnipotent's coming was about one hundred and twenty-four years away.[1] "Omnipotent" (v. 5) means to be all powerful. "Who reigneth" (v. 5) recognizes that Jesus Christ was at this time the administrative God of the earth, the one who was directing the events that were then transpiring. He had been reigning for nearly four thousand years. As Nephi had said, he is "the God of our fathers who were led out of Egypt [by him], out of bondage, and also were preserved by him, yea, the God of Abraham, and of Isaac, and the God of Jacob" (1 Nephi 19:10). "Who was, and is from all eternity to all eternity" (Mosiah 3:5) is proclaiming that his Godhood was attained before this earth's mortal existence, and will continue after the earth is celestialized. Thus he is an eternal God, the Jehovah of the Old Testament.

Jehovah was to "come down from heaven among the children of men, and shall dwell in a tabernacle of clay [mortal body]" (v. 5). Some twenty years earlier, about 148 B.C., a prophet named Abinadi had been burned by apostate Nephites for teaching "that God himself should come down among the children of men." He sealed "the truth of his words by his death" (Mosiah 17:8–20; see also 7:26–28). This doctrine is still not understood in the Christian world today, and will be discussed more fully later.

The mighty miracles Christ would work during his ministry, that

---

[1] Mosiah son of Benjamin began to reign about four hundred and seventy–six years after Lehi left Jerusalem. This would make it 124 B.C., and according to Book of Mormon dating, the length of time until his birth.

are enumerated in general (Mosiah 3:5), are first of all healings of physical infirmities of various kinds. It is important to note that the casting out of devils or evil spirits (v. 6) is listed separately. This listing verifies the existence of devils, and separates them from physical ailments, something that is not always done in the world today. People being possessed or influenced by evil spirits is often labeled as mental illness. However, it must also be recognized that mental illness is not always the influence of evil spirits. Mental illnesses are also caused by physical deficiencies or injuries.

The enumeration of the Savior's personal trials and tribulations (v. 7) are also general. Throughout his life he "was in all points tempted like as we are, yet without sin" (Hebrews 4:15). In other words, he faced every kind of temptation there was. Also, prior to his ministry, after fasting for forty days, he was tempted of the devil in all areas of life.[2] During his ministry, his apostles "continued with [him] in [his] temptations" (Luke 22:28). The pain of body that he suffered probably has reference to his being crucified upon the cross and the events that led up to it. He was arrested and kept up all night without any rest. During this time, "they spit in his face, and buffeted him, and others smote him with the palms of their hands" (Matthew 26:67). "When they had platted a crown of [sharp] thorns, they put it upon his head" (Matthew 27:29), "and scourged him"(John 19:1), and then bearing his [very heavy] cross went forth" to the place of crucifixion" (John 19:17). Following all this "they crucified him"(John 19:18), one of the most painful of all deaths. One of his last words on the cross were "I thirst" (John 19:28). His fatigue was illustrated by Simon the Cyrene; "on him they laid the cross, that he might bear it after Jesus" (Luke 23:26). All of these things were beyond the capacity of man to suffer, "except it be unto death" (Mosiah 3:7). He endured all of these things and then "gave up the ghost [his life]" (Luke 23:46). They did not take it from him, but as

---

[2] Satan appealed to his appetites or passions, to pride and fashion or vanity, and riches of the world and power among men. Nearly every temptation comes in one of these forms according to President David O. McKay. *Gospel Ideals*, [1953], 154–155.

a God, he had "power to lay it down" (John 10:18).

Blood came from every pore when he was in Gethsemane, for "his sweat was as it were great drops of blood falling down to the ground" (Luke 22:44). Luke, a physician, was the only gospel writer to record the sweating of blood, but it is verified by the angel who spoke to King Benjamin. A third witness of his sweating blood is given by the Savior himself. In a revelation to the Prophet Joseph Smith, he said: "Which suffering caused myself, even God, the greatest of all, to tremble because of pain, and to bleed at every pore, and to suffer both body and spirit—and would that I might not drink the bitter cup, and shrink" (D&C 19:18). As the angel told King Benjamin, this suffering was brought about because of "his anguish for the wickedness and the abominations of his people" (Mosiah 3:7).

His name on earth was foreknown (v. 8). It had undoubtedly been revealed to prophets in the old world, but was among the "plain and precious things" taken away (1 Nephi 13:29). The Book of Mormon again bears witness that he would be the Son of God (see 1 Nephi 10:17; 11:7, 18, 21; 13:40). Jacob, son of Lehi, earlier said the great Creator would, in the body, "show himself unto those at Jerusalem" (2 Nephi 9:5); and Nephi had referred to "the Only Begotten of the Father, yea, even the Father of heaven and of earth" (2 Nephi 25:12). Nephi's statement is the most direct and plain reference to Jesus Christ in this role. These references cited above could be read without that concept being plain.

There are three references in the New Testament to Jesus Christ being the Creator. The Gospel of John states: "In the beginning was the Word, and the Word was with God, and the Word was God. The same was in the beginning with God. All things were made by him; and without him was not any thing made that was made" (John 1:1–3). In the epistle to the Colossians, Paul says, "For by him were all things created, that are in heaven, and that are in earth, visible and invisible, whether *they be* thrones, or dominions, or principalities, or powers: all things were created by him, and for him" (Colossians 1:16). In the epistle to the Hebrews, we read, "God, who at sundry times and in divers manners spake in time past unto the fathers by the prophets, Hath in these last days spoken unto us by *his* Son, whom he hath appointed heir of all things, by whom also he made the worlds (Hebrews 1:1–2).

Mary being the name of the mother of Jesus was also foreknown. Nephi had been shown a vision of a virgin being the mother of the Son of God, but he does not name her (see 1 Nephi 11:12–21). Alma said that the Son of God "shall be born of Mary," but it is not clear if the Spirit had told him or if he may have already known this (Alma 7:9–10). If he knew it before, it was probably from the record of King Benjamin's speech. Regardless, the angel of the Lord had very plainly made known the coming birth of Christ to Mary, and who he was.

Mosiah 3:9–13 • Christ Cometh to His Own

9 And lo, he cometh unto his own, that salvation might come unto the children of men even through faith on his name; and even after all this they shall consider him a man, and say that he hath a devil, and shall scourge him, and shall crucify him.

10 And he shall rise the third day from the dead; and behold, he standeth to judge the world; and behold, all these things are done that a righteous judgement might come upon the children of men.

11 For behold, and also his blood atoneth for the sins of those who have fallen by the transgression of Adam, who have died not knowing the will of God concerning them, or who have ignorantly sinned.

12 But wo, wo unto him who knoweth that he rebelleth against God! For salvation cometh to none such except it be through repentance and faith on the Lord Jesus Christ.

13 And the Lord God hath sent his holy prophets among all the children of men, to declare these things to every kindred, nation, and tongue, that thereby whosoever should believe that Christ should come, the same might receive remission of their sins, and rejoice with exceedingly great joy, even as though he had already come among them.

Christ coming to "his own" (v. 9) refers to his being of the tribe of Judah. In "the words of [Moses'] song" (see Deuteronomy 31:30) we read: "When the most High divided to the nations their inheritance, when he separated the sons of Adam, he set the bounds of the people according to the number of the children of Israel. For the LORD's portion *is* his people; Jacob *is* the lot of his inheritance (Deuteronomy 32:8–9). Apparently the numbers of each tribe were determined through pre-mortal organization, and Jesus was born into his afore assigned tribe of Judah. However, the Jewish people would consider him a man and say he had a devil (Mosiah 3:9). The fulfillment of the angel's prophecy was recorded in the gospel of John: "He came unto his own, and his own received him not" (John 1:11).

The angel foretold the resurrection of Christ and his judgment of the world (Mosiah 3:10). After his resurrection, when he appeared to the Nephites, his definition of the gospel included the crucifixion and the judgment.

> 14 And my Father sent me that I might be lifted up upon the cross; and after that I had been lifted up upon the cross, that I might draw all men unto me, that as I have been lifted up by men even so should men be lifted up by the Father, to stand before me, to be judged of their works, whether they be good or whether they be evil—
>
> 15 And for this cause have I been lifted up; therefore, according to the power of the Father I will draw all men unto me, that they may be judged according to their works. [3 Nephi 27:14–15]

During his mortal ministry, he acknowledged his role in the judgment of the world: "For the Father judgeth no man, but hath committed all judgment unto the Son" (John 5:22). Jacob, son of Lehi, also verified that Christ was the judge of all mankind: "O then, my beloved brethren, come unto the Lord, the Holy One. Remember that his paths are righteous. Behold, the way for man is narrow, but it lieth in a straight course before him, and the keeper of the gate is the Holy One of Israel; and he employeth no servant there; and there is none other way save it be by the gate; for he cannot be deceived, for the Lord God is his name (2 Nephi 9:41).

The angel next spoke of the effect of the Atonement upon three groups of people. The first two may be interpreted as the same group, but we will make a distinction between the two. Those who do not know the will of God (Mosiah 3:11) are those who die without the law. Jacob said of this group: "Wherefore, he has given a law; and where there is no law given there is no punishment; and where there is no punishment there is no condemnation; and where there is no condemnation the mercies of the Holy One of Israel have claim upon them, because of the Atonement; for they are delivered by the power of him" (2 Nephi 9:25). Those who "ignorantly sin" (Mosiah 3:11), are those who accept the gospel, but break laws as they are growing in the truth. These were discussed in the previous chapter. The third group is those who rebel against God knowingly. The Atonement does not cover these "except it be through repentance and faith on the Lord Jesus Christ" (v. 12). For the purposes of bringing the rebellious to repentance, the Lord had sent his holy prophets among all people that they might benefit from the Atonement (v. 13). The Atonement was made for all, but there are conditions upon which it is applicable to an individual. The prophets knew he would come and could teach it as though he had already come, just as the angel could teach of his coming to King Benjamin (v. 13). Later Abinadi said: "And now if Christ had not come into the world, speaking of things to come as though they had already come, there could have been no redemption" (Mosiah 16:6).

Mosiah 3:14–16 • The Law of Moses

14 Yet the Lord God saw that his people were a stiffnecked people, and he appointed unto them a law, even the law of Moses.

15 And many signs, and wonders, and types, and shadows showed he unto them, concerning his coming; and also holy prophets spake unto them concerning his coming; and yet they hardened their hearts, and understood not that the law of Moses availeth nothing except it were through the atonement of his blood.

16 And even if it were possible that little children could sin they could not be saved; but I say unto you they are blessed; for behold, as in Adam, or by nature, they fall, even so the blood of Christ atoneth for their sins.

Because the majority of the house of Israel who were led out of Egypt by Moses were stiffnecked, and would not hearken to the Lord through Moses, the Lord gave them a lesser law, called the law of Moses (v. 14). This law was a "schoolmaster to bring [them] to Christ" (Galatians 3:24). It was symbolic of Christ, showing types and shadows of his coming. Notice that there were holy prophets among them (Mosiah 3:15), but the lay people did not hold the priesthood. The Lord "took Moses out of their midst, and the Holy [Melchizedek] Priesthood also" (D&C 84:25). "The lesser priesthood continued" (D&C 84:26), and the Lord told Moses to "separate the Levites from among the children of Israel: and the Levites shall be mine" to carry out the priesthood responsibilities (Numbers 8:14). However, God selected certain qualified men and had the higher priesthood conferred upon them. This doctrine is based on the Prophet Joseph's statement: "All the prophets had the Melchizedek Priesthood and were ordained by God himself" (*TPJS*, 181). The prophets were additional witnesses of Christ and his Atonement (Mosiah 3:15). The law of Moses will be considered further in a later chapter.

A fourth group for whom the Atonement was made is now added. Little children, who are under the age of eight, are also covered by the Atonement. The angel told King Benjamin it was not possible for them to sin (v. 16). As Mormon explained to his son Moroni, "they are not capable of committing sin" (Moroni 8:8). Because of the fall of Adam, they are born into a world of sin, and it is natural, "or by nature" in the angel's words, that "they fall" (Mosiah 3:16). The Lord explained to Adam: "And the Lord spake unto Adam, saying: Inasmuch as thy children are conceived in sin, even so when they begin to grow up, sin conceiveth in their hearts, and they taste the bitter, that they may know to prize the good" (Moses 6:55). Being conceived in sin does not necessarily mean the act of conception, but conceived in a world of sin, or as "they begin to grow up," they may fall. An oft misunderstood scripture is, "Behold, I was shapen in iniquity; and in sin did my mother conceive me" (Psalms 51:5), David's plea for forgiveness in the Bathsheba affair. A later Psalm by David shows that he understood being conceived in sin as born into a world of sin, in the same manner as the Lord told Adam quoted above. David said, "The wicked are estranged from the womb: they go astray as soon as they are born, speaking lies" (Psalms 58:3). The law of Moses could not save the little children, but the atoning blood of Christ in Gethsemane paid the law of justice for the commandments that they break (Mosiah 3:16). The age of accountability for children was revealed to Joseph Smith:

> And again, inasmuch as parents have children in Zion, or in any of her stakes which are organized, that teach them not to understand the doctrine of repentance, faith in Christ the Son of the living God, and of baptism and the gift of the Holy Ghost by the laying on of the hands, when eight years old, the sin be upon the heads of the parents. [D&C 68:25]

Because the Lord's people had changed the ordinance of baptism by immersion to "the washing of children, and the blood of sprinkling" (JST, Genesis 17:5–6), the Lord told Abraham: "And I will establish a covenant of circumcision with thee, and it shall be my covenant between me and thee, and thy seed after thee, in their generations; that thou mayest know for ever that children are not accountable before me until they are eight years old" (JST, Genesis 17:11). He set the age for circumcision at eight days old (Genesis 17:12; JST, Genesis 17:17), symbolic of eight years of age being the years of accountability.

Mosiah 3:17–19 • The Natural Man an Enemy to God

> 17 And moreover, I say unto you, that there shall be no other name given nor any other way nor means whereby salvation can come unto the children of men, only in and through the name of Christ, the Lord Omnipotent.

18 For behold he judgeth, and his judgment is just; and the infant perisheth not that dieth in his infancy; but men drink damnation to their own souls except they humble themselves and become as little children, and believe that salvation was, and is, and is to come, in and through the atoning blood of Christ, the Lord Omnipotent.

19 For the natural man is an enemy to God, and has been from the fall of Adam, and will be, forever and ever, unless he yields to the enticings of the Holy Spirit, and putteth off the natural man and becometh a saint through the atonement of Christ the Lord, and becometh as a child, submissive, meek, humble, patient, full of love, willing to submit to all things which the Lord seeth fit to inflict upon him, even as a child doth submit to his father.

That there is only one name and one means of salvation, "the name of Christ, the Lord Omnipotent," is taught several other places in the Book of Mormon (see 2 Nephi 10:24; Mosiah 16:13; Alma 38:9; Helaman 5:9). Peter taught the same doctrine to the high priest and his kindred in Jerusalem:

10 Be it known unto you all, and to all the people of Israel, that by the name of Jesus Christ of Nazareth, whom ye crucified, whom God raised from the dead, *even* by him doth this man stand here before you whole.

11 This is the stone which was set at nought of you builders, which is become the head of the corner.

12 Neither is there salvation in any other: for there is none other name under heaven given among men, whereby we must be saved. [Acts 4:10–12]

The angel declares that infants are saved through Christ, and adds that man must become as little children to obtain salvation (Mosiah 3:18). Mormon taught the same doctrine to his son Moroni: "Behold I say unto you that this thing shall ye teach—repentance and baptism unto those who are accountable and capable of committing sin; yea, teach parents that they must repent and be baptized, and humble themselves as their little children, and they shall all be saved with their little children" (Moroni 8:10).

The next verse (Mosiah 3:19) is one of the most often quoted and discussed verses in the Book of Mormon. Controversy often arises over who is the natural man, and why he is an enemy to God? These are good questions and need to be answered.

The natural man is the mortal man, or carnal man. The fall of man brought mortality, and "all mankind *became* carnal, sensual, devilish, knowing good from evil, subjecting themselves to the devil" (Mosiah 16:3; emphasis added; see also Moses 6:49). In their fallen state, it is natural to seek the desires and appetites of the flesh (carnal); to follow the instincts of the senses (sensual); and to yield to the temptations of the devil (Figure 1. As Lehi declared, it is "the will of the flesh and the evil which is therein, which giveth the spirit of the devil power to captivate, to bring you down to hell, that he may reign over you in his own kingdom" (2 Nephi 2:28). However, man is born innocent. "Every spirit of man was innocent in the beginning [premortal]; and God having redeemed man from the fall, men became again, in their infant state [mortal], innocent before God. And that wicked one cometh and taketh away light and truth, through disobed-

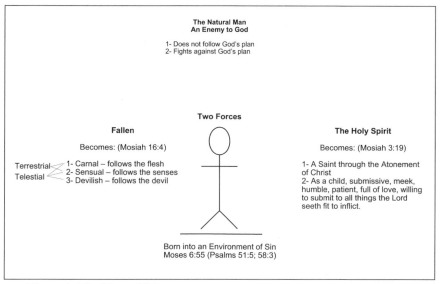

Figure 1. The Natural Man

ience, from the children of men, and because of the tradition of their fathers" (D&C 93:38–39). Alma tells his son Corianton: "And now, my son, all men that are in a state of nature, or I would say, in a carnal state, are in the gall of bitterness and in the bonds of iniquity; they are without God in the world, and they have gone contrary to the nature of God; therefore, they are in a state contrary to the nature of happiness" (Alma 41:11).

The natural man is an enemy to God because he goes "contrary to the nature of God," and opposes the plan of God to bring happiness. The plan of happiness is for men to come unto Christ and be baptized. "The Spirit of Christ is given to every man that he may know good from evil" (Moroni 7:16). As he comes in contact with the gospel, God's messenger, the Holy Ghost (see *TPJS*, 323), will teach him of the baptismal covenant.

> 44 For you shall live by every word that proceedeth forth from the mouth of God.
>
> 45 For the word of the Lord is truth, and whatsoever is truth is light, and whatsoever is light is Spirit, even the Spirit of Jesus Christ.
>
> 46 And the Spirit giveth light to every man that cometh into the world; and the Spirit enlighteneth every man through the world, that hearkeneth to the voice of the Spirit.
>
> 47 And every one that hearkeneth to the voice of the Spirit cometh unto God, even the Father.
>
> 48 And the Father teacheth him of the covenant which he has renewed and confirmed upon you, which is confirmed upon you for your sakes, and not for your sakes only, but for the sake of the whole world.
>
> 49 And the whole world lieth in sin, and groaneth under darkness and under the bondage of sin.
>
> 50 And by this you may know they are under the bondage of sin, because they come not unto me.
>
> 51 For whoso cometh not unto me is under the bondage of sin.
>
> 52 And whoso receiveth not my voice is not acquainted with my voice, and is not of me.

53 And by this you may know the righteous from the wicked, and that the whole world groaneth under sin and darkness even now. [D&C 84:44–53]

Thus, the unbaptized are enemies to God. Also, those who are baptized may lose light and truth through "disobedience . . . and because of the traditions of their fathers" (D&C 93:39; quoted above). Therefore, all people must yield "to the enticings of the Holy Spirit and put off the natural man and become a saint through the Atonement of Christ the Lord, and become as a child" (Mosiah 3:19).

Mosiah 3:20–23 • The Knowledge of the Savior Shall Spread

20 And moreover, I say unto you, that the time shall come when the knowledge of a Savior shall spread throughout every nation, kindred, tongue, and people.

21 And behold, when that time cometh, none shall be found blameless before God, except it be little children, only through repentance and faith on the name of the Lord God Omnipotent.

22 And even at this time, when thou shalt have taught thy people the things which the Lord thy God hath commanded thee, even then are they found no more blameless in the sight of God, only according to the words which I have spoken unto thee.

23 And now I have spoken the words which the Lord God hath commanded me.

The time for the knowledge of the Savior to spread to all nations is underway. It was not accomplished before the apostasy following the earthly ministry of Jesus Christ came about. John the Revelator was shown our generation:

6 And I saw another angel fly in the midst of heaven, having the everlasting gospel to preach unto them that dwell on the earth, and to every nation, and kindred, and tongue, and people,

7 Saying with a loud voice, Fear God, and give glory to him; for the hour of his judgment is come: and worship him that made heaven,

and earth, and the sea, and the fountains of waters. [Revelation 14:6–7]

The Lord told Joseph Smith in November of 1831:

36 And now, verily saith the Lord, that these things might be known among you, O inhabitants of the earth, I have sent forth mine angel flying through the midst of heaven, having the everlasting gospel, who hath appeared unto some and hath committed it unto man, who shall appear unto many that dwell on the earth.

37 And this gospel shall be preached unto every nation, and kindred, and tongue, and people.

38 And the servants of God shall go forth, saying with a loud voice: Fear God and give glory to him, for the hour of his judgment is come;

39 And worship him that made heaven, and earth, and the sea, and the fountains of waters—

40 Calling upon the name of the Lord day and night, saying: O that thou wouldst rend the heavens, that thou wouldst come down, that the mountains might flow down at thy presence. [D&C 133:36–40]

It has been over one hundred and seventy years since that revelation was given, and the work is well under way, but there is still much work to do. The revelation says that the everlasting gospel is to be preached "to every nation, and kindred, and tongue, and people" (Revelation 14:6).

The people of King Benjamin, when they had been taught the words of the angel, were "found no more blameless in the sight of God" (Mosiah 3:22). We too are no more blameless in this generation, because we have received the angels words.

Mosiah 3:24–27 • A Bright Testimony Against this People

24 And thus saith the Lord: They shall stand as a bright testimony against this people, at the judgment day; whereof they shall be

judged, every man according to his works, whether they be good, or whether they be evil.

25 And if they be evil they are consigned to an awful view of their own guilt and abominations, which doth cause them to shrink from the presence of the Lord into a state of misery and endless torment, from whence they can no more return; therefore they have drunk damnation to their own souls.

26 Therefore, they have drunk out of the cup of the wrath of God, which justice could no more deny unto them than it could deny that Adam should fall because of his partaking of the forbidden fruit; therefore, mercy could have claim on them no more forever.

27 And their torment is as a lake of fire and brimstone, whose flames are unquenchable, and whose smoke ascendeth up forever and ever. Thus hath the Lord commanded me. Amen.

Having spoken what the Lord had commanded (v. 23), King Benjamin adds a postscript, under the inspiration of the Lord. The words he had spoken would "stand as a bright testimony against" King Benjamin's subjects (v. 24). The remainder of his words (vv. 25–27) are a confirmation of what the king had said just prior to his quoting the angel (2:32–41; previous chapter), but with one exception. He warns of "endless torment" which is God's punishment (see D&C 19:6–12 quoted above). Therefore, mercy could not pay the demands of justice, when we knowingly break the commandments of God. We would then have to pay our own punishment (see D&C 19:17; quoted above). This doctrine was also written to the Hebrews in the New Testament.

26 For if we sin wilfully after that we have received the knowledge of the truth, there remaineth no more sacrifice for sins,

27 But a certain fearful looking for of judgment and fiery indignation, which shall devour the adversaries.

28 He that despised Moses' law died without mercy under two or three witnesses:

29 Of how much sorer punishment, suppose ye, shall he be thought worthy, who hath trodden under foot the Son of God, and hath counted the blood of the covenant, wherewith he was sanctified,

an unholy thing, and hath done despite unto the Spirit of grace?

30 For we know him that hath said, Vengeance *belongeth* unto me, I will recompense, saith the Lord. And again, The Lord shall judge his people.

31 *It is* a fearful thing to fall into the hands of the living God. [Hebrews 10:26–31]

The angel's warning of "their torment *as* a lake of fire and brimstone" (Mosiah 3:27; emphasis added) is symbolic of the mental anguish they would suffer. The Doctrine and Covenants calls this punishment being "delivered over to the buffetings of Satan until the day of redemption" (D&C 78:12; 82:21; 104:9–10; 132:26). Paul has taught the same doctrine with slightly different wording. He admonished the Corinthian branch leaders of the church to "deliver such an one [guilty of incest] unto Satan for the destruction of the flesh, that the spirit may be saved in the day of the Lord Jesus" (1 Corinthians 5:5). Wherefore, those with knowledge who commit sin still have hope for salvation after having been through endless punishment and having paid the demands of justice. This punishment is the difficult way to pay for sin. Martin Harris, after suffering great mental tribulation over the loss of the early pages of the Book of Mormon manuscript was told: "Wherefore, I command you again to repent, lest I humble you with my almighty power; and that you confess your sins, lest you suffer these punishments of which I have spoken, of which in the smallest, yea, even in the least degree you have tasted at the time I withdrew my Spirit" (D&C 19:20). As Alma told his son Corianton: "Do not suppose, because it has been spoken concerning restoration, that ye shall be restored from sin to happiness. Behold, I say unto you, wickedness never was happiness" (Alma 41:10). Christ has paid for our sins through his Atonement. We need to obey the commandments to receive the benefits of his Atonement.

SACRED WRITING

Prophesying:

Mosiah 3:3–22	The words of an angel to King Benjamin.
Mosiah 3:23–27	King Benjamin's words to his subjects.

Doctrines Learned:

Mosiah 3:4	The Lord (Christ) sometimes answers prayers through the ministering of angels.
Mosiah 3:7	Christ suffered for man's sins causing him to bleed at every pore.
Mosiah 3:8	Christ was the Son of God, an immortal being; and of Mary a mortal woman, thus having a dual nature.
Mosiah 3:9–10	Christ was crucified and resurrected to overcome death (the transgression of Adam).
Mosiah 3:11	Christ's Atonement covers those who sin ignorantly.
Mosiah 3:15	The law of Moses typifies Christ and availeth nothing without the Atonement.
Mosiah 3:16	Little children fall in Adam or by nature, and the blood of Christ atones for their sins.
Mosiah 3:17	There is no other name nor means other than the name of Christ whereby salvation comes.
Mosiah 3:18	Men who humble themselves as little children can be saved through the Atonement.
Mosiah 3:19	The natural man is an enemy to God and has been from the beginning until he yields to the enticings of the Spirit and becometh a Saint.
Mosiah 3:27	The torment of the wicked is *as* a lake of fire and brimstone.

General Authority Quotations

Joseph Fielding Smith • Mosiah 3:7

Greatest suffering was in Gethsemane. We speak of the passion of Jesus Christ. A great many people have an idea that when he was on the cross, and nails were driven into his hands and feet, that was his great suffering. His great suffering was before he ever was placed upon the cross. It was in the Garden of Gethsemane that the blood oozed from the pores of his body: "Which suffering caused myself, even God, the greatest of all, to tremble because of pain, and to bleed at every pore, and to suffer both body and spirit—and would that I might not drink the bitter cup, and shrink."

That was not when he was on the cross; that was in the garden. That is where he bled from every pore in his body. . . .

A mortal man could not have stood it—that is, a man such as we are. I do not care what his fortitude, what his power, there was *no man ever born into this world that could have stood under the weight of the load that was upon the Son of God, when he was carrying my sins and yours* and making it possible that we might escape from our sins. He carried that load for us if we will only accept him as our Redeemer and keep his commandments. Some of us find it so hard, so terribly hard, to do the little things that are asked of us, and yet he was willing to carry all that tremendous load and weight of sin—not his own, for he had no sin. He did it that we might escape. He paid the price, the penalty of our sinning. [*Doctrines of Salvation,* comp. Bruce R. McConkie, 3 vols. (1954–56), 1:130–31]

Brigham Young • Mosiah 3:19

When the Spirit of Revelation from God inspires a man, his mind is opened to behold the beauty, order, and glory of the creation of this earth and its inhabitants, the object of its creation, and the purpose of its Creator in peopling it with his children. He can then clearly understand that our existence here is for the sole purpose of exaltation and restoration to the presence of our Father and God, where we may progress endlessly in the power of godliness. After the mind has thus been illuminated, the ignorance and blindness of the great mass of mankind are more apparent. Yet there is no son or daughter of Adam and Eve who has not incorporated in his organization the priceless gem of endless life, for the endless duration and endless lives which they are approaching.

Every person who will examine his own experience—who will watch closely the leading of his own desires—will learn that the very great majority prefer to do good rather than to do evil, and would pursue a correct course were it not for the evil power that subjects them to sway. In wrong doing, their own consciences condemn them. [*Discourses of Brigham Young*, sel. John A. Widtsoe (1941), 37, 67]

President David O. McKay • Mosiah 3:19

Young people are facing the two great choices in life—the animal plane, in which all created animals move and satisfy their appetites, gratify their passion, perpetuating their kind; or the spiritual realm, which includes the intellectual, the love of beauty, the love of good literature in which we can find " . . . tongues in trees, books in the running brooks, sermons in stones, and good in everything."

There is something higher than the animal life, and up in that spiritual realm there is love—the divinest attribute of the human soul. There is sympathy. There is kindness and there are other attributes.

Someone wrote many years ago that the whole purpose of life might be summed up in these words: "To subdue matter that we might realize the ideal." When I first read that I thought it could be paraphrased to read: The whole purpose of life is to bring under subjection the animal passions, the proclivities and tendencies in order that we might always realize the companionship of God's Holy Spirit. That is the ideal. One chief purpose of life is to overcome evil tendencies, to govern our appetites, to control our passions—anger, hatred, jealousy, immorality. We have to overcome them; we have to subject them, conquest them because God has said: " . . . the Spirit of the Lord doth not dwell in unholy temples" (Helaman 4:24), nor will it " . . . always strive with man . . ." (2 Nephi 26:11). ["Emotional Maturity," *Instructor*, Sept. 1959, 281]

Elder Marion G. Romney • Mosiah 3:19

I know the scriptures say that "the natural man is an enemy to God . . ." (Mosiah 3:19). And so he is when he rejects the promptings of the Spirit and follows the lusts of the flesh. But he is not an enemy to God when he follows the promptings of the Spirit.

I firmly believe that notwithstanding the fact that men, as an incident to mortality, are cast out from the presence of God and deprived of past memories, there still persists in the spirit of every human soul a residuum from his pre-existent spiritual life which instinctively responds to the voice of the Spirit of Christ until and unless inhibited by the free agency of the individual. . . . ["Revelation," *Improvement Era*, June 1964, 506]

Challenges to Eternal Life:

1. Be determined to follow Christ and his plan of salvation that you may obtain salvation.
2. Make a commitment to throw off the natural man (Mosiah 3:19) and yield to the enticings of the Spirit.
3. Study carefully the words of the angel and follow them that you may be found blameless at the judgment day (Mosiah 3:24).
4. Choose a challenge of your own from this reading and apply it to your life.

Chapter Seven

The Effect of King Benjamin's Sermon

Mosiah 4–6

*H*istorical Setting: Following King Benjamin's great sermon, the people fell to the earth for fear of the Lord and cried to the Lord for the mercy of the atoning blood of Christ (Mosiah 4:1–2). The king then continued to speak (Mosiah 4). Following the second part of the sermon, the people entered into a covenant with the Lord (Mosiah 5); and King Benjamin's son, Mosiah, is consecrated as the new king. The consecration took place 476 years after Lehi left Jerusalem, or 124 B.C. (Mosiah 6:4). Three years later King Benjamin passed away (121 B.C.).

Precepts of this Reading:

"If you believe all these things see that ye do them." It is one thing to believe, but another to put your beliefs into practice. King Benjamin speaks of God's attributes and man's need for repentance and forgiveness. [Mosiah 4:10]

I say unto you, I would that ye should remember to retain the name written always in your hearts, that ye are not found on the left hand of God, but that ye hear and know the voice by which ye shall be called, and also, the name by which he shall call you. [Mosiah 5:12]

The subjects of King Benjamin had been spiritually begotten of Christ and are his sons and daughters (5:7). Thus they had taken upon them the name of Christ (5:11). We too should be spiritually begotten of Christ and take his name upon us through repentance. An outline of the three chapters in this reading, as a preparation for a deeper study, follows.

OUTLINE • MOSIAH 4–6

➤ Mosiah 4:1–3   After King Benjamin's speech ended, he looked and saw all had fallen to the earth because of the fear of the Lord.

     a.   They viewed themselves in their own carnal state, even less than the dust of the earth (v. 2).

     b.   They cried with one voice for the atoning blood of Christ to forgive and purify them (v. 2).

     c.   The Spirit of the Lord came upon them and they were filled with joy having received a remission of sins and peace of conscience because of their faith in Jesus Christ (v. 3).

➤ 4:4–30   King Benjamin spoke again to his friends, kindred, and people.

     a.   The knowledge of God's goodness awakened them to a sense of their fallen state (v. 5).

     b.   The knowledge of the Atonement will bring salvation to those who put their trust in the Lord and are diligent in keeping his commandments (v. 6).

     c.   All such men from the fall of Adam to the end of the world may receive salvation (v. 7).

     d.   There were no other conditions whereby salvation will come (vv. 8–10).

        1.   Believe that God is and that he created all things in heaven and earth.

      2.   Believe that he has all wisdom, and all power, both in heaven and earth.

      3.   Believe that man cannot comprehend all that the Lord does.

      4.   Believe that you must repent and ask forgiveness.

      5.   If you believe all these things, see that you do them.

e.   They were told to always retain in remembrance the greatness of God and their own nothingness (v. 11).

      1.   Call on the name of the Lord daily.

      2.   Stand steadfastly in the faith of him who is to come.

f.   If they did this they would always be filled with the love of God, retain a remission of their sins, and grow in the knowledge of him who created them (vv. 12–15).

      1.   Do not injure one another but live peaceably and render to every man his due.

      2.   Do not suffer your children to go hungry or naked, to transgress the laws of God, or fight and quarrel one with another and serve the devil.

      3.   Teach them to walk in truth and soberness, to love and serve one another.

g.   Administer your substance to those in need and not turn the beggar out to perish (vv. 16–23).

      1.   They may say he has brought this misery upon himself and will not give to him, but they need to repent or they will perish.

      2.   We are all beggars and depend on God for our substance and a remission of sins.

      3.   If God grants to them what they ask, they ought to impart to one another.

      4.   If they judge the man and condemn him, their condemnation will be more.

      5.   These things were said to those who were rich in the things of this world.

    h.   The poor who had sufficient and denied the beggar because they had not, should say in their hearts, if I had I would give (vv. 24–25).

        1.   In so doing they will remain guiltless, otherwise they will be condemned.

        2.   They covet that which they do not have.

    i.   Doing these things will retain a remission of their sins, that they may walk guiltless before God (vv. 26–27).

        1.   Impart of their substance according to what you have and help the poor both spiritually and temporally.

        2.   Do all things in wisdom and order, and do not run faster than they have strength.

    j.   He that borrows from his neighbor should return the thing as agreed, or else he commits sin and may cause his neighbor to sin also (v. 28).

    k.   There were many ways and means to sin, they cannot be numbered (vv. 29–30).

        1.   They are to watch themselves, and their thoughts, their words, and their deeds.

        2.   Observe the commandments of God and continue in the faith to the end.

➤ 5:1–5   King Benjamin sent among the people to know if they believed the words he had spoken.

    a.   They cried with one voice that they believed all the words and knew of their surety and truth.

        1.   The Spirit of the Lord had wrought a mighty change in their hearts.

        2.   They had no disposition to do evil but to do good continually.

        3.   Through the Spirit they had received great views of that which was to come.

    b.   They were willing to enter into a covenant to be obedient to God's commandments in all things all the remainder of their days (v. 5).

    1.   That they may not bring unto themselves never-ending torment.

    2.   That they may not drink out of the wrath of God.

➤ 5:6–15   King Benjamin desired to hear these words and told them the covenant they made was a righteous covenant.

a.   Because of the covenant they shall be called the children of Christ, his sons and daughters (v. 7).

    1.   This day he had spiritually begotten you.

    2.   Ye are born of him.

b.   Under his head they were made free and none other could make them free (v. 8).

    1.   No other name can bring salvation.

    2.   All who entered the covenant took upon them the name of Christ.

c.   All who enter the covenant shall be found at the right hand of God and know the name of Christ by which they are called (vv. 9–11).

    1.   Those who do not take the name of Christ must take another name and will be found on the left hand of God.

    2.   The name of Christ was the name King Benjamin promised to given them that should never be blotted out except by transgression.

d.   Remember to always retain the name written on their hearts and hear and know the voice of God (vv. 12–14).

    1.   How can a man know a master whom he hath not served and who is a stranger far from the thoughts and intents on his heart.

    2.   Those not knowing the name by which they are called will be cast out.

e.   Be steadfast and immovable in good works that Christ the Lord God Omnipotent may seal you his (v. 15).

    1.   That they may be brought to heaven and have everlasting salvation and eternal life.

    2.   Eternal life comes through the wisdom, power,

justice, and mercy of him who created all things.

➤ 6:1–2   King Benjamin took the names of all who entered the covenant to keep God's commandments, and all had entered it except little children.

➤ 6:3   King Benjamin consecrated Mosiah, his son, to be king and gave him charge concerning the kingdom.

     a. He appointed priests to teach the people to know the commandments and stir them up to remembrance.

     b. He dismissed the multitude and all returned to their homes.

➤ 6:4–7   Mosiah began to reign in the thirtieth year of his age, about four hundred and seventy-six years since Lehi left Jerusalem.

     a. King Benjamin lived three years and he died (v. 5).

     b. King Mosiah walked in the way of the Lord, and kept his commandments (vv. 6–7).

         1. He caused his people to till the earth.

         2. He also tilled the earth that he might not be a burden to the people.

         3. There was no contention in the land for three years.

Notes and Commentary

Introduction: Two questions should be pertinent to every person who believes in Christ or who desires to learn of him. First, how do I get a remission of my sins; and secondly, if I have received a remission of my sins, how do I retain that blessing in my life? Both of these questions are answered in the two chapters that follow.

Mosiah 4:1–3 • Apply the Atoning Blood of Christ

1 And now, it came to pass that when king Benjamin had made an end of speaking the words which had been delivered unto him by the angel of the Lord, that he cast his eyes round about on the

multitude, and behold they had fallen to the earth, for the fear of the Lord had come upon them.

2 And they had viewed themselves in their own carnal state, even less than the dust of the earth. And they all cried aloud with one voice, saying: O have mercy, and apply the atoning blood of Christ that we may receive forgiveness of our sins, and our hearts may be purified; for we believe in Jesus Christ, the Son of God, who created heaven and earth, and all things; who shall come down among the children of men.

3 And it came to pass that after they had spoken these words the Spirit of the Lord came upon them, and they were filled with joy, having received a remission of their sins, and having peace of conscience, because of the exceeding faith which they had in Jesus Christ who should come, according to the words which king Benjamin had spoken unto them.

The words of the angel spoken by King Benjamin to the multitude had convinced them of their individual need for the blood of the Atonement in their lives. They did not plead for justice, but for mercy because they also understood the angel's words about the natural man (v. 2). We all need to come to that same understanding.

Their cry was answered, and from it we learn how we know if we have received a remission of sins. They were filled with joy and had peace of conscience (v. 3). The Spirit brings inner peace and real joy. The joy had replaced their fear. Their joy was in the glory of the Lord, not in the pleasures of the world. Those who had experienced the Spirit of the Lord in their souls would know of this joy. Ammon, the son of Mosiah described it more fully upon his return from his mission to the Lamanites, "My heart is brim with joy, and I will rejoice in my God" (Alma 26:11). Their faith came from the words of King Benjamin. As Nephi said, "When a man speaketh by the power of the Holy Ghost the power of the Holy Ghost carrieth it unto the hearts of the children of men" (2 Nephi 33:1).

Mosiah 4:4–7 • Salvation Prepared from the Foundation of the World

4 And king Benjamin again opened his mouth and began to speak unto them, saying: My friends and my brethren, my kindred and my people, I would again call your attention, that ye may hear and understand the remainder of my words which I shall speak unto you.

5 For behold, if the knowledge of the goodness of God at this time has awakened you to a sense of your nothingness, and your worthless and fallen state—

6 I say unto you, if ye have come to a knowledge of the goodness of God, and his matchless power, and his wisdom, and his patience, and his long-suffering towards the children of men; and also, the atonement which has been prepared from the foundation of the world, that thereby salvation might come to him that should put his trust in the Lord, and should be diligent in keeping his commandments, and continue in the faith even unto the end of his life, I mean the life of the mortal body—

7 I say, that this is the man who receiveth salvation, through the atonement which was prepared from the foundation of the world for all mankind, which ever were since the fall of Adam, or who are, or who ever shall be, even unto the end of the world.

King Benjamin recognized what had happened to his people. It was a teaching moment and he took advantage of it. He briefly and succinctly summarized their situation. The points of doctrine he taught are essential to appreciate and understand the need for the Atonement. As we understand and turn to the Lord, we may also experience the joy that the king's audience felt.

The king speaks of the people's nothingness, and their worthless and fallen state (v. 5). They are nothing in comparison to God. After viewing "the world and the ends thereof, and all the children of men which are, and which were created;" Moses declared: "Now, for this cause I know that man is nothing, which thing I never had supposed" (Moses 1:8, 10). "The worth of souls is great in the sight of God" (D&C 18:10). "Their souls are precious" (Alma 31:35) "at this time" and at any time (Alma 39:17); but without the blessings of Christ and his gospel, they will be "as dross, which the refiners do cast out, [left over materials that are of no worth]" (Alma 34:29). As discussed in the previous chapter, fallen man is the natural man. He is born innocent and becomes good or evil. He is not depraved or born evil, but is subject to the temptations and evils of the world. He has his agency and is the product of his choices.

King Benjamin told his subjects that a knowledge of God's attributes and the Atonement brings salvation (Mosiah 4:6–7). According to Joseph Smith's *Lectures on Faith*, "a correct idea of his character, perfections, and attributes" is "necessary for any rational and intelligent being to exercise faith in God unto life and salvation" (Lecture 3:3, 2).[1] We will not discuss the individual attributes mentioned by King Benjamin, but refer the reader to some general statements about the attributes from the Lectures on Faith.

> We are indebted to the revelations he has given to us for a correct understanding of his character, perfections, and attributes. Because without the revelations which he has given us, no man searching could find out God (see Job 11:7–9). But as it is written, Eye hath not seen, nor ear heard, neither have entered into the heart of man, the things which God hath prepared for them that love him. But God hath revealed *them* unto us by his Spirit: for the Spirit searcheth all things, yea, the deep things of God. For what man knoweth the things of a man, save the spirit of man which is in him? even so the things of God knoweth no man, but the Spirit of God (1 Corinthians 2:9–11). [Lecture 3:7]

> A little reflection shows that the idea of the existence of these attributes in the Deity is necessary to enable any rational being to exercise faith in him. For without the idea of the existence of these attributes in the Deity, men could not exercise faith in him for life and salvation, seeing that without the knowledge of all things God

---

[1] *Lectures on Faith*, given in Kirtland, Ohio, in the winter of 1835 are questioned by some as being authored by the Prophet Joseph. However, they were given and published under his direction, therefore he was responsible for them. We quote them as an authoritative source.

would not be able to save any portion of his creatures. For it is the knowledge of all things that he has from the beginning to the end that enables him to give that understanding to his creatures by which they are made partakers of eternal life. And if it were not for the idea existing in the minds of men that God has all knowledge, it would be impossible for them to exercise faith in him. [Lecture 4:11]

The Atonement was prepared from the foundation of the world, as King Benjamin mentions twice. Knowing there would be a fall, a Savior was needed to save all mankind from the fall (Mosiah 4:6–7). Jesus Christ identified himself to the brother of Jared as: "I am he who was prepared from the foundation of the world to redeem my people" (Ether 3:14). The apostle Peter wrote telling the meridian church that they were redeemed "with the precious blood of Christ, as of a lamb without blemish and without spot: Who verily was foreordained before the foundation of the world, but was manifest in these last times for you" (1 Peter 1:19–20). We too must trust in the Lord and be diligent in keeping the commandments until the end of our mortal lives (Mosiah 4:6).

Mosiah 4:8–12 • Love God—the First Commandment

8 And this is the means whereby salvation cometh. And there is none other salvation save this which hath been spoken of; neither are there any conditions whereby man can be saved except the conditions which I have told you.

9 Believe in God; believe that he is, and that he created all things, both in heaven and in earth; believe that he has all wisdom, and all power, both in heaven and in earth; believe that man doth not comprehend all the things which the Lord can comprehend.

10 And again, believe that ye must repent of your sins and forsake them, and humble yourselves before God; and ask in sincerity of heart that he would forgive you; and now, if you believe all these things see that ye do them.

11 And again I say unto you as I have said before, that as ye have come to the knowledge of the glory of God, or if ye have known of his goodness and have tasted of his love, and have received a remis-

sion of your sins, which causeth such exceedingly great joy in your souls, even so I would that ye should remember, and always retain in remembrance, the greatness of God, and your own nothingness, and his goodness and long-suffering towards you, unworthy creatures, and humble yourselves even in the depths of humility, calling on the name of the Lord daily, and standing steadfastly in the faith of that which is to come, which was spoken by the mouth of the angel.

12 And behold, I say unto you that if ye do this ye shall always rejoice, and be filled with the love of God, and always retain a remission of your sins; and ye shall grow in the knowledge of the glory of him that created you, or in the knowledge of that which is just and true.

King Benjamin bears testimony, as did Nephi (see 2 Nephi 31:21) and Peter in the New Testament (see Acts 4:12), there is no other salvation or condition of salvation than what he has spoken (v. 8). He tells them what is required to obtain their salvation in relationship to God. They must believe in God (Mosiah 4:9). The *Lectures on Faith* states that "to exercise faith in God unto life and salvation," we must have "the idea that he actually exists" (Lecture 3:2–3). This idea comes to us from the scriptures and from the living prophets. In the words of Joseph Smith: "Faith comes by hearing the word of God, through the testimony of the servants of God; that testimony is always attended by the spirit of prophecy and revelation" (*TPJS*, 148). We have the scriptures and the living prophets available to us today.

God created all things in heaven and earth (v. 9). Therefore he created other worlds. From Moses we learn that "worlds without number have I created" (Moses 1:33). John bore testimony: "He was in the world, and the world was made by him" (John 1:10). Paul taught that "by [Christ] were all things created that are in heaven, and that are in earth" (Colossians 1:16). He also wrote, "by [his Son] also he made the worlds" (Hebrews 1:2).

He has all wisdom (Mosiah 4:9). In modern theology, he is *omniscient*. Paul taught, "In [Christ] are hid all the treasures of wisdom and knowledge" (Colossians 2:3). He has all power (Mosiah

4:9). In modern theology, he is *omnipotent*. Moses was told, "by the word of my power, have I created [all things], which is mine Only Begotten Son" (Moses 1:32). Christ "received all power, both in heaven and on earth" (D&C 93:17). Man cannot comprehend all that God does (Mosiah 4:9). Jacob, son of Lehi, testified that "it is impossible that man should find out all [Christ's] ways. And no man knoweth of his ways save it be revealed unto him" (Jacob 4:8). Isaiah says: "For my thoughts are not your thoughts, neither are your ways my ways, saith the Lord. For as the heavens are higher than the earth, so are my ways higher than your ways, and my thoughts than your thoughts" (Isaiah 55:8–9).[2]

Man must repent and humble himself before God (v. 10). The conditions of repentance will be discussed in a later chapter. The scriptures define humility as to "become as little children" (Mosiah 3:18). Paul reminds us to "be not children in understanding: howbeit in malice be ye children, but in understanding be men" (1 Corinthians 14:20). Alma says the humble "walk after the holy order of God" (Alma 5:54), and are "lowly in heart" (Alma 32:8). Man must also ask God for forgiveness (Mosiah 4:11). It is probably easier to believe these things about God than to do them (v. 10). King Benjamin's precept to his people was to see that they did them. It is also the precept for us to be brought nearer to God (see Joseph Smith, Introduction).

King Benjamin's people had come to a knowledge of God and received a remission of sins (v. 11). To retain that remission of sins he counseled them to retain in remembrance the greatness of God and their own nothingness (v. 11). This was the first thing that he told them to see that they did. They were also to humble themselves and call upon God daily (v. 11). This counsel was not just to pray occasionally, or even just once a day. Amulek counseled to pray "both morning, mid-day, and evening" (Alma 34:21); and Alma told his son

---

[2] While Christ is not identified as the Lord speaking in Isaiah 55, verse 6 of that chapter gives the same invitation as Christ does in D&C 88:62–63: "Seek ye the Lord while he may be found."

Helaman, "Counsel with the Lord in all thy doings, and he will direct thee for good" (Alma 37:27). The third thing they were to do was to stand steadfast "in the faith of that which is to come" (Mosiah 4:11). In other words, they were to study the scriptures and learn the prophecies of the future.

Results

Besides retaining a remission of sins, the above actions will fill you with the love of God. In fact, verses five through twelve instruct us on how to keep the first and great commandment, to "love the Lord thy God with all of thy heart, and with all of thy soul, and with all thy mind" (Matthew 22:37–38). These actions will also bring growth in the knowledge of God, and in the knowledge of truth. It will enable us to "come unto the Father in [Christ's] name, and in due time receive of his fulness." By following these instructions we "shall receive grace for grace" (D&C 93:19–20), and be on the path of eternal progression. We will show of a surety that we love God.

Mosiah 4:13–15 • Love Your Neighbor— the Second Commandment

> 13 And ye will not have a mind to injure one another, but to live peaceably, and to render to every man according to that which is his due.
>
> 14 And ye will not suffer your children that they go hungry, or naked; neither will ye suffer that they transgress the laws of God, and fight and quarrel one with another, and serve the devil, who is the master of sin, or who is the evil spirit which hath been spoken of by our fathers, he being an enemy to all righteousness.
>
> 15 But ye will teach them to walk in the ways of truth and soberness; ye will teach them to love one another, and to serve one another.

The second great commandment is like unto the first: "thou shalt love thy neighbor as thyself" (Matthew 22:39). However, we must love God first in order to grow in the knowledge of how to love our neighbor. As we love God and are filled with his love we will have no mind to injure one another, but to live peaceably and render to every man what is his due (Mosiah 4:13). All people are God's children and should be treated as such. The "principle of freedom in maintaining rights, and privileges, belongs to all men, and is justifiable before [God]," as given in the Constitution of the United States (D&C 98:5).

Our closest and most precious neighbors are our children. We will not suffer [allow] our children to go hungry or naked, transgress the laws of God, and fight and quarrel with one another (Mosiah 4:14). As parents we are obligated to care for their physical needs, to maintain a spiritual atmosphere in our homes and environment, and to avoid contention. The devil "is the father of contention" (3 Nephi 11:29). We are responsible to teach our children to walk in the ways of truth and soberness, to love and serve one another (Mosiah 4:15). The home is the basic unit of the Church and the community. We cannot delegate this responsibility to the schools or the government. They are our primary responsibility.

Mosiah 4:16–23 • Admonition to the Rich of the World

16 And also, ye yourselves will succor those that stand in need of your succor; ye will administer of your substance unto him that standeth in need; and ye will not suffer that the beggar putteth up his petition to you in vain, and turn him out to perish.

17 Perhaps thou shalt say: The man has brought upon himself his misery; therefore I will stay my hand, and will not give unto him of my food, nor impart unto him of my substance that he may not suffer, for his punishments are just—

18 But I say unto you, O man, whosoever doeth this the same hath great cause to repent; and except he repenteth of that which he hath done he perisheth forever, and hath no interest in the kingdom of God.

19 For behold, are we not all beggars? Do we not all depend upon the same Being, even God, for all the substance which we have, for both food and raiment, and for gold, and for silver, and for all the riches which we have of every kind?

20 And behold, even at this time, ye have been calling on his name, and begging for a remission of your sins. And has he suffered that ye have begged in vain? Nay; he has poured out his Spirit upon you, and has caused that your hearts should be filled with joy, and has caused that your mouths should be stopped that ye could not find utterance, so exceedingly great was your joy.

21 And now, if God, who has created you, on whom you are dependent for your lives and for all that ye have and are, doth grant unto you whatsoever ye ask that is right, in faith, believing that ye shall receive, O then, how ye ought to impart of the substance that ye have one to another.

22 And if ye judge the man who putteth up his petition to you for your substance that he perish not, and condemn him, how much more just will be your condemnation for withholding your substance, which doth not belong to you but to God, to whom also your life belongeth; and yet ye put up no petition, nor repent of the thing which thou hast done.

23 I say unto you, wo be unto that man, for his substance shall perish with him; and now, I say these things unto those who are rich as pertaining to the things of this world.

Although the importance of caring for the poor is spoken of often in the Book of Mormon (i.e. 2 Nephi 28:13; Alma 1:27; 4:13; 5:55), King Benjamin's instructions and Jacob 2:13–21 are the only scriptural guidelines given on *how* to care for them. Since all people are the children of God, all our neighbors are His children. The instructions given concerning our neighbors with whom we have association are applicable to all. However, what the Prophet Joseph Smith said about keeping the commandments of God is applicable to what King Benjamin says here: "That which is wrong under one circumstance may be, and often is, right under another" (*TPJS*, 256). The king addresses two different groups, the first being "those who are rich pertaining to the things of this world" (Mosiah 4:23).

King Benjamin speaks of those who stand in need, and the beggars. These are two different groups to whom we should give help. There are those who are in need, but are reticent to ask. King Benjamin focuses upon the beggar, those who make their needs known and ask for help. He speaks first of the attitude of the rich towards the beggar, and later of how to care for him.

There are three major points made by King Benjamin. The rich have no right to judge whether the beggars needs are justified (vv. 17, 22). The apostle James' remarks regarding faith and works are applicable here: "If a brother or sister be naked, and destitute of daily food, And one of you say unto them, Depart in peace, be ye warmed and filled; notwithstanding ye give them not those things which are needful to the body, what doth it profit?" (James 2:15–16). James teaches that after his physical needs are cared for, then he is better prepared to have his spiritual needs helped (see Mosiah 4:26). Those who judge have need to repent for they have no interest in the kingdom of God (v. 18; see also Jacob 2:17–19 discussed in chapter one of this work). The kingdom of God is built by helping others attain the blessings of the Lord.

All of us are beggars, for we depend upon God for our physical as well as our spiritual needs, therefore we ought to help one another (Mosiah 4:19–21). King Benjamin is repeating what he said about eternal indebtedness in his first speech (see Mosiah 2:19–24, 34).

Mosiah 4:24–25 • Admonition to the Poor

24 And again, I say unto the poor, ye who have not and yet have sufficient, that ye remain from day to day; I mean all you who deny the beggar, because ye have not; I would that ye say in your hearts that: I give not because I have not, but if I had I would give.

25 And now, if ye say this in your hearts ye remain guiltless, otherwise ye are condemned; and your condemnation is just for ye covet that which ye have not received.

King Benjamin's second point is now addressed. Those who have sufficient for their needs, but not enough to help others will be judged by their attitude (v. 24). Furthermore, their attitude must come from the heart [internal] and not in meaningless words. Moses taught

"Thou shalt not covet . . . anything that is thy neighbor's" (Exodus 20:21; Mosiah 13:24).

Mosiah 4:26–28 • How to Retain a Remission of Sins

> 26 And now, for the sake of these things which I have spoken unto you—that is, for the sake of retaining a remission of your sins from day to day, that ye may walk guiltless before God—I would that ye should impart of your substance to the poor, every man according to that which he hath, such as feeding the hungry, clothing the naked, visiting the sick and administering to their relief, both spiritually and temporally, according to their wants.
>
> 27 And see that all these things are done in wisdom and order; for it is not requisite that a man should run faster than he has strength. And again, it is expedient that he should be diligent, that thereby he might win the prize; therefore, all things must be done in order.
>
> 28 And I would that ye should remember, that whosoever among you borroweth of his neighbor should return the thing that he borroweth, according as he doth agree, or else thou shalt commit sin; and perhaps thou shalt cause thy neighbor to commit sin also.

King Benjamin's third point is how to retain a remission of sins. First, we must be helped both spiritually and temporally. Therefore, what is right in one situation, may not be so in another. The evils of the dole system were mentioned in chapter one of this work. Not only does the dole not help them spiritually, it harms them. From the beginning the ground was cursed "for thy sake" and "in the sweat of thy face shalt thou eat bread" (Genesis 3:17–19). In modern revelation, the Lord commanded "thou shalt not be idle; for he that is idle shall not eat the bread nor wear the garments of the laborer" (D&C 42:42). Therefore, King Benjamin directs, "see that all these things are done in wisdom and order" (Mosiah 4:27). The wisdom of providing for the needy is to examine the situation and provide opportunities for them to help themselves as the welfare program of the Church directs. For those who are unable to work the Lord has another plan:

15 And it is my purpose to provide for my saints, for all things are mine.

16 But it must needs be done in mine own way; and behold this is the way that I, the Lord, have decreed to provide for my saints, that the poor shall be exalted, in that the rich are made low.

17 For the earth is full, and there is enough and to spare; yea, I prepared all things, and have given unto the children of men to be agents unto themselves.

18 Therefore, if any man shall take of the abundance which I have made, and impart not his portion, according to the law of my gospel, unto the poor and the needy, he shall, with the wicked, lift up his eyes in hell, being in torment. [D&C 104:15–18]

The law of the gospel is the fast offering program. Every adult member of the Church is asked to fast for twenty-four hours and donate the cost of two meals to the Church for the care of the needy. The Bishop or local leader of the Church unit is to use that money for the needy. Excess funds are sent to Church headquarters to help in areas where the needs are not met by local contribution. A man should not be required to run faster than he has strength (Mosiah 4:27), but he should do what his strength allows him to do. Therefore the recipient may be asked to work part-time for the supplement received from the fast offering fund.

The order of the Church for helping the needy is self, family, and Church. Therefore, the motto of "help them to help themselves" should be followed. The father is responsible to provide for his family although circumstances may sometimes alter that role. This responsibility may extend to close relatives, but again should be done in wisdom. To neglect this responsibility is a sin. Paul wrote to Timothy: "But if any provide not for his own, and specially for those of his own house, he hath denied the faith, and is worse than an infidel" (1 Timothy 5:8).

When the law of consecration is lived in the future Zion society, those who are widowed or orphaned may draw upon the Bishop's storehouse.

1 Verily, thus saith the Lord, in addition to the laws of the church concerning women and children, those who belong to the church, who have lost their husbands or fathers:

2 Women have claim on their husbands for their maintenance, until their husbands are taken; and if they are not found transgressors they shall have fellowship in the church.

3 And if they are not faithful they shall not have fellowship in the church; yet they may remain upon their inheritances according to the laws of the land.

4 All children have claim upon their parents for their maintenance until they are of age.

5 And after that, they have claim upon the church, or in other words upon the Lord's storehouse, if their parents have not wherewith to give them inheritances.

6 And the storehouse shall be kept by the consecrations of the church; and widows and orphans shall be provided for, as also the poor. Amen. [D&C 83:1–6]

In the meantime, the Church Welfare Program is to provide for needy members as the circumstances and wisdom dictate.

For those who are not members of the Church but of another church, the government is called upon to help. However, this should not be a dole system, and the government would do well to follow the pattern established by the Church.

King Benjamin's advice on borrowing would fall under the same wisdom category. To borrow implies it will be returned. Not to return something borrowed causes ill feelings and mistrust among neighbors. It may even prompt some act of retaliation such as taking other things from the borrower as a means of payback. This act would be stealing, and so may cause the neighbor to sin (Mosiah 4:28).

Mosiah 4:29–30 • Watch your Thoughts, Words, and Deeds

29 And finally, I cannot tell you all the things whereby ye may

commit sin; for there are divers ways and means, even so many that I cannot number them.

30 But this much I can tell you, that if ye do not watch yourselves, and your thoughts, and your words, and your deeds, and observe the commandments of God, and continue in the faith of what ye have heard concerning the coming of our Lord, even unto the end of your lives, ye must perish. And now, O man, remember, and perish not.

Alma taught: "Our words will condemn us; yea, all our works will condemn us; . . . and our thoughts will also condemn us" (Alma 12:14). The Bible teaches likewise. Jesus said, "For by thy words thou shalt be justified, and by thy words thou shalt be condemned" (Matthew 12:37). He also said "blessed are the pure in heart [thoughts]" (Matthew 5:8); and "knowing their thoughts said, wherefore think ye evil in your hearts" (Matthew 9:4). The Proverbs teach, "For as a man thinketh in his heart, so is he" (Proverbs 23:7). Jesus taught that those who do evil deeds "shall go away into everlasting punishment, but the righteous [those who do good deeds] into life eternal" (Matthew 25:46). Therefore, King Benjamin's admonition to watch "your thoughts, and your words, and your deeds, and observe the commandments of God" (Mosiah 4:30) is timely for every dispensation.

Mosiah 5:1–5 • We Believe All the Words

1 And now, it came to pass that when king Benjamin had thus spoken to his people, he sent among them, desiring to know of his people if they believed the words which he had spoken unto them.

2 And they all cried with one voice, saying: Yea, we believe all the words which thou hast spoken unto us; and also, we know of their surety and truth, because of the Spirit of the Lord Omnipotent, which has wrought a mighty change in us, or in our hearts, that we have no more disposition to do evil, but to do good continually.

3 And we, ourselves, also, through the infinite goodness of God, and the manifestations of his Spirit, have great views of that which is to come; and were it expedient, we could prophesy of all things.

4 And it is the faith which we have had on the things which our king has spoken unto us that has brought us to this great knowledge,

whereby we do rejoice with such exceedingly great joy.

> 5 And we are willing to enter into a covenant with our God to do his will, and to be obedient to his commandments in all things that he shall command us, all the remainder of our days, that we may not bring upon ourselves a never-ending torment, as has been spoken by the angel, that we may not drink out of the cup of the wrath of God.

The response to King Benjamin's question about whether the people believed his words describe being born again. While there are other descriptions of born-again people, there are four characteristics in these verses that seem to be typical of the rebirth experience. The first characteristic is the Spirit of the Lord Omnipotent has wrought a mighty change in our hearts (v. 2). A mighty change suggests a complete turnaround, a totally different life style is the result. Alma asked the Zoramites if they had "experienced this mighty change of heart" (Alma 5:14). Alma the younger was changed from the pain of his sins to his soul being "filled with joy as exceeding as was his pains" (Alma 36:19–20), a mighty change.

The second characteristic is to have no more disposition to do evil, but to do good continually. This change of disposition was also because of the Spirit of the Lord (Mosiah 5:2). From the time of his rebirth, Alma "labored without ceasing, that [he] might bring souls unto repentance" (Alma 36:24). Enos, son of Jacob, after his wrestle "before God [rebirth]," felt "a desire for the welfare of my brethren, the Nephites; wherefore, I did pour out my soul unto God for them" and then "prayed unto [the Lord] with many long strugglings for my brethren, the Lamanites" (Enos 1:2, 9, 11). Both of these reborn people had a desire to do good.

The third characteristic of a born-again person is that by the manifestations of the Spirit, he or she has great views of what is to come (Mosiah 5:3). Compare this with what Jesus taught: "Except a man be born again, he cannot see the kingdom" (John 3:3). Another example: Alma the younger, who when born again, saw "God sitting upon his throne, surrounded with numberless concourses of angels" (Alma 36:22).

The fourth characteristic is a willingness to make a covenant with God to be obedient to his commandments (Mosiah 5:5). The covenant made with God is through the waters of baptism which is followed by the baptism of the Spirit. Jesus taught: "Except a man be born of water and the Spirit, he cannot enter into the kingdom of God" (John 3:5). Joseph Smith said, "Being born again, comes by the Spirit of God through ordinances [baptism of water and confirmation to receive the Holy Ghost]" (*TPJS*, 162). He also said, "It is one thing to see the kingdom of God, and another thing to enter into it. We must have a change of heart to see the kingdom of God, and subscribe the articles of adoption [covenants] to enter therein" (*TPJS*, 328). Alma the younger labored that others "might also be born of God, and be filled with the Holy Ghost" (Alma 36:24).

Although the record does not say that the people of King Benjamin were born again, the evidence given above should leave no doubt.

Mosiah 5:6–11 • The Covenant is a Righteous Covenant

6 And now, these are the words which king Benjamin desired of them; and therefore he said unto them: Ye have spoken the words that I desired; and the covenant which ye have made is a righteous covenant.

7 And now, because of the covenant which ye have made ye shall be called the children of Christ, his sons, and his daughters; for behold, this day he hath spiritually begotten you; for ye say that your hearts are changed through faith on his name; therefore, ye are born of him and have become his sons and his daughters.

8 And under this head ye are made free, and there is no other head whereby ye can be made free. There is no other name given whereby salvation cometh; therefore, I would that ye should take upon you the name of Christ, all you that have entered into the covenant with God that ye should be obedient unto the end of your lives.

9 And it shall come to pass that whosoever doeth this shall be found at the right hand of God, for he shall know the name by which

he is called; for he shall be called by the name of Christ.

10 And now it shall come to pass, that whosoever shall not take upon him the name of Christ must be called by some other name; therefore, he findeth himself on the left hand of God.

11 And I would that ye should remember also, that this is the name that I said I should give unto you that never should be blotted out, except it be through transgression; therefore, take heed that ye do not transgress, that the name be not blotted out of your hearts.

The born again experience gives you another father; you become a son or daughter of Jesus Christ through spiritual adoption (v. 7). He is the father of your eternal life. You have entered into a new family with Christ as your Father. Conditionally, you are free from sin, and also free to obtain salvation in the Celestial Kingdom. You are "in this strait and narrow path which leads to eternal life" (2 Nephi 31:18). The condition, however, is that you must be obedient to the commandments to the end of your mortal life (Mosiah 5:8).

King Benjamin repeats the declaration of the angel (3:17), "there is no other name given whereby salvation cometh" (v. 8). This is the name that King Benjamin promised to give them that could never be changed except by transgression (v. 11; see 1:11). Those who honor that name shall be found at the right hand of God, but those who do not will be called by another name and find himself on the left hand of God (vv. 9–10).

Mosiah 5:12–15 • The Name Written in Your Hearts

12 I say unto you, I would that ye should remember to retain the name written always in your hearts, that ye are not found on the left hand of God, but that ye hear and know the voice by which ye shall be called, and also, the name by which he shall call you.

13 For how knoweth a man the master whom he has not served, and who is a stranger unto him, and is far from the thoughts and intents of his heart?

14 And again, doth a man take an ass which belongeth to his

neighbor, and keep him? I say unto you, Nay; he will not even suffer that he shall feed among his flocks, but will drive him away, and cast him out. I say unto you, that even so shall it be among you if ye know not the name by which ye are called.

15 Therefore, I would that ye should be steadfast and immovable, always abounding in good works, that Christ, the Lord God Omnipotent, may seal you his, that you may be brought to heaven, that ye may have everlasting salvation and eternal life, through the wisdom, and power, and justice, and mercy of him who created all things, in heaven and in earth, who is God above all. Amen.

To retain Christ's name in your heart, you must know his voice. You will come to "know his voice" by serving him because he will direct you through his voice by revelation (vv. 12–13). Those who don't know his voice will be as animals in a strange flock (v. 14).

The born again experience does not guarantee eternal life. King Benjamin says "they should be steadfast and immovable, always abounding in good works, that Christ the Lord God Omnipotent, may seal you his" (v. 15). Those who are immovable as they "press forward with a steadfastness in Christ" (2 Nephi 31:20) will be sealed unto eternal life or have his calling and election made sure. In Peter's words, they have given "diligence to make [their] calling and election sure" (2 Peter 1:10). They are promised to be "brought to heaven" and have "everlasting salvation" (Mosiah 5:15).

Mosiah 6:1–5 • Mosiah Reigns in his Father's Stead

1 And now, king Benjamin thought it was expedient, after having finished speaking to the people, that he should take the names of all those who had entered into a covenant with God to keep his commandments.

2 And it came to pass that there was not one soul, except it were little children, but who had entered into the covenant and had taken upon them the name of Christ.

3 And again, it came to pass that when king Benjamin had made an end of all these things, and had consecrated his son Mosiah to be

a ruler and a king over his people, and had given him all the charges concerning the kingdom, and also had appointed priests to teach the people, that thereby they might hear and know the commandments of God, and to stir them up in remembrance of the oath which they had made, he dismissed the multitude, and they returned, every one, according to their families, to their own houses.

4 And Mosiah began to reign in his father's stead. And he began to reign in the thirtieth year of his age, making in the whole, about four hundred and seventy-six years from the time that Lehi left Jerusalem.

5 And king Benjamin lived three years and he died.

How old King Benjamin was when he delivered his last speech as king is not stated. He was either old or in poor health since his frame trembled "exceedingly while attempting to speak to [his people]" (2:30). Nevertheless, he spoke under the influence of the Spirit because they all fell to the earth after hearing him, and all except little children entered into the covenant and took upon them the name of Christ (v. 2). After he had strengthened his kingdom, he turned it over to his son Mosiah, as he had gathered them to do (v. 3; 1:10; 2:30). He lived three more years and passed to his eternal reward (v. 5).

Mosiah 6:6–7 • The First Three Years of Mosiah's Reign

6 And it came to pass that king Mosiah did walk in the ways of the Lord, and did observe his judgments and his statutes, and did keep his commandments in all things whatsoever he commanded him.

7 And king Mosiah did cause his people that they should till the earth. And he also, himself, did till the earth, that thereby he might not become burdensome to his people, that he might do according to that which his father had done in all things. And there was no contention among all his people for the space of three years.

All that needs be said about the first three years of Mosiah's reign is that he followed the great example of his father Benjamin. He began at age thirty, one hundred and twenty-four years before the coming of Christ.

SACRED WRITING

Preaching Which is Sacred:

Mosiah 4:4–30	King Benjamin to the multitude.
Mosiah 5:6–15	King Benjamin to the multitude.

Revelation Which is Great:

Mosiah 5:2–5	Knowledge given to King Benjamin's people.

Doctrines Learned:

Mosiah 4:3	A knowledge of one's remission of sins comes from a feeling of joy and peace of conscience.
Mosiah 4:11–12	To retain a remission of sins, one must remember the greatness of God and his own nothingness and call on the Lord daily, standing steadfast in the faith.
Mosiah 4:26	We are obligated to help the beggar both spiritually and temporally.
Mosiah 4:27	All things in helping the beggar must be done in wisdom and order and a man is not required to run faster than he has strength.
Mosiah 5:2	Through the Spirit of the Lord comes a mighty change of heart and no disposition to do evil but to do good continually.
Mosiah 5:3	The manifestation of the Spirit gives great views of things to come and enables man to prophesy.
Mosiah 5:7	Those who are born of Christ are spiritually begotten of him becoming his sons and daughters.
Mosiah 5:8	There is no other name whereby salvation comes except Christ's.
Mosiah 5:15	We must continue in good works after rebirth to be sealed by Christ.

General Authority Quotations

President Harold B. Lee • Mosiah 4:3

Brother Romney and I were sitting in the office one day and a young missionary came in. He was getting ready to go on a mission, and he had been interviewed in the usual way and had made confessions of certain transgressions of his youth. But he said to me, "I'm not satisfied by just having confessed. How can I know that I have been forgiven?" In other words, "How do I know that I am born again?" He felt he could not go. As we talked, Brother Romney said: "Son, do you remember what King Benjamin said? He was preaching to some who had been pricked in their hearts because of ' . . . their own carnal state, even to feel themselves less than the dust of the earth. And they all cried aloud with the voice, saying: O have mercy, and apply the atoning blood of Christ that we may receive forgiveness of our sins, and our hearts may be purified; for we believe in Jesus Christ, the Son of God, who created heaven and earth, and all things: who shall come down among the children of men. And it came to pass that after they had spoken these words the Spirit of the Lord came upon them, and they were filled with joy, having received a remission of their sins, and having a peace of conscience, because of their exceeding faith which they had in Jesus Christ . . . !" [Mosiah 4:2, 3]

Brother Romney said to him again, "My son, you wait and pray until you have the peace of conscience because of your faith in Jesus Christ's atonement; and you will know that your sins then have been forgiven." Except for that, as Elder Romney explained, any one of us is impoverished; and we are wondering in a fog until we have had that rebirth. . . .

Now let us confess it, all of us are "sinner anonymous." All of us have done things we ought not to have done, or we have neglected things we should have done; and every one of us has need for repentance. So let us not, as President Woodruff said, spend too much time confessing the other fellow's sins. Ours is the responsibility to find our own need for repentance. ["Teaching the Gospel to Inspire Christ-like Living," *Improvement Era,* June 1963, 222–23]

President Joseph Fielding Smith • Mosiah 4:3

But I would like to call your attention, particularly, to the words of King Benjamin when he met with the people of the Church in a general assembly. You know he built a great tower from which he spoke and his discourse was so powerful and made such an impression upon the great multitude assembled that that generation remained true and faithful all the days of their lives. So it must have been a very powerful presentation. I want to call your attention to one or two things in that great discourse. First let me state that he put the people under a covenant, and the covenant was that they would be true and faithful to the Son of God—and this was at least 124 years before the birth of our Savior. . . .

So powerful was that discourse that these people never forgot it. ["The Fatherhood of Christ," Address to Seminary and Institute faculty, BYU, Provo, Utah, July 17, 1962]

Elder Marion G. Romney • Mosiah 4–5

Webster says the very word "convert" means "to turn from one belief or course to another." That "conversion" is "a spiritual and moral *change* attending a *change* of belief with conviction." As used in the scriptures, "converted" generally implies no merely mental acceptance of Jesus and his teachings but also a motivating faith in him and in his gospel—a faith which works a transformation, an actual *change* in one's understanding of life's meaning and in his allegiance to God—in interest, in thought, and in conduct. While conversion may be accomplished in stages, one is not really converted in the full sense of the term unless and until he is at heart a new person. "Born again" is the scriptural term. . . .

There is a striking example of the change wrought by conversion in Mormon's account of King Benjamin's farewell address. This sermon was so powerful that as Benjamin delivered it the multitude fell to the earth; [Conference Report, Oct. 1963, 23]

President Joseph Fielding Smith • Mosiah 5:7

The Son of God has a perfect right to call us his children, spiritually begotten, and we have a perfect right to look on him as our father who spiritually begot us. [Conference Report, Oct. 1962, 21]

Elder Ezra Taft Benson • Mosiah 4:11–12

Christ is God the Son and possesses every virtue in its perfection. Therefore, the only measure of true greatness is how close a man can become like Jesus. That man is greatest who is most like Christ, and those who love him most will be most like him.

How, then, does a man imitate God, follow his steps, and walk as he walked, which we are commanded to do? We must study the life of Christ, learn his commandments, and do them. God has promised that to follow this course will lead a man to an abundant life and a fullness of joy and the peace and rest which those who are heavy-burdened long for. To learn of Christ necessitates the study of the scriptures and the testimonies of those who know him. We come to know him through prayer and the inspiration and revelation that God has promised to those who keep his commandments. [CR, Oct. 1972, 53]

Challenges to Eternal Life:

1. Based upon Mosiah 4:10, see that you do the things that you believe in.
2. Call upon the Lord daily, and stand steadfast in the faith of that which is to come, thus retaining a remission of your sins (Mosiah 4:11–12).
3. Choose one of the things that is just and true as outlined between Mosiah 4:13–30 and endeavor to improve your attitude and behavior in that one aspect.
4. Choose another challenge or message from this reading and incorporate it into your life.

Chapter Eight

Ammon and His Men
Find Lehi-Nephi

Mosiah 7–8

H istorical setting:

Mosiah 7:1–8 • After Three Years

1 And now, it came to pass that after king Mosiah had had continual peace for the space of three years, he was desirous to know concerning the people who went up to dwell in the land of Lehi-Nephi, or in the city of Lehi-Nephi; for his people had heard nothing from them from the time they left the land of Zarahemla; therefore, they wearied him with their teasings.

2 And it came to pass that king Mosiah granted that sixteen of their strong men might go up to the land of Lehi-Nephi, to inquire concerning their brethren.

3 And it came to pass that on the morrow they started to go up, having with them one Ammon, he being a strong and mighty man, and a descendant of Zarahemla; and he was also their leader.

4 And now, they knew not the course they should travel in the wilderness to go up to the land of Lehi-Nephi; therefore they wandered many days in the wilderness, even forty days did they wander.

5 And when they had wandered forty days they came to a hill, which is north of the land of Shilom, and there they pitched their tents.

6 And Ammon took three of his brethren, and their names were Amaleki, Helam, and Hem, and they went down into the land of Nephi.

7 And behold, they met the king of the people who were in the land of Nephi, and in the land of Shilom; and they were surrounded by the king's guard, and were taken, and were bound, and were committed to prison.

8 And it came to pass when they had been in prison two days they were again brought before the king, and their bands were loosed; and they stood before the king, and were permitted, or rather commanded, that they should answer the questions which he should ask them.

The above account of the sixteen strong men finding the Land of Lehi-Nephi is self explanatory. The events of these two chapters all take place in just over six weeks.

Precepts of This Reading:

But if ye will turn to the Lord with full purpose of heart, and put your trust in him, and serve him with all diligence of mind, if ye do this, he will, according to his own will and pleasure, deliver you out of bondage. [Mosiah 7:33]

The formula for being delivered out of bondage given in this precept will be a theme through the next sixteen chapters of Mosiah and several of the following chapters of this work. An outline of Mosiah 7–8 follows as a preparation for a deeper study.

OUTLINE • MOSIAH 7–8

➢ Mosiah 7:1–7   After three years of continual peace, King Mosiah was desirous to know concerning those who went to dwell in the land of Lehi-Nephi.

a. The people had heard nothing from them since they left the land of Zarahemla, and they wearied the king with their teasing (v. 1).

b. He granted that sixteen strong men might go to the land of Lehi-Nephi to inquire of their brethren (vv. 2–4).

1. They were led by Ammon, a strong and mighty descendant of Zarahemla.

2. They knew not the way and wandered forty days in the wilderness.

c. They came to a hill north of the land of Shilom and pitched their tents (v. 5).

d. Ammon took Amaleki, Helam, and Hem down to the land of Nephi (vv. 6–7).

1. They met the king of the people in the land of Nephi and Shilom.

2. They were surrounded by his guards, were bound and committed to prison.

➤ 7:8–17 After two days they were taken before Limhi, the king. Their bonds were loosed and they were commanded to answer the king's questions.

a. Limhi identified himself as the son of Noah, son of Zeniff who came out of the land of Zarahemla and was made king by the voice of the people (v. 9).

b. He asked why Ammon and his brethren were so bold as to come near the walls when he was outside the city with his guards. He has preserved them rather than put them to death so he could inquire of them (vv. 10–11).

c. Ammon bowed and thanked the king for being permitted to speak (vv. 12–13).

1. If the king had known who he was he would not have had him bound.

2. He is Ammon, a descendant of Zarahemla, come to inquire of Zeniff and those who left.

d. Limhi was exceedingly glad to know the people in Zarahemla are yet alive (vv. 14–16).

1. His people will also rejoice for they are in bondage to the Lamanites.

2. Our brethren (in Zarahemla) will deliver us from the Lamanites and we will be their slaves.

        3.   It is better to be slaves to the Nephites than to pay tribute to the Lamanites.

    e.   Limhi commanded his guards to bring in their brethren into the city that they might eat, drink, and rest (v. 16).

    f.   On the morrow Limhi sent a proclamation for his people to gather to the temple and hear the words he would speak (v. 17).

➤ 7:18–33   The words Limhi spoke after the people gathered

    a.   He comforted his people that the time soon comes when they will not be in subjection to their enemies (v. 18).

    b.   He admonished them to put their trust in the God of Abraham, Isaac, and Jacob (vv. 19–21).

        1.   He delivered the children out of Egypt and provided great miracles.

        2.   He delivered our fathers out of Jerusalem and preserved us until now.

        3.   Our iniquities and abominations had brought us into bondage.

    c.   Zeniff was overzealous to inherit the land and was deceived by the Lamanite king to bring us into bondage (vv. 21–24).

        1.   Their afflictions were great and grievous to be borne.

        2.   Many of their brethren had been slain and blood spilt in vain because of iniquity.

    d.   If they had not fallen into transgression the Lord would not have allowed this evil to come (vv. 25–28).

        1.   Contentions arose and they shed blood among themselves.

        2.   A prophet of the Lord have they slain because he told them of their wickedness, and even that Christ would come.

        3.   He said that Christ was God, the Father of all things, and would take upon him the image of man.

4. Man was created in the image of God, and God would come down and take upon him flesh and blood.

5. They put the prophet to death and did many more things that brought the wrath of God upon them.

e. The Lord had said (concerning bondage) (vv. 29–32):

1. In the day of transgression they will not prosper and their doings will be a stumbling block.

2. If my people sow filthiness they will reap the chaff and its effect will be poison.

3. If my people sow filthiness they will reap the east wind, which brings immediate destruction.

4. The promise of the Lord was fulfilled and the people are smitten and afflicted.

f. If they turn to the Lord with full purpose of heart, trust in him, and serve him, he will, according to his own will and pleasure, deliver them (v. 33).

➤ 8:1–3   Limhi spoke and did many more things which are not written.

a. He told his people all things concerning their brethren in Zarahemla (v. 1).

b. He had Ammon rehearse all that had happened since Zeniff left Zarahemla (v. 2).

c. Ammon rehearsed the last words of King Benjamin to Limhi's people (v. 3).

➤ 8:4–12   Limhi dismissed the people and caused them to return to their homes and Limhi visited with Ammon personally.

a. He had Ammon read the records of his people from the time they left Zarahemla (v. 5).

b. He asked Ammon if he could interpret languages, which he could not. Limhi then told him (vv. 6–12):

1. Forty-three men journeyed into the wilderness to find the land of Zarahemla, got lost and discovered a land among many waters covered with bones of men and beast and ruins of buildings indicating a

numerous host of people.

2. They brought back 24 plates of pure gold filled with engravings, large breast plates of brass and copper, and swords that are rusted and partially perished.

3. No one was able to translate the plates.

4. He asked, do you know of anyone who can translate these and give us a knowledge of this people?

c. Ammon told him of a man who has an instrument called interpreters into which he may look and translate all records of ancient date (vv. 13–14).

1. It is a gift from God.

2. No man can look into them unless he is commanded.

3. Whoso is commanded is called seer.

4. The king in the land of Zarahemla is a man who has been commanded to do these things.

d. King Limhi stated that a seer is greater than a prophet, and Ammon replied that a seer is a revelator and a prophet (vv. 15–18).

1. A gift which is greater can no man have except he possess the power of God, which no man can.

2. A seer can know of things which are past, and are yet to come, and by them are secret things, hidden things, and all things which otherwise would not be known, be made known.

3. God had provided a means whereby man, through faith, can work mighty miracles to benefit his fellow man.

e. King Limhi rejoiced exceedingly and gave thanks to God (vv. 19–21).

1. A great mystery is on these plates and the interpreters have been prepared to unfold these mysteries.

2. How marvelous are the works of the Lord and how blind and impenetrable are the understandings of men who will not seek wisdom.

NOTES AND COMMENTARY

Introduction: What is bondage? The dictionary relates it to servitude, slavery, or compulsion. Most people would think only of physical bondage, but bondage may be mental or social and in various aspects of all three of these areas. What is taught in these chapters is applicable to all kinds of bondage.

Mosiah 7:9–16 • Limhi and Ammon Identified

9 And he said unto them: Behold, I am Limhi, the son of Noah, who was the son of Zeniff, who came up out of the land of Zarahemla to inherit this land, which was the land of their fathers, who was made a king by the voice of the people.

10 And now, I desire to know the cause whereby ye were so bold as to come near the walls of the city, when I, myself, was with my guards without the gate?

11 And now, for this cause have I suffered that ye should be preserved, that I might inquire of you, or else I should have caused that my guards should have put you to death. Ye are permitted to speak.

12 And now, when Ammon saw that he was permitted to speak, he went forth and bowed himself before the king; and rising again he said: O king, I am very thankful before God this day that I am yet alive, and am permitted to speak; and I will endeavor to speak with boldness;

13 For I am assured that if ye had known me ye would not have suffered that I should have worn these bands. For I am Ammon, and am a descendant of Zarahemla, and have come up out of the land of Zarahemla to inquire concerning our brethren, whom Zeniff brought up out of that land.

14 And now, it came to pass that after Limhi had heard the words of Ammon, he was exceedingly glad, and said: Now, I know of a surety that my brethren who were in the land of Zarahemla are yet alive. And now, I will rejoice; and on the morrow I will cause that my people shall rejoice also.

15 For behold, we are in bondage to the Lamanites, and are taxed

with a tax which is grievous to be borne. And now, behold, our brethren will deliver us out of our bondage, or out of the hands of the Lamanites, and we will be their slaves; for it is better that we be slaves to the Nephites than to pay tribute to the king of the Lamanites.

16 And now, king Limhi commanded his guards that they should no more bind Ammon nor his brethren, but caused that they should go to the hill which was north of Shilom, and bring their brethren into the city, that thereby they might eat, and drink, and rest themselves from the labors of their journey; for they had suffered many things; they had suffered hunger, thirst, and fatigue.

Limhi is of the third generation of the people who earlier had left the land of Zarahemla. His being king had come from patriarchal descent, his grandfather having been chosen by the voice of the people (v. 9). A knowledge of the first two generations is given in the following chapters of Mosiah. Limhi's reason for preserving Ammon in his boldness (v. 11), suggests that death to intruders was common. If this supposition is correct, it was probably because of contention between Limhi's people and the Lamanites as will also be shown in the next chapters.

Limhi's great joy was more than learning of the people in Zarahemla being alive (vv. 13–14). As implied in the subsequent speech to his people, it was probably an answer to the king's prayers (v. 33). The king's willingness to be in bondage to the Nephites rather than the Lamanites reminds us of Jesus' parable of the prodigal son (Luke 15:11–32).

Although the message of the parable is somewhat different, both Limhi and the wayward son recognized they were better off before transgression occurred (Mosiah 7:15). The bringing of the twelve other associates of Ammon was mentioned in the historical setting.

Mosiah 7:17–20 • Gathers the People to the Temple

17 And now, it came to pass on the morrow that king Limhi sent

a proclamation among all his people, that thereby they might gather themselves together to the temple, to hear the words which he should speak unto them.

18 And it came to pass that when they had gathered themselves together that he spake unto them in this wise, saying: O ye, my people, lift up your heads and be comforted; for behold, the time is at hand, or is not far distant, when we shall no longer be in subjection to our enemies, notwithstanding our many strugglings, which have been in vain; yet I trust there remaineth an effectual struggle to be made.

19 Therefore, lift up your heads, and rejoice, and put your trust in God, in that God who was the God of Abraham, and Isaac, and Jacob; and also, that God who brought the children of Israel out of the land of Egypt, and caused that they should walk through the Red Sea on dry ground, and fed them with manna that they might not perish in the wilderness; and many more things did he do for them.

20 And again, that same God has brought our fathers out of the land of Jerusalem, and has kept and preserved his people even until now; and behold, it is because of our iniquities and abominations that he has brought us into bondage.

In inviting his people to put their trust in God, Limhi combines four Old Testament incidents, which had been recorded earlier in the brass plates (v. 19). The God of Abraham, Isaac, and Jacob is Jesus Christ (see Exodus 3:14–15; John 8:58; 1 Nephi 19:10). Christ is the Lord who led the children of Israel out of Egypt (Exodus 13:18; 1 Nephi 5:15; 1 Nephi 17:23–25). Moses was commanded of the Lord to part the Red Sea and Israel was able to walk through the Red Sea on dry ground (Exodus 14:21–22; 1 Nephi 4:2; 17:26–27). The Israelites were fed manna in the wilderness that preserved them (Exodus 16:14–15; 1 Nephi 17:28). Some of the many other things that the Lord did for Israel that Limhi does not specify, were mentioned earlier in the Book of Mormon. Moses smote the rock and water came out to quench their thirst (Exodus 17:6; 1 Nephi 17:29). The Lord led them by day [in a cloud], and by night [in a pillar of fire] (Exodus 13:21–22; 1 Nephi 17:30). He destroyed the wicked according to his word, three thousand in one day (Exodus 32:28). He swallowed up in the earth the wicked who followed Korah and two hundred and fifty incense burners on another day (Numbers 16:32–35). Fourteen thousand and seven hundred were destroyed by a plague because of murmuring against Moses (Numbers 16:49). Nephi testified "that according to his word he did destroy them" (1 Nephi 17:31). He also testified that the Lord "sent fiery serpents among them; and after they were bitten, he prepared a way that they might be healed" (1 Nephi 17:41; see Numbers 21:8–9). Indeed, one of the major purposes of the Book of Mormon is "proving to the world that the holy scriptures are true" (D&C 20:11); or that "These last records [the Book of Mormon], which [Nephi] has seen among the Gentiles, shall establish the truth of the first [the Bible]" (1 Nephi 13:40). Limhi also acknowledged the hand of the Lord in bringing his forefathers out of Jerusalem and preserving them in this land (Mosiah 7:20).

Mosiah 7:21–28 • The Cause of Bondage

21 And ye all are witnesses this day, that Zeniff, who was made king over this people, he being over-zealous to inherit the land of his fathers, therefore being deceived by the cunning and craftiness of king Laman, who having entered into a treaty with king Zeniff, and having yielded up into his hands the possessions of a part of the land, or even the city of Lehi-Nephi, and the city of Shilom; and the land round about—

22 And all this he did, for the sole purpose of bringing this people into subjection or into bondage. And behold, we at this time do pay tribute to the king of the Lamanites, to the amount of one half of our corn, and our barley, and even all our grain of every kind, and one half of the increase of our flocks and our herds; and even one half of all we have or possess the king of the Lamanites doth exact of us, or our lives.

23 And now, is not this grievous to be borne? And is not this, our affliction, great? Now behold, how great reason we have to mourn.

24 Yea, I say unto you, great are the reasons which we have to mourn; for behold how many of our brethren have been slain, and their blood has been spilt in vain, and all because of iniquity.

25 For if this people had not fallen into transgression the Lord would not have suffered that this great evil should come upon them. But behold, they would not hearken unto his words; but there arose contentions among them, even so much that they did shed blood among themselves.

26 And a prophet of the Lord have they slain; yea, a chosen man of God, who told them of their wickedness and abominations, and prophesied of many things which are to come, yea, even the coming of Christ.

27 And because he said unto them that Christ was the God, the Father of all things, and said that he should take upon him the image of man, and it should be the image after which man was created in the beginning; or in other words, he said that man was created after the image of God, and that God should come down among the children of men, and take upon him flesh and blood, and go forth upon the face of the earth—

28 And now, because he said this, they did put him to death; and many more things did they do which brought down the wrath of God upon them. Therefore, who wondereth that they are in bondage, and that they are smitten with sore afflictions?

King Limhi cites three reasons for his people being in bondage to the Lamanites. The first reason was Zeniff's [Limhi's grandfather] being overzealous to inherit the land of his father (v. 21). His enthusiasm may be attributed to his knowledge that the land was the first major settlement of Nephi's people after they separated from Laman and Lemuel (2 Nephi 5:8). It was called by Zeniff "the land of Nephi, or the land of our fathers' first inheritance" (Mosiah 9:1). The admonition of King Benjamin may be applicable here: "it is not requisite that a man should run faster than he has strength" (Mosiah 4:27). It is acknowledged that he was referring to physical efforts, but the same is true of intellectual or mental strength. The Lord has cautioned:

8 But, behold, I say unto you, that you must study it out in your mind; then you must ask me if it be right, and if it is right I will cause that your bosom shall burn within you; therefore, you shall feel that it is right.

9 But if it be not right you shall have no such feelings, but you shall have a stupor of thought that shall cause you to forget the thing which is wrong; therefore, you cannot write that which is sacred save it be given you from me. [D&C 9:8–9]

Had Zeniff studied out the Lamanite situation, the Nephites would probably not be paying tribute of one half of all their goods to the Lamanites, nor would many of their brethren have been slain. More will be said of tribute or taxation in a later chapter.

The second reason is mentioned twice; once in the previous verses discussed, "because of our iniquities and abomination" (Mosiah 7:20), and "if this people had not fallen into transgression the Lord would not have suffered [allowed] that this great evil should come upon them." There was contention, even murder, among them (v. 25). The devil "is the father of contention, and he stirreth up the hearts of men to contend, one with another" (3 Nephi 11:29). Great persecutions came upon the Latter-day Saints for the same reason.

6 Behold, I say unto you, there were jarrings, and contentions, and envyings, and strifes, and lustful and covetous desires among them; therefore by these things they polluted their inheritances.

7 They were slow to hearken unto the voice of the Lord their God; therefore, the Lord their God is slow to hearken unto their prayers, to answer them in the day of their trouble. [D&C 101:6–7]

Six months later the redemption of Zion in Jackson County, Missouri was postponed for a little season in the Lord's time "in consequence of transgression of my people" (D&C 101:9).

2 Behold, I say unto you, were it not for the transgressions of my people, speaking concerning the church and not individuals, they might have been redeemed even now.

3 But behold, they have not learned to be obedient to the things which I required at their hands, but are full of all manner of evil, and do not impart of their substance, as becometh saints, to the poor and afflicted among them;

4 And are not united according to the union required by the law of the celestial kingdom;

5 And Zion cannot be built up unless it is by the principles of the law of the celestial kingdom; otherwise I cannot receive her unto myself.

6 And my people must needs be chastened until they learn obedience, if it must needs be, by the things which they suffer. [D&C 105:2–6]

I, the Lord, am bound when ye do what I say; but when ye do not what I say, ye have no promise. [D&C 82:10]

The third reason for bondage to the Lamanites was an extension of the second reason. They had contented and even "shed blood among them" (v. 25), and that included Abinadi the prophet of the Lord, whom we will be introduced to in Mosiah chapter 11 and learn the significance of his martyrdom in Mosiah chapter 17.

Abinadi prophesied of the coming of Christ, and said he was "the God, the Father of all things." He also said he would take upon him the image of man "the image after which man was created in the beginning" and that God [Christ] should come down among the children of men, and take upon him flesh and blood" (v. 27). Almost all of these doctrinal points were made in King Benjamin's great sermon, part of which he was quoting an angel of God (Mosiah 3). It is important to note that the Prophet Joseph Smith was martyred for the same reason—teaching the truth about God, which he learned in "the First Vision."

"It no sooner appeared than I found myself delivered from the enemy which held me bound. When the light rested upon me I saw two Personages, whose brightness and glory defy all description, standing above me in the air. One of them spake unto me, calling me by name and said, pointing to the other—This is My Beloved Son. Hear Him!" [Joseph Smith—History 1:17]

He taught that:

" . . . God himself was once as we are now, and is an exalted man, and sits enthroned in yonder heavens! That is the great secret. If the veil were rent today, and the great God who holds this world in its orbit, and who upholds all worlds and all things by his power, was to make himself visible, —I say, if you were to see him today, you would see him like a man in form—like yourselves in all the person, image, and very form as a man; for Adam was created in the very fashion, image and likeness of God, and received instruction from, and walked, talked and conversed with him, as one man talks and communes with another."

". . . These are incomprehensible ideas to some, but they are simple. It is the first principle of the Gospel to know for a certainty the Character of God, and to know that we may converse with him as one man converse with another, and that he was once a man like us; yea, that God himself, the Father of us all, dwelt on an earth, the same as Jesus Christ himself did; and I will show it from the Bible." [*TPJS*, 345–346]

The Book of Mormon, which the Lord brought forth through Joseph, teaches the fatherhood of Christ (see Mosiah 5:7; 15:1–2; Alma 11:38–40). For these doctrines, Latter-day Saints are accused of not being Christians. As always, the truth will prevail, in the end.

Mosiah 7:29–31 • The Results of Bondage

29 For behold, the Lord hath said: I will not succor my people in the day of their transgression; but I will hedge up their ways that they prosper not; and their doings shall be as a stumbling block before them.

30 And again, he saith: If my people shall sow filthiness they shall reap the chaff thereof in the whirlwind; and the effect thereof is poison.

31 And again he saith: If my people shall sow filthiness they shall reap the east wind, which bringeth immediate destruction.

Limhi quotes three scriptures concerning what the Lord said he would do to people who fall into bondage because of iniquities and abominations. He is apparently quoting things originally recorded on the plates of brass, but that are not identifiable in the present Old Testament. However, the same concepts are taught therein.

The message of the first quote (v. 29) is that the people will not prosper. Their lack of success is because the Lord will not bless [succor] them, and their own efforts, causing them to stumble. The closest present-day biblical quote is from Zechariah (not the prophet of the book by that name; a priest in the days of Joash, king of Judah in the eight hundreds B.C.) who, under the inspiration of the Spirit of God said: "Thus saith God, why transgress ye the commandments of the Lord, that ye cannot prosper? Because ye have forsaken the Lord, he hath also forsaken you" (2 Chronicles 24:20). Jeremiah, the prophet at the time of Lehi's leaving Jerusalem in 600 B.C. also warned: "Therefore thus saith the LORD, Behold, I will lay stumblingblocks before this people, and the fathers and the sons together shall fall upon them; the neighbour and his friend shall perish" (Jeremiah 6:21).

The message of the second quote (Mosiah 7:30) is that people will reap as they sow. Paul, in the New Testament, is known for the same teaching. "Be not deceived; God is not mocked: for whatsoever a man soweth, that shall he also reap. For he that soweth to his flesh shall of the flesh reap corruption; but he that soweth to the Spirit shall of the Spirit reap life everlasting" (Galatians 6:7–8). Paul is probably quoting from the Old Testament, and possibly from the same source as Limhi. The closest present-day Old Testament quote refers to the tribes of northern Israel being taken into Assyria and dispersed among the Gentiles.

> 7 For they have sown the wind, and they shall reap the whirlwind: it hath no stalk: the bud shall yield no meal: if so be it yield, the strangers shall swallow it up.
>
> 8 Israel is swallowed up: now shall they be among the Gentiles as a vessel wherein *is* no pleasure.
>
> 9 For they are gone up to Assyria, a wild ass alone by himself: Ephraim hath hired lovers. [Hosea 8:7–9]

The text suggests Hosea may be quoting from an earlier source. The Lord uses the same symbolism in modern revelation several times in the Doctrine and Covenants.

3 Behold, the field is white already to harvest; therefore, whoso desireth to reap, let him thrust in his sickle with his might, and reap while the day lasts, that he may treasure up for his soul everlasting salvation in the kingdom of God.

4 Yea, whosoever will thrust in his sickle and reap, the same is called of God.

33 Fear not to do good, my sons, for whatsoever ye sow, that shall ye also reap; therefore, if ye sow good ye shall also reap good for your reward. [D&C 6:3–4, 33; see also D&C 11:3–4, 27; 12:3–4; 14:3–4]

The ancient method of harvesting was to cut and stack the grain shocks on the threshing floor, a large level rock on the surface of the earth. The animals would then walk on the shocks to shell the grain. After removing the straw, there would be a pile of grain and chaff, which was the smaller non-grain fragments. Workers would then throw the grain and chaff into the air (winnowing) and the wind would blow away the chaff leaving the grain on the ground to be sacked or stored in bins. A whirlwind would sometime come up and return the chaff into the faces of the workers causing great discomfort. Because of the filthiness that caused the bondage, the analogy is that it would be blown back into the midst of the people and would poison their culture collectively.

The third message (Mosiah 7:31) resulting from the iniquities causing bondage is that the Lord withdraws his blessings through the east wind. In the Middle East, the west wind brings in the life-giving rain from the Mediterranean Sea. The east wind comes off of the desert and brings the heat and drought of destruction or crop failure. While there are no exact quotes like Limhi's (v. 31) in the present Old Testament, the east wind is used in the same context. Joseph, who was sold into Egypt, interpreted the Pharaoh's dream of "seven ears, withered, thin, and blasted with the east wind" as seven years of famine (Genesis 41:23, 27). The Lord, through Jeremiah, said: "I will scatter them as with an east wind before the enemy" (Jeremiah 18:17). The wrath of God (Mosiah 7:28) includes no prosperity, a poisonous environment, and destructive weather conditions mainly because of the withdrawal of his Spirit leaving the people in their natural state of fallen man.

Mosiah 7:32–33 • How to Get Out of Bondage

> 32 And now, behold, the promise of the Lord is fulfilled, and ye are smitten and afflicted.
>
> 33 But if ye will turn to the Lord with full purpose of heart, and put your trust in him, and serve him with all diligence of mind, if ye do this, he will, according to his own will and pleasure, deliver you out of bondage.

Limhi's people were in bondage because of the reasons just given. Their challenge was to get out. He saw Ammon and his companions as an avenue of escape (v. 15), but as a wise leader, he recognizes that they must do their part. He outlines three things for them to do.

First, they must turn to the Lord with full purpose of heart and trust in him (v. 33). No half-hearted effort would suffice. To turn to God is to seek his help in doing things beyond our natural capacity to perform. These are called miracles. Earlier, he had identified God as the God of Abraham, Isaac, and Jacob and cited the great miracles the Lord had done for Israel in bringing them out of bondage in Egypt (v. 19 discussed above). Knowing of or reminding them of these miracles would build their trust in the Lord. As Nephi had taught his unbelieving brothers, "if the Lord has such great power, and has wrought so many miracles among the children of men, how is it he cannot instruct me" (1 Nephi 17:51).

The second thing they must do is serve God in all diligence of mind (Mosiah 7:33). To serve him is to keep his commandments and do his will (see Mosiah 2:17–18). To serve with all diligence of mind is to have an eye single to the glory of God. Such diligence will show you how to serve (see D&C 88:67).

The third thing they must do is to have patience. The people will be delivered according to the Lord's own will and pleasure. He knows what must be done before their delivery from bondage, and when is the best time for that delivery to occur in order to teach his people how to prevent future bondage.

There are two examples of this formula in the following chapters of Mosiah for getting a people out of bondage. Both Limhi's people and Alma's people were delivered through this formula. Those will be discussed later.

Mosiah 8:1–5 • The Past Reviewed

1 And it came to pass that after king Limhi had made an end of speaking to his people, for he spake many things unto them and only a few of them have I written in this book, he told his people all the things concerning their brethren who were in the land of Zarahemla.

2 And he caused that Ammon should stand up before the multitude, and rehearse unto them all that had happened unto their brethren from the time that Zeniff went up out of the land even until the time that he himself came up out of the land.

3 And he also rehearsed unto them the last words which king Benjamin had taught them, and explained them to the people of king Limhi, so that they might understand all the words which he spake.

4 And it came to pass that after he had done all this, that king Limhi dismissed the multitude, and caused that they should return every one unto his own house.

5 And it came to pass that he caused that the plates which contained the record of his people from the time that they left the land of Zarahemla, should be brought before Ammon, that he might read them.

Ammon's purpose in finding Limhi's people was to know what had happened to them since they left Zarahemla (7:1). Fortunately they kept a record of their sojourn and Ammon was able to read it (v. 5). We will also be able to review an abridgment of this record in the following chapters. Limhi was exceedingly glad to learn that the people in Zarahemla were alive and well (7:14), and he undoubtedly wanted to know the condition of their relatives and friends. Ammon's teaching of King Benjamin's last words (v. 3) would certainly have been an incentive for Limhi and his people to seek their freedom.

Mosiah 8:6–12 • Twenty-four Plates of Pure Gold

6 Now, as soon as Ammon had read the record, the king inquired of him to know if he could interpret languages, and Ammon told him that he could not.

7 And the king said unto him: Being grieved for the afflictions of my people, I caused that forty and three of my people should take a journey into the wilderness, that thereby they might find the land of Zarahemla, that we might appeal unto our brethren to deliver us out of bondage.

8 And they were lost in the wilderness for the space of many days, yet they were diligent, and found not the land of Zarahemla but returned to this land, having traveled in a land among many waters, having discovered a land which was covered with bones of men, and of beasts, and was also covered with ruins of buildings of every kind, having discovered a land which had been peopled with a people who were as numerous as the hosts of Israel.

9 And for a testimony that the things that they had said are true they have brought twenty-four plates which are filled with engravings, and they are of pure gold.

10 And behold, also, they have brought breastplates, which are large, and they are of brass and of copper, and are perfectly sound.

11 And again, they have brought swords, the hilts thereof have perished, and the blades thereof were cankered with rust; and there is no one in the land that is able to interpret the language or the engravings that are on the plates. Therefore I said unto thee: Canst thou translate?

12 And I say unto thee again: Knowest thou of any one that can translate? For I am desirous that these records should be translated into our language; for, perhaps, they will give us a knowledge of a remnant of the people who have been destroyed, from whence these records came; or, perhaps, they will give us a knowledge of this very

people who have been destroyed; and I am desirous to know the cause of their destruction.

Limhi's desire to have the twenty-four plates of pure gold interpreted or translated was fulfilled by Mosiah after they were delivered out of bondage to Zarahemla (see Mosiah 28:17). The people identified in the plates were the Jaredites, as known in the Book of Mormon (see Moroni 9:23). Moroni gives us a brief abridgment of these records later, called the book of Ether in the Book of Mormon. We will not discuss them in any detail here.

The land where the bones, plates, and weapon remains were discovered was north of Zarahemla. The forty-three men sent out by Limhi (Mosiah 8:7) apparently passed their destination and went farther north. How far north they went is not known, but a land to the north that had "many waters" is mentioned several times in the Book of Mormon (see Alma 50:29; Helaman 3:3–4; Mormon 6:4). (A correlation with modern geography will not be made here.)

Mosiah 8:13–18 • A Seer, a Revelator, and a Prophet

13 Now Ammon said unto him: I can assuredly tell thee, O king, of a man that can translate the records; for he has wherewith that he can look, and translate all records that are of ancient date; and it is a gift from God. And the things are called interpreters, and no man can look in them except he be commanded, lest he should look for that he ought not and he should perish. And whosoever is commanded to look in them, the same is called seer.

14 And behold, the king of the people who are in the land of Zarahemla is the man that is commanded to do these things, and who has this high gift from God.

15 And the king said that a seer is greater than a prophet.

16 And Ammon said that a seer is a revelator and a prophet also; and a gift which is greater can no man have, except he should possess the power of God, which no man can; yet a man may have great power given him from God.

17 But a seer can know of things which are past, and also of things which are to come, and by them shall all things be revealed, or, rather, shall secret things be made manifest, and hidden things shall come to light, and things which are not known shall be made known by them, and also things shall be made known by them which otherwise could not be known.

18 Thus God has provided a means that man, through faith, might work mighty miracles; therefore he becometh a great benefit to his fellow beings.

The definition of a seer given by Ammon is unique to the Book of Mormon. It must be noted that the statement made by King Limhi, "a seer is greater than a prophet" (v. 15) was corrected by Ammon. He said, "a seer is a revelator and a prophet also" (v. 16). Thus, each word designates a different role. A seer is a one who is commanded of God to look into the interpreters or Urim and Thummim. When the records were taken back to Zarahemla they were translated by King Mosiah. It is apparently Mormon, who comments as he abridges, that the interpreters were prepared from the beginning, "For the purposes of interpreting languages, and whosoever has these things is called seer, after the manner of old time" (Mosiah 28:14–16). An editorial insert from the book of Samuel in the Bible states: "(Beforetime in Israel, when a man went to enquire of God, thus he spake, Come, and let us go to the seer: for *he that is* now *called* a Prophet was beforetime called a Seer)" (1 Samuel 9:9).

There is ample evidence of the Urim and Thummim or the interpreters being used in the days of Aaron through Samuel, which had been lost by the time of Ezra and Nehemiah. Those who polluted the priesthood were not to "eat of the most holy things, till there stood up a priest with Urim and Thummim" (Ezra 2:62–63; Nehemiah 7:64–65). Therefore, the interpreters had been lost, and the editorial insert in Samuel 9:9 was made many years after the time of Samuel. It does imply that Ammon and Mormon's definition of a seer as one who possessed or used the interpreters was correct. The interpreters, or Urim and Thummim, were used to translate languages by the power of God. A seer has "this high gift from God" (Mosiah 8:14).

Joseph Smith was given "power from on high, by the means which were before prepared, to translate the Book of Mormon" (D&C 20:8). Joseph Smith was to "be called a seer, a translator, a prophet, an apostle" in a revelation given on 6 April 1830, the day the Church was organized (D&C 21:1). Being called a seer and a translator suggests a further role of a seer than that of translator. Ammon said that "a gift that is greater can no man have, except he should possess the power of God, which no man can; yet a man may have great power given him from God" (Mosiah 8:16). He then said that "a seer can know of things which are past, and also of things which are to come" (v. 17). This statement suggests there is an additional power granted to a seer besides the translation or interpreting languages. Therefore, it is suggested that a seer is also a revelator; one who receives revelation about things that otherwise could not be known (v. 17). He is also a prophet, one who foretells of things that are to come (v. 17). Thus, God provides miracles to benefit the fellow beings of the seer, revelator and prophet (v. 18).

Ammon says that no man can look into the interpreters unless he is commanded, lest he perish (v. 13). The Urim and Thummim was in ancient Israel kept in the Ark of the Covenant. Those who were to bear it "shall not touch any holy thing [in the ark] lest they die""(Numbers 4:15). When the ark was captured by the Philistines, but later returned because of the plagues that came upon them (see 1 Samuel 4–6), the Lord "smote the men of Beth-Shemesh, because they had looked into the Ark of the Covenant" (1 Samuel 6:19). There seems to be a connection between Ammon's statement and this incident. The person without the gift of God [a seer] could not endure the power of it.

Mosiah 8:19–21 • Preventing Bondage

19 And now, when Ammon had made an end of speaking these words the king rejoiced exceedingly, and gave thanks to God, saying: Doubtless a great mystery is contained within these plates, and these interpreters were doubtless prepared for the purpose of unfolding all such mysteries to the children of men.

20 O how marvelous are the works of the Lord, and how long doth he suffer with his people; yea, and how blind and impenetrable are the understandings of the children of men; for they will not seek wisdom, neither do they desire that she should rule over them!

21 Yea, they are as a wild flock which fleeth from the shepherd, and scattereth, and are driven, and are devoured by the beasts of the forest.

King Limhi recognized that the twenty-four plates contained "a great mystery" and their translation would unfold all mysteries (v. 19). He was referring to more than the mystery of the Jaredite demise. The Jaredites had been destroyed and the people of Limhi had fallen into bondage because they would not follow the commandments of God. God has his prophets keep records that others might avoid the downfall or bondage of mankind. However, many of the children of men do not follow the wisdom that God has provided, but choose the animalistic tendencies of the natural man.

Referring to verse 20, it is often asked why wisdom is referred to in the feminine gender "she." The first nine chapters of Proverbs in the Bible use the same gender. It may be because the female, even in her natural fallen state is more spiritually inclined than the male, or it may be that in the Semitic languages "wisdom" is a feminine noun. Regardless, it is common for the children of men to not seek the wisdom of God nor desire that the wisdom of God be the governing power in their lives (v. 20).[1]

SACRED WRITING

Preaching Which is Sacred:

Mosiah 7:18–33   King Limhi to his people.

Mosiah 8:7–20   The interchange between Ammon and King Limhi.

---

[1] In Alma 42:24, the male pronoun "he" is used to represent justice and "her" is used to represent mercy.

Doctrines Learned:

Mosiah 7:27	Man was created in the image of God.
Mosiah 7:27	God came down and took upon him flesh and blood.
Mosiah 8:13	Translation of languages is a gift from God; no one can translate unless commanded.
Mosiah 8:13	Those who translate are called seers.
Mosiah 8:16	A seer is a revelator and a prophet also.
Mosiah 8:17	A seer can know of things which are past and which are to come, and by them shall all things be revealed.

General Authority Quotations

The Prophet Joseph Smith • Mosiah 8:13

Through the medium of the Urim and Thummim I translated the record, by the gift and power of God. [*HC*, 4:537]

Elder Theodore M. Burton • Mosiah 8:13–17

In the Old Testament there are several Hebrew words, "ro'eh," "hozeh," and "nabhi," all of which are translated by the translators as "prophet." The first two, almost synonymous, from the roots "ra'ah" and "hazah," both meaning "to see," suggest the man of vision and should be properly rendered as "seer." The term "nabhi" from the root "nabha" means "to announce." But if the translator felt that "to see" and "to announce" are synonymous and that they refer to the same thing, then he would so use them. Thus we find that all of these words were used and translated as "prophet" and sometimes the word "prophet" was used where "seer" should have been used. Confusion resulted therefrom, because the translators did not understand that these two words "seer" and "prophet" mean different things; that they have different usages. . . .

Thus, one can trust a seer because a seer may see the heavens open. He may see the great vision of God working in all his majesty. He may see the fulness of truth as it is revealed to him by God who makes no mistakes. The evidence is clear, therefore, and the interpretation is clear. The seer can bear personal testimony, not based on books, not based on tradition, but based on the evidence of things that God himself can reveal to him in an actual experience with Deity. He may receive a revelation from God by actually seeing and hearing and being instructed in the real truth. . . .

There must be someone to whom the people can turn and trust, who can speak for God. God must have someone on earth who can point the way and say, "This is true." How grateful, my brothers, and sisters, we should be that God in the fulness of his grace has given us a living prophet to guide us to Him; evermore that God has given us a seer, for this seer and prophet reveals personal testimony to young and old alike that Jesus is in very deed the risen Savior, the Living God.

Of this I bear sacred testimony, for under conditions too sacred to mention here God has given me witness three times in the temples that David O. McKay is truly and indeed a prophet of God, a seer, and I bear you this testimony that you can trust him and so put your whole faith in Jesus Christ. We must turn from anything which tears us away from God our Father and turn to that which will lead us to him through repentance, through our determination and through our absolute will to do the work of God. . . . [Conference Report, Oct. 1961, 121–22]

Challenges to Eternal Life:

1. Analyze your life and determine if you are subjecting yourself to bondage. If you realize that you are, apply the formula given by king Limhi to become free (Mosiah 7:33).

2. Knowing that there is a prophet, seer, and revelator on the earth today, listen to and study his messages in the general conferences of the Church (Mosiah 8:16–18).

3. Seek to unfold the mysteries of God revealed in the Book of Mormon for our generation through prayerful study (Mosiah 8:19).

4. Select a challenge of your own from this reading and apply it to your life.

Chapter Nine

The Record of Zeniff

Mosiah 9–11:1–19

*H*istorical Setting: The time frame backs up from about 121 B.C. to about 200 B.C. The italicized superscription preceding chapter nine explains:

THE RECORD OF ZENIFF—*An account of his people, from the time they left the land of Zarahemla until the time that they were delivered out of the hands of the Lamanites.* Mormon is abridging the record.

Precepts of this Reading:

Mosiah 9:3 • "[F]or we were slow to remember the Lord our God."

Zeniff was somewhat able to bring his people to remember their God. However, his son Noah, who succeeded him as king, did not walk in the ways of his father. He led the people away from God. Following is an outline of Zeniff's record showing his reign, and then the decline of the people under Noah. This allows the reader to prepare for a deeper study of the principles involved.

OUTLINE • MOSIAH 9–11:1–19

The Record of Zeniff. From the time they left Zarahemla until they were delivered from the Lamanites.

➤ Mosiah 9:1–2   Zeniff was sent as a spy among the Lamanites so that his army might come and destroy them.

    a. He had been taught the languages of the Nephites and had a knowledge of the land of Nephi, or the land of our fathers' first inheritance (v. 1).

    b. He saw that there was good among the Lamanites and that they should not be destroyed (v. 1).

    c. Zeniff contended with his brethren in the wilderness.

        1. Zeniff wanted his ruler to make a treaty with the Lamanites.

        2. The ruler was a blood-thirsty man and commanded that Zeniff be killed.

        3. Zeniff was rescued by the shedding of much blood.

        4. Father fought against father and brother against brother until most of their army was destroyed.

    d. Those spared returned to Zarahemla to relate their events to their wives and children.

➤ 9:3–9   Zeniff, being over-zealous to inherit the land of Nephi, assembled others and started again to possess the land of their fathers.

    a. Zeniff's men were smitten with famine and sore afflictions because they were slow to remember God (v. 3).

    b. After many days they camped where their brethren were slain (v. 4).

    c. Zeniff took four men unto the Lamanite king to see if his party could possess the land in peace (vv. 5–7).

        1. The king covenanted that they might possess the land of Lehi-Nephi, and the city of Shilom.

        2. He commanded his own people to depart out of the land.

    d. Zeniff's people began to build buildings, repair the walls, and till the ground with all manner of seeds and fruits.

    e. They began to multiply and prosper in the city.

➤ 9:10–13   It was the cunning and craftiness of king Laman to attempt to bring Zeniff's people in bondage.

    a.   After twelve years the king grew uneasy that they could not bring them into bondage (v. 11).

    b.   The Lamanites were a lazy and idolatrous people (v. 12).

        1.   They desired to bring Zeniff's people into bondage to glut themselves with others labor.

        2.   They wanted to feast upon the flocks of Zeniff's people.

    c.   The king stirred up his people to wars and contentions with Zeniff's people (v. 13).

➤ 9:14–19   In the thirteenth year, the Lamanites attacked some of Zeniff's people, who fled to the city of Nephi for protection.

    a.   Zeniff's people armed themselves and battled the Lamanites (vv. 16–18).

        1.   They fought with the strength of the Lord.

        2.   The Lord heard their cries and strengthened them.

    b.   Three thousand and forty-three Lamanites were slain and the remainder were driven out (v. 19).

        1.   Zeniff helped bury their dead.

        2.   Two hundred and seventy-nine of Zeniff's brethren were slain.

➤ 10:1–5   King Zeniff's people established the kingdom again and possessed the land in peace for twenty-two years.

    a.   They made weapons of war to defend themselves against the Lamanites (v. 1).

    b.   Guards were set round about the land to defend the people and their flocks (v. 2).

    c.   The men tilled the ground and raised all manner of grain and fruit (v. 4).

    d.   The women spun and worked all manner of fine linen and cloth (v. 5).

➤ 10:6–10   King Laman died and his son reigned in his stead.

    a.   This son stirred up the people in rebellion against Zeniff's people and prepared for war (v. 6).

    b.   Zeniff's spies saw the Lamanites coming up to the north of the land of Shilom heavily armed with shaved heads and leather girdles on their loins (v. 8).

    c.   Zeniff had the women and children hidden in the wilderness and he armed for battle all of his old men and young men who could bear arms according to age (v. 9).

    d.   Zeniff in his old age lead his men up to battle against the Lamanites.

➤ 10:11–19   The Lamanites knew nothing concerning the Lord, but depended on their own strength which was strong as to the strength of men.

    a.   The Lamanites were a wild and ferocious people, blood thirsty, and believed in the traditions of their fathers. They were: (vv. 12–13)

        1.   driven out of Jerusalem because of the iniquity of their fathers.

        2.   wronged by their brethren in the wilderness.

        3.   wronged while crossing the sea.

        4.   wronged in the land of their first inheritance.

    b.   The Lamanites did not understand the dealings of the Lord.

        1.   Nephi was more faithful in keeping the commandments of the Lord and therefore, took the lead (vv. 14–16).

        2.   The Lamanites said Nephi had taken the ruling out of their hands after arriving in the promised land and they sought to kill him.

        3.   The Lamanites were wroth because Nephi followed the Lord's commandments to take the records and go into the wilderness. The Lamanites said he had robbed them.

    c. The Lamanites had taught their children an eternal hatred towards the children of Nephi, to hate, murder, rob, plunder, and destroy them (vv. 17–19).

       1. For this cause King Laman had deceived Zeniff in his promises.

       2. After telling his people these things, Zeniff stimulated his people to go to battle against them.

➤ 10:20–22   Zeniff's people drove the Lamanites out of their land and slew so many they did not number them.

    a. Zeniff's people returned to their own land and began again to tend their flocks and till the land (v. 21).

    b. Zeniff, being old, conferred the kingdom upon one of his sons.

➤ 11:1–15   Zeniff conferred the kingdom on his son Noah, but he did not walk in the ways of his father.

    a. Noah had many wives and concubines and caused his people to commit whoredoms (v. 2).

    b. He laid a tax of one fifth on all their possessions (vv. 3–7).

       1. He did this to support himself and his priests along with their wives and concubines.

       2. He changed the affairs of the kingdom.

       3. In the stead of his father's priests, he consecrated new priests who were lifted up in pride.

       4. They were supported in their laziness and idolatry.

       5. The people labored exceedingly to support iniquity.

       6. The people also had become idolatrous, deceived by the flattering words of the king and priests.

    c. Noah built elegant and spacious buildings and ornamented them with all manner of precious things: (vv. 8–13)

       1. A spacious palace and throne in the midst of it.

2. All manner of fine work within the walls of the temple.

3. The seats of the high priests were ornamented and set above all the others.

4. A breastwork was built to rest their bodies and arms upon while lying and speaking vain words.

5. A very high tower near the temple was built to overlook the Lamanite cities.

6. Many buildings and a high tower were built in the land of Shilom.

d. He placed his heart on riches and spent his time in riotous living with his wives and concubines, as did his priests (v. 14).

e. He planted vineyards, and made wine presses and became a wine bibber (v. 15).

➤ 11:16–19 The Lamanites began to come upon the Nephites in small numbers and slay them while they were tending their flock.

a. The king sent guards, but the Lamanites slew them, drove many of their flocks off, and began to destroy them and exercise hatred toward them (v. 17).

b. The king sent armies who drove the Lamanites back for a time (vv. 18–19).

1. They were lifted up in pride because of their great victory.

2. They boasted in their own strength and delighted in shedding blood.

NOTES AND COMMENTARY

Introduction: Sometime near the beginning of King Benjamin's reign (around 200 B.C.), a number of men left Zarahemla to return to the land of Nephi.

> 27 And now I would speak somewhat concerning a certain number who went up into the wilderness to return to the land of Nephi; for there was a large number who were desirous to possess the land of their inheritance.

28 Wherefore, they went up into the wilderness. And their leader being a strong and mighty man, and a stiffnecked man, wherefore he caused a contention among them; and they were all slain, save fifty, in the wilderness, and they returned again to the land of Zarahemla.

29 And it came to pass that they also took others to a considerable number, and took their journey again into the wilderness.

30 And I, Amaleki, had a brother, who also went with them; and I have not since known concerning them. And I am about to lie down in my grave; and these plates are full. And I make an end of my speaking. [Omni 1:27–30]

Although the first leader is not named, Zeniff became the leader of the second group to leave for the land of Nephi. Fortunately, Zeniff kept a record of their travels..

Mosiah 9:1–3 • Slow to Remember God

1 I, Zeniff, having been taught in all the language of the Nephites, and having had a knowledge of the land of Nephi, or of the land of our fathers' first inheritance, and having been sent as a spy among the Lamanites that I might spy out their forces, that our army might come upon them and destroy them—but when I saw that which was good among them I was desirous that they should not be destroyed.

2 Therefore, I contended with my brethren in the wilderness, for I would that our ruler should make a treaty with them; but he being an austere and a blood-thirsty man commanded that I should be slain; but I was rescued by the shedding of much blood; for father fought against father, and brother against brother, until the greater number of our army was destroyed in the wilderness; and we returned, those of us that were spared, to the land of Zarahemla, to relate that tale to their wives and their children.

3 And yet, I being over-zealous to inherit the land of our fathers, collected as many as were desirous to go up to possess the land, and started again on our journey into the wilderness to go up to the land; but we were smitten with famine and sore afflictions; for we were slow to remember the Lord our God.

Zeniff's recognition of good among the Lamanites (v. 1) indicates that he was a man of moral character. The evil character of the first ruler of the group is shown (v. 2). The ferocious internal fighting of the group is evidence of the Spirit of the Lord having been withdrawn "and the devil [had] power over his own dominion" (D&C 1:35). Joseph Smith saw in vision the same conditions prior to the Second Coming:

> I saw men hunting the lives of their own sons, and brothers murdering brother, women killing their own daughters, and daughters seeking the lives of their mothers. I saw armies arrayed against armies. I saw blood, desolation, fires. The Son of man has said that the mother shall be against the daughter, and the daughter against the mother. These things are at our doors. They will follow the Saints of God from city to city. Satan will rage, and the spirit of the devil is now enraged. I know not how soon these things will take place; but with a view of them, shall I cry peace? No! I will lift up my voice and testify of them. How long you will have good crops, and the famine be kept off, I do not know; when the fig tree leaves, know then that the summer is nigh at hand. [*TPJS*, 161]

The leader of the first group was apparently killed since Zeniff organized a second group to search for the land of Nephi (v. 3). His being over-zealous to inherit the land was apparently passed on to his people. Limhi, two generations later, gives it as a reason for their being in bondage to the Lamanites (Mosiah 7:21). We learn from modern revelation that when a group of people are "slow to hearken unto the voice of the Lord their God; therefore, the Lord their God is slow to hearken unto their prayer, to answer them in the day of their trouble" (D&C 101:7).

Mosiah 9:4–10 • The Cunning and Craftiness of King Laman

> 4 Nevertheless, after many days' wandering in the wilderness we pitched our tents in the place where our brethren were slain, which was near to the land of our fathers.
>
> 5 And it came to pass that I went again with four of my men into the city, in unto the king, that I might know of the disposition of the

king, and that I might know if I might go in with my people and possess the land in peace.

6 And I went in unto the king, and he covenanted with me that I might possess the land of Lehi-Nephi, and the land of Shilom.

7 And he also commanded that his people should depart out of the land, and I and my people went into the land that we might possess it.

8 And we began to build buildings, and to repair the walls of the city, yea, even the walls of the city of Lehi-Nephi, and the city of Shilom.

9 And we began to till the ground, yea, even with all manner of seeds, with seeds of corn, and of wheat, and of barley, and with neas, and with sheum, and with seeds of all manner of fruits; and we did begin to multiply and prosper in the land.

10 Now it was the cunning and the craftiness of king Laman, to bring my people into bondage, that he yielded up the land that we might possess it.

Zeniff must have written his account later on because he did not seem to recognize the Lamanite king's motive at first (v. 10). His colony was prosperous and doing well for some time.

Mosiah 9:11–15 • Lamanites Begin to Slay Them

11 Therefore it came to pass, that after we had dwelt in the land for the space of twelve years that king Laman began to grow uneasy, lest by any means my people should wax strong in the land, and that they could not overpower them and bring them into bondage.

12 Now they were a lazy and an idolatrous people; therefore they were desirous to bring us into bondage, that they might glut themselves with the labors of our hands; yea, that they might feast themselves upon the flocks of our fields.

13 Therefore it came to pass that king Laman began to stir up his people that they should contend with my people; therefore there began to be wars and contentions in the land.

14 For, in the thirteenth year of my reign in the land of Nephi,

away on the south of the land of Shilom, when my people were watering and feeding their flocks, and tilling their lands, a numerous host of Lamanites came upon them and began to slay them, and to take off their flocks, and the corn of their fields.

15 Yea, and it came to pass that they fled, all that were not overtaken, even into the city of Nephi, and did call upon me for protection.

The nature of the Lamanites had not changed since the days of Enos, close to four hundred years.[1] Enos described the Lamanites as being of an "evil nature, that they became wild and ferocious, and a blood-thirsty people, full of idolatry and filthiness" (Enos 1:20). The Lord was "visiting the iniquities of the fathers upon the children unto the third and fourth generation of them that hate me" (Mosiah 13:13; Exodus 20:5). This condition is the natural result of living without the gospel, not the retaliation of an offended God.

Calling upon Zeniff for protection was also a learned behavior of his people. "Wherefore, the people were desirous to retain in remembrance his name. And whoso should reign in his stead were called by the people, second Nephi, third Nephi, and so forth, according to the reigns of the kings; and thus they were called by the people, let them be of whatever name they would. And it came to pass that Nephi died (Jacob 1:11–12). King Benjamin also "did fight with the strength of his own arm, with the sword of Laban" to defend his people (Words of Mormon 1:13).

Mosiah 9:16–19 • Battle in the Strength of the Lord

---

[1] Enos was the son of Jacob, brother of Nephi, who died about 545 B.C. Jacob was around fifteen years younger than Nephi, being born in the wilderness shortly after his parents left Jerusalem. Nephi was "exceeding young" when they left (1 Nephi 2:16). Enos was also young when he had his great rebirth experience and was probably the eldest son since he kept the records after Jacob died. His description of the Lamanites was therefore probably before 500 B.C. Zeniff is speaking of "probably about 160 B.C." (dating in right hand corner of page 167).

16 And it came to pass that I did arm them with bows, and with arrows, with swords, and with cimeters, and with clubs, and with slings, and with all manner of weapons which we could invent, and I and my people did go forth against the Lamanites to battle.

17 Yea, in the strength of the Lord did we go forth to battle against the Lamanites; for I and my people did cry mightily to the Lord that he would deliver us out of the hands of our enemies, for we were awakened to a remembrance of the deliverance of our fathers.

18 And God did hear our cries and did answer our prayers; and we did go forth in his might; yea, we did go forth against the Lamanites, and in one day and a night we did slay three thousand and forty-three; we did slay them even until we had driven them out of our land.

19 And I, myself, with mine own hands, did help to bury their dead. And behold, to our great sorrow and lamentation, two hundred and seventy-nine of our brethren were slain.

The weapons used by the warriors (v. 16) are listed periodically throughout the Book of Mormon, and are always basically the same (i.e. Jarom 1:8; Alma 2:12, 14), but the most important weapon was "the strength of the Lord" (Mosiah 9:17). The law of war given "unto mine ancients" and revealed anew in 1833, commanded the saints not go to battle "save I the Lord commanded them" (D&C 98:33), and if commanded promised to justify their going to battle, "[a]nd I the Lord would fight their battles, and their children's battles" (D&C 98:36–37). The Lamanites suffered almost eleven times more fatalities than the Nephites. Concerning the Nephite deaths in general, Helaman later said of his slain warriors: "Nevertheless, we may console ourselves in this point, that they have died in the cause of their country and of their God, yea, and they are happy" (Alma 56:11).

Concerning the Lamanite fatalities of a later year, Mormon recorded: "Now, they were sorry to take up arms against the Lamanites, because they did not delight in the shedding of blood; yea, and this was not all—they were sorry to be the means of sending so many of their brethren out of this world into an eternal world, unprepared to meet their God" (Alma 48:23). The battle of Zeniff and his people with the Lamanites is an example of the law of war. The Lord was certainly on the Nephites side in this battle.

Mosiah 10:1–5 • Twenty-two Years of Peace

1 And it came to pass that we again began to establish the kingdom and we again began to possess the land in peace. And I caused that there should be weapons of war made of every kind, that thereby I might have weapons for my people against the time the Lamanites should come up again to war against my people.

2 And I set guards round about the land, that the Lamanites might not come upon us again unawares and destroy us; and thus I did guard my people and my flocks, and keep them from falling into the hands of our enemies.

3 And it came to pass that we did inherit the land of our fathers for many years, yea, for the space of twenty and two years.

4 And I did cause that the men should till the ground, and raise all manner of grain and all manner of fruit of every kind.

5 And I did cause that the women should spin, and toil, and work, and work all manner of fine linen, yea, and cloth of every kind, that we might clothe our nakedness; and thus we did prosper in the land—thus we did have continual peace in the land for the space of twenty and two years.

The time period of twenty-two years describing the civil defense against the probability of war seems to be an addition to the previous twelve years of peace. The estimated dates in the lower right hand corner of the Book of Mormon pages considers it that way although the text does not make it clear. Their tilling of the ground and the production of clothing not only brought peace and prosperity, but they were done in keeping with the commandments given to Adam and Eve after being driven out of the Garden of Eden "to eat his bread by the sweat of his brow, as I the Lord had commanded him. And Eve, also, his wife, did labor with him" (Moses 5:1, see also Genesis 3:23–24).

Mosiah 10:6–10 • To Battle in the Strength of the Lord

6 And it came to pass that king Laman died, and his son began to reign in his stead. And he began to stir his people up in rebellion against my people; therefore they began to prepare for war, and to come up to battle against my people.

7 But I had sent my spies out round about the land of Shemlon, that I might discover their preparations, that I might guard against them, that they might not come upon my people and destroy them.

8 And it came to pass that they came up upon the north of the land of Shilom, with their numerous hosts, men armed with bows, and with arrows, and with swords, and with cimeters, and with stones, and with slings; and they had their heads shaved that they were naked; and they were girded with a leathern girdle about their loins.

9 And it came to pass that I caused that the women and children of my people should be hid in the wilderness; and I also caused that all my old men that could bear arms, and also all my young men that were able to bear arms, should gather themselves together to go to battle against the Lamanites; and I did place them in their ranks, every man according to his age.

10 And it came to pass that we did go up to battle against the Lamanites; and I, even I, in my old age, did go up to battle against the Lamanites. And it came to pass that we did go up in the strength of the Lord to battle.

The Lamanites "began to prepare for war" (v. 6) suggests that the Nephite civil defense had caused the Lamanites to hold off their efforts to bring the Nephites into bondage (9:10). The death of the Lamanite king (v. 6) may also have been a factor.

The men being placed in their ranks according to age (v. 9) was apparently a Hebrew custom (see 1 Nephi 18:6). The order being from oldest to youngest is suggested by the first mention of the old men being armed. Their going up in the strength of the Lord is also commented on (9:16–19).

Mosiah 10:11–18 • The Traditions of the Lamanites

11 Now, the Lamanites knew nothing concerning the Lord, nor the strength of the Lord, therefore they depended upon their own strength. Yet they were a strong people, as to the strength of men.

12 They were a wild, and ferocious, and a blood-thirsty people, believing in the tradition of their fathers, which is this—Believing that they were driven out of the land of Jerusalem because of the iniquities of their fathers, and that they were wronged in the wilderness by their brethren, and they were also wronged while crossing the sea;

13 And again, that they were wronged while in the land of their first inheritance, after they had crossed the sea, and all this because that Nephi was more faithful in keeping the commandments of the Lord— therefore he was favored of the Lord, for the Lord heard his prayers and answered them, and he took the lead of their journey in the wilderness.

14 And his brethren were wroth with him because they understood not the dealings of the Lord; they were also wroth with him upon the waters because they hardened their hearts against the Lord.

15 And again, they were wroth with him when they had arrived in the promised land, because they said that he had taken the ruling of the people out of their hands; and they sought to kill him.

16 And again, they were wroth with him because he departed into the wilderness as the Lord had commanded him, and took the records which were engraven on the plates of brass, for they said that he robbed them.

17 And thus they have taught their children that they should hate them, and that they should murder them, and that they should rob and plunder them, and do all they could to destroy them; therefore they have an eternal hatred towards the children of Nephi.

18 For this very cause has king Laman, by his cunning, and lying craftiness, and his fair promises, deceived me, that I have brought this my people up into this land, that they may destroy them; yea, and we have suffered these many years in the land.

The Lamanites being called a strong people as to the strength of men (v. 11) shows their emphasis upon the physical rather than the spiritual side of life. Enos, the second generation of Lehi's people, describes them in similar terms as does Zeniff (v. 12):

> And I bear record that the people of Nephi did seek diligently to restore the Lamanites unto the true faith in God. But our labors were vain; their hatred was fixed, and they were led by their evil nature that they became wild, and ferocious, and a blood-thirsty people, full of idolatry and filthiness; feeding upon beasts of prey; dwelling in tents, and wandering about in the wilderness with a short skin girdle about their loins and their heads shaven; and their skill was in the bow, and in the cimeter, and the ax. And many of them did eat nothing save it was raw meat; and they were continually seeking to destroy us. [Enos 1:20; partially quoted previously]

Without the gospel of Jesus Christ, their evil nature had continued for over three hundred and fifty years.

The traditions of their fathers (v. 12) had originated with Laman and Lemuel, and had been passed down to subsequent generations in spite of their knowing it was wrong. An angel had told Laman and Lemuel "that the Lord hath chosen [Nephi] to be a ruler over you, and this because of your iniquities" (1 Nephi 3:29). Their father Lehi had also corrected their thinking, warned them to "hearken to the voice of Nephi [and] ye shall not perish" and blessed them with "even my first blessing" if they would hearken to him (2 Nephi 1:24–29). In spite of these warnings and promises, shortly after Lehi's death, they sought "to take away [Nephi's] life" using the same excuses that were passed on to the time of Zeniff (2 Nephi 5:3). Although Zeniff's people lived in physical peace, these traditions of the Lamanites caused them much suffering (Mosiah 10:18).

Mosiah 10:19–22 • The Lamanites Driven out of the Land

19 And now I, Zeniff, after having told all these things unto my people concerning the Lamanites, I did stimulate them to go to battle

with their might, putting their trust in the Lord; therefore, we did contend with them, face to face.

20 And it came to pass that we did drive them again out of our land; and we slew them with a great slaughter, even so many that we did not number them.

21 And it came to pass that we returned again to our own land, and my people again began to tend their flocks, and to till their ground.

22 And now I, being old, did confer the kingdom upon one of my sons; therefore, I say no more. And may the Lord bless my people. Amen.

The success of the Nephites in defending against the Lamanites is briefly told, as the reign of Zeniff for about thirty-five years comes to an end. Although the record of his people continues, Mormon apparently copied his account verbatim (chapters 9 and 10), since it is written in the first person. The rest of the record of Zeniff was abridged.

Mosiah 11:1–4 • The Reign of King Noah, Son of Zeniff

1 And now it came to pass that Zeniff conferred the kingdom upon Noah, one of his sons; therefore Noah began to reign in his stead; and he did not walk in the ways of his father.

2 For behold, he did not keep the commandments of God, but he did walk after the desires of his own heart. And he had many wives and concubines. And he did cause his people to commit sin, and do that which was abominable in the sight of the Lord. Yea, and they did commit whoredoms and all manner of wickedness.

3 And he laid a tax of one fifth part of all they possessed, a fifth part of their gold and of their silver, and a fifth part of their ziff, and of their copper, and of their brass and their iron; and a fifth part of their fatlings; and also a fifth part of all their grain.

4 And all this did he take to support himself, and his wives and his concubines; and also his priests, and their wives and their concubines; thus he had changed the affairs of the kingdom.

The description of Noah not walking in "the ways of his father" and his not keeping the commandments of God are basically the same problem (vv. 1–2). Following after the desires of his own heart, he changed the affairs of the kingdom (vv. 2, 5). The first two changes will be considered under this heading, and the last four changes will be considered under Mosiah 11:5–15.

By Noah taking many wives and concubines, he caused others to commit sin, as they followed his example of immorality (v. 2). The Lord told Jacob, brother of Nephi, "there shall not any man among you have save it be one wife; and concubines he shall have none; . . . whoredoms are an abomination before me" (Jacob 2:27–28). The only exception was to "raise up seed unto [the Lord, and] I will command my people" (Jacob 2:30).[2] Noah had not been commanded to take plural wives.

Immorality in any form leads to the breaking up of the family unit. The family is the basic unit of the Church. Satan rejoices in the destruction of the family. He has been so effective in these latter days that the First Presidency and the Twelve issued a proclamation to the Church and to the World[3] as a means of preserving the family. They concluded the proclamation with this warning:

> WE WARN that individuals who violate covenants of chastity, who abuse spouse or offspring, or who fail to fulfill family responsibilities will one day stand accountable before God. Further, we warn that the disintegration of the family will bring upon individuals, communities, and nations the calamities foretold by ancient and modern prophets.
>
> WE CALL UPON responsible citizens and officers of government everywhere to promote those measures designed to maintain and strengthen the family as the fundamental unit of society.

---

[2] See comments in chapter one of this work for the relevance of this statement to our day.

[3] The Family, A PROCLAMATION TO THE WORLD, The First Presidency and the Council of the Twelve Apostles of The Church of Jesus Christ of Latter-day Saints, read by President Gordon B. Hinckley, General Relief Society Meeting, September 23, 1995.

The second change in the affairs of Noah's kingdom was a heavy taxation upon the people, one fifth of all they possessed (v. 3). The amount of taxes seems a warning to us as a nation, and to any nation who possesses this land of promise (see Ether 2:12). The overall taxation in the United States today is almost double the one-fifth tax levied by Noah. While some may argue that Noah's tax was upon all they possessed, not just income or increase, it was indeed a heavy burden that should be a warning to our day. Arguments for the use of the taxes by Noah and for our day will not be paralleled, although some comparison could be made.

Mosiah 11:5–15 • Other Changes in the Affairs of the Kingdom

5 For he put down all the priests that had been consecrated by his father, and consecrated new ones in their stead, such as were lifted up in the pride of their hearts.

6 Yea, and thus they were supported in their laziness, and in their idolatry, and in their whoredoms, by the taxes which king Noah had put upon his people; thus did the people labor exceedingly to support iniquity.

7 Yea, and they also became idolatrous, because they were deceived by the vain and flattering words of the king and priests; for they did speak flattering things unto them.

8 And it came to pass that king Noah built many elegant and spacious buildings; and he ornamented them with fine work of wood, and of all manner of precious things, of gold, and of silver, and of iron, and of brass, and of ziff, and of copper;

9 And he also built him a spacious palace, and a throne in the midst thereof, all of which was of fine wood and was ornamented with gold and silver and with precious things.

10 And he also caused that his workmen should work all manner of fine work within the walls of the temple, of fine wood, and of copper, and of brass.

11 And the seats which were set apart for the high priests, which were above all the other seats, he did ornament with pure gold; and

he caused a breastwork to be built before them, that they might rest their bodies and their arms upon while they should speak lying and vain words to his people.

12 And it came to pass that he built a tower near the temple; yea, a very high tower, even so high that he could stand upon the top thereof and overlook the land of Shilom, and also the land of Shemlon, which was possessed by the Lamanites; and he could even look over all the land round about.

13 And it came to pass that he caused many buildings to be built in the land Shilom; and he caused a great tower to be built on the hill north of the land Shilom, which had been a resort for the children of Nephi at the time they fled out of the land; and thus he did do with the riches which he obtained by the taxation of his people.

14 And it came to pass that he placed his heart upon his riches, and he spent his time in riotous living with his wives and his concubines; and so did also his priests spend their time with harlots.

15 And it came to pass that he planted vineyards round about in the land; and he built wine-presses, and made wine in abundance; and therefore he became a wine-bibber, and also his people.

The replacing of the priests appointed by Zeniff brought a third change in the affairs of the kingdom. In a kingdom sustained by the Lord, the appointments should have been made by revelation. Those whom Zeniff appointed were probably so appointed, but Noah's appointees were his fellow workers in iniquity, and would not have been called by revelation. Although these priests may have been a political body rather than a religious or spiritual group (see Mosiah 27:1), they would still have been appointed by revelation through Zeniff. Political appointments were one of the causes of the apostasy in the Church following the ministry of Christ in the flesh. When Constantine made Christianity the state religion, he made the appointments rather than the church leaders.

The fourth change came when the people became idolatrous, worshipping things other than God, because of the vain and flattering words of the king and his priests (Mosiah 11:7). Vain means useless and flattery is an overstatement of truth for ulterior motives. The priests did "preach and set themselves up for a light unto the world, that they may get gain and praise of the world; but they seek not the welfare of Zion" or their community. Such practice is called priest-craft and is a frequent problem among the Nephites (2 Nephi 26:29; see also Jacob 7:4; Alma 1:3–6; 48:1).

The fifth change was the building of many elegant and spacious buildings (Mosiah 27:8). These monuments were surely intended to become memorials to the leaders so they might boast of their accomplishments. The adorning of the king's throne and the seats of the high priests was not for comfort but for an extension of the idolatrous authority from which they spoke lying and vain words (Mosiah 11:9–11).

The tower near the temple and the one in the land of Shilom were probably for protection from the Lamanites (vv. 12–13). Being able to see them approaching would give them an advantage in preparing to defend themselves. The construction of many buildings in the land of Shilom, which had been a resort town, suggests that the king and his priests wanted a place to go for pleasure. The report of riotous living and spending time with harlots supports this theory.

The consumption of alcohol was the sixth and final change in the affairs of the kingdom that adversely affected the people. The priests are not mentioned, but they most likely were wine bibbers as well as the king (v. 15). Alcohol has destroyed or weakened many nations in the past and is a major problem in the latter days. Thus in just a few years, the Nephites turned from a prosperous and peaceful people who depended upon the Lord to an idolatrous people (v. 7) filled with all manner of wickedness (v. 2).

Mosiah 11:16–19 • The Nephites Boast in their Own Strength

16 And it came to pass that the Lamanites began to come in upon his people, upon small numbers, and to slay them in their fields, and while they were tending their flocks.

17 And king Noah sent guards round about the land to keep them

off; but he did not send a sufficient number, and the Lamanites came upon them and killed them, and drove many of their flocks out of the land; thus the Lamanites began to destroy them, and to exercise their hatred upon them.

18 And it came to pass that king Noah sent his armies against them, and they were driven back, or they drove them back for a time; therefore, they returned rejoicing in their spoil.

19 And now, because of this great victory they were lifted up in the pride of their hearts; they did boast in their own strength, saying that their fifty could stand against thousands of the Lamanites; and thus they did boast, and did delight in blood, and the shedding of the blood of their brethren, and this because of the wickedness of their king and priests.

The Lamanites may have recognized that the Nephites were weakening because they again attempted to bring the Nephites into bondage. Although the Nephites were able to drive them back for a time (v. 18), their victories merely deepened their weakened condition. They became more and more like the Lamanites. They were lifted up in pride, boasted in their own strength rather than in the strength of the Lord, and delighted in shedding the blood of their Lamanite brethren. All of these conditions were brought about because of the wickedness of the king and his priests (v. 19). So much for the recurring argument that the immorality of leaders has no affect on the moral fiber of a nation.

SACRED WRITING

Preaching Which is Sacred:

Mosiah 10:11–19   Zeniff tells his people about the traditions of the Lamanites.

Doctrines Learned:

Mosiah 9:3   Famines and afflictions come when a people are slow to remember the Lord their God.

Mosiah 11:19   The wickedness of leaders affects the moral fiber of a
                    nation.

General Authority Quotations
President Brigham Young • Mosiah 9:17; 10:10–11; 11:19

You never heard me say that I was going to be true to my God; for I know too much of human weakness; but I pray to God to preserve me from falling away—to preserve me in truth. I depend not upon myself; for I know too much of human weakness and of myself to indulge in such remarks.

I derive strength from a superior source. I have been drinking from that source for many years. [*JD*, 5:12–13]

The Family, A Proclamation to the World, The First Presidency and Council of the Twelve Apostles • Mosiah 11:2

THE FAMILY is ordained of God. Marriage between man and woman is essential to His eternal plan. Children are entitled to birth within the bonds of matrimony, and to be reared by a father and mother who honor marital vows with complete fidelity. Happiness in family life is most likely to be achieved when founded upon the teachings of the Lord Jesus Christ. Successful marriages and families are established and maintained on principles of faith, prayer, repentance, forgiveness, respect, love, compassion, work, and wholesome recreation activities. By divine design, fathers are to preside over their families in love and righteousness and are responsible to provide the necessities of life and protection for their families. Mothers are primarily responsible for the nurture of their children. In these sacred responsibilities, fathers and mothers are obligated to help one another as equal partners. Disability, death, or other circumstances may necessitate individual adaptation. Extended families should lend support when needed. [Read by President Gordon B. Hinckley at General Relief Society Meeting, September 23, 1995]

President Spencer W. Kimball • Mosiah 11:2

We warn you against the so-called polygamy cults which would lead you astray. Remember the Lord brought an end to this program many decades ago through a prophet who proclaimed the revelation to the world. People are abroad who would deceive you and bring you much sorrow and remorse. Have nothing to do with those who would lead you astray. It is wrong and sinful to ignore the Lord when he speaks. He has spoken—strongly and conclusively. [Conference Report, Oct. 1974, 5]

Challenges to Eternal Life:

1. In you association with people, follow the example of Zeniff and look for the good in them (9:2), and cultivate those same characteristics in your life.
2. Analyze the traditions of your family (see 10:11–18) and see if they are causing you to disobey the commandments of the Lord. If so, discontinue them in your own family.
3. Meet your problems and decisions of action in the strength of the Lord (10:10), rather than depending upon your own strength (11:19).
4. Choose a challenge of your own from this reading and incorporate it into your life.

Chapter Ten

Christ and the Law of Moses

Mosiah 11:20–29; 12 & 13

*H*istorical Setting: The prophecies of Abinadi are estimated to have been made in about 150 B.C. This date is consistent with the other given dates in the book of Mosiah (see dating in the book of Mosiah—chapter 5). After several years of King Noah's reign, the people were in a general state of wickedness because of the example and administration of the king and his priests (11:19). The Lord sent Abinadi to cry repentance to them, but they sought to take away his life and the Lord delivered him out of their hands (11:26). Two years later (about 148 B.C.) he returned and prophesied again. The majority of the Book of Mormon text for this chapter covers the second time he prophesied.

Precepts of This Reading:

If you teach the law of Moses, why do ye not keep it? [Mosiah 12:29]

I know if ye keep the commandments of God ye shall be saved. [Mosiah 12:33]

I must fulfill the commandments wherewith God has commanded me. [Mosiah 13:4]

Although the Nephites lived the law of Moses, they also lived the higher law of Christ (see 2 Nephi 25:24–30). Therefore, Abinadi's answers to the priests of Noah are very applicable to us today.

An outline of the Book of Mormon chapters discussed in this chapter follows as a preparation for deeper study.

OUTLINE • MOSIAH 11:20–29; 12 & 13

➤ Mosiah 11:20–26   Abinadi, a man among them, began to prophesy. The Lord commanded him to go forth and say "thus saith the Lord."

    a. I have seen their abominations, wickedness, and whoredoms, and except they repent I will visit them in anger (vv. 21–25).

       1. I will deliver them to their enemies and they will be brought into bondage.

       2. They will know I am the Lord their God, and am a jealous God.

       3. None shall deliver them except the Lord, the Almighty God.

       4. When they cry unto me I will be slow to hear them.

       5. Except they repent in sackcloth and ashes, I will not deliver them.

    b. The people were wroth and sought Abinadi's life, but the Lord delivered him (v. 26).

➤ 11:27–29   King Noah asked: Who is Abinadi that he should judge me and my people, and who is the Lord that should bring affliction?

    a. He commanded that Abinadi be brought and slain (v. 28).

    b. The people hardened their hearts and sought to take him (v. 29).

    c. King Noah hardened his heart and did not repent (v. 29).

➤ 12:1–8   After two years, Abinadi was commanded by the Lord to go and prophesy many things to the Lord's people because they had not hearkened to his word.

a. He came among them in disguise (v. 1).

b. They had not repented of their evil doings, therefore the Lord would visit them in his anger (v. 1).

c. This generation shall be brought into bondage and be smitten, driven, and slain, and the vultures, dogs and wild beasts will eat their flesh (v. 2).

d. King Noah shall be valued as a garment in a hot furnace and know that the Lord is God (v. 3).

e. The people will be smitten with afflictions, famine, and pestilence that will cause them to howl all the day long (vv. 4–7).

   1. They will have burdens lashed upon their backs and be driven as a dumb ass.

   2. The Lord will send hail, the east wind, and insects will devour their grain.

   3. All this will come because of their iniquities and abominations.

f. Except they repent they will be utterly destroyed from the earth (v. 8).

   1. They will leave a record behind them.

   2. Other nations shall possess the land.

➤ 12:9–12 The people were angry and carried Abinadi before the king and said:

a. Abinadi has prophesied evil and said God will destroy this people (v. 9).

b. The king's life shall be as a garment in a furnace of fire (v. 10).

c. The king shall be as a dry stalk in a field that is run over and trodden down (v. 11).

d. The king shall be as a fully ripe thistle driven forth by the wind (v. 12).

e. Abinadi has pretended the Lord has spoken it, and that it will come except we repent (v. 12).

➤ 12:13–16   The people asked what evil the king had done, or the people, that they should be judged or condemned by God or this man?

   a. The people are guiltless, the king has not sinned and this man has lied (v. 14).

   b. We shall not come into bondage or be taken captive (v. 15).

   c. Here is the man, do with him as seemeth thee good.

➤ 12:17–37   King Noah cast Abinadi into prison and commanded the priests to gather and hold a council to determine what to do.

   a. The priests brought Abinadi before them to question him that they might cross him and have something wherewith to accuse him (vv. 18–19).

      1. Abinadi answered boldly and to their astonishment.

      2. He withstood them in all their questions and confounded them in their words.

   b. The priests asked the meaning of what is written (Isaiah 52:7–10) (vv. 20–21).

   c. Abinadi asked if they are priests, and pretend to teach the people, and to understand prophesying, why do they ask him? (vv. 25–27)

      1. He warned them of perverting the ways of the Lord for not teaching these things if they understood them.

      2. He said they had not applied their hearts to understanding and were not wise.

   d. Abinadi asked what the priests teach the people and they said the law of Moses. Abinadi asked (vv. 27–30):

      1. Why they did not keep it?

      2. Why did they set their hearts on riches?

      3. Why did they commit whoredoms and spend their strength with harlots?

    4.   Why did they cause this people to sin that the Lord sent me to prophecy?

    5.   They know that I spoke the truth and ought to tremble before God.

  e.   They will be smitten for they claim to teach the law of Moses and what do they know about the law of Moses? (vv. 31–36)

    1.   Abinadi asked: Doth salvation come by the law of Moses? They answered yes.

    2.   Abinadi said if they kept the commandments given to Moses in the Mount of Sinai they would be saved (He then quoted the first two of the ten commandments quoting Exodus 20:2–4).

  f.   Abinadi said they had not done this nor taught this people that they should do it (v. 37).

➤ 13:1–5   The King (Noah) commanded his priests to slay Abinadi, accusing him of being mad.

  a.   The priests attempted to lay hands on him but he withstood them (v. 2).

  b.   Abinadi told them not to touch him or God would smite them (vv. 3–4).

    1.   He had not yet delivered the message God sent him to deliver.

    2.   He had not answered what they requested of him.

    3.   He must fulfill the commandment of God and because he told the truth they were angry.

  c.   The people of King Noah dared not lay hands on him for his face shone with exceeding luster, even as Moses while speaking with the Lord on Sinai (v. 5).

➤ 13:6–24   Abinadi spoke with power and authority from God continuing his words.

  a.   Ye have not power to slay me so I will continue my message (vv. 7–8).

    1.   It cuts you to your hearts because I tell you the truth.

    2.   My words fill you with wonder, amazement, and anger.

  b.   I finish my message and then it matters not where I go, if I am saved (v. 9).

  c.   What you do to me shall be a shadow and type of things to come (v. 10).

  d.   Abinadi read the remainder of the ten commandments of God for they were not written in their hearts. They had studied and taught iniquity the most part of their lives. (He read Exodus 20:4–17.)

➤ 13:25–35   Abinadi testified that they had not taught these things to the people or God would not have sent him to prophesy.

  a.   The priests claimed that salvation came by the law of Moses. Abinadi responded: (vv. 27–33)

    1.   It is expedient to keep the law of Moses as yet, but the time will come when it will not be expedient.

    2.   The law of Moses alone will not bring salvation, but the Atonement only.

    3.   It was expedient for a strict law to be given to Israel because they were stiffnecked, quick to do iniquity but slow to remember God.

    4.   It was a law of ordinances and performances to keep strictly from day to day to keep them in remembrance of their duty to God.

    5.   All of these things were types of things to come.

    6.   They had not understood the law and that they could not be saved but by the redemption of God.

  b.   Moses and all the prophets prophesied concerning the coming of the Messiah to redeem his people (vv. 33–35).

    1.   They said God himself would come down in the form of a man and go forth in mighty power.

    2.   He would bring forth the resurrection from the dead and he himself shall be oppressed and afflicted.

NOTES AND COMMENTARY

Introduction: What does God do when his people forsake him? He sends a prophet or prophets among them: "Surely the Lord God will do nothing, until he revealeth his secret unto his servants the prophets" (JST, Amos 3:7). Abinadi is a good example of how the Lord uses his prophets to warn the people.

Mosiah 11:20–25 • The Lord Commands Abinadi to Prophesy

20 And it came to pass that there was a man among them whose name was Abinadi; and he went forth among them, and began to prophesy, saying: Behold, thus saith the Lord, and thus hath he commanded me, saying, Go forth, and say unto this people, thus saith the Lord—Wo be unto this people, for I have seen their abominations, and their wickedness, and their whoredoms; and except they repent I will visit them in mine anger.

21 And except they repent and turn to the Lord their God, behold, I will deliver them into the hands of their enemies; yea, and they shall be brought into bondage; and they shall be afflicted by the hand of their enemies.

22 And it shall come to pass that they shall know that I am the Lord their God, and am a jealous God, visiting the iniquities of my people.

23 And it shall come to pass that except this people repent and turn unto the Lord their God, they shall be brought into bondage; and none shall deliver them, except it be the Lord the Almighty God.

24 Yea, and it shall come to pass that when they shall cry unto me I will be slow to hear their cries; yea, and I will suffer them that they be smitten by their enemies.

25 And except they repent in sackcloth and ashes, and cry mightily to the Lord their God, I will not hear their prayers, neither will I deliver them out of their afflictions; and thus saith the Lord, and thus hath he commanded me.

Abinadi was a man among them (v. 20). The Lord either sends an existing prophet from another area or chooses a new one. In either case he is chosen from among the people. Amos was chosen from "among the herdsmen of Tekoa" and sent to Northern Israel (8th century B.C.) to prophesy (Amos 1:1). The people rejected him and Amos responded: "Then answered Amos, and said to Amaziah, I *was* no prophet, neither *was* I a prophet's son; but I *was* an herdman, and a gatherer of sycamore fruit: And the LORD took me as I followed the flock, and the LORD said unto me, Go, prophesy unto my people Israel" (Amos 7:14–15). He was a herdman prior to this calling; he "was no prophet." He was not in line to become a prophet because of his lineage or heredity (not the son of a prophet). He was a common, everyday herdsman and fruit laborer when his call came to him. We have no record of Abinadi's call, but it was undoubtedly similar. However, there was no prophet within immediate traveling distance for the Lord to send, and the Lord knew Abinadi was qualified to become a prophet, so he was chosen. With the mantle of the Lord upon him, he was courageous and effective.

There are two kinds of prophecies: conditional and unconditional. The conditional is what will happen if certain requirements are or are not met. The unconditional prophecy is what is going to happen regardless of the reaction of the people. The conditional prophecy is usually given first and followed by the unconditional one if the first requirements are not met.

Abinadi's first prophecy is conditional. The people must repent of their abominations and whoredoms (Mosiah 11:20), or they will be brought into bondage to their enemies the Lamanites. They would also be afflicted (v. 21) because of their breaking the second of the Ten Commandments, "to not make unto thee any graven images" (Exodus 20:5). The Nephites had become an idolatrous people (Mosiah 11:7). There were two conditions foretold: the Lord is the only one who can deliver them, and the Lord will be slow to hear their cries and prayers. They have rejected his mercy and so justice will run its course. The second commandment states that their iniquities will last unto the third and fourth generation if they continue to hate the

Lord. This condition is the natural effect of not turning to the Lord. "There is a law irrevocably decreed in heaven before the foundation of this world, upon which all blessings are predicated" (D&C 130:20). However, those who love him will be blessed regardless of their generation if they love him "and [keep his] commandments" (Exodus 20:6).

Mosiah 11:26–29 • The Lord Delivered Abinadi

26 Now it came to pass that when Abinadi had spoken these words unto them they were wroth with him, and sought to take away his life; but the Lord delivered him out of their hands.

27 Now when king Noah had heard of the words which Abinadi had spoken unto the people, he was also wroth; and he said: Who is Abinadi, that I and my people should be judged of him, or who is the Lord, that shall bring upon my people such great affliction?

28 I command you to bring Abinadi hither, that I may slay him, for he has said these things that he might stir up my people to anger one with another, and to raise contentions among my people; therefore I will slay him.

29 Now the eyes of the people were blinded; therefore they hardened their hearts against the words of Abinadi, and they sought from that time forward to take him. And king Noah hardened his heart against the word of the Lord, and he did not repent of his evil doings.

The Lord's delivering Abinadi from the angry mob will be commented on later. King Noah rejected Abinadi's words and also the Lord. His response (v. 27) was the same as Cain's when his mother (Eve) asked that he not reject the Lord's words: "Who is the Lord that I should know him" (Moses 5:16). King Noah was successful in stirring up the people to anger and seeking the life of Abinadi (Mosiah 11:28–29).

Mosiah 12:1–8 • Abinadi Comes in Disguise

1 And it came to pass that after the space of two years that Abinadi came among them in disguise, that they knew him not, and

began to prophesy among them, saying: Thus has the Lord commanded me, saying—Abinadi, go and prophesy unto this my people, for they have hardened their hearts against my words; they have repented not of their evil doings; therefore, I will visit them in my anger, yea, in my fierce anger will I visit them in their iniquities and abominations.

2 Yea, wo be unto this generation! And the Lord said unto me: Stretch forth thy hand and prophesy, saying: Thus saith the Lord, it shall come to pass that this generation, because of their iniquities, shall be brought into bondage, and shall be smitten on the cheek; yea, and shall be driven by men, and shall be slain; and the vultures of the air, and the dogs, yea, and the wild beasts, shall devour their flesh.

3 And it shall come to pass that the life of king Noah shall be valued even as a garment in a hot furnace; for he shall know that I am the Lord.

4 And it shall come to pass that I will smite this my people with sore afflictions, yea, with famine and with pestilence; and I will cause that they shall howl all the day long.

5 Yea, and I will cause that they shall have burdens lashed upon their backs; and they shall be driven before like a dumb ass.

6 And it shall come to pass that I will send forth hail among them, and it shall smite them; and they shall also be smitten with the east wind; and insects shall pester their land also, and devour their grain.

7 And they shall be smitten with a great pestilence—and all this will I do because of their iniquities and abominations.

8 And it shall come to pass that except they repent I will utterly destroy them from off the face of the earth; yet they shall leave a record behind them, and I will preserve them for other nations which shall possess the land; yea, even this will I do that I may discover the abominations of this people to other nations. And many things did Abinadi prophesy against this people.

Why did Abinadi go to all the trouble of disguising himself and then promptly identify himself in his opening statement? The answer is he needed the disguise to get inside the city. The people were seeking his life, but he had been commanded of the Lord (v. 1) and put his trust in him. Later he indicates he may have had an inclination of his being put to death (vv. 13:2–9).

Abinadi now gives an unconditional prophecy from the Lord. It had been two years, and Noah and his people had not met the conditions of repentance given in the previous prophecy (11:20–25). This generation—the following ones would be given an opportunity to repent—would be brought into bondage and suffer the foretold afflictions (vv. 2, 4–7). In addition, the life of King Noah, the major instigator of their wickedness, would be of no value. His death by fire is implied (v. 3), but not specifically stated as yet because of another somewhat conditional prophecy to be given later (see 13:10). There is a conditional prophecy, directed to the people, added to the unconditional future bondage: "except they repent I will utterly destroy them from off the face of the earth." However, they would leave a record behind them as a conditional prophecy for those who later possessed the land (v. 8). The record referred to is the one Mormon is now abridging, the Record of Zeniff. Mormon's abridgment is thus a conditional prophecy to the people of the latter days. If the people of the land of the Americas do not keep the Lord's commandments, they will go into bondage and eventually be destroyed from the face of the land.

Mosiah 12:9–16 • Bound and Carried Before the King

9 And it came to pass that they were angry with him; and they took him and carried him bound before the king, and said unto the king: Behold, we have brought a man before thee who has prophesied evil concerning thy people, and saith that God will destroy them.

10 And he also prophesieth evil concerning thy life, and saith that thy life shall be as a garment in a furnace of fire.

11 And again, he saith that thou shalt be as a stalk, even as a dry stalk of the field, which is run over by the beasts and trodden under foot.

12 And again, he saith thou shalt be as the blossoms of a thistle, which, when it is fully ripe, if the wind bloweth, it is driven forth upon the face of the land. And he pretendeth the Lord hath spoken

it. And he saith all this shall come upon thee except thou repent, and this because of thine iniquities.

13 And now, O king, what great evil hast thou done, or what great sins have thy people committed, that we should be condemned of God or judged of this man?

14 And now, O king, behold, we are guiltless, and thou, O king, hast not sinned; therefore, this man has lied concerning you, and he has prophesied in vain.

15 And behold, we are strong, we shall not come into bondage, or be taken captive by our enemies; yea, and thou hast prospered in the land, and thou shalt also prosper.

16 Behold, here is the man, we deliver him into thy hands; thou mayest do with him as seemeth thee good.

Abinadi's captors now claim to be retelling his prophecies to the king (vv. 9–12), Mormon, however, did not include these prophecies in his abridgment (v. 8).[1] The rationalization offered by the captors of the king's and priests' innocence (vv. 13–15) is an example of the modern "spin" tactics of today: attack the accuser rather than answer the accusation. It reminds us also of the devil's tactics outlined by Nephi: "stir them up to anger against that which is good. And others will he pacify, and lull them into carnal security, that they will say: All is well in Zion; yea, Zion prospereth, all is well" (2 Nephi 28:20–21).

Mosiah 12:17–24 • Abinadi Confounds the Priests

17 And it came to pass that king Noah caused that Abinadi should be cast into prison; and he commanded that the priests should gather themselves together that he might hold a council with them what he should do with him.

18 And it came to pass that they said unto the king: Bring him

---

[1] For further evidence of Mormon not including all of Abinadi's prophecies see Mosiah 7:27 and Mormon 1:19.

hither that we may question him; and the king commanded that he should be brought before them.

19 And they began to question him, that they might cross him, that thereby they might have wherewith to accuse him; but he answered them boldly, and withstood all their questions, yea, to their astonishment; for he did withstand them in all their questions, and did confound them in all their words.

20 And it came to pass that one of them said unto him: What meaneth the words which are written, and which have been taught by our fathers, saying:

21 How beautiful upon the mountains are the feet of him that bringeth good tidings; that publisheth peace; that bringeth good tidings of good; that publisheth salvation; that saith unto Zion, Thy God reigneth;

22 Thy watchmen shall lift up the voice; with the voice together shall they sing; for they shall see eye to eye when the Lord shall bring again Zion;

23 Break forth into joy; sing together ye waste places of Jerusalem; for the Lord hath comforted his people, he hath redeemed Jerusalem;

24 The Lord hath made bare his holy arm in the eyes of all the nations, and all the ends of the earth shall see the salvation of our God?

Abinadi faces the priests of Noah, and through the inspiration of the Lord, he confounds "them in all their words" (v. 19). He is an example of what Jesus told his disciples would happen as they were confronted with the hypocrisy of the Pharisees. "And when they bring you unto the synagogues, and *unto* magistrates, and powers, take ye no thought how or what thing ye shall answer, or what ye shall say: For the Holy Ghost shall teach you in the same hour what ye ought to say" (Luke 12:11–12). The Holy Ghost was certainly with Abinadi.

Having failed to cross up Abinadi, one of the priests asks the meaning of Isaiah 52:7–10 (Mosiah 12:21–24). This question, on the good tidings that bring peace, opened the door for Abinadi to leave the priests without excuse for their teachings to their people. At the same time Abinadi was magnifying his priesthood (see Jacob 1:19). Abinadi does not answer the question of the meaning of the Isaiah passage at this time, but he does so later.

Mosiah 12:25–37 • What Teach Ye This People?

25 And now Abinadi said unto them: Are you priests, and pretend to teach this people, and to understand the spirit of prophesying, and yet desire to know of me what these things mean?

26 I say unto you, wo be unto you for perverting the ways of the Lord! For if ye understand these things ye have not taught them; therefore, ye have perverted the ways of the Lord.

27 Ye have not applied your hearts to understanding; therefore, ye have not been wise. Therefore, what teach ye this people?

28 And they said: We teach the law of Moses.

29 And again he said unto them: If ye teach the law of Moses why do ye not keep it? Why do ye set your hearts upon riches? Why do ye commit whoredoms and spend your strength with harlots, yea, and cause this people to commit sin, that the Lord has cause to send me to prophesy against this people, yea, even a great evil against this people?

30 Know ye not that I speak the truth? Yea, ye know that I speak the truth; and you ought to tremble before God.

31 And it shall come to pass that ye shall be smitten for your iniquities, for ye have said that ye teach the law of Moses. And what know ye concerning the law of Moses? Doth salvation come by the law of Moses? What say ye?

32 And they answered and said that salvation did come by the law of Moses.

33 But now Abinadi said unto them: I know if ye keep the commandments of God ye shall be saved; yea, if ye keep the commandments which the Lord delivered unto Moses in the mount of Sinai, saying:

34 I am the Lord thy God, who hath brought thee out of the land of Egypt, out of the house of bondage.

35 Thou shalt have no other God before me.

36 Thou shalt not make unto thee any graven image, or any likeness of any thing in heaven above, or things which are in the earth beneath.

37 Now Abinadi said unto them, Have ye done all this? I say unto you, Nay, ye have not. And have ye taught this people that they should do all these things? I say unto you, Nay, ye have not.

Under the Mosaic law, the Sanhedrin was "the Jewish senate and the highest native court in both civil and ecclesiastical matters."[2] The priests of Noah were probably considered to have that same authority. Abinadi is merely reminding them of their role when he asks, why do you "desire to know of me what these things mean?" (v. 25). He then calls them to repentance and asks "what teach ye this people?" (vv. 26–27). Their answer is an affirmation of their need to repent.

To the priest's response that they teach the law of Moses, Abinadi again calls them to repentance for not living the law they teach (vv. 28–29). Abinadi declares to the priests that they know he is speaking the truth (v. 30). He knew this in the same way that Alma knew the hearts of the people of Gideon: "I know that ye believe them; and the way that I know that ye believe them is by the manifestation of the Spirit which is in me" (Alma 7:17). Although Noah's priests knew they were not keeping the law, they really didn't understand the law as Abinadi's next question revealed: "Doth salvation come by the law of Moses?" (Mosiah 12:31). To their positive response, Abinadi acknowledges the commandments given to Moses on Sinai as a source of salvation (vv. 32–33), but accuses them of not living the first two of the ten commandments given there, nor teaching them to the people (vv. 34–37). He is then interrupted by the king's reaction.

Mosiah 13:1–10 •Abinadi Protected Until the Message Completed

1 And now when the king had heard these words, he said unto his

---

[2] LDS Bible Dictionary, 769.

priests: Away with this fellow, and slay him; for what have we to do with him, for he is mad.

2 And they stood forth and attempted to lay their hands on him; but he withstood them, and said unto them:

3 Touch me not, for God shall smite you if ye lay your hands upon me, for I have not delivered the message which the Lord sent me to deliver; neither have I told you that which ye requested that I should tell; therefore, God will not suffer that I shall be destroyed at this time.

4 But I must fulfil the commandments wherewith God has commanded me; and because I have told you the truth ye are angry with me. And again, because I have spoken the word of God ye have judged me that I am mad.

5 Now it came to pass after Abinadi had spoken these words that the people of king Noah durst not lay their hands on him, for the Spirit of the Lord was upon him; and his face shone with exceeding luster, even as Moses' did while in the mount of Sinai, while speaking with the Lord.

6 And he spake with power and authority from God; and he continued his words, saying:

7 Ye see that ye have not power to slay me, therefore I finish my message. Yea, and I perceive that it cuts you to your hearts because I tell you the truth concerning your iniquities.

8 Yea, and my words fill you with wonder and amazement, and with anger.

9 But I finish my message; and then it matters not whither I go, if it so be that I am saved.

10 But this much I tell you, what you do with me, after this, shall be as a type and a shadow of things which are to come.

This is the first mention of the king being present, but he had heard all he wanted to hear. The king's order to take Abinadi away could not be carried out (vv. 1–2). The Lord had delivered him out of the hands of the enemy two years before (11:26), and he was protecting him this time. From this second encounter, we learn a great principle. The Lord's servants will be protected until their mission is completed (vv. 3–4). The Prophet Joseph Smith acknowledged this same protection:

> The Lord Almighty has preserved me until today. He will continue to preserve me by the united faith and prayers of the Saints, until I have fully accomplished my mission in this life, and so firmly established the dispensation of the fulness of the priesthood in the last days, that all the powers of earth and hell can never prevail against it. [*TPJS*, 258; see also 328]

Having read the account in the plates of brass, Mormon, or whoever kept the record of Zeniff during the wicked reign of King Noah, must have known of the ancient account where the face of Moses reflected the Spirit of the Lord.

> 29 And it came to pass, when Moses came down from mount Sinai with the two tables of testimony in Moses' hand, when he came down from the mount, that Moses wist not that the skin of his face shone while he talked with him.
>
> 30 And when Aaron and all the children of Israel saw Moses, behold, the skin of his face shone; and they were afraid to come nigh him. [Exodus 34:29–30]

The Book of Mormon verifies the King James translation of this passage, and also clears up a controversy among biblical scholars.

The Catholic translators of the Douay Version followed the pattern of the Septuagint Bible by translating the same verse as follows:

> "And they knew not his face was horned from the conversation with the Lord. And Aaron and the children of Israel seeing the face of Israel horned, were afraid to come near." Because of this faulty interpretation, the great sculptor Michelangelo put horns on his famous statue of Moses! The Book of Mormon again comes to the support of its companion scripture, the Bible, and clarifies an area of

controversy; the face of Moses "shone" when he came off the
mount.[3]

Abinadi's words of truth spoken "with power and authority from
God" (v. 8) cut to the hearts of King Noah's people (vv. 7–8) because,
as Nephi said, "the guilty taketh the truth to be hard" (1 Nephi 16:2).
That same power and authority restrained the people enabling Abinadi
to finish his mission. Abinadi's attitude of having no concern for his
physical life if he obtained eternal salvation (Mosiah 13:9) was also
reflected by the Prophet Joseph: "I shall not be sacrificed until my
time comes; then I shall be offered freely" (*TPJS*, 274). Abinadi now
adds a conditional prophecy. Whatever the king and his people shall
do to Abinadi will be a type and shadow of what will come upon them
(v. 10). The fulfillment of these words in every aspect will be seen as
the Book of Mormon account continues.

Mosiah 13:11–26 • The Remainder of the Commandments

11 And now I read unto you the remainder of the commandments
of God, for I perceive that they are not written in your hearts; I
perceive that ye have studied and taught iniquity the most part of
your lives.

12 And now, ye remember that I said unto you: Thou shall not
make unto thee any graven image, or any likeness of things which
are in heaven above, or which are in the earth beneath, or which are
in the water under the earth.

13 And again: Thou shalt not bow down thyself unto them, nor
serve them; for I the Lord thy God am a jealous God, visiting the
iniquities of the fathers upon the children, unto the third and fourth
generations of them that hate me;

14 And showing mercy unto thousands of them that love me and
keep my commandments.

---

[3] Daniel H. Ludlow, *A Companion To Your Study of the Book of Mormon*, [1977], 183.

15 Thou shalt not take the name of the Lord thy God in vain; for the Lord will not hold him guiltless that taketh his name in vain.

16 Remember the sabbath day, to keep it holy.

17 Six days shalt thou labor, and do all thy work;

18 But the seventh day, the sabbath of the Lord thy God, thou shalt not do any work, thou, nor thy son, nor thy daughter, thy man-servant, nor thy maid-servant, nor thy cattle, nor thy stranger that is within thy gates;

19 For in six days the Lord made heaven and earth, and the sea, and all that in them is; wherefore the Lord blessed the sabbath day, and hallowed it.

20 Honor thy father and thy mother, that thy days may be long upon the land which the Lord thy God giveth thee.

21 Thou shalt not kill.

22 Thou shalt not commit adultery. Thou shalt not steal.

23 Thou shalt not bear false witness against thy neighbor.

24 Thou shalt not covet thy neighbor's house, thou shalt not covet thy neighbor's wife, nor his man-servant, nor his maid-servant, nor his ox, nor his ass, nor anything that is thy neighbor's.

25 And it came to pass that after Abinadi had made an end of these sayings that he said unto them: Have ye taught this people that they should observe to do all these things for to keep these commandments?

26 I say unto you, Nay; for if ye had, the Lord would not have caused me to come forth and to prophesy evil concerning this people.

To have the commandments written in your hearts is a prevalent Old Testament concept. Isaiah invites "the people in whose heart is written my law" to hearken (Isaiah 51:7). Jeremiah, whose record was only partly upon the plates of brass (see 1 Nephi 5:13), quotes the Lord: "I will put my law in their inward parts, and write it upon their hearts" (Jeremiah 31:33). Paul quotes the prophecy of Jeremiah (Hebrews 8:8–10) and paraphrases it to the Corinthians (2 Corinthians 3:3). A Proverb advises to "write [the commandments] upon the table of thine heart" (3:3). The priests of Noah had chosen iniquity rather than following this symbolic internalizing of the commandments.

Abinadi quotes the last nine of the Ten Commandments as given to Moses on Mount Sinai (Mosiah 13:12–24), as he had intended to do before he was interrupted by the king (v. 1). The first two commandments were quoted before (12:34–36), and he repeated the second one as a reminder of what he had said (v. 12). There are no significant differences in the text of Exodus (20:2–17) and the Book of Mormon text. The first four commandments are concerning man's relationship to God, and the last six commandments are concerning man's relationship to his neighbor. This break down supports Jesus' answer to the lawyer's question:

> 36 Master, which *is* the great commandment in the law?
>
> 37 Jesus said unto him, Thou shalt love the Lord thy God with all thy heart, and with all thy soul, and with all thy mind.
>
> 38 This is the first and great commandment.
>
> 39 And the second *is* like unto it, Thou shalt love thy neighbour as thyself.
>
> 40 On these two commandments hang all the law and the prophets. [Matthew 22:36–40]

The Lord having sent Abinadi to prophesy unto them, he accuses the priests of not teaching their people these commandments (Mosiah 13: 25–26).

Mosiah 13:27–35 • Salvation Does Not Come by the Law of Moses

> 27 And now ye have said that salvation cometh by the law of Moses. I say unto you that it is expedient that ye should keep the law of Moses as yet; but I say unto you, that the time shall come when it shall no more be expedient to keep the law of Moses.
>
> 28 And moreover, I say unto you, that salvation doth not come by the law alone; and were it not for the atonement, which God himself shall make for the sins and iniquities of his people, that they must unavoidably perish, notwithstanding the law of Moses.

29 And now I say unto you that it was expedient that there should be a law given to the children of Israel, yea, even a very strict law; for they were a stiffnecked people, quick to do iniquity, and slow to remember the Lord their God;

30 Therefore there was a law given them, yea, a law of performances and of ordinances, a law which they were to observe strictly from day to day, to keep them in remembrance of God and their duty towards him.

31 But behold, I say unto you, that all these things were types of things to come.

32 And now, did they understand the law? I say unto you, Nay, they did not all understand the law; and this because of the hardness of their hearts; for they understood not that there could not any man be saved except it were through the redemption of God.

33 For behold, did not Moses prophesy unto them concerning the coming of the Messiah, and that God should redeem his people? Yea, and even all the prophets who have prophesied ever since the world began—have they not spoken more or less concerning these things?

34 Have they not said that God himself should come down among the children of men, and take upon him the form of man, and go forth in mighty power upon the face of the earth?

35 Yea, and have they not said also that he should bring to pass the resurrection of the dead, and that he, himself, should be oppressed and afflicted?

Abinadi returns to the question of whether salvation comes by the law of Moses. The reason they would no longer be required to keep the law (v. 27) was that Christ had come to fulfill the law. As Nephi had taught, they were to "look forward with steadfastness unto Christ, until the law shall be fulfilled. For, for this end was the law given" (2 Nephi 25:24–25). The apostle Paul taught the same doctrine: "Wherefore the law was our schoolmaster *to bring us* unto Christ, that we might be justified by faith. But after that faith is come, we are no longer under a schoolmaster" (Galatians 3:24–25). Therefore, salvation did not come by the law alone, but Christ would make an atonement for the sins and iniquities of his people when he came (Mosiah 13:28).

During the four thousand Old Testament years, the gospel had been revealed to dispensational prophets from Adam down to the time of Moses (between 1400 and 1200 B.C.). Moses also offered the gospel to his people, but they rejected it (see D&C 84:23–24), and the Lord gave them a lesser law. The law of Moses was a strict law because of the nature of the people at the time it was given (Mosiah 13:29). Paul taught: "It was added because of transgression" (Galatians 3:19). Joseph Smith said: "It was added to the gospel, since we learn that they had the gospel preached to them" (*TPJS*, 60; see Galatians 3:8). Thus it was a good law, one needed for that time period. A law of performances and ordinances (Mosiah 13:30), it was called "the law of carnal commandments" (D&C 84:27; Hebrews 7:16). Hebrews further described it: "*Which stood* only in meats and drinks, and divers washings, and carnal ordinances, imposed *on them* until the time of reformation (Hebrews 9:10). Their daily reminder through performances and ordinances (Mosiah 13:30) was because of being slow to remember God (v. 29). Today, sacrament ordinance is performed weekly in remembrance of the body and blood of Christ for the Resurrection and Atonement (see 3 Nephi 18:5–11).

The ordinances of the law were types of things to come [through Christ] (Mosiah 13:31). The sacrifices were symbolic of the sacrifice of Christ. For example, they were to be "made without blemish" (Leviticus 1:3). Christ "was in all points tempted like as we are, yet without sin" (Hebrews 4:15). They were to be offered "of his own voluntary will" (Leviticus 1:3). Christ voluntarily "gave up the Ghost" when his mission was finished (John 19:26). They were to not "break any bone of [the animal]" (Numbers 9:12). When the soldiers came "and saw that he was already dead, they broke not his legs" (John 19:33) (see Table 4).

Table 4
Law of Moses

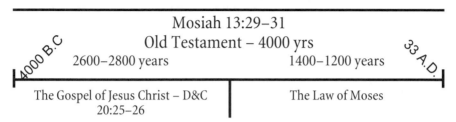

The Gospel of Jesus Christ – D&C 20:25–26	The Law of Moses
The Plan of Salvation – Moses 6:58–62	No Salvation

1. Be born again into the Kingdom of Heaven
  a. Water – keep the commandments (covenant)
  b. Spirit – Justified (cleansed)
  c. Blood of Only Begotten – sanctified (receive the Comforter because of the Atonement)
2. Peaceable things of immortal glory
3. The truth of all things
4. Quickeneth all things, maketh alive
5. Knoweth all things, hath power according to wisdom, mercy, truth, justice and judgment.
	1. Ten commandments (Mosiah 12:33 –13:24)
	2. Performances and ordinances observe strictly day to day
	Carnal commandments (D&C 84:27)
	  a. meats and drinks (Lev. 11, Num. 6:3, Deut. 14)
	  b. diverse washings (Lev. 15, Col. 2:16)
	  c. carnal ordinances (Deut. 22–23)
	3. Types and shadows of things to come (Christ. Galatians 3:24).
	Exodus 12:5–12; Moses 6:63

In summary, Abinadi explained to King Noah and his priests that the law of Moses they were to keep included the Ten Commandments and strict daily ordinances and performances. They were to keep them in remembrance of God, symbolic of Christ who would come to make the Atonement and bring about the redemption of all mankind. He decried that they do not understand the law they have professed (v. 32). Furthermore, he reminded them that Moses and *all* of the prophets had prophesied of these things (v. 33; emphasis added). He told the priests that they should be teachers of the message of the prophets to their people. These prophecies consisted, to one degree or another, of two major themes: first, God himself [Jesus Christ] was to come to the earth in the form of a [mortal] man and go forth in mighty power; and second, he would bring to pass the resurrection of the dead, and be oppressed and afflicted [make the Atonement] (v. 35). Abinadi then quoted the prophet Isaiah to prove his point. Isaiah's prophecy of the mission of Christ is the subject of the following chapter.

SACRED WRITING

Preaching Which is Sacred:

Mosiah 12:25–13:35   Abinadi's interchange with the priests of Noah.

Prophesying:

Mosiah 11:20–25   Abinadi's conditional prophecy of the Nephite bondage.

Mosiah 12:1–8   Abinadi's prophecy of unconditional bondage and conditional prophesy of destruction.

Mosiah 13:10   Abinadi prophesies of his death being a type and a shadow of King Noah's death.

Doctrines Learned:

Mosiah 11:20–22; 12:8   Some prophecies are conditional.

Mosiah 11:25   The Lord will not hear the prayers nor deliver the wicked from their afflictions.

Mosiah 12:27   Some prophecies are unconditional.

Mosiah 13:3, 7   God will not allow a prophet to be slain until his message is delivered and his mission completed.

Mosiah 13:28   Salvation did not come by the law of Moses alone but pointed to the Atonement of Christ.

Mosiah 13:33   All the prophets have prophesied of the coming of the Messiah.

General Authority Quotations

Pres. Joseph Fielding Smith • Mosiah 12:34–36; 13:11–24

Some people have the idea that the Ten Commandments were first given by Moses when he directed the children of Israel and formulated their code of laws. This is not the case. These great commandments are from the beginning and were understood in righteous communities in the days of

Adam. They are, in fact, fundamental parts of the gospel of Jesus Christ, and the gospel in its fulness was first given to Adam. [*Doctrines of Salvation*, comp. Bruce R. McConkie, 3 vols. (1954–56), 1:96]

After Moses had led the children of Israel out of Egypt, through the Red Sea, to the Sinaitic Peninsula, the Lord instructed Moses to ascend Mount Sinai for the purpose of receiving instruction. Moses, obedient to the call, ascended the Mount and there was instructed for a period of forty days. The gospel was given to Moses, and Moses was instructed in turn to explain the truths of the gospel to his people.

When Moses descended he witnessed the Israelites engaging in revelry, idolatry and lasciviousness. Moses, in disgust, dashed to the ground and broke the tables of stone which contained the Ten Commandments and the gospel of Jesus Christ.

The Lord later instructed Moses to return to the Mount with two other tables of stone, similar to the first, to receive a new set of instructions. In the "Inspired Version" of the Bible this is explained:

"And the Lord said unto Moses, Hew thee two other tables of stone, like unto the first, and I will write upon them also, the words of the law, according as they were written at the first on the tables which thou brakest; but it shall not be according to the first, for I will take away the priesthood out of their midst; therefore my holy order, and the ordinances thereof, shall not go before them; for my presence shall not go up in their midst, lest I destroy them" (Exodus 34:1). [*Improvement Era*, 44: 523]

Challenges to Eternal Life:

1. Commit yourself to be as courageous as Abinadi in defending the truths of the gospel of Jesus Christ (Mosiah 12:19).
2. As members of "the one and only true and living Church" (D&C 1:30), begin or continue a study program that you may understand and be able to explain the gospel to others (Mosiah 12:25).
3. Review the Ten Commandments as the basic laws of salvation and determine to keep them (Mosiah 12:33).
4. Choose a challenge of your own from this reading and apply it to your life.

Chapter Eleven

Abinadi Testifies of Christ

Mosiah 14–16

*H*istorical Setting: See the Historical Setting of chapter 10.

Precepts of This Reading:

> For behold, did not Moses prophesy unto them concerning the coming of the Messiah, and that God should redeem his people? Yea, and even all the prophets who have prophesied ever since the world began—have they not spoken more or less concerning these things? [Mosiah 13:33]

Although this precept was addressed to people living under the law of Moses, it is just as applicable to us, who are living under the higher law of Christ as it was to them. An outline of the chapter of Isaiah quoted by Abinadi, and his commentary that follows, presented below as a preparation for deeper study.

OUTLINE • MOSIAH 14–16

➢ Mosiah 14:1–3 The Jews will reject the mission of the Savior.

    a. They will not believe the testimony of the prophets. (v. 1).

    b. They will not believe the miracles that attest to his divinity (v. 1).

    c.   Christ will be raised up before the Father as a mortal (v. 2).

    d.   The Jews will despise and reject him (v. 3).

➤14:4–9   The Savior will suffer these things to save the world.

    a.   The world will esteem him to be smitten of God (v. 4).

    b.   All will have gone astray and will need his Atonement (v. 6).

    c.   He will be afflicted and oppressed, but will not retaliate (v. 7).

    d.   His life will be cut short upon the earth (v. 8).

    e.   He will be buried with the wicked and the rich (v. 9).

➤ 14:10–11   Christ's sacrifice will be a free will offering.

    a.   He will see his seed, or those who will accept his Atonement (v. 10).

    b.   He will satisfy the demands of justice (v. 11).

➤ 14:12   Christ will be exalted and extolled because he will fulfill his mission.

    a.   He will divide his glory with the strong.

    b.   He will voluntarily give his life.

    c.   He will suffer to gain an understanding of people.

    d.   He will pay the price for the Atonement.

➤ 15:1–5   Abinadi taught that God himself shall come down among the children of men and redeem his people.

    a.   Because he dwells in the flesh he shall be called the Son of God, subjecting his flesh to the will of the Father, being the Father and the Son (vv. 2–3).

        1.   The Father because he was conceived by the power of God.

        2.   The Son because of the flesh.

    b.   The Father and Son is one God, the very Eternal Father of heaven and earth (v. 4).

    c.   The flesh becomes subject to the Spirit or the Son to

the Father, being one God (v. 5).

1. Suffereth temptation but yields not.

2. Suffereth to be mocked, scourged, cast out, and disowned by his people.

➤ 15:6–9 After working many might miracles, Christ shall be led, even as Isaiah said, as a sheep before the shearer is dumb, so he opened not his mouth.

    a. He shall be led, crucified, and slain, the flesh becoming subject to the Spirit, the will of the Son swallowed up in the will of the Father (vv. 7–8).

        1. God breaketh the bands of death, gaining victory over death.

        2. The Son is given power to make intercession for the children of men.

    b. Ascending into heaven, Christ's bowels of mercy being filled with compassion, he stands betwixt the children of men and justice (v. 9).

        1. He redeemed them by breaking the bands of death and taking upon himself their iniquity and transgressions.

        2. He satisfied the demands of justice.

➤ 15:10–31 Christ's generation will be declared when he makes his soul an offering for sin and sees his seed.

    a. Those who hearken and believe in the words of the prophets that prophesied of the Lord are his seed and heirs to the Kingdom of God (vv. 11–13). They are:

        1. Those whose sins he has borne.

        2. Those for whom he died to redeem them from their transgressions.

        3. The prophets who have not fallen into transgression.

    b. The prophets are they who have published peace and have salvation and brought good tidings (vv. 14–18).

        1. How beautiful upon the mountains were their feet.

2. How beautiful upon the mountains are those who are still publishing peace.

3. How beautiful upon the mountains are those who shall hereafter publish peace.

c. How beautiful upon the mountains are the feet of the founder of peace, the Lord who has redeemed his people (vv. 19–20).

1. Were it not for the redemption, prepared from the foundation of the world, all mankind must perish.

2. The bands of death shall be broken, the Son reigneth and has power over death, and brings to pass the resurrection of the dead.

d. There comes a first resurrection of those who have been, who are, and shall be until the resurrection of Christ (vv. 21–25).

1. The prophets, those who believed their words, or all those that kept the commandments of God.

2. They are raised to dwell with God and have eternal life through Christ.

3. Those who have died before Christ came, in their ignorance, not having salvation declared to them.

4. Little children also have eternal life.

e. The Lord redeems none that rebel against him and die in their sins, have known the commandments of God and do not keep them (vv. 26–27).

1. They ought to tremble, the Lord cannot redeem such for he cannot deny himself.

2. He cannot deny justice when it has its claim.

f. The time comes when salvation shall be declared to every nation, kindred, tongue, and people (Abinadi then quotes Isaiah 52:8–10).

➤ 16:1–15   Abinadi stretched forth his hand and said: the time comes when all shall see the salvation of the Lord, see eye to eye, and confess before God that his judgments are just.

a. The wicked will be cast out and have cause to howl,

weep, wail and gnash their teeth because they would not hearken to the voice of the Lord (vv. 2–3).

   1. They are carnal, sensual, and devilish, and the devil has power over them.

   2. That old serpent did beguile our first parents, which was the cause of their fall.

   3. The fall was the cause of all mankind becoming carnal, sensual, and devilish, knowing evil from good, and subjecting themselves to the devil.

b. All mankind were lost and would be endlessly lost had God not redeemed them from their lost and fallen state (vv. 4–5).

   1. He that persists in his own carnal nature, and rebels against God remains in his fallen state and the devil has all power over him.

   2. He is as though there was no redemption made, being an enemy to God.

   3. The devil was an enemy to God.

c. If Christ had not come, speaking as though he had already come, there could have been no redemption (v. 6).

d. If Christ had not risen or broken the bands of death, there could have been no resurrection (v. 7).

   1. There is a resurrection and the sting of death is swallowed up in Christ (vv. 7–9).

   2. He is the light and life of the world, an endless light that cannot be darkened.

   3. A life which is endless that there can be no more death.

e. This mortal shall put on immortality and be brought before the bar of God to be judged (vv. 10–12).

   1. If they be good to the resurrection of endless life and happiness.

   2. If they be evil to the resurrection of endless damnation, delivered up to the devil.

(a) Gone according to their own wills and desires.

(b) Never having called upon the Lord while the arms of mercy were extended to them.

(c) Commanded to repent and they would not repent.

f. The people ought to tremble and repent of your sins and remember that only through Christ are ye saved (v. 13).

g. If the priests teach the law of Moses teach they should also, that it is a shadow of things to come (vv. 14–15).

1. Teach that redemption comes through Christ the Lord.

2. Christ is the very Eternal Father.

NOTES AND COMMENTARY

Introduction: Abinadi was a lone witness to the priests of Noah of the coming of Jesus Christ in the form of a man among the children of men. He testified that all of the prophets had foretold this marvelous advent and then quoted Isaiah as a second witness of the coming of the Messiah (Mosiah 13:33–35). The requirement of the law of Moses was thus fulfilled. "One witness shall not rise up against a man for any iniquity, or for any sin, in any sin that he sinneth: at the mouth of two witnesses, or at the mouth of three witnesses, shall the matter be established" (Deuteronomy 19:15).

Isaiah 53 is a well-known prophecy among Christians and Jews. Christians generally interpret it as a prophecy of the life and suffering of Jesus Christ. The Jewish interpretation is that Isaiah is describing the suffering of the entire nation of Israel, not a specific person. Abinadi's commentary sustains the Christian interpretation with details not found in the writings of other Christians. Abinadi's commentary on Isaiah 53 (Mosiah 15), although sometimes confusing to Church members, amplifies the beautiful message of Isaiah. Abinadi's great doctrinal insights and explanations of the true role of Jesus Christ are textual proofs that "Jesus is the Christ, the Eternal God"

(Book of Mormon title page). Mosiah's version of Isaiah is identical to the Old Testament text, except for a few words that will be identified and commented on as they appear.

Mosiah 14:1 (Isaiah 53:1) • Isaiah an Example of All Prophets

> Yea, even doth not Isaiah say: Who hath believed our report, and to whom is the arm of the Lord revealed?

Although Abinadi does not comment directly on this verse, the context in which he quotes it makes his interpretation clear. He had just declared that all of the prophets since the world began have testified of Christ. To support this statement, he said, "Yea, even doth not Isaiah say" and proceeded to quote the entirety of Isaiah 53. Clearly Abinadi understands this passage not as a prophesy of suffering Israel, but a prophecy of Jesus Christ, of whom all the prophets have testified. And yet, the people were not receptive to Isaiah's prophecies of Christ, to Abinadi's, or witness, to the testimonies of the other prophets. It was the hard hearts of the people and their lack of understanding of the law that brought Isaiah to cry, "Who hath believed our report?"

Other scriptures support Abinadi's interpretation. For example, Jacob, the brother of Nephi, prophesied "that none of the prophets have written, nor prophesied, save they have spoken concerning this Christ" (Jacob 7:11; see also 4:4–6). The Savior himself, when he ministered in the flesh, showed how the law of Moses, the Prophets, and the Psalms [the three divisions of the Hebrew bible] all foretold of him (Luke 24:27; 44). Paul's Epistle to the Romans confirmed that many of the people would not accept the testimony of the ancient prophets. He said, "But they would have not all obeyed the gospel" (Romans 10:16), and quoted the first phrase of Isaiah 53:1 to support his statement. Thus, both the Book of Mormon and the Bible give us the correct meaning of Isaiah's words "who hath believed our report?"

Abinadi also said: "God himself shall come among the children of men, and take upon him the form of a man" (Mosiah 13:34). Isaiah referred to Christ by the title Immanuel, which means "God with us" (see Isaiah 7:14; 8:8). While is no record of other prophets referring to him by this name, they might have done so because "many plain and precious things were taken away from the [Bible]" (1 Nephi 13:28).

Abinadi does not comment on the last half of Isaiah 53:1, "and to whom is the arm of the Lord revealed?" However, John interprets the many miracles that Jesus did among the Jews during his sojourn in the flesh as a fulfillment of Isaiah's words that the arm of the Lord would be revealed: "But though he had done so many miracles before them, yet they believed not on him: That the saying of Esaias the prophet might be fulfilled, which he spake, Lord, who hath believed our report? and to whom hath the arm of the Lord been revealed?" (John 12:37–38). The performance of miracles exhibited his power as the Son of God. Thus the people rejected the written testimony of their Redeemer as well as the physical evidence provided by his miracles. Although both testimonies were rejected, the two types of witnesses established the divinity of the Messiah.

The same symbolism is used to show his power in the latter days: "And I would, my brethren, that ye should know that all the kindreds of the earth cannot be blessed unless he shall make bare his arm in the eyes of the nations. Wherefore, the Lord God will proceed to make bare his arm in the eyes of all the nations, in bringing about his covenants and his gospel unto those who are of the house of Israel" (1 Nephi 22:10–11).

It is also used to show his power at the time of his appearance to the Jews.

> 43 And the remnant shall be gathered unto this place;
>
> 44 And then they shall look for me, and, behold, I will come; and they shall see me in the clouds of heaven, clothed with power and great glory; with all the holy angels; and he that watches not for me shall be cut off.

45 But before the arm of the Lord shall fall, an angel shall sound his trump, and the saints that have slept shall come forth to meet me in the cloud.

46 Wherefore, if ye have slept in peace blessed are you; for as you now behold me and know that I am, even so shall ye come unto me and your souls shall live, and your redemption shall be perfected; and the saints shall come forth from the four quarters of the earth.

47 Then shall the arm of the Lord fall upon the nations. [D&C 45:43–47]

Mosiah 14:2 (Isaiah 53:2) • The Childhood of Jesus

For he shall grow up before him as a tender plant, and as a root out of dry ground; he hath no form nor comeliness; and when we shall see him there is no beauty that we should desire him.

This verse gives only a vague picture of Christ and his nature on earth. It does not describe his physical appearance, but rather teaches that people would misjudge him because they were expecting their Messiah to come in a more glorious or supernatural way. However, Abinadi teaches quite specifically about Christ and his nature. In Mosiah 15:2–4 Abinadi comments on the nature of Christ as both the Father and the Son: "And because he dwelleth in flesh he shall be called the Son of God, and having subjected the flesh to the will of the Father, being the Father and the Son—"(Mosiah 15:2). Jesus Christ attained Godhood in the pre-mortal life as stated by the Apostle John: "In the beginning was the gospel preached through the Son. And the gospel was the word, and the word was with the Son, and the Son was with God, and the Son was of God. The same was in the beginning with God" (JST, John 1:1–2).

Christ was "the God of Abraham, and of Isaac, and the God of Jacob" (1 Nephi 19:10), and the leader of the children of Israel out of Egypt (see 1 Corinthians 10:1–4). Jesus' coming among humankind begins with his birth and childhood. Isaiah had previously foretold the Redeemer's birth (see Isaiah 7:14; 9:6), and in Isaiah 53 he describes his childhood. When studied in its context, Abinadi's commentary provides a beautiful explanation of the life, the nature, and the roles of our Lord and Savior as he came "down among the children of men" (Mosiah 15:1).

Returning to Mosiah 15:2, Abinadi's specific commentary is difficult to understand on a first or even a second reading. "And because he dwelleth in flesh he shall be called the Son of God, and having subjected the flesh to the will of the Father, being the Father and the Son" (Mosiah 15:2). This verse refers to Jesus' mortal ministry, when he would come to earth as a mortal and be called the Son of God; however, he would subject himself while in his mortal tabernacle to do the will of his Father in Heaven. The will of the Father was that Christ "be lifted up upon the cross; and after that [he] had been lifted up upon the cross, that [he] might draw all men unto [him], that as [he had] been lifted up by men even so should men be lifted up by the Father, to stand before [him], to be judged of their works, whether they be good or whether they be evil" (3 Nephi 27:14). In other words, the Father's will was for Christ to come and atone for all humankind. Thus while he would live upon the earth as the Son of God, he would carry out the will of the Father, and through divine investiture of authority would represent the Father. Therefore, he would be the Father and the Son while living upon the earth.

The above explanation by Abinadi in verse 2 qualifies as a commentary on the first phrase of Mosiah 14:2 (Isaiah 53:2): "For he shall grow up before him as a tender plant, and as a root out of dry ground." By substituting nouns for pronouns, we get a clearer picture: "For he [Christ] shall grow up before him [Elohim] as a tender plant." A tender plant is one that must be given special care by the gardener. It may need to be covered at night to protect it from frost, uncovered during the day to enable it to absorb the light and sunshine, and watered at frequent or regular hours. In like manner, the Father cared for his Son throughout his early childhood.

Luke recalls that "the child [Jesus] grew, and waxed strong in spirit, filled with wisdom: and the grace of God was upon him" (Luke

2:40). At age 12, he went with his parents on their annual passover trek to the temple. Upon their return, Jesus tarried behind—unknown to his parents. They supposed he was with others of the traveling group. Missing him at the end of the first day's journey, they spent three days searching for him and found him conversing with the learned doctors of Judaism (see Luke 2:41–48). In response to his mother's mild chastisement, he responded, "How is it that ye sought me? Wist ye not that I must be about my Father's business? And they understood not the saying which he spake unto them" (Luke 2:49–50). Even his mother seems not to have known the extent to which Heavenly Father had cared for him as a tender plant.

The phrase, "root out of dry ground," may be interpreted as Christ growing up in apostate Judaism. In Revelation 22:16, Christ identifies himself as "the root and the offspring of David." Both Mary his mother and Joseph his stepfather were descendants of David and of the lineage of Judah (see Matthew 1:1–17; Luke 3:23:38). Judah, as a nation, was spiritually barren and could not give him the nurturing he needed to prepare him for his ministry. Instead, his Heavenly Father nurtured him. His nurturing was perfect and prepared Christ for his ministry in due time. Joseph Smith taught that Jesus was prepared for his ministry long before he was thirty years of age, but waited to begin his ministry until the Father directed him.

> When still a boy He had all the intelligence necessary to enable Him to rule and govern the kingdom of the Jews, and could reason with the wisest and most profound doctors of law and divinity, and make their theories and practice to appear like folly compared with the wisdom He possessed; but He was a boy only, and lacked physical strength even to defend His own person; and was subject to cold, to hunger and to death. [*TPJS*, 392]

Being thus prepared, he carried out the will of the Father when the time came for him to fulfill his ministry.[1]

Having referred to the ministry of Jesus, Abinadi comments on the nature of the Son of God during mortality that would enable him to finalize his ministry by bringing about the Resurrection. Christ was: "The Father, because he was conceived by the power of God; and the Son, because of the flesh; thus becoming the Father and Son" (Mosiah 15:3). Because he was conceived by an immortal being, his divine Father in Heaven, Jesus had immortality as a part of his own nature. Because he was born of a mortal woman, he was also part mortal. Being mortal he was subject to death and had power to lay down his life; being immortal he had power to break the bands of death, or take up his life. This is clearly taught to the Jews during his earthly ministry: "Therefore doth my Father love me, because I lay down my life, that I might take it again. No man taketh it from me, but I lay it down of myself. I have power to lay it down, and I have power to take it again. This commandment have I received of my Father" (John 10:17–18).

Possessing the power of the Father enabled him to overcome the grave and bring about the Resurrection. Through his dual nature he was the Father and Son, being immortal as well as mortal.

Abinadi's explanation of Christ's nature seems to be a commentary on the latter part of Isaiah 53:2; which says "He hath no form nor comeliness; and when we shall see him there is no beauty that we should desire him" (Mosiah 14:2). That Jesus had "no form nor comeliness" is the prophet Isaiah's way of saying that he looked like a normal Jewish boy, and was not distinctive in his looks although he was the Son of God. People in Nazareth did not look upon him as different from his brothers and sisters or other children in the community. They referred to him as "the carpenter's son" (Matthew

---

[1] Under the law of Moses, the Levite sons, those who held the priesthood, were to serve in the work of the tabernacle at the age of thirty (see Numbers 4:34), although there was apparently an apprenticeship beginning at age twenty-five (see Numbers 8:24). This may be the reason the ministry of Jesus began at age thirty. He always lived the law of Moses to the letter.

13:54–56) or "the son of Joseph whose father and mother we know" (John 6:42). His having "no beauty that we should desire him" is not an indication of ugliness or plainness, but is an example of poetic parallelism, a repetition of the same thought. It was another expression of the fact that he looked like any other child growing up in Nazareth. Abinadi's commentary explains how this was possible: Christ was both mortal and the divine Son of God.

After describing the dual nature of the mortal Messiah, Abinadi adds one more dimension to his description of the Savior: "And they are one God, yea, the very Eternal Father of heaven and of earth" (Mosiah 15:4). This verse is a summation of the two previous verses spoken by Abinadi. The one God referred to is Jesus Christ. The plural "they" refers to the dual roles in his ministry and to his dual nature as the Father and the Son. He is the Son of God, but by divine investiture of authority he represents the Father in his ministry. Having immortality and mortality in his nature he has power over life and death. Thus he has all power in heaven and in earth. He is the divine Son of God with all the attributes of his Father to make the Atonement and bring about the Resurrection. His is in the role of the Father and the Son, and he is thus one God.[2]

Abinadi's statement that Christ is "the very Eternal Father of heaven and of earth" (Mosiah 15:4) undoubtedly refers to the creative power of Christ as the Father of this earth and of other earths in the heavens. That Christ created this and other worlds is repeatedly taught in the New Testament (see John 1:3, 10; Colossians 1:16; Hebrews 1:2). It is also confirmed in modern scripture (see D&C 14:9; 76:24;

---

[2] It should be kept in mind that Abinadi is not instructing prospective members of the Church. He is accusing, chastising, and refuting a group of apostate priests who claim to be scriptural authorities. Recall his words to them earlier: "And now Abinadi said unto them: Are you priests, and pretend to teach this people, and to understand the spirit of prophesying, and yet desire to know of me what these things mean? I say unto you, wo be unto you for perverting the ways of the Lord! For if ye understand these things ye have not taught them; therefore, ye have perverted the ways of the Lord" (Mosiah 12:25–26).

93:10; Moses 1:31–33). A diagram of Abinadi's teaching in Mosiah 15:2–4 would be thus:

Table 5

SUMMARY OF ABINADI'S COMMENTARY OF ISAIAH 53:2

A. How Christ is Both the Father and the Son

	The Father	The Son
Christ's Ministry Provides the Atonement	He is the Father because he does the will of the Father (Mosiah 15:2).	He is the Son because he dwelt in the flesh (Mosiah 15:2).
Christ's Nature Provides the Resurrection	He was immortal because he was conceived by the power of God (Mosiah 15:3).	He was mortal because he was born of a mortal mother with the power to lay down life (Mosiah 15:3).

B. Christ's Dual Nature

Christ's Role Jesus is the Creator of Heaven and Earth	There is one God—Jesus Christ (Mosiah 15:4)

The prophet Abinadi has masterfully shown the apostate priests the role of Christ as the Father by divine investiture of authority and the divine nature that would enable him to atone for the sins of humankind and provide for their resurrection. In addition, he testifies that Christ is the Father in his role as the Creator of heaven and earth.

The complex definition of Jesus Christ given by Abinadi is really quite simple and beautiful when seen in the light of Abinadi's commentary on Isaiah, which is supported by modern revelation. In a revelation to Joseph Smith, that may have been originally of the record of John, the Lord proclaimed: "And that I am in the Father, and the Father in me, and the Father and I are one— The Father because he gave me of his fullness, and the Son because I was in the world and made flesh my tabernacle, and dwelt among the sons of men" (D&C 93:3–4). This shows that John, as well as Abinadi, and certainly all of the prophets, knew and appreciated the role of Jesus Christ.

Other Book of Mormon prophets also understood and taught the position of Christ as fulfilling the role of the Father as well as the Son. Nephi, son of Lehi, taught that "there is a God, and he is Christ, and he cometh in the fulness of his own time" (2 Nephi 11:7). Amulek taught the repentant lawyer Zeezrom that there is only one God who is the Son of God and that "he is the very Eternal Father of heaven and of earth, and all things which in them are; he is the beginning and the end, the first and the last" (Alma 11:39; see Mosiah 14:26–40).

In the meridian of time, as Nephi prayed on behalf of his people concerning the coming of the sign of Christ's birth as prophesied by Samuel the Lamanite, the voice of the Lord came to Nephi saying that the sign would be given that night and that on the morrow he would come into the world to fulfill what the prophets had spoken and made known from the foundation of the world. He further testified that he would come "to do the will, both of the Father and of the Son—of the Father because of me, and of the Son because of my flesh" (3 Nephi 1:13–14). And as a last example, hundreds of years before the Nephite prophets taught these truths, the Lord appeared to the brother of Jared and identified himself as "he who was prepared from the foundation of the world to redeem [his] people. Behold, I am Jesus Christ. I am the Father and the Son. In me shall all mankind have life, and that eternally, even they who shall believe on my name" (Ether 3:14). Thus we see that this eternal truth of Christ's true position was taught throughout the history of the Nephites and among the Jaredites as well. Hopefully, as we understand the role of Jesus Christ as the Father and the Son as taught in the Book of Mormon, we will also appreciate more fully the subtitle of the Book of Mormon: "Another Testament of Jesus Christ."

A further verification of Christ's various roles as the Father was given in "A Doctrinal Exposition by the First Presidency and the Twelve" on 30 June 1916. On this occasion, the Brethren gave detailed information and scriptural evidence about the four uses of the term *Father* that appear in the scriptures. Their exposition is really the key to understanding Mosiah 15. Because of the length and detail of this exposition, its four major points are here listed. It is given in full under "General Authority Quotations" at the end of the chapter.

1. Father as literal parent: Hebrews 12:9; Ether 3:14
2. Father as Creator: Ether 4:7; Mosiah 15:4; Alma 11:38–39
3. Jesus Christ, the Father of those who abide in his gospel: John 17:6–12, 20–24; D&C 9:1; 25:1; 34:3; 121:7
4. Jesus Christ, the Father by divine investiture of authority: John 14:28; Revelation 22:8, 9; D&C 93:21

All the scriptural uses of the term *Father* thus refer to Jesus Christ, except our being the spirit offspring of our Father in Heaven. The title page of the Book of Mormon declares that a major purpose of the book is "the convincing of the Jew and Gentile that Jesus is the Christ, the Eternal God" (see also 2 Nephi 26:12–13). Understanding Abinadi's commentary on Isaiah helps fulfill this major purpose.

Mosiah 14:3–5 (Isaiah 53:3–5) • Despised and Rejected of Men

> 3 He is despised and rejected of men; a man of sorrows, and acquainted with grief; and we hid as it were our faces from him; he was despised, and we esteemed him not.
>
> 4 Surely he has borne our griefs, and carried our sorrows; yet we did esteem him stricken, smitten of God, and afflicted.
>
> 5 But he was wounded for our transgressions, he was bruised for our iniquities; the chastisement of our peace was upon him; and with his stripes we are healed.

Abinadi gives but one verse of commentary:

> And thus the flesh becoming subject to the Spirit, or the Son to

> the Father, being one God, suffereth temptation, and yieldeth not to the temptation, but suffereth himself to be mocked, and scourged, and cast out, and disowned by his people. [Mosiah 15:5]

Here Abinadi explains Isaiah's prophecy of Christ's ministry. Not only would Christ be rejected and humiliated, but he would also be tempted. However, he will not yield to temptation. This comment by Abinadi helps us better understand the Savior's ministry and also the perfect example he set as part of the overall Atonement for humankind. As he commanded the Nephites, we are also to be the manner of beings that he was in his ministry (see 3 Nephi 27:27). We must be "willing to submit to all things which the Lord seeth fit to inflict upon [us], even as a child doth submit to his father" (Mosiah 3:19), or, as Abinadi says, submit our flesh to the Spirit as the Son did to the Father.

The writings of the New Testament Apostles also support Abinadi's commentary. Matthew paraphrased Isaiah 53:4—"Himself took our infirmities, and bare our sicknesses"—to show its fulfillment in Jesus' casting out devils and healing the sick in Capernaum (Matthew 8:16–17). Paul taught the Hebrews that Jesus "was in all points tempted like as we are, yet without sin" (Hebrews 4:15). And Peter quotes or paraphrases parts of Isaiah 53:4–5 and equates it with Jesus' being on the cross: "Who his own self bare our sins in his own body on the tree, that we, being dead to sins, should live unto righteousness: by whose stripes ye were healed" (1 Peter 2:24). While his mission culminated on the cross, his entire life and particularly his ministry was one of temptation: being mocked, scourged, cast out, and disowned by his people. Mark records that Jesus taught his disciples "that the Son of man must suffer many things, and be rejected of the elders, and of the chief priests, and scribes, and be killed" (Mark 8:31). With the support of these scriptures, we may conclude that Abinadi gave us a briefer but very accurate commentary of the Savior's ministry.

Mosiah 14:6 (Isaiah 53:6) •
All Have Gone Astray

> All we, like sheep, have gone astray; we have turned every one
> to his own way; and the Lord hath laid on him the iniquities of us all.

Peter quotes the first part of this verse and adds: "but are now returned unto the Shepherd and Bishop of our souls" (1 Peter 2:24–25). Paul wrote: "For all have sinned, and come short of the glory of God" (Romans 3:23, see also 1 John 1:8). Thus all who lived on this earth have sinned except Christ who took upon him all of our sins.

Abinadi explains the relationship between Christ and the Father after he had completed his ministry: "Having ascended into heaven, having the bowels of mercy; being filled with compassion towards the children of men; standing betwixt them and justice; having broken the bands of death, taken upon himself their iniquity and their transgressions, having redeemed them, and satisfied the demands of justice" (Mosiah 15:9).

This commentary sheds further light on the role of Jesus Christ as the Father and the Son. Having suffered for all humankind's sins, Jesus Christ fulfilled the demands of justice in his role as the Father. His compassion to those who repent illustrates his role as the Son since his mercy satisfies the demands of justice. While the New Testament tells us that the Atonement was accomplished, we must turn to the Book of Mormon to enlarge our understanding of the roles of mercy and justice. Other passages of the Book of Mormon such as Amulek's testimony to the apostate Zoramites (see Alma 34:15–16), and Alma's instructions to his wayward son Corianton (see Alma 42) give us more enlightenment on these principles of mercy and justice. An analysis of these references will be left to another time.

Mosiah 14:7 (Isaiah 53:7) • Brought as a Lamb to the Slaughter

> He was oppressed, and he was afflicted, yet he opened not his mouth; he is brought as a lamb to the slaughter, and as a sheep before her shearers is dumb so he opened not his mouth.

Isaiah prophecies here of Jesus' being judged before Pilate and Herod. Abinadi's commentary on this verse is little more than a repetition of Isaiah.

> And after all this, after working many mighty miracles among the children of men, he shall be led, yea, even as Isaiah said, as a sheep before the shearer is dumb, so he opened not his mouth." [Mosiah 15:6]

The New Testament records Jesus' actual appearance before Pilate and Herod. While Jesus did answer Pilate, he did so only sparingly, and on one occasion he gave him no answer (see John 19:9). When Pilate sent him to Herod, Jesus answered him not a word. Herod could only retaliate by mocking him (see Luke 23:8–11). Peter described the trials this way: "Who, when he was reviled, reviled not again; when he suffered, he threatened not; but committed himself to him that judgeth righteously" (1 Peter 2:23). Isaiah's prophecy was fulfilled. The eunuch that Philip found in Gaza was reading Isaiah 53:7–8, and when Philip testified of Jesus he was baptized (see Acts 8:26–38).

Mosiah 14:8 (Isaiah 53:8) • Cut Off from the Living

> He was taken from prison and from judgment; and who shall declare his generation? For he was cut off out of the land of the living; for the transgressions of my people was he stricken.

This verse contains the prophecy of Christ's crucifixion and death. In his commentary (Mosiah 15:7–13), Abinadi elaborates on the death of the Savior, speaking of the Resurrection following the Crucifixion and then answering Isaiah's question: "Who shall declare his generation?" Abinadi first comments on the Savior's crucifixion and death, "Yea, even so he shall be led, crucified, and slain, the flesh becoming subject even unto death, the will of the Son being swallowed up in the will of the Father" (Mosiah 15:7), and then he concludes, "And thus God breaketh the bands of death, having gained the victory over death; giving the Son power to make intercession for the children of men" (Mosiah 14:8). In the New Testament we find the concept of breaking the bands of death and gaining a victory in Paul's First Epistle to the Corinthians; however, Paul is quoting what "is written" (1 Corinthians 15:54–55). Where was it written? Some have supposed it to be a quotation from Hosea 13:14, but if so, the Hosea text has been greatly modified. It seems more logical that this quote is a part "of the many plain and precious things which have been taken out of the [Bible]" (1 Nephi 13:29). Nonetheless, it was known to Old Testament prophets that the Resurrection of Christ would break the bands of death, and gain victory over the grave. Abinadi would probably not have coined a phrase so close to what Paul was reading from the Hebrew Bible. Of course the Spirit could have dictated the same words, but it seems most logical that both Paul and Abinadi were quoting from an earlier text which has since been lost.

After speaking of the Resurrection and Atonement of Christ (Mosiah 15:8–9; quoted previously), Abinadi answers the question posed by Isaiah: "And now I say unto you, who shall declare his generation?" (Mosiah 14:8). "And now I say unto you, who shall declare his generation? Behold, I say unto you, that when his soul has been made an offering for sin he shall see his seed. And now what say ye? And who shall be his seed?" (Mosiah 15:10). Abinadi combines his answer to the question, "who shall declare his generation'" with Isaiah's declaration that when Christ made "his soul an offering for sin, he shall see his seed." The question and the declaration go hand in hand. Those who are "spiritually begotten" of Christ through being born again are adopted as "his sons and daughters" (Mosiah 5:7; see also Galatians 4:1–7; Romans 8:14–17; and the Exposition by the First Presidency and the Twelve cited above). Thus the adopted, born-again sons and daughters of Jesus Christ will declare the message of the gospel that Jesus Christ was sent to the earth to redeem all humankind. Following his death, Christ's Apostles and others were to take this message to all the world (see Mark 16:15–16). Abinadi explains at some length who these messengers will be, the prophets and those who have accepted and lived their message:

> 11 Behold I say unto you, that whosoever has heard the words of the prophets, yea, all the holy prophets who have prophesied concerning the coming of the Lord—I say unto you, that all those who have hearkened unto their words, and believed that the Lord would redeem his people, and have looked forward to that day for a remission of their sins, I say unto you, that these are his seed, or they are the heirs of the kingdom of God.
>
> 12 For these are they whose sins he has borne; these are they for whom he has died, to redeem them from their transgressions. And now, are they not his seed?
>
> 13 Yea, and are not the prophets, every one that has opened his mouth to prophesy, that has not fallen into transgression, I mean all the holy prophets ever since the world began? I say unto you that they are his seed. [Mosiah 15:11–13]

Mosiah 14:9 (Isaiah 53:9) • His Grave with the Wicked

> And he made his grave with the wicked, and with the rich in his death; because he had done no *evil*, neither was any deceit in his mouth.

Abinadi does not comment on this verse from Isaiah. Did the priests understand it? Jesus was crucified between two thieves (see Matthew 27:38; Mark 15:27; Luke 23:32–33; John 19:18). He was buried in the tomb of a rich man, Joseph of Arimathaea (see Matthew 27:57–60; Mark 15:42–46; Luke 23:50–53; John 19:38–42). Isaiah's announcement that he had done "no evil" (emphasis added) is the only word change between the text of the King James Bible and the Book of Mormon. The KJV records, "He had done no violence." "No evil" is consistent with Abinadi's earlier declaration that he yielded not to temptation (Mosiah 15:5). No "deceit in his mouth" proclaims that he spoke the truth at all times. Peter varies slightly the same Isaiah passage: "Neither was *guile* found in his mouth" (1 Peter 2:23; emphasis added). The translation into English may account for the word differences. The message is clear. There was no reason or basis that justified his Crucifixion. However, his death was not only foreknown but "was foreordained before the foundation of the world" (1 Peter 1:20; see also Ether 3:14). Isaiah understood this clearly.

Mosiah 14:10 (Isaiah 53:10) • His Soul and Offering for Sin

> Yet it pleased the Lord to bruise him; he hath put him to grief; when thou shalt make his soul an offering for sin he shall see his seed, he shall prolong his days, and the pleasure of the Lord shall prosper in his hand.

The wording of the opening phrase of this verse may have two meanings depending on the interpretation of the word *Lord,* as capitalized in the Book of Mormon text. In the King James text, the word is all in capital letters, LORD. Some would interpret this to mean Jehovah, and others would interpret it to refer to Elohim. Since there are no original manuscripts, the correct interpretation can only be determined by the context. Through the years, scribes have altered the word for God back and forth to fit their own understanding.[3] If the person referred to as Lord is Elohim, then the phrase would read that it pleased Elohim to bruise Christ or allow him to suffer affliction and grief as part of the Atonement. This interpretation was nicely summarized by John in his Gospel: "For God so loved the world, that he gave his only begotten Son, that whosoever believeth in him should not perish, but have everlasting life" (John 3:16).

If the word *Lord* is interpreted to refer to Jehovah, then it would

---

[3] Illustrations of the variant use of the word *God* may be seen in a comparison of the almost identical Psalms 14 and 53, or in Psalm 110 and Matthew's quotation of it in Matthew 22:44. It seems apparent that scribes have pondered and altered these quotations to fit their private interpretation of the text.

read that it pleased Jehovah to bruise Christ. Since Jehovah is the Old Testament name for Christ, this may sound like an impossible interpretation. However, it could be interpreted to say that Christ was willing to suffer to bring about the Atonement. This second interpretation is sustained in modern revelation. In a revelation to Orson Pratt, Jesus Christ identified himself as he "who so loved the world that he gave his own life, that as many as would believe might become the sons of God" (D&C 34:1–3). Perhaps both interpretations are valid. Certainly Elohim was the author of the plan of salvation that provided for a Savior (see Abraham 3:27–28; Moses 4:1–2), and, as revealed to Orson Pratt, Christ did make a free-will offering.

The offering of Christ's soul for sin was done in the Garden of Gethsemane. "The spirit and the body are the soul of man" (D&C 88:15). There he suffered as a God "temptations, and pain of body, hunger, thirst and fatigue [of the body], even more than man can suffer, except it be unto death; for behold, blood cometh from every pore, so great shall be his anguish [of the spirit] for the wickedness and abominations of his people" (Mosiah 3:7; see also 2 Nephi 9:20–21; Alma 7:11; and Luke 22:44). As he paid this all-encompassing price for sin, he apparently had a panoramic view of all the world's experiences, past, present, and future, and, in some way, beyond our comprehension, he placed himself in the position of every inhabitant of the earth, that he might satisfy the demands of justice for the punishment of every broken law of humankind. He was able to prolong his days, at least in a figurative sense, in order to pass through this agonizing ordeal for the entire period of the earth's habitation by mortal beings, from Adam to the final scene. With the payment of this eternal debt, the pleasure (will) of the Lord (Jehovah or Christ) and LORD (Elohim) was fulfilled, and Christ prospered by fulfilling the mission of his Atonement. With the sacrifice of his soul and the end of his mortal life, Christ's seed became responsible for prolonging his days in another way, that of carrying on his mission. His seed, as stated above, are the prophets and teachers of the gospel and all who accept the gospel message (Mosiah 15:10–13; quoted previously).

Mosiah 14:11 (Isaiah 53:11) •
The Travail of His Soul

> He shall see the travail of his soul, and shall be satisfied; by his knowledge shall my righteous servant justify many; for he shall bear their iniquities.

An understanding of this verse comes by substituting nouns for the pronouns. From the context of the verse, it is clear that Elohim shall see the travail of Jesus Christ's soul and shall be satisfied. Jesus suffered in Gethsemane and there took "upon himself [the people's] iniquity and their transgressions, having redeemed them, and satisfied the demands of justice" (Mosiah 15:9). Jesus' knowledge of the sins of all humankind (see 2 Nephi 9:20) and his sinlessness—"a righteous servant"—enabled him to make an eternal sacrifice. Many people will thus may be justified and obtain salvation because Jesus paid for their sins. Some have interpreted the servant's justifying of "many" as evidence that Jesus, in his foreknowledge, only suffered for those who he knew would repent. This interpretation is not consistent with Jacob's declaration that Jesus "suffereth the pains of all men, yea, the pains of every living creature, both men, women, and children, who belong to the family of Adam" (2 Nephi 9:21); or with Jacob and Amulek's pronouncement that the Atonement must be an infinite atonement (see 2 Nephi 9:7), in other words, an infinite and eternal sacrifice (see Alma 34:10). Samuel the Lamanite taught that the Atonement brought *all* humankind back into the presence of God (Helaman 14:17). However, Jacob taught that only those who repent, are baptized, and have perfect faith in the Holy One of Israel will be saved—and if not they will be damned (see 2 Nephi 9:23–24). Therefore, although Jesus paid for the sins of all humankind, not all will meet the criteria for obtaining the blessings of eternal life.

> 16 For behold, I, God, have suffered these things for all, that they might not suffer if they would repent;
>
> 17 But if they would not repent they must suffer even as I;
>
> 18 Which suffering caused myself, even God, the greatest of all,

to tremble because of pain, and to bleed at every pore, and to suffer both body and spirit—and would that I might not drink the bitter cup, and shrink— [D&C 19:16–18]

Those who do not meet the criteria will be part of the fulfillment of Isaiah's further prophecy, which follows.

Mosiah 14:12 (Isaiah 53:12) • Divide the Spoil with the Strong

> Therefore will I divide him a portion with the great, and he shall divide the spoil with the strong; because he hath poured out his soul unto death; and he was numbered with the transgressors; and he bore the sins of many, and made intercession for the transgressors.

In context, Elohim, or Heavenly Father, is still speaking in this verse. Because Jesus had fulfilled his role as the Redeemer of humankind, he "ascended into heaven" (Mosiah 15:9) and took his position "on the right hand of the Father" in the council of the Gods (D&C 20:24). In turn, Jesus is willing to divide his blessings, or spoils—a term referring to what was obtained after winning a battle—with those who accept and remain strong in the gospel. He taught this principle to his disciples at the end of his ministry: "Ye are they which have continued with me in my temptations. And I appoint unto you a kingdom, as my Father hath appointed unto me; That ye may eat and drink at my table in my kingdom, and sit on thrones judging the twelve tribes of Israel" (Luke 22:28–30).

Jesus was able to do this because he had poured out his soul unto death, or had freely given his life that "I might take it again. No man taketh it from me, but I lay it down of myself" (John 10:17–18). In accomplishing this momentous task, he was numbered with the transgressors, or suffered the most degrading of deaths at that time.[4] Prior to his death, he had gone to Gethsemane and there, as Isaiah foretold, bore the sins of those who repented and also paid for those

---

[4] Bruce R. McConkie, *Doctrinal New Testament Commentary*, [1965], 1:814–816.

who ignorantly sinned. As explained earlier, Christ paid for the sins of all humankind, both the repentant and unrepentant, but the context of Isaiah describes only those who benefitted from the Atonement by repenting of their sins. Having completed his prophecy of Christ's suffering, Isaiah returned to prophecy of the gathering of Israel (Isaiah 54), the subject he had left to insert this inspiring and now well-known prophecy of Christ's mission.

Mosiah 15:1–13 • Abinadi
Comments on Isaiah

Abinadi's Thesis: Mosiah 13:33–35

Abinadi speaks in ...	Commenting on ...	Other Commentary
Mosiah 14:33–34	Isaiah 53:1	Rom. 10:16; John 12:37–38
15:1	(Mosiah 14:1)	
15:2	53:2a (14:2)	Luke 2:40–50
15:3	53:2b (14:2)	Rev. 22:16; Matt. 13:55–56; John 6:42
15:4	53:2 (14:2)	
15:5	53:3–5	3 Nephi 27:27; Mosiah 3:19; Matt. 8:16–17; Heb. 4:15; 1 Peter 2:24; Mark 8:31
15:9	53:6	Alma 34:15–16; chapter 42
15:6	53:7	
15:7–8	53:8	1 Cor. 15:54–55; Mosiah 5:7
15:11–13	53:10b	

Abinadi returns to the original question posed by one of Noah's apostate priests about the meaning of Isaiah 52:7–10. "How beautiful upon the mountains are the feet of him that bringeth good tidings; that publisheth peace; that bringeth good tidings of good; that publisheth salvation; that saith unto Zion, Thy God reigneth" (Mosiah 12:21). Abinadi's commentary on this verse constitutes the rest of Mosiah 15. Because of Abinadi's extensive discussion of Isaiah 53, King Noah's priests are prepared to understand not only the meaning of this verse in question, but also the plan of salvation. Abinadi's commentary begins with an interpretation of Isaiah 52:7 and ends with a call to repentance.

Mosiah 15:14–17 • The Publishers of Peace

> 14 And these are they who have published peace, who have brought good tidings of good, who have published salvation; and said unto Zion: Thy God reigneth!
>
> 15 And O how beautiful upon the mountains were their feet!
>
> 16 And again, how beautiful upon the mountains are the feet of those that are still publishing peace!
>
> 17 And again, how beautiful upon the mountains are the feet of those who shall hereafter publish peace, yea, from this time henceforth and forever!

Abinadi had already established the idea that the seed of Christ are those spiritually begotten of him as the Father of their eternal lives (vv. 10–13). He now states that these same servants are the publishers of peace and how beautiful upon the mountains were their feet and the feet of those who are now and who will yet publish peace. True peace comes only from the gospel, so those who travel (upon their feet) to preach the gospel upon the mountains of the earth are beautiful in the eyes of the people who accept their message (vv. 14–17).

Mosiah 15:18–19 • The Lord, the Founder of Peace

These verses refer to the founder of that peace—Jesus Christ. Without him there would be no peace. In Abinadi's words:

> 18 And behold, I say unto you, this is not all. For O how beautiful upon the mountains are the feet of him that bringeth good tidings, that is the founder of peace, yea, even the Lord, who has redeemed his people; yea, him who has granted salvation unto his people;
>
> 19 For were it not for the redemption which he hath made for his people, which was prepared from the foundation of the world, I say

unto you, were it not for this, all mankind must have perished.

Mosiah 15:20–25 • The First Resurrection

20 But behold, the bands of death shall be broken, and the Son reigneth, and hath power over the dead; therefore, he bringeth to pass the resurrection of the dead.

21 And there cometh a resurrection, even a first resurrection; yea, even a resurrection of those that have been, and who are, and who shall be, even until the resurrection of Christ—for so shall he be called.

22 And now, the resurrection of all the prophets, and all those that have believed in their words, or all those that have kept the commandments of God, shall come forth in the first resurrection; therefore, they are the first resurrection.

23 They are raised to dwell with God who has redeemed them; thus they have eternal life through Christ, who has broken the bands of death.

24 And these are those who have part in the first resurrection; and these are they that have died before Christ came, in their ignorance, not having salvation declared unto them. And thus the Lord bringeth about the restoration of these; and they have a part in the first resurrection, or have eternal life, being redeemed by the Lord.

25 And little children also have eternal life.

Christ broke the bands of death and, as the Son of God, he reigns and has power over the dead that he may bring about their resurrection (v. 20). The first resurrection includes those who "have been, and who are, and who shall be, even until the resurrection of Christ" (v. 21). It includes the prophets and those who have believed in their words and kept the commandments. They will dwell with Christ, who redeemed them, and have eternal life (vv. 22–23). The first resurrection also includes those who died in ignorance before Christ came, not having had salvation declared to them (v. 24). Although Abinadi does not expound upon this group, Peter and modern revelation qualify their salvation upon the condition of their accepting the gospel in the spirit world: "For Christ also hath once suffered for sins, the just for the unjust, that he might bring us to God, being put to death in the flesh, but quickened by the Spirit: By which also he went and preached unto the spirits in prison; Which sometime were disobedient, when once the longsuffering of God waited in the days of Noah, while the ark was a preparing, wherein few, that is, eight souls were saved by water" (1 Peter 3:18–20). Peter commented further: "Who shall give account to him that is ready to judge the quick and the dead. For for this cause was the gospel preached also to them that are dead, that they might be judged according to men in the flesh, but live according to God in the spirit" (1 Peter 4:5–6). The Prophet Joseph Smith saw in vision and heard:

> 7 Thus came the voice of the Lord unto me, saying: All who have died without a knowledge of this gospel, who would have received it if they had been permitted to tarry, shall be heirs of the celestial kingdom of God;
>
> 8 Also all that shall die henceforth without a knowledge of it, who would have received it with all their hearts, shall be heirs of that kingdom;
>
> 9 For I, the Lord, will judge all men according to their works, according to the desire of their hearts. [D&C 137:7–9]

Abinadi also announces that little children shall have eternal life (Mosiah 15:25). Joseph Smith adds his witness: "And I also beheld that all children who die before they arrive at the years of accountability are saved in the celestial kingdom of heaven" (D&C 137:10).

Mosiah 15:26–27 • No Part in the First Resurrection

> 26 But behold, and fear, and tremble before God, for ye ought to tremble; for the Lord redeemeth none such that rebel against him and die in their sins; yea, even all those that have perished in their sins ever since the world began, that have wilfully rebelled against God, that have known the commandments of God, and would not keep them; these are they that have no part in the first resurrection.
>
> 27 Therefore ought ye not to tremble? For salvation cometh to none such; for the Lord hath redeemed none such; yea, neither can

the Lord redeem such; for he cannot deny himself; for he cannot deny justice when it has its claim.

Abinadi closes his commentary on Isaiah 52:7 with a warning to those who rebel against Christ and die in their sins, those who have known the commandments and would not keep them. These ought to tremble and fear, for salvation does not come to such, and justice will claim them instead of mercy.

Mosiah 15:28–31 • All Shall See Salvation

28 And now I say unto you that the time shall come that the salvation of the Lord shall be declared to every nation, kindred, tongue, and people.

29 Yea, Lord, thy watchmen shall lift up their voice; with the voice together shall they sing; for they shall see eye to eye, when the Lord shall bring again Zion.

30 Break forth into joy, sing together, ye waste places of Jerusalem; for the Lord hath comforted his people, he hath redeemed Jerusalem.

31 The Lord hath made bare his holy arm in the eyes of all the nations; and all the ends of the earth shall see the salvation of our God.

The next verses questioned by the wicked priests (Mosiah 12:22–24; Isaiah 52:8–10) were now interpreted as a future event by Abinadi. The salvation of the Lord will come to all peoples (Mosiah 15:28). The Book of Mormon text is essentially the same as the KJV except for the capitalization of LORD. Isaiah's declaration that salvation would come when the Lord would bring again (gather) Zion (v. 29), and when the Lord comforted (gathered) his people in Jerusalem (v. 30), designates the two major gathering places of the latter days. It also sheds light upon the reference to the mountains where peace is published, or, in other words, where the gospel will be taught. Both Zion and Jerusalem are designated, in scripture, as the tops of the mountains (Isaiah 40:9; 1 Nephi 19:13; 2 Nephi 12:2;

D&C 133:12–13). While the gospel will eventually be taught to all peoples (Mosiah 15:31), the major centers of administering the gospel will be from Zion (the Americas) and Jerusalem. The people who accept the gospel shall see eye to eye and confess that God's judgments are just because they will understand the gospel taught by the prophets and the missionaries.

Mosiah 16:1–6 • They are Carnal, Sensual, and Devilish

1 And now, it came to pass that after Abinadi had spoken these words he stretched forth his hand and said: The time shall come when all shall see the salvation of the Lord; when every nation, kindred, tongue, and people shall see eye to eye and shall confess before God that his judgments are just.

2 And then shall the wicked be cast out, and they shall have cause to howl, and weep, and wail, and gnash their teeth; and this because they would not hearken unto the voice of the Lord; therefore the Lord redeemeth them not.

3 For they are carnal and devilish, and the devil has power over them; yea, even that old serpent that did beguile our first parents, which was the cause of their fall; which was the cause of all mankind becoming carnal, sensual, devilish, knowing evil from good, subjecting themselves to the devil.

4 Thus all mankind were lost; and behold, they would have been endlessly lost were it not that God redeemed his people from their lost and fallen state.

5 But remember that he that persists in his own carnal nature, and goes on in the ways of sin and rebellion against God, remaineth in his fallen state and the devil hath all power over him. Therefore, he is as though there was no redemption made, being an enemy to God; and also is the devil an enemy to God.

6 And now if Christ had not come into the world, speaking of things to come as though they had already come, there could have been no redemption.

Abinadi proceeds to warn those who have become wicked, carnal, sensual, and devilish because of the Fall. That they became carnal, sensual, and devilish tells us that they were not originally that way. We learn from modern revelation:

> 38 Every spirit of man was innocent in the beginning; and God having redeemed man from the fall, men became again, in their infant state, innocent before God.

> 39 And that wicked one cometh and taketh away light and truth, through disobedience, from the children of men, and because of the tradition of their fathers. [D&C 93:38–39]

As the Lord told Adam:

> 55 And the Lord spake unto Adam, saying: Inasmuch as thy children are conceived in sin, even so when they begin to grow up, sin conceiveth in their hearts, and they taste the bitter, that they may know to prize the good.

> 56 And it is given unto them to know good from evil; wherefore they are agents unto themselves, and I have given unto you another law and commandment. [Moses 6:55–56]

It is natural for man to follow their carnal and sensual instincts. Thus, "the natural man is an enemy to God" (Mosiah 3:19). To be carnal is to follow the flesh. To be sensual is to follow the senses. While these ways are not always bad, without following Christ and the guidance of the Spirit the best one may become is among the "honorable men of the earth," who will become only terrestrial beings (D&C 76:75). They will not be sanctified. However, if they follow Satan, they will become devilish and telestial beings at best. As Lehi told his son Jacob:

> And not choose eternal death, according to the will of the flesh and the evil which is therein, which giveth the spirit of the devil power to captivate, to bring you down to hell, that he may reign over you in his own kingdom. [2 Nephi 2:29]

Therefore, a person may become carnal and sensual and yet not devilish, for a person will not be come devilish except by yielding to the temptations of the devil through the flesh and the senses.

Abinadi speaks of Christ as though he had already come (Mosiah 16:6). The coming of Christ, and the fulfilling of his mission had been assured by Heavenly Father. There was no question of it happening. He was to be the source of salvation for all, to see and know (v. 1).

Mosiah 16:7–12 • The Grave has no Victory, Death has no Sting

> 7 And if Christ had not risen from the dead, or have broken the bands of death that the grave should have no victory, and that death should have no sting, there could have been no resurrection.
>
> 8 But there is a resurrection, therefore the grave hath no victory, and the sting of death is swallowed up in Christ.
>
> 9 He is the light and the life of the world; yea, a light that is endless, that can never be darkened; yea, and also a life which is endless, that there can be no more death.
>
> 10 Even this mortal shall put on immortality, and this corruption shall put on incorruption, and shall be brought to stand before the bar of God, to be judged of him according to their works whether they be good or whether they be evil—
>
> 11 If they be good, to the resurrection of endless life and happiness; and if they be evil, to the resurrection of endless damnation, being delivered up to the devil, who hath subjected them, which is damnation—
>
> 12 Having gone according to their own carnal wills and desires; having never called upon the Lord while the arms of mercy were extended towards them; for the arms of mercy were extended towards them, and they would not; they being warned of their iniquities and yet they would not depart from them; and they were commanded to repent and yet they would not repent.

The Resurrection was also assured: "As in Adam all die, even so in Christ shall all be made alive" (1 Corinthians 15:22). What Abinadi prophesied (Mosiah 16:8–9) was verified by the Savior in his ministry. At the Feast of the Tabernacles, also called the Feast of Lights, he testified: "Then spake Jesus again unto them, saying, I am the light of the world: he that followeth me shall not walk in darkness, but shall have the light of life" (John 8:12). He later testified to Thomas, one of the Twelve: Jesus saith unto him, I am the way, the truth, and the life: no man cometh unto the Father, but by me" (John 14:6).

To the Nephites, after his Resurrection, he testified: "I am the light and the life of the world. I am Alpha and Omega, the beginning and the end" (3 Nephi 9:18). Paul proclaimed the same concept of immortality as did Abinadi (Mosiah 16:10): "It is sown in dishonour; it is raised in glory: it is sown in weakness; it is raised in power" (1 Corinthians 15:43). Christ and Paul testified of the judgment bar:

> 27 And hath given him authority to execute judgment also, because he is the Son of man.
>
> 28 Marvel not at this: for the hour is coming, in the which all that are in the graves shall hear his voice,
>
> 29 And shall come forth; they that have done good, unto the resurrection of life; and they that have done evil, unto the resurrection of damnation. [John 5:27–29; see also D&C 76:15–17]
>
> 10 For we must all appear before the judgment seat of Christ; that every one may receive the things *done* in *his* body, according to that he hath done, whether *it be* good or bad. [2 Corinthians 5:10]

Mosiah 16:13–15 • Redemption Cometh Through Christ

> 13 And now, ought ye not to tremble and repent of your sins, and remember that only in and through Christ ye can be saved?
>
> 14 Therefore, if ye teach the law of Moses, also teach that it is a shadow of those things which are to come—
>
> 15 Teach them that redemption cometh through Christ the Lord, who is the very Eternal Father. Amen.

Abinadi's closing comments to Noah's wicked priests are still as applicable to us as they were to them, except we are not living the law of Moses. We still must teach and be taught that redemption comes through Christ our Lord who is the very Eternal Father.

SACRED WRITING

Preaching Which is Sacred:

Mosiah 15:1–16:15   Abinadi's interpretation of Isaiah.

Revelation Which is Great:

Mosiah 14 (Isaiah 53)   Isaiah's prophecy of the birth, youth, and mission of Christ.

Doctrines Learned:

Mosiah 15:1	Jesus was a God before he came to the earth.
Mosiah 15:2–3	Jesus was the Son because he dwelt in the flesh and was the literal son of Mary.
Mosiah 15:2–3	Jesus was the Father because he did the will of Heavenly Father and was his literal Son.
Mosiah 15:4	Jesus is the very Eternal Father of heaven and of earth.
Mosiah 15:8–9	Jesus broke the bands of death and satisfied the demands of justice, therefore he can exercise mercy.
Mosiah 15:10–13	Jesus' seed are those who have heard the prophets and hearkened to their words as well as the prophets themselves.
Mosiah 16:3	The fall was the cause of mankind becoming carnal, sensual, and devilish, subjecting themselves to the devil.
Mosiah 16:7	Christ broke the bands of death and gained victory over the grave.
Mosiah 16:10	The mortal body shall, in the resurrection, put on immortality; and the corruptible body shall put on incorruption.
Mosiah 16:15	Redemption comes through Christ the Lord, who is the very Eternal Father.

General Authority Quotations

President Joseph Fielding Smith • Mosiah 14:2

Did not Christ grow up as a tender plant? There was nothing about him to cause people to single him out. In appearance he was like man; and so it is expressed here by the prophet that he had no form or comeliness, that is, he was not so distinctive, so different from others that people would recognize him as the Son of God. He appeared as a mortal man. [*Doctrines of Salvation*, comp. Bruce R. McConkie, 3 vols. (1954–56), 1:23]

The First Presidency • Mosiah 15:1–4

The Father and The Son: A Doctrinal Exposition by the First Presidency and The Twelve [June 30, 1916]

> *The scriptures plainly and repeatedly affirm that God is the Creator of the earth and the heavens and all things that in them are. In the sense so expressed the Creator is an Organizer. God created the earth as an organized sphere; but He certainly did not create, in the sense of bringing into primal existence, the ultimate elements of the materials of which the earth consists, for "the elements are eternal."* [D&C 93:33]

> *So also life is eternal, and not created; but life, or the vital force, may be infused into organized matter, though the details of the process have not been revealed unto man. For illustrative instances see Genesis 2:7; Moses 3:7; and Abraham 5:7. Each of these scriptures states that God breathed into the body of man the breath of life. See further Moses 3:19, for the statement that God breathed the breath of life into the bodies of the beasts and birds. God showed unto Abraham "the intelligences that were organized before the world was"; and by "intelligences" we are to understand personal "spirits" (Abraham 3:22, 23); nevertheless, we are expressly told that "Intelligence" that is, "the light of truth was not created or made, neither indeed can be."* [D&C 93:29]

> *The term "Father" as applied to Deity occurs in sacred writ with plainly different meanings. Each of the four signifi-*

cations specified in the following treatment should be care-fully segregated.

1. "Father" as Literal Parent

Scriptures embodying the ordinary signification—literally that of Parent—are too numerous and specific to require citation. The purport of these scriptures is to the effect that God the Eternal Father, whom we designate by the exalted name-title "Elohim," is the literal Parent of our Lord and Savior Jesus Christ, and of the spirits of the human race. Elohim is the Father in every sense in which Jesus Christ is so designated, and distinctively He is the Father of spirits. Thus we read in the Epistle to the Hebrews: "Furthermore we have had fathers of our flesh which corrected us, and we gave them reverence; shall we not much rather be in subjection unto the Father of spirits, and live?" (Hebrews 12:9). In view of this fact we are taught by Jesus Christ to pray: "Our Father which art in heaven, Hallowed be thy name."

Jesus Christ applies to Himself both titles, "Son" and "Father." Indeed, he specifically said to the brother of Jared: "Behold, I am Jesus Christ. I am the Father and the Son" (Ether 3:14). *Jesus Christ is the Son of Elohim both as spiritual and bodily offspring; that is to say, Elohim is literally the Father of the spirit of Jesus Christ and also of the body in which Jesus Christ performed His mission in the flesh, and which body died on the cross and was afterward taken up by the process of resurrection, and is now the immortalized tabernacle of the eternal spirit of our Lord and Savior. No extended explanation of the title "Son of God" as applied to Jesus Christ appears necessary.*

2. "Father" as Creator

A second scriptural meaning of "Father" is that of Creator, e.g., in passages referring to any one of the Godhead as "The Father of the heavens and of the earth and all things that in them are." [Ether 4:7; see also Alma 11:38–39 and Mosiah 15:4]

God is not the Father of the earth as one of the worlds in

*space, nor of the heavenly bodies in whole or in part, nor of
the inanimate objects and the plants and the animals upon the
earth, in the literal sense in which He is the Father of the
spirits of mankind. Therefore, scriptures that refer to God in
any way as the Father of the heavens and the earth are to be
understood as signifying that God is the Maker, the Orga-
nizer, the Creator of the heavens and the earth.*

*With this meaning, as the context shows in every case,
Jehovah, who is Jesus Christ the Son of Elohim, is called "the
Father," and even "the very eternal Father of heaven and of
earth" (see passages before cited, and also Mosiah 16:15).
With analogous meaning Jesus Christ is called "The Everlasting Father" (Isaiah 9:6; compare 2 Nephi 19:6). The descrip-
tive titles "Everlasting" and "Eternal" in the foregoing texts
are synonymous.*

*That Jesus Christ, whom we also know as Jehovah, was the
executive of the Father, Elohim, in the work of creation is set
forth in the book* "Jesus the Christ" chapter 4. *Jesus Christ,
being the Creator, is consistently called the Father of heaven
and earth in the sense explained above; and since His cre-
ations are of eternal quality He is very properly called the
Eternal Father of heaven and earth.*

3. Jesus Christ the "Father" of Those Who Abide in His Gospel

*A third sense in which Jesus Christ is regarded as the
"Father" has reference to the relationship between Him and
those who accept His Gospel and thereby become heirs of
eternal life. Following are a few of the scriptures illustrating
this meaning.*

*In the fervent prayer offered just prior to His entrance into
Gethsemane, Jesus Christ supplicated His Father in behalf of
those whom the Father had given unto Him, specifically the
apostles, and, more generally, all who would accept and
abide in the Gospel through the ministry of the apostles. Read
in the Lord's own words the solemn affirmation that those for
whom He particularly prayed were His own, and that His
Father had given them unto Him: "I have manifested thy*

name unto the men which thou gavest me out of the world: thine they were, and thou gavest them me; and they have kept thy word. Now they have known that all things whatsoever thou hast given me are of thee. For I have given unto them the words which thou gavest me; and they have received them, and have known surely that I came out from thee, and they have believed that thou didst send me. I pray for them: I pray not for the world, but for them which thou hast given me; for they are thine. And all mine are thine, and thine are mine; and I am glorified in them. And now I am no more in the world, but these are in the world, and I come to thee. Holy Father, keep through thine own name those whom thou hast given me, that they may be one as we are. While I was with them in the world, I kept them in thy name: those that thou gavest me I have kept, and none of them is lost, but the son of perdition; that the scripture might be fulfilled." [John 17:6–12]

And further: "Neither pray I for these alone, but for them also which shall believe on me through their word; That they all may be one; as thou, Father, art in me, and I in thee, that they also may be one in us: that the world may believe that thou hast sent me. And the glory which thou gavest me I have given them; that they may be one, even as we are one: I in them, and thou in me, that they may be made perfect in one; and that the world may know that thou hast sent me, and hast loved them, as thou hast loved me. Father, I will that they also, whom thou hast given me, be with me where I am; that they may behold my glory, which thou hast given me: for thou lovedst me before the foundation of the world." [John 17:20–24]

To His faithful servants in the present dispensation the Lord has said: "Fear not, little children; for you are mine, and I have overcome the world, and you are of them that my Father hath given me." [D&C 50:41]

Salvation is attainable only through compliance with the laws and ordinances of the Gospel; and all who are thus saved become sons and daughters unto God in a distinctive sense. In a revelation given through Joseph the Prophet to Emma Smith the Lord Jesus addressed the woman as "My daughter," and said: "for verily I say unto you, all those who

receive my gospel are sons and daughters in my kingdom"
(D&C 25:1). In many instances the Lord has addressed men
as His sons (e.g. D&C 9:1; 34:3; 121:7).

   That by obedience to the Gospel men may become sons of
God, both as sons of Jesus Christ, and, through Him, as sons
of His Father, is set forth in many revelations given in the
current dispensation. Thus we read in an utterance of the
Lord Jesus Christ to Hyrum Smith in 1829: "Behold, I am
Jesus Christ, the Son of God. I am the life and light of the
world. I am the same who came unto mine own and mine own
received me not; but verily, verily, I say unto you, that as
many as receive me, to them will I give power to become the
sons of God, even to them that believe on my name. Amen"
(D&C 11:28–30). To Orson Pratt the Lord spoke through
Joseph the Seer, in 1830: "My son Orson, hearken and hear
and behold what I, the Lord God, shall say unto you, even
Jesus Christ your Redeemer; the light and the life of the
world; a light which shineth in darkness and the darkness
comprehendeth it not; who so loved the world that he gave his
own life, that as many as would believe might become the sons
of God: wherefore you are my son" (D&C 34:1–3). *In 1830*
the Lord thus addressed Joseph Smith and Sidney Rigdon:
"Listen to the voice of the Lord your God, even Alpha and
Omega, the beginning and the end, whose course is one
eternal round, the same today as yesterday, and forever. I am
Jesus Christ, the Son of God, who was crucified for the sins
of the world, even as many as will believe on my name, that
they may become the sons of God, even one in me as I am one
in the Father, as the Father is one in me, that we may be one"
(D&C 35:1–2). Consider also the following given in 1831:
"Hearken and listen to the voice of him who is from all
eternity to all eternity, the Great I am, even Jesus Christ, the
light and the life of the world; a light which shineth in dark-
ness and the darkness comprehendeth it not: the same which
came in the meridian of time unto mine own, and mine own
received me not; but to as many as received me, gave I power
to become my sons, and even so will I give unto as many as
will receive me, power to become my sons" (D&C 39:1–4).
In a revelation given through Joseph Smith in March, 1831,
we read: "For verily I say unto you that I am Alpha and

Omega, the beginning and the end, the light and the life of the world-a light that shineth in darkness and the darkness comprehendeth it not. I came unto mine own, and mine own received me not; but unto as many as received me, gave I power to do many miracles, and to become the sons of God, and even unto them that believed on my name gave I power to obtain eternal life. " [D&C 45:7–8]

A forceful exposition of this relationship between Jesus Christ as the Father and those who comply with the requirements of the Gospel as His children was given by Abinadi, centuries before our Lord's birth in the flesh: "And now I say unto you. Who shall declare his generation? Behold, I say unto you, that when his soul has been made an offering for sin, he shall see his seed. And now what say ye? And who shall be his seed? Behold I say unto you, that whosoever has heard the words of the prophets, yea, all the holy prophets who have prophesied concerning the coming of the Lord; I say unto you, that all those who have hearkened unto their words, and believed that the Lord would redeem his people, and have looked forward to that day for a remission of their sins; I say unto you, that these are his seed, or they are the heirs of the kingdom of God: for these are they whose sins he has borne; these are they for whom he has died to redeem them from their transgressions. And now, are they not his seed? Yea, and are not the prophets, every one that has opened his mouth to prophesy, that has not fallen into transgression; I mean all the holy prophets ever since the world began? I say unto you that they are his seed. " [Mosiah 15:10–13]

In tragic contrast with the blessed state of those who become children of God through obedience to the Gospel of Jesus Christ is that of the unregenerate, who are specifically called the children of the devil. Note the words of Christ, while in the flesh, to certain wicked Jews who boasted of their Abrahamic lineage: "If ye were Abraham's children, ye would do the works of Abraham. . . . Ye do the deeds of your father. . . . If God were your Father, ye would love me. . . . Ye are of your father the devil, and the lusts of your father ye will do" (John 8:39, 41, 42, 44). *Thus Satan is designated as the father of the wicked, though we cannot assume any personal relationship of parent and children as existing between him and them. A combined illustration showing that the righteous are the children of God and the wicked the children of the devil appears in the parable of the Tares: "The good seed are the children of the kingdom; but the tares are the children of the wicked one."* [Matthew 13:38]

Men may become children of Jesus Christ by being born anew-born of God, as the inspired word states: "He that committeth sin is of the devil; for the devil sinneth from the beginning. For this purpose the Son of God was manifested, that he might destroy the works of the devil. Whosoever is born of God doth not commit sin; for his seed remaineth in him: and he cannot sin, because he is born of God. In this the children of God are manifest, and the children of the devil: whosoever doeth not righteousness is not of God, neither he that loveth not his brother." [1 John 3:8–10]

Those who have been born unto God through obedience to the Gospel may by valiant devotion to righteousness obtain exaltation and even reach the status of godhood. Of such we read: "Wherefore, as it is written, they are gods, even the sons of God" (D&C 76:58; compare 132:20, and contrast paragraph 17 in same section; see also paragraph 37). *Yet, though they be gods they are still subject to Jesus Christ as their Father in this exalted relationship; and so we read in the paragraph following the above quotation: "and they are Christ's, and Christ is God's."* [76:59]

By the new birth—that of water and the Spirit—mankind may become children of Jesus Christ, being through the means by Him provided "begotten sons and daughters unto God" (D&C 76:24). *This solemn truth is further emphasized in the words of the Lord Jesus Christ given through Joseph Smith in 1833: "And now, verily I say unto you, I was in the beginning with the Father, and am the firstborn; and all those who are begotten through me are partakers of the glory of the same, and are the Church of the Firstborn"* (D&C 93:21, 22). *For such figurative use of the term "begotten" in application to those who are born unto God see Paul's explanation: "for in Christ Jesus I have begotten you through the gospel"* (1 Cor. 4:15). An analogous instance of sonship attained by righteous service is found in the revelation relating to the order and functions of Priesthood, given in 1832: "For whoso is faithful unto the obtaining of these two priesthoods of which I have spoken, and the magnifying their calling, are sanctified by the Spirit unto the renewing of their bodies: they become the sons of Moses and of Aaron and the seed of Abraham, and the church and kingdom, and the elect of God." [D&C 84:33, 34]

If it be proper to speak of those who accept and abide in the Gospel as Christ's sons and daughters—and upon this matter the scriptures are explicit and cannot be gainsaid nor denied—it is consistently proper to speak of Jesus Christ as the Father of the righteous, they having become His children and He having been made their Father through the second birth—the baptismal regeneration.

4. Jesus Christ the "Father" By Divine Investiture of Authority

A fourth reason for applying the title "Father" to Jesus Christ is found in the fact that in all His dealings with the human family Jesus the Son has represented and yet represents Elohim His Father in power and authority. This is true of Christ in His preexistent, antemortal, or unembodied state, in the which He was known as Jehovah; also during His embodiment in the flesh; and during His labors as a disembodied spirit in the realm of the dead; and since that period in His resurrected state. To the Jews He said: "I and my Father are one" (John 10:30; see also 17:11, 22); yet He declared "My Father is greater than I" (John 14:28); and further, "I am come in my Father's name" (John 5:43; see also 10:25). The same truth was declared by Christ Himself to the Nephites (see 3 Nephi 20:35 and 28:10), and has been reaffirmed by revelation in the present dispensation (D&C 50:43). Thus the Father placed His name upon the Son; and Jesus Christ spoke and ministered in and through the Father's name; and so far as power, authority, and Godship are concerned His words and acts were and are those of the Father.

We read, by way of analogy, that God placed His name

upon or in the Angel who was assigned to special ministry unto the people of Israel during the exodus. Of that Angel the Lord said: "Beware of him, and obey his voice, provoke him not; for he will not pardon your transgressions: for my name is in him." [Exodus 23:21]

The ancient apostle, John, was visited by an angel who ministered and spoke in the name of Jesus Christ. As we read: "The Revelation of Jesus Christ, which God gave unto him, to shew unto his servants things which must shortly come to pass; and he sent and signified it by his angel unto his servant John" (Revelation 1:1). *John was about to worship the angelic being who spoke in the name of the Lord Jesus Christ, but was forbidden: "And I John saw these things, and heard them. And when I had heard and seen, I fell down to worship before the feet of the angel which showed me these things. Then saith he unto me, See thou do it not: for I am thy fellowservant, and of thy brethren the prophets, and of them which keep sayings of this book: worship God"* (Revelation 22:8, 9). *And then the angel continued to speak as though he were the Lord Himself: "And, behold, I come quickly; and my reward is with me, to give every man according as his work shall be. I am Alpha and Omega, the beginning and the end, the first and the last" (verses 12, 13). The resurrected Lord, Jesus Christ, who had been exalted to the right hand of God His Father, had placed His name upon the angel sent to John, and the angel spoke in the first person, saying "I come quickly," "I am Alpha and Omega," though he meant that Jesus Christ would come, and that Jesus Christ was Alpha and Omega.*

None of these considerations, however, can change in the least degree the solemn fact of the literal relationship of Father and Son between Elohim and Jesus Christ. Among the spirit children of Elohim the firstborn was and is Jehovah or Jesus Christ to whom all others are juniors. Following are affirmative scriptures bearing upon this great truth. Paul, writing to the Colossians, says of Jesus Christ: "Who is the image of the invisible God, the firstborn of every creature: for by him were all things created, that are in heaven, and that are in earth, visible and invisible, whether they be thrones, or dominions, or principalities, or powers; all things were created by him, and for him: and he is before all things, and by him all things consist. And he is the head of the body, the church: who is the beginning, the firstborn from the dead; that in all things he might have the preeminence. For it pleased the Father that in him should all fullness dwell" (Colossians 1:15–19). *From this scripture we learn that Jesus Christ was "the firstborn of every creature" and it is evident that the seniority here expressed must be with respect to antemortal existence, for Christ was not the senior of all mortals in the flesh. He is further designated as "the firstborn from the dead" this having reference to Him as the first to be resurrected from the dead, or as elsewhere written "the firstfruits of them that slept"* (1 Corinthians 15:20, see also verse 23); *and "the first begotten of the dead"* (Revelation 1:5; compare Acts 26:23). *The writer of the Epistle to the Hebrews affirms the status of Jesus Christ as the firstborn of the spirit children of His Father, and extols the preeminence of the Christ when tabernacled in flesh: "And again, when he bringeth in the firstbegotten into the world, he saith, And let all the angels of God worship him"* (Hebrews 1:6; read the preceding verses). *That the spirits who were juniors to Christ were predestined to be born in the image of their Elder Brother is thus attested by Paul: "And we know that all things work together for good to them that love God, to them who are the called according to his purpose. For whom he did foreknow, he also did predestinate to be conformed to the image of his Son, that he might be the firstborn among many brethren"* (Romans 8:28, 29). *John the Revelator was commanded to write to the head of the Laodicean church, as the words of the Lord Jesus Christ: "These things saith the Amen, the faithful and true witness, the beginning of the creation of God"* (Revelation 3:14). *In the course of a revelation given through Joseph Smith in May, 1833, the Lord Jesus Christ said as before cited: "And now, verily I say unto you, I was in the beginning with the Father, and am the Firstborn"* (D&C 93:21). *A later verse makes plain the fact that human beings generally were similarly existent in spirit state prior to their embodiment in the flesh: "Ye were also in the beginning with the Father; that which is Spirit, even the Spirit of truth"* (verse 23).

There is no impropriety, therefore, in speaking of Jesus Christ as the Elder Brother of the rest of human kind. That He is by spiritual birth Brother to the rest of us is indicated in Hebrews: "Wherefore in all things it behoved him to be made like unto his brethren, that he might be a merciful and faithful high priest in things pertaining to God, to make reconciliation for the sins of the people" (Hebrews 2:17). *Let it not be forgotten, however, that He is essentially greater than any and all others, by reason (1) of His seniority as the oldest or firstborn; (2) of His unique status in the flesh as the offspring of a mortal mother and of an immortal, or resurrected and glorified, Father; (3) of His selection and foreordination as the one and only Redeemer and Savior of the race; and (4) of His transcendent sinlessness.*

Jesus Christ is not the of the spirits who have taken or yet shall take bodies upon this earth, for He is one of them. He is The , as they are sons and daughters of Elohim. So far as the stages of eternal progression and attainment have been made known through divine revelation, we are to understand that only resurrected and glorified beings can become parents of spirit offspring. Only such exalted souls have reached maturity in the appointed course of eternal life; and the spirits born to them in the eternal worlds will pass in due sequence through the several stages or estates by which the glorified parents have attained exaltation. (Messages of the First Presidency, James R. Clark [5:26–34]; The Articles of Faith, James E. Talmage [Appendix 2, 466–73])

President Joseph Fielding Smith • Mosiah 15:1–4

Having subjected himself to the will of the Father and offering a sacrifice to give us life, he became a father to us. Is it not the Father that gives the life in the flesh?—"And having subjected the flesh to the will of the Father, being the Father and the Son." Now that ought to be clear to anybody, but it is very, very confusing to many of our missionaries, and our most wicked enemies take advantage of it. [He quotes Mosiah 15:1–4]

Now I do not know why anyone should be confused particularly on that. He is both Father and Son. That is, the Savior is Father and Son. The Father because he gave us life, the Son because he was begotten by the Father.

["The Fatherhood of Christ." Address to Seminary and Institute of Religion Faculty, BYU, Provo, Utah, July 17, 1962]

Challenges to Eternal Life:

1. Make a commitment to listen to General Conference and read the addresses of the General Authorities in the *Ensign*, then follow their counsel as living prophets (Mosiah 15:11).

2. Seek the guidance of the Spirit rather than following the carnal nature of our fallen state (Mosiah 16:3, 5).

3. When you teach in the Church programs and activities emphasize that redemption comes only through Christ (Mosiah 16:15).

4. Choose a challenge of your own from this reading and apply it to your life.

Chapter Twelve

Alma Organizes the Church

Mosiah 17–18; 23:1–19

*H*istorical Setting: Following Abinadi's courageous testimony before King Noah and his priests, Alma, one of the priests pleads in behalf of Abinadi but is cast out. The king sends his servants to slay Alma, but he flees for his own safety. These chapters tell us what happened to Abinadi, and the activities of Alma after he fled. The estimated time period is about 147 B.C.

Precepts of this Reading:

> Now I say unto you, if this be the desire of your hearts, what have you against being baptized in the name of the Lord, as a witness before him that ye have entered into a covenant with him, that ye will serve him and keep his commandments, that he may pour out his Spirit more abundantly upon you? [Mosiah 18:10]

Mosiah chapter 18 is the best explanation of the covenant made in the waters of baptism found in the scriptures. Every member of the Church and every prospective member should understand this covenant. As a preparation for further study, an outline of the chapters in this reading follows.

OUTLINE • MOSIAH 17–18; 23:1–19

➤ 17:1–10   King Noah commanded the priests to put Abinadi to death.

     a.   Alma, a young man who was a descendant of Nephi, believed Abinadi's words and pleaded with the king to let Abinadi go in peace (v. 2).

     b.   The king had Alma cast out and sent his servants to slay him (v. 3).

     c.   Alma fled from them and hid, and he wrote all the words Abinadi had spoken (v. 4).

     d.   The king's guards surround Abinadi, bind him, and cast him into prison (v. 5).

     e.   After three days, having counseled with the priests, King Noah brings Abinadi before him again (v. 6).

        1.   Abinadi is accused of teaching that God would come down among men.

        2.   Unless Abinadi recalls all his words, he will be put to death.

     f.   Abinadi refuses to recall his words because they are true (vv. 9–10).

        1.   He allowed himself to fall into the king's hands that the king might know they are true.

        2.   He will suffer even until death that his words will stand as a testimony against the king.

        3.   If the king slays him, he sheds innocent blood that shall also stand as a testimony against him at the last day.

➤ 17:11–19   King Noah feared Abinadi's words and was about to release him for he feared the judgements of God would come upon him.

     a.   The priests accuse Abinadi of reviling the king. The king is stirred up to anger and delivers Abinadi to be slain (v. 12).

     b.   They bind him and scourge his skin with faggots even unto death (vv. 13–19).

      1. As the flames scorch him, Abinadi prophesies that the priests' seed would cause many who believed in the salvation of God to suffer the pains of death by fire as had Abinadi.

      2. The priests would be afflicted with diseases and be smitten and driven as a wild flock is driven by wild beasts.

      3. The priests would be taken by their enemies and suffer death by fire.

      4. God's vengeance will come upon those who destroy his people.

      5. Abinadi asks God to receive his soul.

➤ 17:20   Abinadi fell having suffered death by fire.

    a. He was put to death because he would not deny the commandments of God.

    b. He sealed the truth of his words by his death.

➤ 18:1–6   Alma, having fled from King Noah's servants, went about teaching the words of Abinadi.

    a. He taught the coming of the resurrection and redemption of the people through Christ (v. 2).

    b. He taught privately to as many as would come that it might not come to the knowledge of the king. Many did believe his words (v. 3).

    c. Those who believed him gathered to a place called Mormon to hear his words (vv. 4–6).

      1. It was named by the king, being in the borders of the land infested at seasons by wild beasts.

      2. There was a fountain of pure water and a thicket of small trees where Alma hid himself in the daytime from the searches of the king.

➤ 18:7–16   After many days a goodly number were gathered at the place of Mormon to hear the words of Alma.

    a. Alma taught them repentance and redemption, and faith on the Lord (vv. 7–9).

1. Ye are desirous to come into the fold of God and be called his people and bear one another's burdens.

2. Ye are willing to mourn with those that mourn and comfort those that stand in need of comfort.

3. Ye are willing to stand as witnesses of God at all times, in all things, and in all places until death.

4. Ye will then be redeemed of God, numbered in the first resurrection and have eternal life.

b. Alma asks: what have ye against being baptized as a witness that ye have entered a covenant with the Lord?

1. To serve him and keep his commandments.

2. That he may pour his Spirit more abundantly upon you.

c. The people clapped for joy and said they desired to be baptized (v. 11).

d. Alma took Helam into the water and cried unto the Lord to pour out his Spirit upon his servant, and the Spirit came upon him and he said: (v. 12–16).

1. Helam, I baptize thee, having authority from God, as a testimony that ye have entered a covenant to serve him until the death of your mortal body.

2. May the Spirit of the Lord be poured out upon you and grant you eternal life.

3. Alma and Helam were buried in the water and came forth filled with the Spirit.

4. Alma baptized another according to the first but did not bury himself in the water.

e. About two hundred and four souls were baptized in the waters of Mormon and filled with the grace of God.

➤ 18:17–29   Those baptized were called the Church of God or the Church of Christ.

a. Whosoever was baptized by the power and authority of God were added to the Church (v. 17–22).

b. Alma, having authority from God, ordained one priest

to every fifty of their number to preach and teach them pertaining to the Kingdom of God (v. 18).

    1. They were to teach only what Alma and the holy prophets had taught.

    2. They should teach nothing save repentance and faith on the Lord.

    3. He commanded there be no contention, but that they be of one faith and one baptism, knit together in unity and love.

    4. They become the children of God.

c. He commanded them to observe the sabbath and keep it holy and to give thanks daily to God (v. 23).

d. The priests were to labor with their own hands for their support (v. 24).

e. One day a week was set apart to assemble together and teach the people and to worship the Lord (v. 25).

f. The priests were not to depend upon the people for their support but were to receive the grace of God for their labors (v. 26).

g. The people of the Church were to impart of their substance according to their ability, and to give to those who had not (v. 27–28).

    1. It was according to their own free will and good desires before God.

    2. It was given to the priests in need and to every needy, naked soul.

h. They walked uprightly before God, imparting both temporally and spiritually to one another according to their needs and wants (v. 29).

➤ 18:30–35 These things were all done in Mormon, in the forest near the waters of Mormon.

a. This place is beautiful to those who there came to the knowledge of their Redeemer (v. 30).

b. These things were done in the border of the land so

they would not come to the knowledge of the king (v. 31).

   c.   The king discovered a movement among his people and sent his servants to watch them (v. 32).

   d.   They were discovered and the king said Alma was stirring up the people to rebellion and sent his army to destroy them (v. 33).

   e.   Alma and his people were apprised of the army and departed into the wilderness with about four hundred and fifty souls (vv. 34–35).

Superscription (of Alma 23). The account of Alma and his people driven into the wilderness by King Noah.

➤ 23:1–5   Alma was warned of the Lord that the armies would come, and the people departed with their flocks and grain.

   a.   The Lord strengthened them that the army could not overtake them (v. 2).

   b.   They traveled eight days to a very beautiful and pleasant land of pure water.

      1.   They pitched their tents, tilled the ground and built buildings.

      2.   They were industrious and labored exceedingly.

➤ 23:6–15   The people desired Alma to be their king, but he declined and taught them.

   a.   It is not expedient to have a king, for the Lord has said: Ye shall not esteem one flesh above another, or one man shall not think himself above another (v. 7).

   b.   If you could always have just men to be your king, it would be well to have a king (v. 8–9).

      1.   The iniquity of king Noah and his priests should be remembered.

      2.   Alma was also caught in this snare and did many abominable things for which he repented.

   c.   After much tribulation, Alma was heard by the Lord and made an instrument in his hands to bring many to the knowledge of the truth (v. 10).

d. Alma does not glory in his doing this for he is unworthy to glory of himself (v. 11).

e. They had been oppressed by king Noah and in bondage to him and his priests (v. 12).

f. They were delivered out of this bondage by the power of God (v. 13).

1. Stand fast in this liberty wherewith you are made free.

2. Trust no man to be a king over you.

g. Trust no man to be your teacher or minister, except he be a man of God (v. 14).

h. Alma taught them to love their neighbor as themselves and to have no contention among them (v. 15).

➤ 23:16–19 Alma was their high priest and the founder of their church.

a. None received authority to teach or preach except from Alma (v. 17).

1. He consecrated all their priests and teachers.

2. None but just men were consecrated.

b. The priests and teacher did watch over their people and nourish them with things pertaining to righteousness (v. 18).

c. They began to prosper in the land and called the land Helam.

NOTES & COMMENTARY

Introduction: "Apostasy" and "Restoration" are two words commonly used in the Church. Apostasy is an internal corruption of a religious faith. Restoration is to bring back that which had been lost or taken away. As used in the Church, "apostasy" represents the corruption or falling away of the Church of Jesus Christ established in the meridian of time sometime after his advent on earth. The "restoration" refers to the authority to establish the Church in the latter days with "the same organization that existed in the primitive Church" (Articles of Faith 6). There were hundreds of years that elapsed between these two movements. However, we witness both an apostasy and a restoration in this reading. The reign of King Noah brought about an apostasy within one generation, and Alma restores the Church shortly thereafter.

Mosiah 17:1–5 • Alma Writes All the Words of Abinadi

1 And now it came to pass that when Abinadi had finished these sayings, that the king commanded that the priests should take him and cause that he should be put to death.

2 But there was one among them whose name was Alma, he also being a descendant of Nephi. And he was a young man, and he believed the words which Abinadi had spoken, for he knew concerning the iniquity which Abinadi had testified against them; therefore he began to plead with the king that he would not be angry with Abinadi, but suffer that he might depart in peace.

3 But the king was more wroth, and caused that Alma should be cast out from among them, and sent his servants after him that they might slay him.

4 But he fled from before them and hid himself that they found him not. And he being concealed for many days did write all the words which Abinadi had spoken.

5 And it came to pass that the king caused that his guards should surround Abinadi and take him; and they bound him and cast him into prison.

As stated before, we do not know who kept the record of King Noah's reign that Mormon is abridging; but Alma writes the works of Abinadi that constitute the account of the past two or more years (v. 4, Mosiah 11:20–16:15). Alma was a young man (v. 2) but was old enough to have been on the council of priests advising the king, and thus was present during the time of Abinadi's prophesying. Alma's courage reflects his character. His ancestry may also have been a contributing factor. The wrath of the king against Abinadi and Alma

(vv. 1, 3, 5) further indicates the cause of the apostasy that had taken place.

Mosiah 17:6–12 • Abinadi Refuses to Recall His Words

> 6 And after three days, having counseled with his priests, he caused that he should again be brought before him.
>
> 7 And he said unto him: Abinadi, we have found an accusation against thee, and thou art worthy of death.
>
> 8 For thou hast said that God himself should come down among the children of men; and now, for this cause thou shalt be put to death unless thou wilt recall all the words which thou hast spoken evil concerning me and my people.
>
> 9 Now Abinadi said unto him: I say unto you, I will not recall the words which I have spoken unto you concerning this people, for they are true; and that ye may know of their surety I have suffered myself that I have fallen into your hands.
>
> 10 Yea, and I will suffer even until death, and I will not recall my words, and they shall stand as a testimony against you. And if ye slay me ye will shed innocent blood, and this shall also stand as a testimony against you at the last day.
>
> 11 And now king Noah was about to release him, for he feared his word; for he feared that the judgments of God would come upon him.
>
> 12 But the priests lifted up their voices against him, and began to accuse him, saying: He has reviled the king. Therefore the king was stirred up in anger against him, and he delivered him up that he might be slain.

The accusation against Abinadi was the same as brought against the prophet Joseph Smith. They both had taught the truth about God— Jesus Christ. Abinadi apparently could have escaped, but was willing to seal his testimony with his blood (v. 9, 10). This was the situation with Joseph Smith:" When Joseph went to Carthage to deliver himself up to the pretended requirements of the law, two or three days previous to his assassination, he said: 'I am going like a lamb to the slaughter; but I am calm as a summer's morning; I have a conscience void of offense towards God, and towards all men. I SHALL DIE INNOCENT, AND IT SHALL YET BE SAID OF ME—HE WAS MURDERED IN COLD BLOOD.'—(D&C 135:4)

King Noah's yielding to the pressure of the priests reminds us of Jesus before Pilate. "And from thenceforth Pilate sought to release him: but the Jews cried out, saying, If thou let this man go, thou art not Caesar's friend: whosoever maketh himself a king speaketh against Caesar. When Pilate therefore heard that saying, he brought Jesus forth, and sat down in the judgment seat in a place that is called the Pavement, but in the Hebrew, Gabbatha" (John 19:12–13). Both King Noah and Pilate "should not have feared man more than God" (D&C 3:7). Both will be accountable at the last day for the testimonies borne to them (Mosiah 17:10).

Mosiah 17:13–20 • Abinadi Seals His Testimony With Blood

13 And it came to pass that they took him and bound him, and scourged his skin with faggots, yea, even unto death.

14 And now when the flames began to scorch him, he cried unto them, saying:

15 Behold, even as ye have done unto me, so shall it come to pass that thy seed shall cause that many shall suffer the pains that I do suffer, even the pains of death by fire; and this because they believe in the salvation of the Lord their God.

16 And it will come to pass that ye shall be afflicted with all manner of diseases because of your iniquities.

17 Yea, and ye shall be smitten on every hand, and shall be driven and scattered to and fro, even as a wild flock is driven by wild and ferocious beasts.

18 And in that day ye shall be hunted, and ye shall be taken by the hand of your enemies, and then ye shall suffer, as I suffer, the pains of death by fire.

19 Thus God executeth vengeance upon those that destroy his people. O God, receive my soul.

20 And now, when Abinadi had said these words, he fell, having suffered death by fire; yea, having been put to death because he would not deny the commandments of God, having sealed the truth of his words by his death. [Mosiah 17:13–20]

True to the very end, Abinadi expands on the prophesies he had uttered earlier (Mosiah 12:3–7, 13:10). Before, only the king was told he would die by fire or the same type of death as Abinadi. Now he adds that the seed of the priests' would administer death the same way to the people of God (Mosiah 17:15). What will come upon the priests seed because of these deaths are then enumerated (vv. 16–18). A continued study of the Book of Mormon will reveal the fulfillment of Abinadi's prophesy to every detail he gave. His final plea was for God to receive his soul (v. 19). That plea must have been answered because he fulfilled his mission before the Lord allowed him to be destroyed. Again, there is a parallel to the Prophet Joseph. Joseph said: "I shall not be sacrificed until my time comes; then I shall be sacrificed freely" (*TPJS*, 274).

Mormon ends the account of Abinadi by saying: "Yea, having been put to death because he would not deny the commandments of God, having sealed the truth of his words by his death" (v. 20). After the death of Joseph Smith, the Lord revealed to his successor Brigham Young similar words:

34 Thy brethren have rejected you and your testimony, even the nation that has driven you out;

35 And now cometh the day of their calamity, even the days of sorrow, like a woman that is taken in travail; and their sorrow shall be great unless they speedily repent, yea, very speedily.

36 For they killed the prophets, and them that were sent unto them; and they have shed innocent blood, which crieth from the ground against them.

37 Therefore, marvel not at these things, for ye are not yet pure; ye can not yet bear my glory; but ye shall behold it if ye are faithful in keeping all my words that I have given you, from the days of Adam to Abraham, from Abraham to Moses, from Moses to Jesus and his apostles, and from Jesus and his apostles to Joseph Smith,

whom I did call upon by mine angels, my ministering servants, and by mine own voice out of the heavens, to bring forth my work;

38 Which foundation he did lay, and was faithful; and I took him to myself.

39 Many have marveled because of his death; but it was needful that he should seal his testimony with his blood, that he might be honored and the wicked might be condemned.

40 Have I not delivered you from your enemies, only in that I have left a witness of my name?

41 Now, therefore, hearken, O ye people of my church; and ye elders listen together; you have received my kingdom.

42 Be diligent in keeping all my commandments, lest judgments come upon you, and your faith fail you, and your enemies triumph over you. So no more at present. Amen and Amen. [D&C 136:34–42]

In a somewhat different situation, the Lord turns to his newly called servant Alma.

Mosiah 18:1–6 • Alma at the Waters of Mormon

1 And now, it came to pass that Alma, who had fled from the servants of king Noah, repented of his sins and iniquities, and went about privately among the people, and began to teach the words of Abinadi—

2 Yea, concerning that which was to come, and also concerning the resurrection of the dead, and the redemption of the people, which was to be brought to pass through the power, and sufferings, and death of Christ, and his resurrection and ascension into heaven.

3 And as many as would hear his word he did teach. And he taught them privately, that it might not come to the knowledge of the king. And many did believe his words.

4 And it came to pass that as many as did believe him did go forth to a place which was called Mormon, having received its name from the king, being in the borders of the land having been infested, by times or at seasons, by wild beasts.

5 Now, there was in Mormon a fountain of pure water, and Alma

resorted thither, there being near the water a thicket of small trees, where he did hide himself in the daytime from the searches of the king.

6 And it came to pass that as many as believed him went thither to hear his words.

The work of God will continue as long as there are people who are receptive to his word. It is only when, collectively, the "people had rejected every word of God, and they were ripe in iniquity" (1 Nephi 17:35, see also Genesis 15:16) that he totally withdraws his Spirit and "the judgements of God will overtake the wicked; and it is by the wicked that the wicked are punished" (Mormon 4:5). Alma secretly carried on the work of God to those who did believe in his words (Mosiah 18:2–3). Abinadi had planted, Alma watered, "but God gave the increase" (1 Corinthians 3:6)

Mosiah 18:7–11 • The Desire of the Peoples' Hearts

7 And it came to pass after many days there were a goodly number gathered together at the place of Mormon, to hear the words of Alma. Yea, all were gathered together that believed on his word, to hear him. And he did teach them, and did preach unto them repentance, and redemption, and faith on the Lord.

8 And it came to pass that he said unto them: Behold, here are the waters of Mormon (for thus were they called) and now, as ye are desirous to come into the fold of God, and to be called his people, and are willing to bear one another's burdens, that they may be light;

9 Yea, and are willing to mourn with those that mourn; yea, and comfort those that stand in need of comfort, and to stand as witnesses of God at all times and in all things, and in all places that ye may be in, even until death, that ye may be redeemed of God, and be numbered with those of the first resurrection, that ye may have eternal life—

10 Now I say unto you, if this be the desire of your hearts, what have you against being baptized in the name of the Lord, as a witness before him that ye have entered into a covenant with him, that ye will serve him and keep his commandments, that he may pour out his

Spirit more abundantly upon you?

11 And now when the people had heard these words, they clapped their hands for joy, and exclaimed: This is the desire of our hearts.

Alma teaches them the first principles of the gospel: faith in the Lord and redemption from their sins through repentance (v. 7). If the people desire to come into the fold of God and to be called his people (v. 8), they enter into the family of Christ. As stated previously, Christ is the Father of our eternal life. Through the baptism of the Holy Ghost, they would be "spiritually begotten . . . and born of him and . . . become his sons and his daughters" (Mosiah 5:7). They would "take upon [them] the name of Christ, by baptism" (2 Nephi 31:13). Christ becomes their family name, and they are thereafter brothers and sisters in the gospel. They accept certain responsibilities towards those who have become their brothers and sisters. They are to share the burdens that come, that one member is not overwhelmed, but all share the responsibilities (Mosiah 18:8). As Paul told the Galatians "Bear ye one another's burdens, and so fulfill the law of Christ" (6:2). When one member of the family has cause to mourn, the whole family is to mourn together and extend comforts toward one another. To both family members and those who are not family members, they are to stand as witnesses of the family of Christ (v. 9). This will strengthen the family and extend and invitation for others to become adopted or spiritually begotten into the family. This witness is to be given at all times; every day of the week, and every hour and minute of the day. It is to be given through their conduct, in all things, in their occupations or businesses, their social engagements, their recreational activities, and their spiritual gatherings. It is to be given in their travels and activities among all cultures and localities and in every environment. These witnesses are to continue "even to death" (v. 9).

The family of Christ is a covenant family (v. 10). As with the prophesies of the prophets, the promises are both conditional and unconditional. The conditional promises are based on eternal law. "There is a law, irrevocably decreed in heaven before the foundations of this world, upon which all blessings are predicated— And when we obtain any blessing from God, it is by obedience to that law upon which it is predicated" (D&C 130:20–21).

The unconditional promises are also eternal, "I , the Lord, am bound when ye do what I say; but when ye do not what I say, ye have no promise" (D&C 82:10). If family members keep their commitments, they will be redeemed [forgiven of their sins] and come forth in the first resurrection and have eternal life (Mosiah 18:9). They are also promised to have the Spirit poured out more abundantly if they keep the commandments (v. 10). Thus the Lord takes care of their past [sins], present [the Spirit], and future [the first resurrection and Eternal Life].

A father, as the head of the household, designates to his children various tasks he expects them to perform. Christ, as the head of His family, directs his family members to serve and to keep his commandments (v. 10). These directions may come through personal revelation or through his servants; "whether by mine own voice or the voice of my servants, it is the same" (D&C 1:38). As King Benjamin taught, "when ye are in the service of your fellow beings, ye are only in the service of your God" (Mosiah 2:17). We serve others to perfect ourselves. As Jesus taught in his mortal ministry, "he that is greatest among you, let him be your servant" (Matthew 23:11). We serve also "for the perfecting of the Saints, for the work of the ministry, for the edifying of the body of Christ" (Ephesians 4:12). However, we must serve as Christ, our family Father, directs us to serve, "it must be done in mine own way" (D&C 104:16).

A father also establishes rules by which the family is governed. As the family head, Christ has given the scriptures or his commandments to govern his children. To obtain eternal life, the member of Christ's family must be "willing to submit to all things which the Lord seeth fit to inflict upon him, even as a child doth submit to his father" (Mosiah 3:19).

As in a temporal contract or covenant, the baptismal covenant requires witnesses and an official validation. In the Church today, and probably in Alma's day as well (see D&C 20:25–26), other members of Christ's family view the baptism to assure it is performed properly, and the validation comes by the ordinance being sealed by the Holy Spirit of Promise (see D&C 132:7). The reaction of those who assembled and heard Alma's explanation of the baptismal covenant is indicative of their having received a witness of the Holy Ghost that his words were true. They desired to enter the covenant (Mosiah 18:11).

A summary of the covenant of baptism is given in the accompanying table on page 408, "The Purpose and Covenant of Baptism." Additional points and scriptures are added:

Mosiah 18:12–17 • Alma Baptizes Helam and Others

> 12 And now it came to pass that Alma took Helam, he being one of the first, and went and stood forth in the water, and cried, saying: O Lord, pour out thy Spirit upon thy servant, that he may do this work with holiness of heart.

> 13 And when he had said these words, the Spirit of the Lord was upon him, and he said: Helam, I baptize thee, having authority from the Almighty God, as a testimony that ye have entered into a covenant to serve him until you are dead as to the mortal body; and may the Spirit of the Lord be poured out upon you; and may he grant unto you eternal life, through the redemption of Christ, whom he has prepared from the foundation of the world.

> 14 And after Alma had said these words, both Alma and Helam were buried in the water; and they arose and came forth out of the water rejoicing, being filled with the Spirit.

> 15 And again, Alma took another, and went forth a second time into the water, and baptized him according to the first, only he did not bury himself again in the water.

16 And after this manner he did baptize every one that went forth to the place of Mormon; and they were in number about two hundred and four souls; year, and they were baptized in the waters of Mormon, and were filled with the grace of God.

17 And they were called the church of God, or the church of Christ, from that time forward. And it came to pass that whosoever was baptized by the power and authority of God was added to his church.

Several questions arise over the baptism of Helam by Alma. First, where did Alma get his authority. President Joseph Fielding Smith responded to this question:

> In the case of Alma and his priesthood, we are left to surmise that he legally and divinely received it before the days of King Noah. We read that Zeniff, the father of Noah, was a righteous man. Alma evidently received the priesthood in the days of Zeniff, and at no time did he fully accept the teachings nor with full purpose to follow the counsels and procedures of Noah and his wicked priests. It was Alma who was deeply touched at the scathing denunciation of the Prophet Abinadi. Moreover it was Alma who recorded them, for he believed thoroughly in what Abinadi had declared and he turned from whatever transgression he had committed and set forth with a repentant spirit to gather together all those who were willing to accept the teachings of the martyred prophet.[1]

---

[1] *Answers to Gospel Questions*, comp. Joseph Fielding Smith Jr., 5 vols. [1957–66], 3:203–04.

Table 6

The Purpose and Covenant of Baptism

1. Remission of Sins • 2 Nephi 31:4–5; Alma 7:14.

2. Admittance by covenant into the Church and Kingdom of God on earth • 2 Nephi 31:6–8, 13; Mosiah 5:5, 18:10; Alma 7:15–16.

A Covenant is a Binding or Solemn Agreement to Do or Keep from Doing

MAN'S PART
(Baptism = signature)*

A. Come into the fold of God— Mosiah 18:8 (The name of Christ—your family) Mosiah 1:11–12; 5:10–11

B. Bear one another's (family members) burdens— Mosiah 18:8–9

   1. Mourn with those that mourn

   2. Comfort those that need comfort

C. Stand as a Witness (to family and non-family) Mosiah 18:9

   1. At all times

   2. In all things

   3. In all places

D. Serve Him (Christ —by helping perfect the Saints, Mosiah 2:17) Mosiah 18:10

E. Keep His (Christ's) commandments— Mosiah 18:10 (follow directions of the father —family head)

GOD'S PART
(Atonement = signature)

A. Redeemed of God— Mosiah 18:9. Remission of past sins (past life)

B. Numbered with first Resurrection— Mosiah 18:9 and Eternal Life (future life)

C. Pour out his Spirit— Mosiah 18:10 (present life)

[Note the complete coverage]

---

*The covenant must be witnessed by others and validated by the Holy Spirit of Promise (Seal of Approval). D&C 132:7. Validation requires: (1) faith and repentance 2 Nephi 30:2; and (2) A broken heart and a contrite spirit Moroni 6:1–3, compare D&C 20:37.

Secondly, why is the baptismal prayer different than the set prayer given in the Book of Mormon when Christ visited the Nephites (3 Nephi 11:25–26) or in the Doctrine and Covenants (20:73–74)? Alma was one of the priests of Noah who had gone into apostasy. He may not have known or remembered the prayer and so used the prayer to the best of his memory. He did have the essential parts: the authority from God and the method of immersion. The last part of the prayer seems to be more of a blessing that was added to the prayer. It should be remembered that "the Spirit of the Lord was upon him as he baptized Helam."

Thirdly, why did Alma immerse himself with Helam? This question was also answered by President Smith:

> If he [Alma] had authority to baptize that is evidence that he had been baptized. Therefore, when Alma baptized himself with Helam that was not a case of Alma baptizing himself, but merely as a token to the Lord of his humility and full repentance. In Alma 5:3 we learn that Alma [the younger] was consecrated the high priest over the Church under his father. Now Alma did not organize the Church with the idea that they had not church before that time. They had a church from the days of Lehi and Alma only set things in order.[2]

The two hundred and four souls who were baptized were called the Church of God, or the Church of Christ (Mosiah 18:16–17). There is no mention of the Church being organized. This implies, as President Smith said, that "Alma only set things in order." In further support of this statement, when Mormon was abridging the record of Third Nephi, he said Alma established "the first church which was established among them *after their transgression*" (3 Nephi 5:12; emphasis added). It should be remembered that at this time Mosiah was a prophet, seer, and revelator in the land of Zarahemla (see Mosiah 8:13–17). We will read later that Ammon, who came from the land of Zarahemla, declined from baptizing the people of Limhi, not because he didn't have authority, but because he considered "himself

---

[2] *Answers to Gospel Questions* [1960], 4:162.

an unworthy servant" (Mosiah 21:33). There was indeed a Church and the priesthood among the main branch of the Nephites.

Mosiah 18:18–22 • Alma Sets the Church In Order

> 18 And it came to pass that Alma, having authority from God, ordained priests; even one priest to every fifty of their number did he ordain to preach unto them, and to teach them concerning the things pertaining to the kingdom of God.
>
> 19 And he commanded them that they should teach nothing save it were the things which had been spoken by the mouth of the holy prophets.
>
> 20 Yea, even he commanded them that they should preach nothing save it were repentance and faith on the Lord, who had redeemed his people.
>
> 21 And he commanded them that there should be no contention one with another, but that they should look forward with one eye, having their hearts knit together in unity and in love one towards another.
>
> 22 And thus he commanded them to preach. And thus they became the children of God.

In regards to setting the church in order, President Joseph F. Smith, in speaking of offices in the Melchizedek Priesthood remarked:

> ... if it were necessary, though I do not expect the necessity will ever arise, and there was no man left on earth holding the Melchizedek Priesthood, except an elder—that elder, by the inspiration of the Spirit of God and by the direction of the Almighty, could proceed, and should proceed, to organize the Church of Jesus Christ in all its perfection, because he holds the Melchizedek Priesthood. [3]

Why Alma ordained "one priest to every fifty of their number" (Mosiah 18:18) is not stated. Perhaps a similar organization was

---

[3] Joseph F. Smith, *Gospel Doctrine,* 11th ed. [1959], 148.

followed by Zeniff who may have learned it from the plates of brass. Moses had "the Holy Priesthood, which he received under the hand of his father-in-law, Jethro" (D&C 84:6). Moses followed his counsel in making "heads over the people, rulers of thousands, rulers of hundreds, rulers of fifties, and rulers of tens" (Exodus 18:21–25). Having only two hundred and four people, Alma may have begun at the fifties division set up by Moses. The principle of teaching nothing but what the prophets had taught he had learned from Abinadi (see Mosiah 14:33; 15:11–16), or from the Spirit of the Lord that was upon him. To preach nothing but repentance and faith on the Lord (Mosiah 18:20) is similar to the modern revelation that the thing "of the most worth unto you will be to declare repentance unto this people, that you may bring souls unto [Christ]" (D&C 15:6). Faith is implied in the statement. Having "one faith and one baptism" (Mosiah 18:21) may also have been taken from the plates of brass. Paul taught it to the Ephesians (4:5) and may have been quoting from the Old Testament as he so often did. Alma's organization was successful, they become the children of God (v. 22).

Mosiah 18:23–26 • Observe the Sabbath Day

23 And he commanded them that they should observe the sabbath day, and keep it holy, and also every day they should give thanks to the Lord their God.

24 And he also commanded them that the priests whom he had ordained should labor with their own hands for their support.

25 And there was one day in every week that was set apart that they should gather themselves together to teach the people, and to worship the Lord their God, and also, as often as it was in their power, to assemble themselves together.

26 And the priests were not to depend upon the people for their support; but for their labor they were to receive the grace of God, that they might wax strong in the Spirit, having the knowledge of God, that they might teach with power and authority from God.

The people of Alma have two days of the week devoted to the

Lord in addition to daily prayer (vv. 23). They were to keep the Sabbath Day holy and there was at least another day in each week set apart for teaching (v. 25). This practice reminds us of the auxiliary organizations of our day and of religious education programs. They also had a lay priesthood, as we do today. Those called to minister to the Church worked with their own hands for support rather than depending on the people for their livelihood (vv. 24, 26). The priests were encouraged to labor for the Spirit that they might teach with power and authority from God (v. 26).

Mosiah 18:27–30 • A Welfare Program

27 And again Alma commanded that the people of the church should impart of their substance, every one according to that which he had; if he have more abundantly he should impart more abundantly; and of him that had but little, but little should be required; and to him that had not should be given.

28 And thus they should impart of their substance of their own free will and good desires towards God, and to those priests that stood in need, yea, and to every needy, naked soul.

29 And this he said unto them, having been commanded of God; and they did walk uprightly before God, imparting to one another both temporally and spiritually according to their needs and their wants.

30 And now it came to pass that all this was done in Mormon, yea, by the waters of Mormon, in the forest that was near the waters of Mormon; yea, the place of Mormon, the waters of Mormon, the forest of Mormon, how beautiful are they to the eyes of them who there came to the knowledge of their Redeemer; yea, and how blessed are they, for they shall sing to his praise forever. [Mosiah 18:27–30]

Alma did not advocate a dole system, but one somewhat like the present welfare program of the Church. The principles that governed the program were ability to give (v. 27), agency and a good conscience before God (v. 28); and helping others both temporally and spiritually (v. 29). These principles were advocated by King Benjamin (see Mosiah 2) and discussed in that chapter so will only be listed here.

The waters and place of Mormon were certainly beautiful to any resident or traveler, and it was also spiritually beautiful to those who came to a knowledge of their Redeemer in that place. It was much like the mission field of today where the young men and young women serve, each one feeling it was the best mission in the Church, and it was for them. It was like the sacred places in Church history: the sacred grove in New York, the Whitney Store or Temple in Kirkland, Ohio, the John Johnson home in Hiram, Ohio where the vision of the degrees of glory was given, or Nauvoo or Independence, Missouri. It was like the mount of Beatitudes, the mount of transfiguration, Gethsemane, or the Garden Tomb in Jerusalem where the Savior had great experiences. In these places, the Spirit of the Lord still dwells, and so it must have done in the place of Mormon. An appreciation and understanding of the covenants made in the waters of baptism will produce our own spiritual waters of Mormon in our hearts.

Mosiah 18:31–35 • Alma and His People Depart into the Wilderness

31 And these things were done in the borders of the land, that they might not come to the knowledge of the king.

32 But behold, it came to pass that the king, having discovered a movement among the people, sent his servants to watch them. Therefore on the day that they were assembling themselves together to hear the word of the Lord they were discovered unto the king.

33 And now the king said that Alma was stirring up the people to rebellion against him; therefore he sent his army to destroy them.

34 And it came to pass that Alma and the people of the Lord were apprized of the coming of the king's army; therefore they took their tents and their families and departed into the wilderness.

35 And they were in number about four hundred and fifty souls. [Mosiah 18:31–35]

The moving of four hundred and fifty people with tents and

families is not an easy task, but Alma, of all people, knew the temperament of the King Noah and what the consequences would be if they stayed. Therefore, they departed. For the moment, we will skip the next four chapters (19–22) and follow Alma and his people.

Mosiah 23:1–5 • The Lord Did Strengthen Them

> 1 Now Alma, having been warned of the Lord that the armies of king Noah would come upon them, and having made it known to his people, therefore they gathered together their flocks, and took of their grain, and departed into the wilderness before the armies of king Noah.
>
> 2 And the Lord did strengthen them, that the people of king Noah could not overtake them to destroy them.
>
> 3 And they fled eight days' journey into the wilderness.
>
> 4 And they came to a land, yea, even a very beautiful and pleasant land, a land of pure water.
>
> 5 And they pitched their tents, and began to till the ground, and began to build buildings; yea, they were industrious, and did labor exceedingly. [Mosiah 23:1–5]

We learn from this section that the Lord warned Alma that the armies of Noah would come upon him. So the Lord did strengthen Alma and his peoples, thus preventing Noah's armies from overtaking them (vv. 1–2). The traveling distance of eight days (v. 3) may be significant geographically and will be discussed later. The land where they settled had the same characteristics as the place of Mormon, which they left—a very beautiful and pleasant place, a land of pure water (v. 4, compare 18:5, 30).

Mosiah 23:6–15 • The People Desire a King

> 6 And the people were desirous that Alma should be their king, for he was beloved by his people.
>
> 7 But he said unto them: Behold, it is not expedient that we

should have a king; for thus saith the Lord: Ye shall not esteem one flesh above another, or one man shall not think himself above another; therefore I say unto you it is not expedient that ye should have a king.

8 Nevertheless, if it were possible that ye could always have just men to be your kings it would be well for you to have a king.

9 But remember the iniquity of king Noah and his priests; and I myself was caught in a snare, and did many things which were abominable in the sight of the Lord, which caused me sore repentance;

10 Nevertheless, after much tribulation, the Lord did hear my cries, and did answer my prayers, and has made me an instrument in his hands in bringing so many of you to a knowledge of his truth.

11 Nevertheless, in this I do not glory, for I am unworthy to glory of myself.

12 And now I say unto you, ye have been oppressed by king Noah, and have been in bondage to him and his priests, and have been brought into iniquity by them; therefore ye were bound with the bands of iniquity.

13 And now as ye have been delivered by the power of God out of these bonds; yea, even out of the hands of king Noah and his people, and also from the bonds of iniquity, even so I desire that ye should stand fast in this liberty wherewith ye have been made free, and that ye trust no man to be a king over you.

14 And also trust no one to be your teacher nor your minister, except he be a man of God, walking in his ways and keeping his commandments.

15 Thus did Alma teach his people, that every man should love his neighbor as himself, that there should be no contention among them.

The advantages and disadvantages of a kingship form of government will be discussed more fully in chapter 15 of this work. However, Alma lays the foundation for that discussion. The Lord either revealed to Alma (or he had read in the scriptures) the Lord's admonition not to esteem one flesh above another or for one man not to think himself above another (v. 7), as is typical of a monarchy. Noah was the prime example of that kind of king (v. 9). Nevertheless, if you could always have a just man for your king it would be well (v. 8). Nephi, King Benjamin, and the Mosiah kings, although not mentioned by Alma, are examples of just men being king.

Alma was the victim of King Noah's wicked reign although he does not enumerate what he did. He does acknowledge the sore repentance he went through before leading his people to the truth (v. 10). His great humility is apparent (v. 11). Alma's people were also victims of this tyrant (v. 12). Acknowledging the Lord's hand in their deliverance from bondage to freedom, Alma admonishes them to stand fast in their liberty and not to trust any man to lead them either politically or spiritually, except he be a man of God (vv. 13–14). These people had just experienced what Jesus taught, "Ye shall know the truth and the truth shall make you free" (John 8:32). Having come to know their Redeemer, he taught them the second great commandment, to love their neighbor (v. 15).

Mosiah 23:15–19 • Prosperity in the Land of Helam

15 Thus did Alma teach his people, that every man should love his neighbor as himself, that there should be no contention among them.

16 And now, Alma was their high priest, he being the founder of their church.

17 And it came to pass that none received authority to preach or to teach except it were by him from God. Therefore he consecrated all their priests and all their teachers; and none were consecrated except they were just men.

18 Therefore they did watch over their people, and did nourish them with things pertaining to righteousness.

19 And it came to pass that they began to prosper exceedingly in the land; and they called the land Helam.

Alma and his priests practiced what they had been taught and the result was prosperity. We will leave Alma's people in their prosperous circumstances and return now to the people of King Noah.

SACRED WRITING

Preaching Which is Sacred:

Mosiah 18:7–20	Alma to the people he had gathered to the place of Mormon.
Mosiah 23:7–14	Alma to the people in the land of Helam.

Revelation Which is Great:

Mosiah 23:1	Alma is warned of the Lord of the coming of Noah's army.

Doctrines Learned:

Mosiah 17:20	Prophets are sometimes required to seal their testimony with their death.
Mosiah 18:8–10	Baptism is a covenant between man and God. Man agrees to keep the commandments, God promises redemption and resurrection unto eternal life.

General Authority Quotes

President Brigham Young • Mosiah 18:10

All Latter-day Saints enter the new and everlasting covenant when they enter this Church. The covenant to cease sustaining, upholding and cherishing the kingdom of the Devil and the kingdoms of this world. They enter the new and everlasting covenant to sustain the Kingdom of God and no other kingdom. They take a vow of the most solemn kind, before the heavens and earth, and that, too, upon the validity of their own salvation, that they will sustain truth and righteousness instead of wickedness and falsehood, and build up the Kingdom of God, instead of the kingdoms of this world. [*Discourses of Brigham Young*, sel. John A. Widtsoe (1951), 160]

Joseph Smith the Prophet • Mosiah 18:18, 23:9–10

Whenever there has been a righteous man on earth unto whom God revealed His work and gave power and authority to administer in His name. And where there is a priest of God—a minister who has power and authority from God to administer in the ordinances of the gospel and officiate in the priesthood of God— there is the kingdom of God. And, in consequence of rejecting the Gospel of Jesus Christ and the Prophets whom God hath sent, the judgments of God have rested upon people, cities, and nations, in various ages of the world, which was the case with the cities of Sodom and Gomorrah, that were destroyed from rejecting the Prophets . . .

Where there is no kingdom of God there is no salvation. What constitutes the kingdom of God? Where there is a prophet, a priest or a righteous man unto whom God gives His oracles, there is the kingdom of God; and where the oracles of God are not, there the kingdom of God is not. [*Teachings of the Prophet Joseph Smith*, sel. Joseph Fielding Smith (1976), 271–272]

Challenges for Eternal Life:

1. Choose a part of the baptismal covenant and note how the Lord's part is fulfilled as you fulfill yours (Mosiah 18:10).
2. As a member of Christ's family, think of the need and the responsibility you have to another member of the family and give them the help they need (Mosiah 18:9).
3. Determine to be a witness of God at all times, in all places, and in all things (Mosiah 18:9).
4. Pray that you might be an instrument in the Lord's hand in bringing someone to the knowledge of the truth (Mosiah 23:10).
5. Choose a challenge of your own from this reading assignment and apply it to your life.

Chapter Thirteen

Deliverance from Bondage

Mosiah 19–22; 23:20–39

H *istorical Setting*: There are three locations in the book of Mosiah and many flashbacks in the story line. The main body of Nephites are in the land of Zarahemla. The Nephites under King Noah are in the land of Lehi-Nephi, the main land of the Lamanites. The Nephite people of Alma are in the land of Helam close to midway between the land of Lehi-Nephi and the land of Zarahemla. We begin with the people of Noah in the land of Lehi-Nephi about 145 B.C. (Mosiah 19:1–21; 22). Ammon and his fifteen associates leave the land of Zarahemla in about 121 B.C. They are taken captive by the Nephites who are in bondage to the Lamanites, and Limhi son of Noah is the king of the Nephites (Mosiah 7). The story line is with this group until they return to the land of Zarahemla (Mosiah 21:21–22:16). We then go to the land of Helam and follow their deliverance out of bondage to the Lamanites and their return to the land of Zarahemla about 120 B.C. (Mosiah 23:20–24:25).

Precept of this reading:

21 Nevertheless the Lord seeth fit to chasten his people; yea, he trieth their patience and their faith.

22 Nevertheless—whosoever putteth his trust in him the same shall be lifted up at the last day. Yea, and thus it was with this people.

23 For behold, I will show unto you that they were brought into
bondage, and none could deliver them but the Lord their God, yea,
even the God of Abraham and Isaac and of Jacob. [Mosiah 23:21–23]

The formula for deliverance from bondage was outlined in chapter
8. Limhi gave a four-step process (Mosiah 7:33 summarized below).

1. Turn to the Lord with full purpose of heart.
2. Put your trust in him.
3. Serve him with all diligence of mind.
4. According to his own will and pleasure, he will deliver you.

That the formula works is exemplified in the experiences of
Limhi's and Alma's people. An outline of the chapters telling of these
experiences follows as a preparation for a deeper study.

OUTLINE • MOSIAH 19–22; 23:20–39

➤ Mosiah 19:1–8   King Noah returned to the land of Nephi having
searched in vain for Alma and his people.

    a. There began to be a division among the people (v. 2).

    b. The lesser part began to threaten the king and great
contention arose (v. 3).

    c. Gideon, a strong man and an enemy to the king, swore
he would kill the king (vv. 4–5).

        1. He fought with the king and was about to over-
power him.

        2. The king fled and got upon the tower near the
temple.

    d. The king saw the Lamanite army within the borders of
the land (vv. 6–8).

        1. The king plead with Gideon to spare him for the
Lamanites were about to destroy them.

        2. The king was more concerned with his life than
with the peoples lives.

        3. Gideon spared the king.

➤ 19:9–17   King Noah commanded the people to flee before the Lamanites. He led them into the wilderness with the women and children.

    a.   The Lamanites overtook them and began to slay them (v. 10).

    b.   King Noah commanded the men to leave their wives and children and flee (vv. 11–12).

        1.   Many would not leave their wives and children.

        2.   Others fled leaving their wives and children.

    c.   Those who remained caused their daughters to plead with the Lamanites to spare them (vv. 11–12).

        1.   The Lamanites had compassion being charmed by the women's beauty.

        2.   The Nephites were carried back captive to the land of Nephi.

        3.   The Nephites agreed to deliver King Noah into the Lamanite hands.

        4.   The Nephites agreed to deliver one-half of their possessions: gold, silver, and precious things.

        5.   The Nephites agreed to pay tribute to the Lamanites from year to year.

    e.   Limhi, one of Noah's sons, was desirous that his father not be killed (vv. 17–18).

        1.   Limhi was not ignorant of his father's iniquities.

        2.   Limhi was a just man.

➤ 19:18–26   Gideon sent men into the wilderness to search for King Noah and those who were with him.

    a.   They met all the people in the wilderness, except the king and his priests (v. 18).

    b.   They had sworn to return to the land, and if their sons and daughters had been slain they would seek revenge and perish with them (v. 19).

    c.   The king commanded them not to return, and they put him to death by fire (vv. 20–25).

1. The priests fled as they were about to put the king to death.

2. The people were about to return to the land of Nephi when they met Gideon's men.

3. The men of Gideon informed them of the conditions of bondage to the Lamanites.

4. They all returned to the land of Nephi rejoicing after they told Gideon what had happened.

5. The king of the Lamanites made an oath that his people would not slay them.

d. Limhi was made king by the voice of the people. He made an oath with the Lamanite king to pay a tribute of one-half of their possessions (v. 26).

➢ 19:27–29 Limhi established the kingdom and there was peace among the people.

a. The king of the Lamanites set guards about the land (v. 28).

b. The guards were supported out of the Nephite tribute (v. 28).

c. Limhi had peace in his kingdom for two years (v. 29).

➢ 20:1–5 Twenty-four of the Lamanite daughters were carried captive into the wilderness by the priests of Noah.

a. The daughters had gathered in a place called Shemlon to sing and dance (v. 1).

b. The priests of Noah were ashamed to return to the city of Nephi and feared they would be slain (vv. 2–5).

1. They discovered the Lamanite daughters and watched them.

2. When there were but a few of them, they came out of hiding and took them.

➢ 20:6–7 The Lamanites were angry thinking it was the people of Limhi who took their daughters and the king led his army to the land of Nephi to destroy them.

a. King Limhi discovered their preparation for war from his tower (v. 8).

b. He gathered his people in the fields and forests to wait for the Lamanites (v. 8).

c. When the Lamanites came up, the people of Limhi fell on them, and a battle took place (vv. 9–11).

    1. Limhi's people, though only half as numerous, drove back the Lamanites.

    2. They fought like dragons for their wives and children.

d. They found the Lamanite king wounded and left among the dead (vv. 12–15).

    1. They bound up his wounds and brought him to Limhi desiring permission to kill him.

    2. Limhi refused and asked the king why they had broken their oath and had come up against them.

    3. The king said it was because they had carried their daughters away.

e. Limhi was not aware of the daughters being carried away. He searched among his people saying the guilty ones would perish (v. 16).

f. Gideon, the king's captain, suggested it was the priests of Noah who stolen the daughters (vv. 17–22).

    1. He asked Limhi to tell the Lamanite king of these things that the Lamanites may be pacified.

    2. The Lamanites were preparing to come again with their numerous hosts and destroy them.

    3. The words of Abinadi were fulfilled because they did not hearken to the Lord's words.

    4. Gideon asked that they pacify the Lamanite king because it was better to be in bondage than to be killed.

g. Limhi told the Lamanite king of Gideon's suggestion and the king was pacified (vv. 23–26).

    1. The Lamanite king swore an oath that the Laman-

ites would not slay the Nephites if they met them without arms.

2. The Lamanite king led the Nephites to meet the Lamanites without arms.

3. The Lamamite king bowed down and pled in behalf of the Nephites.

4. The Lamanites were pacified and returned with their king to their own lands.

➤ 21:1–5   Limhi and his people returned to the land of Nephi and dwelt in peace.

a. The Lamanites were stirred up to anger and came into the Nephite borders (vv. 2–31).

1. They did not slay them because of the oath their king had made.

2. They smote them, exercised authority over them, put heavy burdens on them, and drove them.

b. Their afflictions fulfilled the word of the Lord (v. 4).

c. They were surrounded by the Lamanites and could not be delivered (v. 5).

➤ 21:6–22   The people murmured and desired to go to battle. The king granted them their desire.

a. They put on their armor and went forth against the Lamanites (v. 7).

b. The Lamanites drove them back and slew many (v. 8).

c. There was great mourning among the people of Limhi (vv. 9–10).

1. The widows, sons and daughters, and brothers mourned for their dead.

2. Many widows cried mightily from day to day.

d. The continual cries stirred up the people of Limhi to go to battle again, but they were driven back (v. 11).

e. They went the third time and suffered in like manner (v. 12).

f. They humbled themselves, submitted to their bondage,

but cried mightily all day long that God would deliver them from their afflictions (vv. 14–15).

1. The Lord was slow to hear their cries because of their iniquities.

2. The Lord did hear their cries and softened the hearts of the Lamanites and they eased their burdens.

3. The Lord did not see fit to deliver them at this time.

g. The people of Limhi prospered by degrees in raising grain, flocks, and herds that they suffered no hunger (vv. 16–17).

1. There were a greater number of women than men.

2. King Limhi commanded that every man imparted to the support of the widows and children.

h. The people of Limhi kept in a body and the king would not go outside the city walls without guards (vv. 18–21).

1. They watched the land round about that they might take the priests who had stolen the Lamanite daughters.

2. They desired to punish them, for they came by night and stole grain and precious things.

i. There were no more disturbances between the Lamanites and the Nephites until Ammon and his brethren came into the land.

➤ 21:23–31 King Limhi and his guards discovered Ammon and his brethren outside the walls of the city and supposed them to be the priests of Noah.

a. Ammon and his brethren were cast into prison and would nave been put to death were they the priests of Noah (v. 23).

b. The king rejoiced to find they were from the land of Zarahemla (v. 24).

c. The king had sent a small number of men to find the

land of Zarahemla but they had gotten lost (vv. 25–27).

1. They found a land covered with the dry bones of a people who had been destroyed.

2. They supposed it was the land of Zarahemla, and they returned to the land of Nephi a few days before Ammon came.

3. They brought a record of the people whose bones they found engraven on plates of ore.

d. King Limhi and Ammon rejoiced that King Mosiah had a gift from God to interpret languages.

e. Ammon and his brethren were filled with sorrow over so many of their brethren having been slain and others being led into iniquity (vv. 29–31).

1. King Noah had caused his people to commit sins and iniquity.

2. The people mourned the death of Abinadi.

3. They mourned that Alma's people had departed after forming the church and knew not where they had fled.

4. They would gladly have joined Alma's people for they also had entered into a covenant to serve God and keep his commandments.

➤ 21:32–36   Since the coming of Ammon, Limhi and his people had entered into a covenant to serve God and keep his commandments.

a. They were desirous to be baptized, but none in the land had authority from God (vv. 33–35).

1. Ammon declined baptizing them, considering himself an unworthy servant.

2. Limhi's people did not form a church, waiting for the Spirit of the Lord.

3. They desired to become as Alma and his brethren.

4. They desired to be baptized as a witness and testimony of their willingness to serve God.

b. Ammon, Limhi and his people studied ways to be

delivered out of Lamanite bondage (v. 36).

➤ 22:1–8   Ammon and king Limhi consulted with the people on ways to be delivered from bondage.

    a. They concluded that the only way was to take their families and depart into the wilderness. They could not contend with the Lamanites (v. 2).

    b. Gideon asked the king to consider his way for his people to leave uninterrupted (vv. 3–8).

        1. The Lamanite guards at the back pass are drunken at night.

        2. The people were to gather together their animals.

        3. Gideon would pay the last tribute of wine to the Lamanites and they would be drunk.

        4. The people would pass through the secret pass while the guards were drunk.

        5. They would depart with their families and animals into the wilderness and travel around the land of Shilom.

➤ 22:9–13   The king hearkened to Gideon's words.

    a. The flocks were gathered, and the tribute of wine was sent plus a present of wine that they might drink freely (v. 10).

    b. The people departed by night and were led by Ammon toward Zarahemla (vv. 11–13).

        1. They took all their gold, silver, precious things, and provisions that they could carry.

        2. After many days they arrived in the land of Zarahemla.

    c. They joined Mosiah's people and became his subjects (v. 13).

➤ 22:14   King Mosiah received them with joy.

    a. He received Limhi's records.

    b. He received the other records that Limhi's people had found.

➤ 22:15–16   The Lamanites found the people of Limhi had departed and
              sent an army to pursue them.

              a.   After two days they could no longer follow their tracks
                    (v. 16).

              b.   They were lost in the wilderness (v. 16).

➤ 23:20–24   The people of Alma multiplied and prospered exceedingly
              in the land of Helam. They built a city called the city of
              Helam.

              a.   The Lord saw fit to chasten his people and try their
                    patience and their faith (v. 21).

              b.   Nevertheless, those who put their trust in him will be
                    lifted up at the last day (v. 22).

              c.   Mormon said he would show that none could deliver
                    from bondage but the God of Abraham, Isaac, and
                    Jacob (vv. 23–24).

                    1.   God did deliver them and show his mighty power.

                    2.   There was much rejoicing among the people.

➤ 23:25–29   While tilling the land about the land of Helam, a Lamanite
              army came in the border of the land.

              a.   The people gathered to the city being much frightened
                    (v. 26).

              b.   Alma exhorted them to remember the Lord and he
                    would deliver them (v. 27).

              c.   They cried unto the Lord that he would soften the
                    hearts of the Lamanites and spare them and their fami-
                    lies (v. 28).

              d.   The Lord softened the Lamanites hearts (v. 29).

                    1.   Alma and his people delivered themselves into the
                          hands of the Lamanites.

                    2.   The Lamanites took possession of the land of
                          Helam.

➤ 23:30–39   The army of the Lamanites became lost in following

Limhi's people and found the priests of Noah in a place called Amulon.

a. The leader of the priests was called Amulon (v. 32).

b. Amulon pled with the Lamanites, and sent their wives, the Lamanite daughters, to plead with them not to destroy their husbands (vv. 33–35).

    1. The Lamanites had compassion because of the wives.

    2. The people of Amulon joined the Lamanites to search for the land of Nephi.

    3. They discovered the land of Helam possessed by Alma's people.

c. The Lamanites promised Alma that they would grant them life and liberty if they would lead them to the land of Nephi (vv. 36–38).

    1. After they showed them the way, they did not keep their promise.

    2. They set guards about the land of Helam to watch Alma and his people.

    3. Part of the Lamanites went to the land of Nephi and part of them remained to guard the land of Helam and brought with them their wives and children.

e. The king of the Lamanites appointed Amulon to be the king and ruler over the land of Helam, but he could do nothing contrary to the will of the Lamanite king (v. 39).

➤ 24:1–7   Amulon gained favor with the king of the Lamanites who granted that he and his brethren be appointed teachers over all the people.

a. The Lamanites had taken possession of all the lands and appointed kings over each land (vv. 2–3).

    1. The king over all the Lamanites was Laman, named after his father. He was king over a numerous people.

   b. The king appointed teachers in every land, thus the
       Nephite language began to be taught among all the
       Lamanites (vv. 4–6).

       1. They were a friendly people but knew not God.

       2. The brethren of Amulon did not teach about God,
           the law of Moses, or the words of Abinadi.

       3. They taught them to keep records and to write to
           one another.

   c. The Lamanites began to increase in riches, to trade
       with one another, and to be wise and cunning as to the
       ways of the world (v. 7).

       1. They delighted in wickedness and plunder.

       2. They did not do such among their own brethren.

➤ 24:8–17   Amulon began to exercise authority over Alma and his
             brethren and to persecute them and their children.

   a. Amulon knew that Alma had been one of the king's
       priests and that he had believed Abinadi's words and
       was driven out by the king (v. 9).

       1. Amulon was subject to king Laman yet exercised
           authority over Alma's people.

       2. Amulon put tasks and taskmasters over them.

   b. So great were the afflictions of Alma's people that they
       cried mightily to God (vv. 10–12).

       1. Amulon commanded them to stop their cries and
           put guards over them, killing those found calling
           upon God.

       2. Alma's people did not raise their voices but poured
           out their hearts to him.

       3. The Lord knew the thoughts of their hearts.

   c. The voice of the Lord came to them and said he knew
       the covenant they had made to him. He covenanted to
       deliver them out of bondage (vv. 13–15).

       1. The Lord would ease their burdens that they would
           not feel them.

       2. They would stand as witnesses for God hereafter

and know that the Lord visits his people in their afflictions.

   3.   Their burdens were made light and the Lord strengthened them.

  d.   Their faith and patience were so great that the voice of the Lord came again saying I will deliver you out of bondage on the morrow (vv. 16–17).

    1.   Alma was to go before the people.

    2.   The Lord would go with them and deliver them.

➤ 24:18–25   In the night time, Alma and his people gathered all their flocks and grain.

  a.   The Lord caused a deep sleep to come upon the Lamanites (v. 19).

  b.   Alma's people departed and traveled all day into the wilderness (vv. 20–22).

    1.   They pitched their tents in a valley and called it the valley of Alma.

    2.   They poured out their thanks to God for easing their burdens and delivering them.

    3.   None could have delivered them but the Lord their God.

    4.   All the men, women, and children who could speak praised God.

  c.   The Lord told Alma to get this people out of the land (v. 23).

    1.   The Lamanites had awakened and were pursuing them.

    2.   The Lord would stop them that they come no farther than the valley.

  d.   They departed out of the valley into the wilderness (vv. 24–25).

    1.   After traveling twelve days, they arrived in the land of Zarahemla.

    2.   King Mosiah received them with joy.

Notes and Commentary

Introduction: Abinadi had made several unconditional prophecies concerning King Noah and his people. Every one of these prophecies was fulfilled. Since the people separated into different groups they were fulfilled at different times. The fulfillment of some are recorded in these chapters which we will note.

Mosiah 19:1–8 • Gideon spares the life of King Noah

1 And it came to pass that the army of the king returned, having searched in vain for the people of the Lord.

2 And now behold, the forces of the king were small, having been reduced, and there began to be a division among the remainder of the people.

3 And the lesser part began to breathe out threatenings against the king, and there began to be a great contention among them.

4 And now there was a man among them whose name was Gideon, and he being a strong man and an enemy to the king, therefore he drew his sword, and swore in his wrath that he would slay the king.

5 And it came to pass that he fought with the king; and when the king saw that he was about to overpower him, he fled and ran and got upon the tower which was near the temple.

6 And Gideon pursued after him and was about to get upon the tower to slay the king, and the king cast his eyes round about towards the land of Shemlon, and behold, the army of the Lamanites were within the borders of the land.

7 And now the king cried out in the anguish of his soul, saying: Gideon, spare me, for the Lamanites are upon us, and they will destroy us; yea, they will destroy my people.

8 And now the king was not so much concerned about his people as he was about his own life; nevertheless, Gideon did spare his life. [Mosiah 19:1–8]

The Nephite people were becoming discontented with their self-serving king. The departure of Alma and his people had probably encouraged others to resist. Although it was the lesser part (vv. 2–3), a new leader named Gideon emerges among them. We will hear more of him later. The character of Noah is further exposed. His concern for his own life is natural, but the plot thickens.

Mosiah 19:9–15 • King Noah the Coward

9 And the king commanded the people that they should flee before the Lamanites, and he himself did go before them, and they did flee into the wilderness, with their women and their children.

10 And it came to pass that the Lamanites did pursue them, and did overtake them, and began to slay them.

11 Now it came to pass that the king commanded them that all the men should leave their wives and their children, and flee before the Lamanites.

12 Now there were many that would not leave them, but had rather stay and perish with them. And the rest left their wives and their children and fled.

13 And it came to pass that those who tarried with their wives and their children caused that their fair daughters should stand forth and plead with the Lamanites that they would not slay them.

14 And it came to pass that the Lamanites had compassion on them, for they were charmed with the beauty of their women.

15 Therefore the Lamanites did spare their lives, and took them captives and carried them back to the land of Nephi, and granted unto them that they might possess the land, under the conditions that they would deliver up king Noah into the hands of the Lamanites, and deliver up their property, even one half of all they possessed, one half of their gold, and their silver, and all their precious things, and thus they should pay tribute to the king of the Lamanites from year to year. [Mosiah 19:9–15]

What kind of leader, or what man, would desert his wife and children and flee from an enemy? Both Noah and his priests left wives and children. Fortunately, there were some courageous men among them who used their brains instead of their brawn against impossible odds (vv. 12–13). It may appear that these courageous men were willing to sacrifice or barter their daughters, but they undoubtedly knew the nature of the Lamanites, who would have defended their daughters from physical or moral harm. The offer of bondage is now presented. They were already paying a fifth-part of all they possessed to the Lamanite king (Mosiah 11:3), but now it would be increased to one-half from year to year (Mosiah 19:15).

Mosiah 19:16–24 • King Noah
Put to Death by Fire

16 And now there was one of the sons of the king among those that were taken captive, whose name was Limhi.

17 And now Limhi was desirous that his father should not be destroyed; nevertheless, Limhi was not ignorant of the iniquities of his father, he himself being a just man.

18 And it came to pass that Gideon sent men into the wilderness secretly, to search for the king and those that were with him. And it came to pass that they met the people in the wilderness, all save the king and his priests.

19 Now they had sworn in their hearts that they would return to the land of Nephi, and if their wives and their children were slain, and also those that had tarried with them, that they would seek revenge, and also perish with them.

20 And the king commanded them that they should not return; and they were angry with the king, and caused that he should suffer, even unto death by fire.

21 And they were about to take the priests also and put them to death, and they fled before them.

22 And it came to pass that they were about to return to the land of Nephi, and they met the men of Gideon. And the men of Gideon told them of all that had happened to their wives and their children; and that the Lamanites had granted unto them that they might possess the land by paying a tribute to the Lamanites of one half of all they possessed.

23 And the people told the men of Gideon that they had slain the king, and his priests had fled from them farther into the wilderness.

24 And it came to pass that after they had ended the ceremony, that they returned to the land of Nephi, rejoicing, because their wives and their children were not slain; and they told Gideon what they had done to the king. [Mosiah 19:16–24]

Gideon, who sent men into the wilderness to "hunt" for the king and his men, would have captured the king and turned him over to the Lamanites, to spare the Nephite lives (v. 15, 18). However, other men, who had deserted their wives and children, had second thoughts and fulfilled the prophecy of Abinadi. At Abinadi's death he had foretold that the king and his priests would be "hunted"and "suffer, even as I suffer, the pains of death by fire" (Mosiah 17:18). The king had been put to death by fire, and the priests were about to be, but fled (Mosiah 19:20–21). The priests were later captured and put to death by fire (see Alma 25:8–12). Earlier Abinadi had prophesied that "Thus saith the Lord . . . the life of King Noah shall be valued as a garment in a hot furnace; for he shall that I am the Lord" (Mosiah 12:2–3). His own people had placed no value on his life. They considered his reign as king and cast him into the fire as a useless worn-out garment. The "ceremony" they preformed (Mosiah 19:24) is not explained. It may have been some form of a thanksgiving sacrifice unto God.

Mosiah 19:25–29 • Bondage to the Lamanites

25 And it came to pass that the king of the Lamanites made an oath unto them, that his people should not slay them.

26 And also Limhi, being the son of the king, having the kingdom conferred upon him by the people, made oath unto the king of the Lamanites that his people should pay tribute unto him, even one half of all they possessed.

27 And it came to pass that Limhi began to establish the kingdom and to establish peace among his people.

28 And the king of the Lamanites set guards round about the land, that he might keep the people of Limhi in the land, that they might

not depart into the wilderness; and he did support his guards out of the tribute which he did receive from the Nephites.

29 And now king Limhi did have continual peace in his kingdom for the space of two years, that the Lamanites did not molest them nor seek to destroy them. [Mosiah 19:25–29]

The oath made with the Lamanite king by the newly appointed King Limhi (vv. 25–26) fulfilled another of Abinadi's prophecies. The Lord had said through him: "This generation, because of their iniquities, shall be brought into bondage" (Mosiah 12:2). Further details of the prophecy were not fulfilled until after the two years of peace (Mosiah 19:29). These details will be discussed at the time of their fulfillment.

Mosiah 20:1–11 • The Twenty-four Lamanite Daughters

1 Now there was a place in Shemlon where the daughters of the Lamanites did gather themselves together to sing, and to dance, and to make themselves merry.

2 And it came to pass that there was one day a small number of them gathered together to sing and to dance.

3 And now the priests of king Noah, being ashamed to return to the city of Nephi, yea, and also fearing that the people would slay them, therefore they durst not return to their wives and their children.

4 And having tarried in the wilderness, and having discovered the daughters of the Lamanites, they laid and watched them;

5 And when there were but few of them gathered together to dance, they came forth out of their secret places and took them and carried them into the wilderness; yea, twenty and four of the daughters of the Lamanites they carried into the wilderness.

6 And it came to pass that when the Lamanites found that their daughters had been missing, they were angry with the people of Limhi, for they thought it was the people of Limhi.

7 Therefore they sent their armies forth; yea, even the king himself went before his people; and they went up to the land of Nephi to destroy the people of Limhi.

8 And now Limhi had discovered them from the tower, even all their preparations for war did he discover; therefore he gathered his people together, and laid wait for them in the fields and in the forests.

9 And it came to pass that when the Lamanites had come up, that the people of Limhi began to fall upon them from their waiting places, and began to slay them.

10 And it came to pass that the battle became exceedingly sore, for they fought like lions for their prey.

11 And it came to pass that the people of Limhi began to drive the Lamanites before them; yet they were not half so numerous as the Lamanites. But they fought for their lives, and for their wives, and for their children; therefore they exerted themselves and like dragons did they fight. [Mosiah 20:1–11]

The Nephites were probably inspired to fight as they did because of the fear of being annihilated. Had either side known the facts, there may have been no battle at all.

Mosiah 20:12–16 • Why the Oath Was Broken

12 And it came to pass that they found the king of the Lamanites among the number of their dead; yet he was not dead, having been wounded and left upon the ground, so speedy was the flight of his people.

13 And they took him and bound up his wounds, and brought him before Limhi, and said: Behold, here is the king of the Lamanites; he having received a wound has fallen among their dead, and they have left him; and behold, we have brought him before you; and now let us slay him.

14 But Limhi said unto them: Ye shall not slay him, but bring him hither that I may see him. And they brought him. And Limhi said unto him: What cause have ye to come up to war against my people? Behold, my people have not broken the oath that I made unto you; therefore, why should ye break the oath which ye made unto my people?

15 And now the king said: I have broken the oath because thy people did carry away the daughters of my people; therefore, in my

anger I did cause my people to come up to war against thy people.

16 And now Limhi had heard nothing concerning this matter; therefore he said: I will search among my people and whosoever has done this thing shall perish. Therefore he caused a search to be made among his people. [Mosiah 20:12–16]

The probable cause for Limhi's not slaying the injured king was a desire to know why the oath was broken (v. 14). Oaths were sacred in both cultures (see 1 Nephi 4:30–35). The sacredness of oaths is shown in Limhi's determination to find who was responsible for the act (Mosiah 20:16).

Mosiah 20:17–22 • Gideon Solves the Mystery

17 Now when Gideon had heard these things, he being the king's captain, he went forth and said unto the king: I pray thee forbear, and do not search this people, and lay not this thing to their charge.

18 For do ye not remember the priests of thy father, whom this people sought to destroy? And are they not in the wilderness? And are not they the ones who have stolen the daughters of the Lamanites?

19 And now, behold, and tell the king of these things, that he may tell his people that they may be pacified towards us; for behold they are already preparing to come against us; and behold also there are but few of us.

20 And behold, they come with their numerous hosts; and except the king doth pacify them towards us we must perish.

21 For are not the words of Abinadi fulfilled, which he prophesied against us—and all this because we would not hearken unto the words of the Lord, and turn from our iniquities?

22 And now let us pacify the king, and we fulfil the oath which we have made unto him; for it is better that we should be in bondage than that we should lose our lives; therefore, let us put a stop to the shedding of so much blood.

Gideon again demonstrates his leadership. He seems to have

followed the formula given to Oliver Cowdery:

> 8 But, behold, I say unto you, that you must study it out in your mind; then you must ask me if it be right, and if it is right I will cause that your bosom shall burn within you; therefore, you shall feel that it is right.

> 9 But if it be not right you shall have no such feelings, but you shall have a stupor of thought that shall cause you to forget the thing which is wrong; therefore, you cannot write that which is sacred save it be given you from me. [D&C 9:8–9]

The convictions Gideon had were true and could have come to him from the Lord. Gideon's reasoning that it was better to be in bondage than to lose their lives (Mosiah 20:22) is not always true, but was in this case. The Lord knows "the end from the beginning" (Abraham 2:8; Isaiah 46:10), and the fulfilling of prophecy and the sacredness of keeping the oath were considered as more important than death at this time. The Lord's will was what needed to be known, and Gideon seems to have known what it was for the Nephites in their situation.

Mosiah 20:23–26 • The Lamanites Are Pacified

> 23 And now Limhi told the king all the things concerning his father, and the priests that had fled into the wilderness, and attributed the carrying away of their daughters to them.

> 24 And it came to pass that the king was pacified towards his people; and he said unto them: Let us go forth to meet my people, without arms; and I swear unto you with an oath that my people shall not slay thy people.

> 25 And it came to pass that they followed the king, and went forth without arms to meet the Lamanites. And it came to pass that they did meet the Lamanites; and the king of the Lamanites did bow himself down before them, and did plead in behalf of the people of Limhi.

> 26 And when the Lamanites saw the people of Limhi, that they were without arms, they had compassion on them and were pacified

towards them, and returned with their king in peace to their own land. [Mosiah 20:23–26]

The Lamanite king was an honorable man. Here again he uses the oath for an assurance to the Nephites, and the Lamanites were responsive to his pleading.

Mosiah 21:1–4 • The Word of the Lord Fulfilled

1 And it came to pass that Limhi and his people returned to the city of Nephi, and began to dwell in the land again in peace.

2 And it came to pass that after many days the Lamanites began again to be stirred up in anger against the Nephites, and they began to come into the borders of the land round about.

3 Now they durst not slay them, because of the oath which their king had made unto Limhi; but they would smite them on their cheeks, and exercise authority over them; and began to put heavy burdens upon their backs, and drive them as they would a dumb ass—

4 Yea, all this was done that the word of the Lord might be fulfilled. [Mosiah 21:1–4]

The Lamanites kept their oath not to slay the Nephites, but the prophecy of Abinadi was fulfilled (vv. 3–4). The Lord told him that "I will smite this my people with sore afflictions . . . they shall have burdens lashed upon their backs, and they shall be driven before like a dumb ass" (Mosiah 12:4–5).

Mosiah 21:5–13 • The Nephites Defeated Three Times

5 And now the afflictions of the Nephites were great, and there was no way that they could deliver themselves out of their hands, for the Lamanites had surrounded them on every side.

6 And it came to pass that the people began to murmur with the king because of their afflictions; and they began to be desirous to go against them to battle. And they did afflict the king sorely with their

complaints; therefore he granted unto them that they should do according to their desires.

7 And they gathered themselves together again, and put on their armor, and went forth against the Lamanites to drive them out of their land.

8 And it came to pass that the Lamanites did beat them, and drove them back, and slew many of them.

9 And now there was a great mourning and lamentation among the people of Limhi, the widow mourning for her husband, the son and the daughter mourning for their father, and the brothers for their brethren.

10 Now there were a great many widows in the land, and they did cry mightily from day to day, for a great fear of the Lamanites had come upon them.

11 And it came to pass that their continual cries did stir up the remainder of the people of Limhi to anger against the Lamanites; and they went again to battle, but they were driven back again, suffering much loss.

12 Yea, they went again even the third time, and suffered in the like manner; and those that were not slain returned again to the city of Nephi.

13 And they did humble themselves even to the dust, subjecting themselves to the yoke of bondage, submitting themselves to be smitten, and to be driven to and fro, and burdened, according to the desires of their enemies. [Mosiah 21:5–13]

The afflictions suffered by the Nephites were so great that they fulfilled another part of Abinadi's prophecy: "I shall cause that they shall howl all the day long" (Mosiah 12:4; compare vv. 9–11). After the third attempt to drive the Lamanites out of the land they were "compelled to be humble" (v. 13; compare Alma 32:13–14); but this humility was not sufficient.

Mosiah 21:14–17 • Why the Nephites Were Not Delivered

14 And they did humble themselves even in the depths of humil-

ity; and they did cry mightily to God; yea, even all the day long did they cry unto their God that he would deliver them out of their afflictions.

15 And now the Lord was slow to hear their cry because of their iniquities; nevertheless the Lord did hear their cries, and began to soften the hearts of the Lamanites that they began to ease their burdens; yet the Lord did not see fit to deliver them out of bondage.

16 And it came to pass that they began to prosper by degrees in the land, and began to raise grain more abundantly, and flocks, and herds, that they did not suffer with hunger.

17 Now there was a great number of women, more than there was of men; therefore King Limhi commanded that every man should impart to the support of the widows and their children, that they might not perish with hunger; and this they did because of the greatness of their number that had been slain. [Mosiah 21:14–17]

Their compelled humility (v. 13) did not fully bring about the first condition for being delivered from bondage. They did "turn to the Lord" (v. 14). However, they may not yet have done so "with full purpose of heart; and put their trust in him" (Mosiah 7:33). The text does not tell us to what degree they had turned to or trusted in him, the second condition of being delivered. Neither were they meeting the third condition of being delivered; to "serve him with all diligence of mind" (Mosiah 7:33). Therefore, "the Lord was slow to hear their cry because of their iniquities" (Mosiah 21:15).

As Nephites began improving, the Lord did soften the Lamanites hearts to ease the Nephites burdens (v. 15). The fourth condition, the Lord's "own will and pleasure" had not yet come to fruition (Mosiah 7:33). To prosper by degrees (Mosiah 21:16) suggests they were gradually turning their hearts more to the Lord and putting more trust in him, but the Lord had one more objective. The widows and children needed to be delivered also. When these were provided for, the Lord would act (v. 17).

Mosiah 21:18–24 • Ammon and His Brethren Come into the Land

18 Now the people of Limhi kept together in a body as much as it was possible, and secured their grain and their flocks;

19 And the king himself did not trust his person without the walls of the city, unless he took his guards with him, fearing that he might by some means fall into the hands of the Lamanites.

20 And he caused that his people should watch the land round about, that by some means they might take those priests that fled into the wilderness, who had stolen the daughters of the Lamanites, and that had caused such a great destruction to come upon them.

21 For they were desirous to take them that they might punish them; for they had come into the land of Nephi by night, and carried off their grain and many of their precious things; therefore they laid wait for them.

22 And it came to pass that there was no more disturbance between the Lamanites and the people of Limhi, even until the time that Ammon and his brethren came into the land.

23 And the king having been without the gates of the city with his guard, discovered Ammon and his brethren; and supposing them to be priests of Noah therefore he caused that they should be taken, and bound, and cast into prison. And had they been the priests of Noah he would have caused that they should be put to death.

24 But when he found that they were not, but that they were his brethren, and had come from the land of Zarahemla, he was filled with exceedingly great joy. [Mosiah 21:18–24]

The Nephites had been in bondage to the Lamanites some twenty years. Although the disturbances between the two groups had subsided (v. 22), the Nephites were still bothered by the defected priests of Noah (vv. 20–21). Ammon and his brethren were God-sent. Had the Lord inspired them to come? "They wearied (King Mosiah) with their teasings" in Zarahemla (Mosiah 7:1). This indicates some prodding by another source. Ammon's words to King Limhi of being "thankful before God" (Mosiah 7:12–13) gives a hint, if only slightly, that it was a mission for them not just a curiosity about their departed brethren from whom they had not heard. Furthermore, Limhi's "exceedingly great joy" (Mosiah 21:24) suggests that he looked upon them as an answer to prayer. Any one or all three of these incidents support the idea of God playing a part in the men from the land of Zarahemla coming to the land of Lehi-Nephi.

Mosiah 21:25–28 • A Record of Another People Found

> 25 Now king Limhi had sent, previous to the coming of Ammon, a small number of men to search for the land of Zarahemla; but they could not find it, and they were lost in the wilderness.
>
> 26 Nevertheless, they did find a land which had been peopled; yea, a land which was covered with dry bones; yea, a land which had been peopled and which had been destroyed; and they, having supposed it to be the land of Zarahemla, returned to the land of Nephi, having arrived in the borders of the land not many days before the coming of Ammon.
>
> 27 And they brought a record with them, even a record of the people whose bones they had found; and it was engraven on plates of ore.
>
> 28 And now Limhi was again filled with joy on learning from the mouth of Ammon that king Mosiah had a gift from God, whereby he could interpret such engravings; yea, and Ammon also did rejoice. [Mosiah 21:25–28]

The record engraved on metal plates found by the men sent out by King Limhi was an account of the Jaredites. They were commented on previously (Mosiah 8:7–13). The translation of these records will be commented on later in this work.

Mosiah 21:29–36 • The Nephites Wait For the Spirit of the Lord

> 29 Yet Ammon and his brethren were filled with sorrow because so many of their brethren had been slain;
>
> 30 And also that king Noah and his priests had caused the people

to commit so many sins and iniquities against God; and they also did mourn for the death of Abinadi; and also for the departure of Alma and the people that went with him, who had formed a church of God through the strength and power of God, and faith on the words which had been spoken by Abinadi.

31 Yea, they did mourn for their departure, for they knew not whither they had fled. Now they would have gladly joined with them, for they themselves had entered into a covenant with God to serve him and keep his commandments.

32 And now since the coming of Ammon, king Limhi had also entered into a covenant with God, and also many of his people, to serve him and keep his commandments.

33 And it came to pass that king Limhi and many of his people were desirous to be baptized; but there was none in the land that had authority from God. And Ammon declined doing this thing, considering himself an unworthy servant.

34 Therefore they did not at that time form themselves into a church, waiting upon the Spirit of the Lord. Now they were desirous to become even as Alma and his brethren, who had fled into the wilderness.

35 They were desirous to be baptized as a witness and a testimony that they were willing to serve God with all their hearts; nevertheless they did prolong the time; and an account of their baptism shall be given hereafter.

36 And now all the study of Ammon and his people, and king Limhi and his people, was to deliver themselves out of the hands of the Lamanites and from bondage.

As covenant people themselves (v. 31), Ammon and his associates mourned over the afflictions and iniquities of their fellow Nephites. They would have gladly borne the burdens with Alma's people, but they had departed into the wilderness (vv. 29–31; compare Mosiah 18:8–9).

Since the arrival of Ammon and his brethren, King Limhi and his people had covenanted to serve God and keep his commandments, and were desirous to be baptized as had Alma's people. But none in the land had authority to perform this ordinance, and Ammon considered himself unworthy (Mosiah 21:32–34). Ammon's reasons for feeling unworthy are not specified. One cannot help but wonder about the Lord's involvement in this attitude. As suggested earlier, perhaps Ammon and his companions were chosen by King Mosiah because of their ability to survive in the wilderness. They may not have been spiritual giants. The Lord uses people according to their abilities. Another possibility is that Ammon was worthy, but the Lord inspired him to decline lest the Nephites lose their incentive to return to Zarahemla following their baptism.

While these possibilities cannot be positively ascertained, it is evident that Limhi's people were now turning to the Lord with full purpose of heart and putting their trust in him (Mosiah 7:33). Their trust is exemplified in their devoted study towards finding a deliverance from bondage. As mentioned before, the Lord has instructed us to study things out in our minds as a part of the revelatory process (see comments under Mosiah 20:17–22). Limhi's people recognized the Lord's timetable and began "waiting upon the Spirit of the Lord" (Mosiah 21:34).

Mosiah 22:1–12 • Gideon's Plan of Deliverance

1 And now it came to pass that Ammon and king Limhi began to consult with the people how they should deliver themselves out of bondage; and even they did cause that all the people should gather themselves together; and this they did that they might have the voice of the people concerning the matter.

2 And it came to pass that they could find no way to deliver themselves out of bondage, except it were to take their women and children, and their flocks, and their herds, and their tents, and depart into the wilderness; for the Lamanites being so numerous, it was impossible for the people of Limhi to contend with them, thinking to deliver themselves out of bondage by the sword.

3 Now it came to pass that Gideon went forth and stood before the king, and said unto him: Now O king, thou hast hitherto hear-

kened unto my words many times when we have been contending with our brethren, the Lamanites.

4 And now O king, if thou hast not found me to be an unprofitable servant, or if thou hast hitherto listened to my words in any degree, and they have been of service to thee, even so I desire that thou wouldst listen to my words at this time, and I will be thy servant and deliver this people out of bondage.

5 And the king granted unto him that he might speak. And Gideon said unto him:

6 Behold the back pass, through the back wall, on the back side of the city. The Lamanites, or the guards of the Lamanites, by night are drunken; therefore let us send a proclamation among all this people that they gather together their flocks and herds, that they may drive them into the wilderness by night.

7 And I will go according to thy command and pay the last tribute of wine to the Lamanites, and they will be drunken; and we will pass through the secret pass on the left of their camp when they are drunken and asleep.

8 Thus we will depart with our women and our children, our flocks, and our herds into the wilderness; and we will travel around the land of Shilom.

9 And it came to pass that the king hearkened unto the words of Gideon.

10 And king Limhi caused that his people should gather their flocks together; and he sent the tribute of wine to the Lamanites; and he also sent more wine, as a present unto them; and they did drink freely of the wine which king Limhi did send unto them.

11 And it came to pass that the people of king Limhi did depart by night into the wilderness with their flocks and their herds, and they went round about the land of Shilom in the wilderness, and bent their course towards the land of Zarahemla, being led by Ammon and his brethren.

12 And they had taken all their gold, and silver, and their precious things, which they could carry, and also their provisions with them, into the wilderness; and they pursued their journey. [Mosiah 22:1–12]

Once more Gideon, the stalwart defender of righteousness, comes into the picture. His study resulted in a plan to pay a tribute of wine to the Lamanites, and while they were drunken to escape through a secret pass (vv. 6–9). The plan worked perfectly. The people of Limhi were delivered from bondage by the hand of the Lord only after they followed the four-step repentance process given to them by King Limhi (vv. 9–12). Note that Ammon and his brethren led them back to Zarahemla. This was the suggested reason for the Lord inspiring them to find the people in the land of Lehi-Nephi in the first place.

Mosiah 22:13–16 • Arrival
In the Land of Zarahemla

13 And after being many days in the wilderness they arrived in the land of Zarahemla, and joined Mosiah's people, and became his subjects.

14 And it came to pass that Mosiah received them with joy; and he also received their records, and also the records which had been found by the people of Limhi.

15 And now it came to pass when the Lamanites had found that the people of Limhi had departed out of the land by night, that they sent an army into the wilderness to pursue them;

16 And after they had pursued them two days, they could no longer follow their tracks; therefore they were lost in the wilderness.

These verses are self-explanatory. We now return to Alma's people in the land of Helam.

Mosiah 23:20–24 • Mormons
Editorial Comments

20 And it came to pass that they did multiply and prosper exceedingly in the land of Helam; and they built a city, which they called the city of Helam.

21 Nevertheless the Lord seeth fit to chasten his people; yea, he trieth their patience and their faith.

22 Nevertheless—whosoever putteth his trust in him the same

shall be lifted up at the last day. Yea, and thus it was with this people.

23 For behold, I will show unto you that they were brought into bondage, and none could deliver them but the Lord their God, yea, even the God of Abraham and Isaac and of Jacob.

24 And it came to pass that he did deliver them, and he did show forth his mighty power unto them, and great were their rejoicings. [Mosiah 23:20–24]

As an editorial comment, Mormon once more brings the reader to the subject of bondage into which Alma's people fell after prospering in the land of Helam. Mormon depicted their afflictions as a chastening of the Lord and a trial of their patience and faith (the unconditional prophecy). He further declared that those who trusted in the Lord would be lifted up at the last day. He also said that Alma's people fell into bondage, a fulfillment of Abinadi's prophecy to another part of the people (Mosiah 12:2). Mormon gives us the precept of chapter 13 in these verses summarized here as "none could deliver them but . . . the God of Abraham, Isaac, and Jacob (Mosiah 23:23). Although Mormon's declaration is similar to King Limhi's formula, we will follow the king's formula to show how and when Limhi's people were delivered (see figure 2 on page 460).

Mosiah 23:25–29 • The Lamanites Take Possession of the Land

25 For behold, it came to pass that while they were in the land of Helam, yea, in the city of Helam, while tilling the land round about, behold an army of the Lamanites was in the borders of the land.

26 Now it came to pass that the brethren of Alma fled from their fields, and gathered themselves together in the city of Helam; and they were much frightened because of the appearance of the Lamanites.

27 But Alma went forth and stood among them, and exhorted them that they should not be frightened, but that they should remember the Lord their God and he would deliver them.

28 Therefore they hushed their fears, and began to cry unto the Lord that he would soften the hearts of the Lamanites, that they

would spare them, and their wives, and their children.

29 And it came to pass that the Lord did soften the hearts of the Lamanites. And Alma and his brethren went forth and delivered themselves up into their hands; and the Lamanites took possession of the land of Helam. [Mosiah 23:25–29]

As Alma's people were tilling their lands in Helam, an army of the Lamanites approached them (v. 25). In fright they fled to the city (v. 26). Alma admonished them to remember the Lord and they would be delivered (v. 27). This fits Limhi's instructions to trust in the Lord. The people cried unto the Lord that he would soften the hearts of the Lamanites (v. 28). This is the same as Limhi's formula for turning to the Lord with full purpose of heart. That Alma's people did this is evident in the record. The Lord did soften the hearts of the Lamanites (v. 29).

Mosiah 23:30–39 • Amulon and His Brethren Join the Lamanites

30 Now the armies of the Lamanites, which had followed after the people of king Limhi, had been lost in the wilderness for many days.

31 And behold, they had found those priests of king Noah, in a place which they called Amulon; and they had begun to possess the land of Amulon and had begun to till the ground.

32 Now the name of the leader of those priests was Amulon.

33 And it came to pass that Amulon did plead with the Lamanites; and he also sent forth their wives, who were the daughters of the Lamanites, to plead with their brethren, that they should not destroy their husbands.

34 And the Lamanites had compassion on Amulon and his brethren, and did not destroy them, because of their wives.

35 And Amulon and his brethren did join the Lamanites, and they were traveling in the wilderness in search of the land of Nephi when they discovered the land of Helam, which was possessed by Alma and his brethren.

36 And it came to pass that the Lamanites promised unto Alma and his brethren, that if they would show them the way which led to the land of Nephi that they would grant unto them their lives and their liberty.

37 But after Alma had shown them the way that led to the land of Nephi the Lamanites would not keep their promise; but they set guards round about the land of Helam, over Alma and his brethren.

38 And the remainder of them went to the land of Nephi; and a part of them returned to the land of Helam, and also brought with them the wives and the children of the guards who had been left in the land.

39 And the king of the Lamanites had granted unto Amulon that he should be a king and a ruler over his people, who were in the land of Helam; nevertheless he should have no power to do anything contrary to the will of the king of the Lamanites. [Mosiah 23:30–39]

The Lamanite army was in pursuit of King Limhi's people, but had become lost (v. 30). They found the priests of Noah who had stolen the Lamanite daughters (Mosiah 20). These priests were accompanying the Lamanite army. After breaking their promise to Alma (Mosiah 23:36–37), the Lamanites placed Amulon, the leader of the priests, in command of the Lamanite people in the land of Helam, although under the jurisdiction of the Lamanite king (v. 39). Thus, he was also over Alma's people. His appointment brought about the condition of bondage upon Alma's people.

Mosiah 24:1–7 • Amulon and His Brethren Appointed Teachers

1 And it came to pass that Amulon did gain favor in the eyes of the king of the Lamanites; therefore, the king of the Lamanites granted unto him and his brethren that they should be appointed teachers over his people, yea, even over the people who were in the land of Shemlon, and in the land of Shilom, and in the land of Amulon.

2 For the Lamanites had taken possession of all these lands; therefore, the king of the Lamanites had appointed kings over all these lands.

3 And now the name of the king of the Lamanites was Laman, being called after the name of his father; and therefore he was called king Laman. And he was king over a numerous people.

4 And he appointed teachers of the brethren of Amulon in every land which was possessed by his people; and thus the language of Nephi began to be taught among all the people of the Lamanites.

5 And they were a people friendly one with another; nevertheless they knew not God; neither did the brethren of Amulon teach them anything concerning the Lord their God, neither the law of Moses; nor did they teach them the words of Abinadi;

6 But they taught them that they should keep their record, and that they might write one to another.

7 And thus the Lamanites began to increase in riches, and began to trade one with another and wax great, and began to be a cunning and a wise people, as to the wisdom of the world, yea, a very cunning people, delighting in all manner of wickedness and plunder, except it were among their own brethren. [Mosiah 24:1–7]

The priests of Amulon were further commissioned to teach the Nephite language to the Lamanites. The language of one or both had changed over the four hundred years of being a separate peoples. Again, we ask whether the Lord's hand was not involved in this assignment? While they did not teach the law of Moses or the words of Abinadi (v. 5), which they were not qualified to teach anyway, did they not prepare the way for the future Nephite missionaries, the sons of Mosiah, to proclaim the gospel among the Lamanites? With both languages they could understand each other and converse. The Lord being involved in the teaching of the Nephite language seems very plausible.

Mosiah 24:8–15 • Amulon Exercises Authority and Persecutes the Nephites

8 And now it came to pass that Amulon began to exercise authority over Alma and his brethren, and began to persecute him, and cause that his children should persecute their children.

9 For Amulon knew Alma, that he had been one of the king's

priests, and that it was he that believed the words of Abinadi and was driven out before the king, and therefore he was wroth with him; for he was subject to king Laman, yet he exercised authority over them, and put tasks upon them, and put task-masters over them.

10 And it came to pass that so great were their afflictions that they began to cry mightily to God.

11 And Amulon commanded them that they should stop their cries; and he put guards over them to watch them, that whosoever should be found calling upon God should be put to death.

12 And Alma and his people did not raise their voices to the Lord their God, but did pour out their hearts to him; and he did know the thoughts of their hearts.

13 And it came to pass that the voice of the Lord came to them in their afflictions, saying: Lift up your heads and be of good comfort, for I know of the covenant which ye have made unto me; and I will covenant with my people and deliver them out of bondage.

14 And I will also ease the burdens which are put upon your shoulders, that even you cannot feel them upon your backs, even while you are in bondage; and this will I do that ye may stand as witnesses for me hereafter, and that ye may know of a surety that I, the Lord God, do visit my people in their afflictions.

15 And now it came to pass that the burdens which were laid upon Alma and his brethren were made light; yea, the Lord did strengthen them that they could bear up their burdens with ease, and they did submit cheerfully and with patience to all the will of the Lord. [Mosiah 24:8–15]

As Amulon knew that Alma had once been a priest of Noah and had believed in the words of Abinadi, he began to put tasks upon Alma's people and placed taskmasters over them (vv. 8–9). As Alma had previously admonished his people to do, they turned to God and began to cry mightily (v. 10). Amulon commanded them to stop such crying and placed guards over them to prevent it. Alma's people then secretly poured out their hearts to the Lord their God and, God did know the thoughts of their hearts (vv. 10–11). They certainly had put their trust in him. He rewarded that trust with an acknowledgment of their covenant to him and his covenant to deliver them from bondage (v. 13). They had served him in accordance with their covenant. He in return promised to ease their burdens insomuch that they would not feel them. The burdens being lightened was be a witness to them and to others that the Lord does visit his people in their afflictions (v. 14).The Lord fulfilled his promise, as he always does, and strengthened them to bear up their burdens. They submitted cheerfully, and with patience, to the will of the Lord (v. 15).

Mosiah 24:16–23 • The People of Alma Are Delivered

16 And it came to pass that so great was their faith and their patience that the voice of the Lord came unto them again, saying: Be of good comfort, for on the morrow I will deliver you out of bondage.

17 And he said unto Alma: Thou shalt go before this people, and I will go with thee and deliver this people out of bondage.

18 Now it came to pass that Alma and his people in the night-time gathered their flocks together, and also of their grain; yea, even all the night-time were they gathering the flocks together.

19 And in the morning the Lord caused a deep sleep to come upon the Lamanites, yea, and all their task-masters were in a profound sleep.

20 And Alma and his people departed into the wilderness; and when they had traveled all day they pitched their tents in a valley, and they called the valley Alma, because he led their way in the wilderness.

21 Yea, and in the valley of Alma they poured out their thanks to God because he had been merciful unto them, and eased their burdens, and had delivered them out of bondage; for they were in bondage, and none could deliver them except it were the Lord their God.

22 And they gave thanks to God, yea, all their men and all their women and all their children that could speak lifted their voices in the praises of their God.

23 And now the Lord said unto Alma: Haste thee and get thou and

this people out of this land, for the Lamanites have awakened and do pursue thee; therefore get thee out of this land, and I will stop the Lamanites in this valley that they come no further in pursuit of this people.

The people served the Lord and turned to him in trust. However, the due time of the Lord did not come quickly. Perhaps the Lord was instituting a physical conditioning program in preparation for their extremely strenuous thirteen-day flight to the land of Zarahemla. The terrain was undoubtedly rough and the Lamanites would be in hot pursuit. Without this conditioning, would Alma's people, including women and children, have been able to endure the trip, as well as to outrun the Lamanite army? Probably not without the Lord's help. The Lord caused a deep sleep to come upon the Lamanites and all their taskmasters to give the Nephites a head start (v. 19). He further promised to halt the Lamanites in the valley wherein the Nephites had pitched camp (v. 23). The people had complied with their covenant and the Lord delivered his people.

Mosiah 24:24–25 • Alma and His People Arrive in Zarahemla

24 And it came to pass that they departed out of the valley, and took their journey into the wilderness.

25 And after they had been in the wilderness twelve days they arrived in the land of Zarahemla; and king Mosiah did also receive them with joy. [Mosiah 24:24–25]

We learn from Alma's travels that the land of Lehi-Nephi and the land of Zarahemla were separated by twenty-one days of strenuous travel. Alma, under pursuit of the Lamanites, and with over four hundred people traveled for eight days before settling in the land of Helam (Mosiah 23:3). In leaving the land of Helam, they traveled one day to the valley of Alma (Mosiah 24:20), and another twelve days to arrive in Zarahemla (v. 25). They also had animals and supplies with them (Mosiah 24:18). These calculations are important in plotting Book of Mormon geography, but we must also remember that geography lessons were not important to the recorders of the Book of Mormon plates. It was the precepts such as deliverance from bondage that was their main concern.

One of the purposes of the Book of Mormon is to warn us of the situations and experiences that were among the Nephites so that we may not avoid like situations and experiences. There are many other kinds of bondage in addition to physical bondage. A person may be bound by intellectual pursuits, financial extensions, social customs, or others. The formula is essentially the same for deliverance from all these conditions, and there is none but the God of Abraham, Isaac, and Jacob who can and will deliver his people (see Mosiah 7:19; 23:23 and comments above). However, much more important is the admonition to prevent such bondage from occurring in our lives. The Book of Mormon suggests some preventions.

Ammon informed King Limhi that Mosiah, the king of Zarahemla, was a prophet, seer, and revelator who could "know of things which are past, and also of things which are to come" (Mosiah 8:16–17). He also had an instrument which gave him the ability to translate records of an unknown language such as those of the records found by the Limhi expedition of forty-three men (Mosiah 8:13–14). These we know were the Jaredite records. The Jaredites had fallen into similar bondage as the Nephites and certainly their unabridged account gave inspired direction to the Nephites on how to avoid future bondage. In modern times, we too had a prophet, seer, and revelator, Joseph Smith who translated the Book of Mormon from an unknown language, known as reformed Egyptian, with a Urim and Thummim (see Mormon 9:32–33). We can learn from the Book of Mormon just as the Nephites may have learned from the Jaredites. Our challenge is to study and follow the precepts taught in that sacred record.

SACRED WRITING

Revelation which is great:

Mosiah 24:13–14; 16–17; 23

The Lord directs Alma and his people.

Doctrines Learned:

Mosiah 20:21; 21:4   The word of the Lord through his prophets is always fulfilled.

General Authority Quotations

The author is unaware of specific General Authority quotes that refer directly to these chapters in Mosiah. However, since they involve several kinds of bondage and several things that lead to it, it is suggested that we read the general conference addresses of the President of the Church after each conference. As an example, excerpts from President Gordon B. Hinckley's address in October 2002 follows.

We urge, in the strongest terms possible, that fathers and mothers regard most seriously this opportunity and challenge to make of Monday evening a time sacred to the family.

Brethren, I wish to urge again the importance of self-reliance on the part of every individual Church member and family.

None of us knows when a catastrophe might strike. Sickness, injury, unemployment may effect any of us.

We have a great welfare program with facilities for such things as grain storage in various areas. It is important that we do this. But the best place to have some food set aside is within our homes, together with a little money in savings. The best welfare program is our own welfare program. Five or six cans of wheat in the home are better than a bushel in the welfare granary.

I do not predict any impending disaster. I hope that there will not be one. But prudence should govern our lives. Everyone who owns a home recognizes the need for fire insurance. We hope and pray that there will never be a fire. Nevertheless, we pay for insurance to cover such a catastrophe, should it occur.

We ought to do the same with reference to family welfare.

We can begin ever so modestly. We can begin with a one-week's food supply and gradually build it to a month, and then to three months. I am speaking now of food to cover basic needs. As all of you recognize, this counsel is not new. But I fear that so many feel that a long term food supply is so far beyond their reach that they make no effort at all.

Get out of debt and rid yourself of terrible bondage that debt brings.

Discipline yourselves in matters of spending, in matters of borrowing, in practices that lead to bankruptcy and the agony that comes therewith.

Too many are being caught in the web of immorality and all of the bitter fruit that flows from it. To the boys who are here tonight-the young men-I wish to say in the strongest language of which I am capable, stay away from moral inequity. You know what is right and wrong. You cannot use ignorance as an excuse for unacceptable behavior.

How can you possibly think that you can become involved in immoral practices and then go into the mission field as a representative of the Lord Jesus Christ? Do you suppose that you can be worthy to go to the house of the Lord, there to be married for time and eternity, if you have indulged in such practices?

Stay away from the erotic stuff of the Internet. It can only pull you down. It can lead to your destruction.

May I again mention a matter with which I have dealt at length in the past. I speak of evil and despicable sin of child abuse.

We cannot tolerate it. We will not tolerate it. Anyone who abuses a child may expect Church discipline as well as possible legal action.

Child abuse is an affront toward God. Jesus spoke of the beauty and innocence of children. To anyone who has as inclination that could lead to the abuse of children, I say in the strongest language of which I am capable, discipline yourself. Seek help before you do injury to a child and bring ruin upon yourself.

Challenges to Eternal Life:

1. Analyze your life to see what bondage (subjection to influence, force, or compulsion) you are under and follow the formula given by king Limhi to overcome it (Mosiah 7:33).

2. Remember that none can deliver you but the God of Abraham, Isaac, and Jacob.

3. Remember that the Lord sees fit to chasten his people and try their patience and faith, but those who trust in the Lord will be lifted up at the last day (Mosiah 23:21–22).

4. Recognize that the Lord may have us prosper by degrees. We should acknowledge he is doing so or will do so (Mosiah 21:16).

5. Choose a challenge of your own from this reading and apply it to your life.

Reading Sequence
Mosiah 19:1–21:22
Mosiah 7–8
Mosiah 21:22–22:16
Mosiah 23:20–24:25

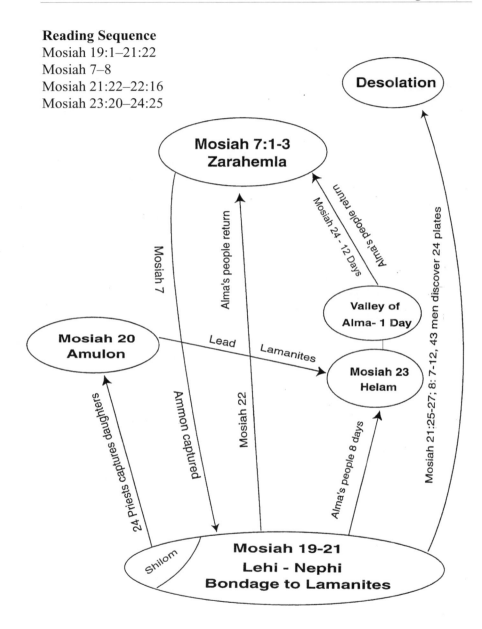

Figure 2. Kings Formula

Chapter Fourteen

The Mission of the Church

Mosiah 25–27

*H*istorical Setting: The last chapters of Mosiah (25–29) cover about thirty years, from about 120 B.C. to 91 B.C. The three chapters of this reading (25–27) cover the majority of these years. With the arrival of the people of Limhi and the people of Alma in the land of Zarahemla the church is restructured and established more firmly.

Precept of These Chapters:

> "And the Lord did pour out his Spirit upon them, and they were blessed, and prospered in the land" (Mosiah 25:24).

The Lord was with the church and through revelation helped to strengthen it.

An outline of the chapters in this reading follows as a preparation for further study.

OUTLINE • MOSIAH 25–27

➤ Mosiah 25:1–4　King Mosiah, son of Benjamin, gathered all the people of Nephi and all the people of Zarahemla into two bodies.

　　　　a.　The people of Nephi were not as numerous as the

people of Zarahemla who was a descendant of Mulek (v. 2)

b.   The people of Nephi and Mukek in Zarahemla were not as numerous as the Lamanites (vv. 2–3).

➤ 25:5–13   Mosiah, son of Benjamin, read all the records of Zeniff and the record of Alma to his people.

a.   The people who remained were struck with wonder and amazement (vv. 7–11).

1.   In beholding those who were delivered from bondage, they were filled with joy.

2.   They were filled with sorrow over those who were slain.

3.   They gave thanks to God for his goodness in delivering Alma's people.

4.   They had anguish for the souls of the sinful and polluted state of the Lamanites.

b.   The children of Amulon and their brethren who had taken Lamanite wives, being displeased with the conduct of their fathers, would no longer be called by their father's names (vv. 12–13).

1.   They took the name of Nephi.

2.   They were numbered among those called Nephites.

➤ 25:14–18   Mosiah, son of Benjamin, desired Alma to speak. Alma went from one body of people to another preaching repentance and faith on the Lord.

a.   He exhorted the people of Limhi to remember that it was the Lord who delivered them (v. 16).

b.   King Limhi and his people were desirous to be baptized (vv. 17–18).

1.   Alma baptized them after the manner of his baptizing at the waters of Mormon.

2.   As many as were baptized belonged to the church of God.

➤ 25:19–24   Mosiah, son of Benjamin, granted Alma the authority to establish churches throughout all the land of Zarahemla.

a.   He gave Alma power to ordain priests and teachers over every church (vv. 19–21).

    1.   The people were too numerous to be governed by one teacher or to hear the word of God in one assembly.

    2.   They assembled in different bodies called churches. The priests and teachers taught the word received from Alma.

b.   There were seven churches, but they were one church, even the church of God (vv. 22–23).

    1.   Nothing was preached but repentance and faith in God.

    2.   Those who desired to take upon them the name of Christ joined the church.

c.   Those in the church were called the people of God (v. 24).

    1.   The Lord poured out his Spirit upon them.

    2.   They were blessed and called the people of God.

➤ 26:1–5   Many of the rising generation did not understand the words of King Benjamin and did not believe the traditions of their fathers.

a.   The unbelievers did not believe in the resurrection of the dead or in the coming of Christ (v. 2).

b.   They could not understand the words of God, and their hearts were hardened (v. 3).

c.   They would not be baptized or join the church (v. 4).

    1.   They were a separate people, as to their faith, and remained in their carnal and sinful state.

    2.   They would not call upon the Lord their God.

d.   They were not as numerous as the people of God, but because of dissensions they became more numerous (v. 5).

➤ 26:6–9   Many church members were deceived by the flattering words of the unbelievers, which caused them to commit many sins.

    a.   It was expedient that the members be admonished by the church for their sins (v. 6).

    b.   The teachers brought them before the priests who brought them before Alma (vv. 7–9).

        1.   Alma was the high priest having authority over the church.

        2.   Many witnesses testified of their wickedness before Alma.

➤ 26:10–12   Alma delivered them to the king because he had never before had this problem.

    a.   Alma informed the king of their iniquities, and of the witnesses, and asked the king to judge them (v. 11).

    b.   King Mosiah said that Alma was to judge them (v. 12).

➤ 26:13–32   Alma was troubled and he inquired of the Lord. The voice of the Lord came to him.

    a.   Alma and those baptized in the waters of Mormon were blessed because of their faith in Abinadi's words (vv. 15–16).

    b.   Alma was blessed because he established a church for the Lord's people (vv. 17–18).

        1.   The people would be blessed who were willing to bear the Lord's name.

        2.   They would be called by his name and are his people.

    c.   Alma is blessed because he inquired concerning the transgressor (v. 19).

    d.   The Lord covenanted with Alma, his servant, that he shall have eternal life (vv. 20–21).

        1.   Alma is to gather the Lord's sheep.

        2.   He that hears the Lord's voice shall be his sheep.

        3.   They are to be received into the church, and the Lord will also receive them.

      e. Those baptized unto repentance into the Lord's church will be freely forgiven (vv. 22–28).

          1. The Lord will take upon him the sins of the world.

          2. The Lord created them.

          3. Those who believe are granted a place at the Lord's right hand and shall know him.

          4. When the second trump sounds, those that never knew the Lord shall stand before him and know he is God, but shall not be redeemed.

          5. The Lord will confess that he never knew them, and they shall depart into everlasting fire.

          6. Those that will not hear the Lord's voice shall not be received into his church nor be received by him at the last day.

      f. Whosoever transgresses against the Lord shall be judged by the sins committed (vv. 29–32).

          1. Those who confess before Alma and the Lord and repent in sincerity of heart, Alma shall forgive and they will be forgiven by the Lord also.

          2. As often as the Lord's people repent, he will forgive their trespasses against him.

          3. You should also forgive one another your trespasses, or you bring condemnation upon yourself.

          4. Those who will not repent shall not be numbered among the Lord's people.

➤ 26:33–39   Alma wrote down the Lord's words that he might judge the people of the church according to the commandments of God.

      a. Alma judged those that had been taken in iniquity (vv. 34–36).

          1. Those who repented and confessed their sins were numbered among the people of the church.

          2. The names of those who did not confess and repent were blotted out of the church.

      b. Alma regulated all the affairs of the church (v. 37).

1. There began to be peace and prosperity in the church.
2. Many were received by God and many were baptized.

c. Alma and all those in the church walked in all diligence, taught the word of God, and suffered afflictions and persecutions by those who did not belong to the church (vv. 38–39).

   1. They did admonish their brethren.
   2. They were all admonished by the word of God according to the sins committed.
   3. They were commanded of God to pray without ceasing and give thanks in all things.

➤ 27:1–7   The church members began to complain to their leaders because of the persecutions by the unbelievers.

a. The church complained to Alma, Alma complained to King Mosiah, son of Benjamin, and the king consulted with his priests (v. 1).

b. Mosiah, son of Benjamin, sent a proclamation throughout the land that the unbelievers should not persecute those who belonged to the church (vv. 2–5).

   1. All the churches had a strict command of no persecutions among them, and to have equality among all men.
   2. No pride or haughtiness should disturb their peace.
   3. Every man should esteem his neighbor as himself, laboring with their own hands for their support.
   4. Priests and teachers should labor with their own hands for their support, except for sickness or much want.
   5. They did abound in the grace of God.

c. There began to be much peace. The people became numerous and scattered abroad upon the earth (vv. 6–7).

   1. They extended north, south, east, and west, build-

ing cities and villages in all quarters of the land.

2. The Lord visited them, they prospered, and became a large and wealthy people.

➤ 27:8–17   The sons of Mosiah and Alma, son of Alma, were numbered among the unbelievers.

a. Alma, son of Alma, became a very wicked and idolatrous man (vv. 8–9).

1. He was a man of many words, speaking much flattery to lead people into iniquities.

2. He became a great hindrance to the prosperity of the church of God.

b. As Alma, son of Alma, was going about secretly with the sons of Mosiah seeking to destroy the church, an angel of the Lord appeared to them (vv. 10–12).

1. The angel descended in a cloud and spoke with a voice of thunder that caused the earth to shake.

2. In astonishment, they fell to the earth and understood not his words.

c. The angel cried again for Alma, son of Alma, to stand, and asked why he persecuted the church (v. 13).

1. The Lord has said, this is my church and I will establish it.

2. Nothing shall overthrow the church, save the transgressions of my people.

d. The angel said the Lord had heard the prayers of the people and of Alma his father (v. 14).

1. His father had prayed with much faith for him to come to a knowledge of the truth.

2. The angel had come to convince him of the power and authority of God, and to answer the prayers of his father.

e. The angel asked if Alma, son of Alma, could dispute the power of God (v. 15).

1. The angel's voice shook the earth.

2. Alma could behold the angel sent from God.

f. The angel told Alma, son of Alma, to remember the captivity of their fathers and their deliverance from bondage (v. 16).

g. Alma, son of Alma, was told to seek to destroy the church no more, even if he would destroy himself.

h. The angel departed (v. 17).

➤ 27:18–22 Alma, son of Alma, and those with him fell to the earth in great astonishment.

a. They had seen an angel whose voice had shaken the earth, and they knew it was by the power of God (v. 18).

b. Alma, son of Alma, became dumb that he could not open his mouth and so weak that he could not move his hands (vv. 19–20).

1. He was taken to his father by those who were with him, and they rehearsed all that had happened.

2. His father rejoiced for he knew it was the power of God.

c. Alma, the father, gathered a multitude to witness what the Lord had done for his son and those with him (vv. 21–22).

➤ 27:23–31 Alma caused the priests to assemble together, and they began to fast and to pray.

a. They desired the eyes of the people to see and know of the goodness and glory of God (v. 22).

b. After two days and two nights, Alma, son of Alma, received his strength and stood and spoke (vv. 23–27).

1. He testified that he had repented, been redeemed, and born of the Spirit.

2. The Lord said to him that all mankind must be born again, changed from their carnal and fallen state to a state of righteousness, and become his sons and his daughters.

3. Thus they become new creatures and inherit the kingdom of God.

        4.   Unless they are born again, they must be cast off, and Alma was about to be cast off.

   c.   After wading through much tribulation and repenting nigh unto death, Alma, son of Alma, had been snatched out of an everlasting burning and born of God through his mercy (vv. 28–29).

        1.   His soul had been redeemed from the gall of bitterness and the bonds of iniquity.

        2.   He had been in darkness but now beheld the marvelous light of God.

        3.   He was racked with eternal torment, but now his soul pained no more.

   d.   Alma, son of Alma, had rejected his Redeemer and denied what his father had spoken (vv. 30–31).

        1.   Christ will come and manifest himself unto all.

        2.   Every knee shall bow and every tongue confess before him.

        3.   At the last day, all men shall stand to be judged of him, and they will confess he is God.

        4.   Those who live without God will confess that his judgment is just, and will tremble.

➤ 27:32–37   Alma, son of Alma, and those who were with him traveled about the land and published what they had seen and heard.

   a.   They imparted much consolation to the church, confirming their faith (v. 33).

   b.   The four sons of Mosiah who were with Alma, son of Alma, were Ammon, Aaron, Omner, and Himni (v. 34).

   c.   These sons zealously strived to repair the injuries they had done (v. 35).

        1.   They confessed their sins.

        2.   They published the things they had seen.

        3.   They explained the prophecies and scriptures.

   d.   They were instruments in the hands of God to bring

many to the knowledge of the truth and of their Redeemer (v. 36).

e.   They were blessed for they published peace (v. 37).

NOTES AND COMMENTARY

Introduction: In the April 1981 General Conference of the Church, President Spencer W. Kimball said:

> My brothers and sisters, as the brethren of the First Presidency and the Twelve have meditated upon and prayed about the great latter-day work the Lord has given us to do, we are impressed that the mission of the Church is three-fold:
>
> • to proclaim the gospel of the Lord Jesus Christ to every nation, kindred, tongue and people;
>
> • to perfect the Saints by preparing them to receive the ordinances of the gospel and by instruction and discipline to gain exaltation.
>
> • to redeem the dead by performing vicarious ordinances of the gospel for those who have lived on the earth.
>
> All three are part of one work—to assist our Father in Heaven and his Son, Jesus Christ, in their grand and glorious mission "to bring to pass the immortality and eternal life of man." [Moses 1:39]

That the work of the Church has always been essentially the same was revealed to the Prophet Joseph Smith when the latter-day Church was established.

> That as many as would believe and be baptized in his holy name, and endure in faith to the end, should be saved—
>
> Not only those who believed after he came in the meridian of time, in the flesh, but all those from the beginning, even as many as were before he came, who believed in the words of the holy prophets, who spake as they were inspired by the gift of the Holy Ghost, who truly testified of him in all things, should have eternal life. [D&C 20:25–26]

There is one exception:

It appears very clear in all that was written in the Old Testament, or in the Book of Mormon pertaining to the history of Israel, that nothing in any way conveys the thought that vicarious work was performed in those early times for the dead. It seems to be a very clear and logical conclusion for one to reach that until the Son of God had finished his preparation for the salvation of man and to bring to pass the resurrection of the dead, there could be no ordinances or labor of any kind pertaining to the resurrection and redemption of mankind that could be performed for the dead.[1]

The work of Alma and his associates at this time focused on the perfection of the Saints in the land of Zarahemla.

Mosiah 25:1–6 • The Records Read to the People

1 And now king Mosiah caused that all the people should be gathered together.

2 Now there were not so many of the children of Nephi, or so many of those who were descendants of Nephi, as there were of the people of Zarahemla, who was a descendant of Mulek, and those who came with him into the wilderness.

3 And there were not so many of the people of Nephi and of the people of Zarahemla as there were of the Lamanites; yea, they were not half so numerous.

4 And now all the people of Nephi were assembled together, and also all the people of Zarahemla, and they were gathered together in two bodies.

5 And it came to pass that Mosiah did read, and caused to be read, the records of Zeniff to his people; yea, he read the records of the people of Zeniff, from the time they left the land of Zarahemla until they returned again.

6 And he also read the account of Alma and his brethren, and all their afflictions, from the time they left the land of Zarahemla until the time they returned again.

The descendants of Nephi would include the people of Limhi and

---

[1] Joseph Fielding Smith, *Answers to Gospel Questions,* [1972], 5:94–95.

the people of Alma who had returned to the land of Zarahemla. The only numbers given of these two groups is the four hundred and fifty who separated themselves from King Noah and followed Alma in about 145 B.C. (Mosiah 18:35). This separation happened twenty-four years earlier than their gathering on this occasion. The people of Alma were a minority in 145 B.C., so the people of Limhi must have been a few thousand.

The descendants of Mulek and also some of Nephi (see Omni 1:19), in the land of Zarahemla, were more than the people of Nephi (Mosiah 25:2) in 120 B.C. Therefore, the total number would have been several thousand, yet they were not half as numerous as the Lamanites (v. 3). Another help to the estimation of numbers is given in about 87 B.C., about thirty-three years later. In a battle between the Amlicites (apostate Nephites) and the Nephites which would include the people of Zarahemla (see v. 13); there were over twelve thousand five hundred Amlicites and over six thousand five hundred Nephites killed, or over nineteen thousand deaths (see Alma 2:19). Fifty-eight years would include about three generations of population growth. The deaths, although staggering, do not seem to represent even half of the total population a generation and a half after the gathering of Mosiah's people with Limhi's and Alma's mentioned in the verses under consideration here. Again we conclude that the total number gathered was several thousand.

The public reading of the records (Mosiah 25:5–6) was certainly a solidifying factor for the three groups, as the following verses will show.

Mosiah 25:7–13 • Mulekites Numbered With the Nephites

7 And now, when Mosiah had made an end of reading the records, his people who tarried in the land were struck with wonder and amazement.

8 For they knew not what to think; for when they beheld those

that had been delivered out of bondage they were filled with exceedingly great joy.

9 And again, when they thought of their brethren who had been slain by the Lamanites they were filled with sorrow, and even shed many tears of sorrow.

10 And again, when they thought of the immediate goodness of God, and his power in delivering Alma and his brethren out of the hands of the Lamanites and of bondage, they did raise their voices and give thanks to God.

11 And again, when they thought upon the Lamanites, who were their brethren, of their sinful and polluted state, they were filled with pain and anguish for the welfare of their souls.

12 And it came to pass that those who were the children of Amulon and his brethren, who had taken to wife the daughters of the Lamanites, were displeased with the conduct of their fathers, and they would no longer be called by the names of their fathers, therefore they took upon themselves the name of Nephi, that they might be called the children of Nephi and be numbered among those who were called Nephites.

13 And now all the people of Zarahemla were numbered with the Nephites, and this because the kingdom had been conferred upon none but those who were descendants of Nephi.

The Nephite joys, sorrows, and concerns for the welfare of the souls of the Lamanites strongly supports the conclusion that the people of Zarahemla were already members of the church, as suggested above. The taking of the name of Nephi by the children of Amulon and his brethren (v. 12) also suggests their desire to be affiliated with the people of God. There is no specific record of the kingdom belonging to only the Nephites, but it must have been a political guideline given when Mosiah the first was "appointed to be their king" (Omni 1:19; see also Mosiah 29:6).

Mosiah 25:14–18 • The People of Limhi Are Baptized

14 And now it came to pass that when Mosiah had made an end

of speaking and reading to the people, he desired that Alma should also speak to the people.

15 And Alma did speak unto them, when they were assembled together in large bodies, and he went from one body to another, preaching unto the people repentance and faith on the Lord.

16 And he did exhort the people of Limhi and his brethren, all those that had been delivered out of bondage, that they should remember that it was the Lord that did deliver them.

17 And it came to pass that after Alma had taught the people many things, and had made an end of speaking to them, that king Limhi was desirous that he might be baptized; and all his people were desirous that they might be baptized also.

18 Therefore, Alma did go forth into the water and did baptize them; yea, he did baptize them after the manner he did his brethren in the waters of Mormon; yea, and as many as he did baptize did belong to the church of God; and this because of their belief on the words of Alma.

Although Alma appears to be the catalyst for the desire of King Limhi and his peoples to be baptized (v. 17), the king had wanted to be baptized in the land of Lehi-Nephi, but Ammon had declined "considering himself an unworthy servant" (Mosiah 22:33).

Mosiah 25:19–24 • Seven Churches Established In the Land

19 And it came to pass that king Mosiah granted unto Alma that he might establish churches throughout all the land of Zarahemla; and gave him power to ordain priests and teachers over every church.

20 Now this was done because there were so many people that they could not all be governed by one teacher; neither could they all hear the word of God in one assembly;

21 Therefore they did assemble themselves together in different bodies, being called churches; every church having their priests and their teachers, and every priest preaching the word according as it was delivered to him by the mouth of Alma.

22 And thus, notwithstanding there being many churches they

were all one church, yea, even the church of God; for there was nothing preached in all the churches except it were repentance and faith in God.

23 And now there were seven churches in the land of Zarahemla. And it came to pass that whosoever were desirous to take upon them the name of Christ, or of God, they did join the churches of God;

24 And they were called the people of God. And the Lord did pour out his Spirit upon them, and they were blessed, and prospered in the land.

The seven churches that Alma was granted authority to establish were from among all of the members of the church people who had gathered to the land of Zarahemla (v. 19). As noted before, Mosiah, son of Benjamin, was a seer as well as "a revelator and a prophet also" (Mosiah 8:16). The seven churches were the same church of God (v. 22). It was apparently comparable to the organization of a stake in the Church today. There is no significance to the number seven, but was so divided because of geographical or numerical expediency for the time and place. The Lord pouring out his Spirit upon them (v. 24) verifies that the organization had the Lord's approval.

Mosiah 26:1–6 • Many of the Rising Generation Do Not Believe

1 Now it came to pass that there were many of the rising generation that could not understand the words of king Benjamin, being little children at the time he spake unto his people; and they did not believe the tradition of their fathers.

2 They did not believe what had been said concerning the resurrection of the dead, neither did they believe concerning the coming of Christ.

3 And now because of their unbelief they could not understand the word of God; and their hearts were hardened.

4 And they would not be baptized; neither would they join the church. And they were a separate people as to their faith, and re-

mained so ever after, even in their carnal and sinful state; for they would not call upon the Lord their God.

5 And now in the reign of Mosiah they were not half so numerous as the people of God; but because of the dissensions among the brethren they became more numerous.

6 For it came to pass that they did deceive many with their flattering words, who were in the church, and did cause them to commit many sins; therefore it became expedient that those who committed sin, that were in the church, should be admonished by the church. [Mosiah 26:1–6]

It is usually "the traditions of their fathers" that take away light and truth (D&C 93:39; see also Alma 9:16), but with many of the Nephite rising generation it was their failure to believe their fathers (Mosiah 26:1). These same people could not understand the word of God because the Spirit of the Lord had left them (see 2 Nephi 32:7). Neither could they call upon the Lord their God because the evil spirit "teacheth [a man] not to pray" (2 Nephi 32:8). Iniquity brings dissension among a people (see Alma 53:9), and when it is among the brethren (Mosiah 26:5) the opposition to the people of God grows and gives strength to groups supported by Satan (see 3 Nephi 2:18). Throughout the record of the Book of Mormon, many Nephites became "Lamanites because of their dissensions" (D&C 10:48).

Flattery (Mosiah 26:6) is another constant threat to the people of God. Sherem, the anti-Christ, (mentioned in Jacob 7:4) "could use much flattery, and much power of speech, according to the power of the devil." King Noah deceived many with "vain and flattering words" (Mosiah 11:7). Korihor, another anti-Christ, brought "many souls down to destruction" with his lying and flattering words (Alma 30:47). Amalickiah, one very wicked man, "led away the hearts of many people to do wickedly" (Alma 46:10). Thus it was expedient that the unbelievers among the church in Alma's day be admonished by the church (Mosiah 26:6). Through instruction and discipline, one of the missions of the Church today, such conditions may be overcome.

Mosiah 26:7–12 • Alma Given Authority Over the Church

7 And it came to pass that they were brought before the priests, and delivered up unto the priests by the teachers; and the priests brought them before Alma, who was the high priest.

8 Now king Mosiah had given Alma the authority over the church.

9 And it came to pass that Alma did not know concerning them; but there were many witnesses against them; yea, the people stood and testified of their iniquity in abundance.

10 Now there had not any such thing happened before in the church; therefore Alma was troubled in his spirit, and he caused that they should be brought before the king.

11 And he said unto the king: Behold, here are many whom we have brought before thee, who are accused of their brethren; yea, and they have been taken in divers iniquities. And they do not repent of their iniquities; therefore we have brought them before thee, that thou mayest judge them according to their crimes.

12 But king Mosiah said unto Alma: Behold, I judge them not; therefore I deliver them into thy hands to be judged.

The small congregation in the wilderness had not been exposed such to problems within the church. As the church grew, Alma was experiencing many internal problems. As Alma turns to King Mosiah for help, he learns another great lesson: there is a separation between church and state. Alma had been delegated the authority to administer the affairs of the church (v. 8). Transgressions and sins against the commandments of God, as given to the church, were to be handled by the church.

Mosiah 26:13–19 • The Voice of the Lord to Alma

13 And now the spirit of Alma was again troubled; and he went and inquired of the Lord what he should do concerning this matter, for he feared that he should do wrong in the sight of God.

14 And it came to pass that after he had poured out his whole soul to God, the voice of the Lord came to him, saying:

15 Blessed art thou, Alma, and blessed are they who were baptized in the waters of Mormon. Thou art blessed because of thy exceeding faith in the words alone of my servant Abinadi.

16 And blessed are they because of their exceeding faith in the words alone which thou hast spoken unto them.

17 And blessed art thou because thou hast established a church among this people; and they shall be established, and they shall be my people.

18 Yea, blessed is this people who are willing to bear my name; for in my name shall they be called; and they are mine.

19 And because thou hast inquired of me concerning the transgressor, thou art blessed.

The voice of the Lord did not come to Alma until he had poured out his whole soul to God (v. 14). His was not a rote or formal prayer but a communication of soul to soul. After listening to Alma's plea for help, the Lord comforted his troubled soul (v. 13) by giving two reasons for the people being blessed, and three reasons why Alma was blessed. The people were blessed because they had been baptized in the waters of Mormon after exercising exceeding faith in the words of Alma alone, only one witness (vv. 15–16). They were further blessed for their willingness to bear the name of Christ as members of his church (vv. 17–18).

Alma was blessed because he had exercised exceeding faith in Abinadi's words alone, only one witness (v. 15). He had shown that he was "determined to serve [Christ] at all hazards" (*TPJS*, 150). Alma was further blessed because he had established the Lord's church, giving the people the opportunity to be instructed and to become his people (v. 17). He was also blessed because he had inquired concerning the transgressor (v. 19). "The worth of souls is great in the sight of God" (D&C 18:10).

Mosiah 26:20–24 • The Lord's Covenant With Alma

20 Thou art my servant; and I covenant with thee that thou shalt have eternal life; and thou shalt serve me and go forth in my name, and shalt gather together my sheep.

21 And he that will hear my voice shall be my sheep; and him shall ye receive into the church, and him will I also receive.

22 For behold, this is my church; whosoever is baptized shall be baptized unto repentance. And whomsoever ye receive shall believe in my name; and him will I freely forgive.

23 For it is I that taketh upon me the sins of the world; for it is I that hath created them; and it is I that granteth unto him that believeth unto the end a place at my right hand.

24 For behold, in my name are they called; and if they know me they shall come forth, and shall have a place eternally at my right hand.

The Lord's covenant with Alma promising eternal life is known as the more sure word of prophecy or having his calling and election made sure. On May 17th, 1843, The Prophet Joseph Smith instructed: "The more sure word of prophecy means a man's knowing that he is sealed up unto eternal life, by revelation and the spirit of prophecy, through the power of the Holy Priesthood. It is impossible for a man to be saved in ignorance" (D&C 131:5–6). Peter admonished the New Testament Saints to make their calling and election sure. "But he that lacketh these things is blind, and cannot see afar off, and hath forgotten that he was purged from his old sins. Wherefore the rather, brethren, give diligence to make your calling and election sure: for if ye do these things, ye shall never fall" (2 Peter 1:10–11).

To have one's calling and election made sure is to receive the second Comforter. The Prophet Joseph Smith explained:

The Doctrine of Election. St. Paul exhorts us to make our calling and election sure. This is the sealing power spoken of by Paul in other places.

"13 In whom ye also trusted, that after ye heard the word of truth, the Gospel of your salvation: in whom also after that ye believed, ye were sealed with that Holy Spirit of promise,

"14 Which is the earnest of our inheritance until the redemption of the purchased possession, unto the praise of His glory, that we may be sealed up unto the day of redemption." — Ephesians, 1st chapter.

This principle ought (in its proper place) to be taught, for God hath not revealed to Joseph, but what he will make known to the Twelve, and even the least Saint may know all things as fast as he is able to bear them, for the day must come when no man need say to his neighbor, Know ye the Lord; for all shall know Him (who remain from the least to the greatest. How is this to be done? It is to be done by this sealing power, and the other Comforter spoken of, which will be manifest by revelation. [*TPJS*, 149][2]

Being assured of eternal life does not end one's service and responsibilities in the kingdom or the Church. In fact it will increase them. Alma is instructed to serve the Lord by gathering his sheep (Mosiah 26:20). This assignment is also one of the missions of the Church: to "proclaim the gospel of Jesus Christ." Those who receive the word of God will be received into the church (vv. 21–22). They will have been prepared to receive some of the ordinances necessary for exaltation, another mission of the church, and will be prepared to receive further ordinances. Having become a part of Christ's family by taking his name upon them, they will come to know him and have a place eternally at his right hand (vv. 23–24).

Mosiah 26:25–28 • Those Who Will Not Hear His Voice

25 And it shall come to pass that when the second trump shall sound then shall they that never knew me come forth and shall stand before me.

26 And then shall they know that I am the Lord their God, that

---

[2] For further comments of the Prophet Joseph Smith on the Second Comforter see chapter 3, quoted under Enos 1:25–27.

I am their Redeemer; but they would not be redeemed.

27 And then I will confess unto them that I never knew them; and they shall depart into everlasting fire prepared for the devil and his angels.

28 Therefore I say unto you, that he that will not hear my voice, the same shall ye not receive into my church, for him I will not receive at the last day.

The second trump is mentioned in both the Doctrine and Covenants and the book of Revelation. In the Doctrine and Covenants, it signals the resurrection of the terrestrial beings (see D&C 88:99). The first trump speaks of the celestial resurrection. The third and fourth trumps speak of the assigning of spirits of telestial beings and sons of perdition to the spirit world for one thousand years (see D&C 88:96–102). In the book of Revelation, the first through the fourth angel speak of the destruction of various parts of the earth and changes to the sun and the moon (see Revelation 8:6–13). Therefore, there is no correlation between the angels mentioned in the Doctrine and Covenants and the book of Revelation. The book of Revelation is describing the destruction of the telestial beings from the earth in preparation for the Second Coming. The other two parts that are not destroyed are the celestial and terrestrial beings. This interpretation is supported by the revelation given to Joseph Smith explaining the book of Revelation.

Q. What are we to understand by the sounding of the trumpets, mentioned in the 8th chapter of Revelation?

A. We are to understand that as God made the world in six days, and on the seventh day he finished his work, and sanctified it, and also formed man out of the dust of the earth, even so, in the beginning of the seventh thousand years will the Lord God sanctify the earth, and complete the salvation of man, and judge all things, and shall redeem all things, except that which he hath not put into his power, when he shall have sealed all things, unto the end of all things; and the sounding of the trumpets of the seven angels are the preparing and finishing of his work, in the beginning of the seventh thousand years—the preparing of the way before the time of his coming. [D&C 77:12]

The sanctifying of the earth and the completion of the salvation of man will include the destruction of the wicked or the telestial beings from the earth. This work of destruction will be cut short by the teaching of the gospel to as many as will hear his voice. This interpretation is also supported by modern revelation.

> 94 And another angel shall sound his trump, saying: That great church, the mother of abominations, that made all nations drink of the wine of the wrath of her fornication, that persecuteth the saints of God, that shed their blood—she who sitteth upon many waters, and upon the islands of the sea—behold, she is the tares of the earth; she is bound in bundles; her bands are made strong, no man can loose them; therefore, she is ready to be burned. And he shall sound his trump both long and loud, and all nations shall hear it.
>
> 95 And there shall be silence in heaven for the space of half an hour; and immediately after shall the curtain of heaven be unfolded, as a scroll is unfolded after it is rolled up, and the face of the Lord shall be unveiled;
>
> 96 And the saints that are upon the earth, who are alive, shall be quickened and be caught up to meet him. [D&C 84:96–98]

The context of the Mosiah verses above fit into this explanation.

Mosiah 26:29–33 • The Transgressors Judged According to Their Sins

> 29 Therefore I say unto you, Go; and whosoever transgresseth against me, him shall ye judge according to the sins which he has committed; and if he confess his sins before thee and me, and repenteth in the sincerity of his heart, him shall ye forgive, and I will forgive him also.
>
> 30 Yea, and as often as my people repent will I forgive them their trespasses against me.
>
> 31 And ye shall also forgive one another your trespasses; for verily I say unto you, he that forgiveth not his neighbor's trespasses

when he says that he repents, the same hath brought himself under condemnation.

32 Now I say unto you, Go; and whosoever will not repent of his sins the same shall not be numbered among my people; and this shall be observed from this time forward.

33 And it came to pass when Alma had heard these words he wrote them down that he might have them, and that he might judge the people of that church according to the commandments of God.

To be judged "according to the sins . . . committed" (v. 29) tells us that some sins are more serious than others, and thus require more serious consequences or conditions of repentance. The law of the Church revealed to Joseph Smith in 1831 gives several guidelines for dealing with various sins (see D&C 42:18–28; 74–93). The law of Moses also prescribed various judgments for different sins (see Exodus 21–23).

Two confessions were required for forgiveness of sins: one to Alma, the Lord's representative, and one to the Lord himself. The same requirement is given for the Church today. The Bishop is the judge in Israel.

71 Nevertheless, a high priest, that is, after the order of Melchizedek, may be set apart unto the ministering of temporal things, having a knowledge of them by the Spirit of truth;

72 And also to be a judge in Israel, to do the business of the church, to sit in judgment upon transgressors upon testimony as it shall be laid before him according to the laws, by the assistance of his counselors, whom he has chosen or will choose among the elders of the church. [D&C 107:71–72]

As the judge in Israel, the bishop forgives the sin in behalf of the Church, judging whether or not the person is worthy to serve in the Church. After his resurrection, Jesus told his disciples, "Receive ye the Holy Ghost" and then said: "Whose soever sins ye remit, they are remitted unto them; *and* whose soever *sins* ye retain, they are retained" (John 20:23). The Holy Ghost will direct the Lord's servants if and when the sinner is to be forgiven. Of course, the eternal status of the sinner is determined by the Lord.

> O then, my beloved brethren, come unto the Lord, the Holy One. Remember that his paths are righteous. Behold, the way for man is narrow, but it lieth in a straight course before him, and the keeper of the gate is the Holy One of Israel; and he employeth no servant there; and there is none other way save it be by the gate; for he cannot be deceived, for the Lord God is his name. [2 Nephi 9:41]

As explained by President J. Reuben Clark, there is a difference between confession and admission:

> By this you ye may know if a man repenteth of his sins—behold, he will confess them and forsake them. [D&C 58:43]

> I would like to point out that to me there is a great difference between confessions, and admission after transgression is proved. I doubt much the efficacy of an admission as a confession.

> In the ancient days, men made sacrifice that they might be forgiven. Today we are told that we must bring to the Lord for our forgiveness a humble heart and a contrite spirit. As to forgiveness, the Lord has said,

> "I, the Lord will forgive whom I will forgive, but of you it is required to forgive all men" (D&C 64:10). Which means, as I understand it, that where there is repentance, we shall forgive and receive into fellowship the repentant transgressor, leaving to God the final disposition of the sin.[3]

The sincerity of repentance (v. 29) may be known by confession rather than admission (D&C 58:43 as quoted above by President Clark).

To forgive the sinner as often as he repents (v. 30) was also taught by the Savior in his mortal ministry: "Then came Peter to him, and said, Lord, how oft shall my brother sin against me, and I forgive him? till seven times? Jesus saith unto him, I say not unto thee, Until seven times: but, Until seventy times seven" (Matthew 18:21–22).

---

[3] CR, April 1950, 166–67.

The requirement of forgiving one another your trespasses (Mosiah 26:31) was also taught by the Savior in what is known as the Lord's prayer. "And forgive us our debts, as we forgive our debtors" (Matthew 6:11; 3 Nephi 13:11). The Savior commented following the prayer: "For if ye forgive men their trespasses, your heavenly Father will also forgive you; But if ye forgive not men their trespasses neither will your Father forgive your trespasses" (Matthew 6:14–15; 3 Nephi 13:14–15).

Some sins are serious enough to require excommunication or being cast out of the Church (see D&C 42:18–28; 75–93 also referred to above). Such a requirement has two purposes: First, to protect the name of the Church, and secondly to give the sinner an opportunity to begin anew the plan to gain eternal life. Therefore, he or she should not be forgotten.

> 30 Nevertheless, ye shall not cast him out from among you, but ye shall minister unto him and shall pray for him unto the Father, in my name; and if it so be that he repenteth and is baptized in my name, then shall ye receive him, and shall minister unto him of my flesh and blood.
>
> 31 But if he repent not he shall not be numbered among my people, that he may not destroy my people, for behold I know my sheep, and they are numbered.
>
> 32 Nevertheless, ye shall not cast him out of your synagogues, or your places of worship, for unto such shall ye continue to minister; for ye know not but what they will return and repent, and come unto me with full purpose of heart, and I shall heal them; and ye shall be the means of bringing salvation unto them. [3 Nephi 18:30–32; see also Moroni 6:7–8]

Alma's recording these instructions from the Lord (Mosiah 26:33) is another witness to the judging that takes place in the Church today.

Mosiah 26:34–39 • Alma Regulates All the Affairs of the Church

> 34 And it came to pass that Alma went and judged those that had

been taken in iniquity, according to the word of the Lord.

35 And whosoever repented of their sins and did confess them, them he did number among the people of the church;

36 And those that would not confess their sins and repent of their iniquity, the same were not numbered among the people of the church, and their names were blotted out.

37 And it came to pass that Alma did regulate all the affairs of the church; and they began again to have peace and to prosper exceedingly in the affairs of the church, walking circumspectly before God, receiving many, and baptizing many.

38 And now all these things did Alma and his fellow laborers do who were over the church, walking in all diligence, teaching the word of God in all things, suffering all manner of afflictions, being persecuted by all those who did not belong to the church of God.

39 And they did admonish their brethren; and they were also admonished, every one by the word of God, according to his sins, or to the sins which he had committed, being commanded of God to pray without ceasing, and to give thanks in all things.

The following of the Lord's instruction brought both peace and prosperity to the church (v. 30). The "righteous are favored of God" and "he loveth those who will have him to be their God" (1 Nephi 17:35–40).

Mosiah 27:1–7 • A Strict Command of No Persecution

1 And now it came to pass that the persecutions which were inflicted on the church by the unbelievers became so great that the church began to murmur, and complain to their leaders concerning the matter; and they did complain to Alma. And Alma laid the case before their king, Mosiah. And Mosiah consulted with his priests.

2 And it came to pass that king Mosiah sent a proclamation throughout the land round about that there should not any unbeliever persecute any of those who belonged to the church of God.

3 And there was a strict command throughout all the churches that

there should be no persecutions among them, that there should be an equality among all men;

4 That they should let no pride nor haughtiness disturb their peace; that every man should esteem his neighbor as himself, laboring with their own hands for their support.

5 Yea, and all their priests and teachers should labor with their own hands for their support, in all cases save it were in sickness, or in much want; and doing these things, they did abound in the grace of God.

6 And there began to be much peace again in the land; and the people began to be very numerous, and began to scatter abroad upon the face of the earth, yea, on the north and on the south, on the east and on the west, building large cities and villages in all quarters of the land.

7 And the Lord did visit them and prosper them, and they became a large and wealthy people.

As stated previously, the Nephites had a proper separation of church and state; but they worked together as a people of God. King Mosiah recognized the need of religious freedom (v. 2), and Alma taught it in the church (vv. 3–4). We are reminded of persecutions in the time of Joseph Smith that brought forth this declaration: "We claim the privilege of worshiping Almighty God according to the dictates of our own conscience, and allow all men the same privilege, let them worship how, where, or what they may" (11th Article of Faith).

The Lord also revealed the same esteem for neighbors in our day as he revealed to Alma, and felt it was important enough to repeat. "And let every man esteem his brother as himself, and practice virtue and holiness before me. And again I say unto you, let every man esteem his brother as himself" (D&C 38:24–25).

The time period describing the growth of the cities and villages is not given (Mosiah 27:6–7). Alma had established peace and prosperity within the church, but persecution came from those not in the church. The persecution was probably a result of the prosperity in the church bringing envy to the unbelievers. The persecutions would suggest at least a few years separating the two periods of peace and prosperity. Both periods appropriately give credit to the Lord for these blessed conditions (v. 7; see also 26:37–39).

Mosiah 27:8–12 • Alma and the Sons of Mosiah

8 Now the sons of Mosiah were numbered among the unbelievers; and also one of the sons of Alma was numbered among them, he being called Alma, after his father; nevertheless, he became a very wicked and an idolatrous man. And he was a man of many words, and did speak much flattery to the people; therefore he led many of the people to do after the manner of his iniquities.

9 And he became a great hinderment to the prosperity of the church of God; stealing away the hearts of the people; causing much dissension among the people; giving a chance for the enemy of God to exercise his power over them.

10 And now it came to pass that while he was going about to destroy the church of God, for he did go about secretly with the sons of Mosiah seeking to destroy the church, and to lead astray the people of the Lord, contrary to the commandments of God, or even the king—

11 And as I said unto you, as they were going about rebelling against God, behold, the angel of the Lord appeared unto them; and he descended as it were in a cloud; and he spake as it were with a voice of thunder, which caused the earth to shake upon which they stood;

12 And so great was their astonishment, that they fell to the earth, and understood not the words which he spake unto them.

What led Alma, son of Alma, and the sons of Mosiah to be rebellious is not mentioned, but much learning is suggested by association with "many words" and "flattery," as discussed above (v. 8). Jacob, brother of Nephi, warned earlier:

28 O that cunning plan of the evil one! O the vainness, and the frailties, and the foolishness of men! When they are learned they

think they are wise, and they hearken not unto the counsel of God, for they set it aside, supposing they know of themselves, wherefore, their wisdom is foolishness and it profiteth them not. And they shall perish.

29 But to be learned is good if they hearken unto the counsels of God. [2 Nephi 9:28–29]

Isaiah likewise warned of pseudo-intellectualism: "Wo unto the wise in their own eyes and prudent in their own sight!" (2 Nephi 15:21).

The enemy of God is Satan. His power over Alma, son of Alma, and Mosiah's four sons was obtained because they were breaking God's commandments (Mosiah 27:8). The Prophet Joseph Smith said: "The devil has no power over us only as we permit him. The moment we revolt at anything that comes from God, the devil takes power" (*TPJS*, 181). One of the purposes of angels appearing to men "is to call them to repentance" (Moroni 7:31). God and angels have greater power than Satan. The angel descending as it were in a cloud was apparently seen by all or some of those five people for it to be recorded. No one else was present. The voice of thunder causing the earth to shake (Mosiah 27:11), along with a glorious man in mid air descending without falling, was certainly evidence to them that the power of God was causing them to be overcome.

Mosiah 27:13–18 • The Words of an Angel to Alma

13 Nevertheless he cried again, saying: Alma, arise and stand forth, for why persecutest thou the church of God? For the Lord hath said: This is my church, and I will establish it; and nothing shall overthrow it, save it is the transgression of my people.

14 And again, the angel said: Behold, the Lord hath heard the prayers of his people, and also the prayers of his servant, Alma, who is thy father; for he has prayed with much faith concerning thee that thou mightest be brought to the knowledge of the truth; therefore, for this purpose have I come to convince thee of the power and authority of God, that the prayers of his servants might be answered according to their faith.

15 And now behold, can ye dispute the power of God? For behold, doth not my voice shake the earth? And can ye not also behold me before you? And I am sent from God.

16 Now I say unto thee: Go, and remember the captivity of thy fathers in the land of Helam, and in the land of Nephi; and remember how great things he has done for them; for they were in bondage, and he has delivered them. And now I say unto thee, Alma, go thy way, and seek to destroy the church no more, that their prayers may be answered, and this even if thou wilt of thyself be cast off.

17 And now it came to pass that these were the last words which the angel spake unto Alma, and he departed.

18 And now Alma and those that were with him fell again to the earth, for great was their astonishment; for with their own eyes they had beheld an angel of the Lord; and his voice was as thunder, which shook the earth; and they knew that there was nothing save the power of God that could shake the earth and cause it to tremble as though it would part asunder.

Another purpose for angels appearing to man is shown in the angels words that nothing would overthrow the church except the transgression of the people (v. 13). Angels may be sent to protect the church from apostasy. Alma, son of Alma, was told to quit trying to destroy the church even if he would destroy himself (v. 16). Alma had his agency, but there were enough righteous people in the church for the Lord to send a protector for them.

Angels show "themselves unto men of strong faith" (Moroni 7:30). In this case it was the faith of Alma, the first, that brought the angel (Mosiah 27:14). The father's prayers were for the son to "be brought to a knowledge of the truth" (v. 14). He did not ask for the Lord to send an angel, but the Lord selected the way to answer the prayer. God knows how the people will respond, and that some people are not capable of enduring an angel's presence. The angel's words were brief, to the point and affective. Alma son of Alma learned of the power and authority of God from this experience.

Mosiah 27:19–23 • Alma Becomes Dumb

19 And now the astonishment of Alma was so great that he became dumb, that he could not open his mouth; yea, and he became weak, even that he could not move his hands; therefore he was taken by those that were with him, and carried helpless, even until he was laid before his father.

20 And they rehearsed unto his father all that had happened unto them; and his father rejoiced, for he knew that it was the power of God.

21 And he caused that a multitude should be gathered together that they might witness what the Lord had done for his son, and also for those that were with him.

22 And he caused that the priests should assemble themselves together; and they began to fast, and to pray to the Lord their God that he would open the mouth of Alma, that he might speak, and also that his limbs might receive their strength—that the eyes of the people might be opened to see and know of the goodness and glory of God.

23 And it came to pass after they had fasted and prayed for the space of two days and two nights, the limbs of Alma received their strength, and he stood up and began to speak unto them, bidding them to be of good comfort:

The mission of the Church was and is to prepare the members to receive the ordinances necessary for exaltation, and here it was beginning to come about. Through the prayers of his father, Alma, son of Alma, was now ready to be baptized by fire and the Holy Ghost. He had certainly been baptized by water as a youth, being the son of the head of the church, but had not been baptized by the Spirit. Two days and two nights of purging (v. 23) is not the usual way of being baptized by fire, but Alma, son of Alma, was not the usual person. He needed a cleansing of intense fire to purge out the old creature. The assembling of the priests to fast and pray (v. 22) had involved the church in his cleansing, both as participants and as observers of God's power.

Mosiah 27:24–29 • The Words
of Alma, Son of Alma

24 For, said he, I have repented of my sins, and have been redeemed of the Lord; behold I am born of the Spirit.

25 And the Lord said unto me: Marvel not that all mankind, yea, men and women, all nations, kindreds, tongues and people, must be born again; yea, born of God, changed from their carnal and fallen state, to a state of righteousness, being redeemed of God, becoming his sons and daughters;

26 And thus they become new creatures; and unless they do this, they can in nowise inherit the kingdom of God.

27 I say unto you, unless this be the case, they must be cast off; and this I know, because I was like to be cast off.

28 Nevertheless, after wading through much tribulation, repenting nigh unto death, the Lord in mercy hath seen fit to snatch me out of an everlasting burning, and I am born of God.

29 My soul hath been redeemed from the gall of bitterness and bonds of iniquity. I was in the darkest abyss; but now I behold the marvelous light of God. My soul was racked with eternal torment; but I am snatched, and my soul is pained no more.

The rebirth experience was described following the speech of King Benjamin (see Alma 5). Even though Alma, son of Alma, says all mankind must be born again of God (Mosiah 27:25; see also Alma 5:49), since all physical births are uniquely different, rebirths may also be individually unique. However, there are certain fundamental likenesses in both births. Thus we will follow the description of Alma, son of Alma, being born again. He first says that the born again one must be changed from their carnal and fallen state to a state of righteousness (v. 25). This is the "mighty change in us or in our hearts" spoken of by King Benjamin (Mosiah 5:2). The change is a complete turnaround of our desires and our actions. Alma, son of Alma, had farther to turn than most people. Therefore, his rebirth was unusual.

The second point of Alma, son of Alma, is that the born again person is redeemed of God, becoming his son and daughter (Mosiah 27:25). King Benjamin said his subjects were "the children of Christ, his sons and daughters" having been "spiritually begotten of him" (Mosiah 5:7). Being "new creatures," Alma, son of Alma, says, was required to "inherit the kingdom of God" (Mosiah 27:26). The closest parallel to King Benjamin's description is the reborn person having "great views of that which is to come" (Mosiah 5:3). The Savior included both Alma, son of Alma, and King Benjamin's description in defining the born again person.

> 3 Jesus answered and said unto him, Verily, verily, I say unto thee, Except a man be born again, he cannot see the kingdom of God.
>
> 4 Nicodemus saith unto him, How can a man be born when he is old? can he enter the second time into his mother's womb, and be born?
>
> 5 Jesus answered, Verily, verily, I say unto thee, Except a man be born of water and *of* the Spirit, he cannot enter into the kingdom of God. [John 3:3–5][4]

Alma, son of Alma, speaks of his repenting nigh unto death and being snatched out of an everlasting burning and eternal torment (Mosiah 27:28–29). King Benjamin spoke of being "willing to enter into a covenant with our God to do his work, and to be obedient to his commandments," that "we may not bring upon ourselves a never ending torment" (Mosiah 5:5). Alma probably suffered severely because of the seriousness of his past sins. However, there is a difference between everlasting, eternal punishment, and never-ending torment. In the Doctrine and Covenants, the Lord revealed the differences to the Prophet Joseph Smith:

> 6 Nevertheless, it is not written that there shall be no end to this torment, but it is written *endless torment.*
>
> 7 Again, it is written *eternal damnation;* wherefore it is more

---

[4] See Joseph Smith's comments about this statement, as quoted under Mosiah 5:3 in this commentary, p. 259.

express than other scriptures, that it might work upon the hearts of the children of men, altogether for my name's glory.

8 Wherefore, I will explain unto you this mystery, for it is meet unto you to know even as mine apostles.

9 I speak unto you that are chosen in this thing, even as one, that you may enter into my rest.

10 For, behold, the mystery of godliness, how great is it! For, behold, I am endless, and the punishment which is given from my hand is endless punishment, for Endless is my name. Wherefore—

11 Eternal punishment is God's punishment.

12 Endless punishment is God's punishment. [D&C 19:6–12]

Mosiah 27:30–31 • Alma, Son of Alma Confesses

30 I rejected my Redeemer, and denied that which had been spoken of by our fathers; but now that they may foresee that he will come, and that he remembereth every creature of his creating, he will make himself manifest unto all.

31 Yea, every knee shall bow, and every tongue confess before him. Yea, even at the last day, when all men shall stand to be judged of him, then shall they confess that he is God; then shall they confess, who live without God in the world, that the judgment of an everlasting punishment is just upon them; and they shall quake, and tremble, and shrink beneath the glance of his all-searching eye.

Alma, son of Alma, concludes by confessing that he rejected the Redeemer, but testifies that he will come and manifest himself to all. Every knee shall bow and every tongue confess that he is God. All who live without God will suffer an everlasting punishment (vv. 30–31). Both Alma, son of Alma, and King Benjamin are speaking of the Second Coming of Christ and the final judgment of all mankind. The experiences Alma, son of Alma, described before were those he had previously suffered.

Mosiah 27:32–37 • Alma, Son of Alma, and Others Travel Throughout the Land

32 And now it came to pass that Alma began from this time forward to teach the people, and those who were with Alma at the time the angel appeared unto them, traveling round about through all the land, publishing to all the people the things which they had heard and seen, and preaching the word of God in much tribulation, being greatly persecuted by those who were unbelievers, being smitten by many of them.

33 But notwithstanding all this, they did impart much consolation to the church, confirming their faith, and exhorting them with long-suffering and much travail to keep the commandments of God.

34 And four of them were the sons of Mosiah; and their names were Ammon, and Aaron, and Omner, and Himni; these were the names of the sons of Mosiah.

35 And they traveled throughout all the land of Zarahemla, and among all the people who were under the reign of king Mosiah, zealously striving to repair all the injuries which they had done to the church, confessing all their sins, and publishing all the things which they had seen, and explaining the prophecies and the scriptures to all who desired to hear them.

36 And thus they were instruments in the hands of God in bringing many to the knowledge of the truth, yea, to the knowledge of their Redeemer.

37 And how blessed are they! For they did publish peace; they did publish good tidings of good; and they did declare unto the people that the Lord reigneth.

It is not clear how many people were with Alma at the time of the angel's appearance, but for certain four of the sons of Mosiah were present. Others were rebelling, but may not have been present. Their travels throughout the land was a step in their repentance. They were seeking to make restitution for rebelling against God and his church. While restitution for some sins is impossible or difficult to make directly, indirect restitution can be made by endeavoring to keep others from making similar mistakes. The sons of Mosiah were trying to correct the damage they had caused to come upon the church (v. 35). They were successful with many. Mormon concludes his abridgment of this section by commenting on their work of teaching throughout the land (v. 37) through paraphrasing Isaiah's prophecy of publishing peace (Isaiah 52:7).

SACRED WRITING

Revelation which is Great:

Mosiah 26:15–32	The Lord to Alma concerning transgressors in the church.
Mosiah 27:11, 13–16	An angel calling Alma, son of Alma, to repentance.
Mosiah 27:24–31	Alma, son of Alma, relates his rebirth to his father and the priests.

Doctrines Learned:

Mosiah 26:20	A man may have his calling and election made sure in this life.
Mosiah 26:21–22	Baptism is for entrance into the Church and for forgiveness of sins.
Mosiah 26:23–24	Those called by Christ's name and who know him shall have an eternal place at the right hand of God.
Mosiah 26:25	At the second trump, those who never knew Christ as their God will depart into everlasting fire prepared for the devil and his angels.
Mosiah 26:28	Those who will not hear Christ's voice are not to be received into his Church.
Mosiah 26:29	Man is judged by his sins. Those who confess their sins before the Lord and the Church shall be forgiven by the Church and the Lord.
Mosiah 26:30	The Lord will forgive his people as often as they repent.
Mosiah 26:31	Those who will not forgive others are brought under condemnation.

Mosiah 27:2–4	There should be freedom of religion among all men, equality, and no persecution.
Mosiah 27:5	Priests and teachers should labor for their own support.
Mosiah 27:13	Nothing shall overthrow the Church but transgression.
Mosiah 27:14	Angels minister because of the faith of others.
Mosiah 27:14–16	Angels may be sent to convince people of the power and authority of God, but they have their agency to choose to repent.
Mosiah 27:25	All mankind must be born again, changed from their fallen state to a state of righteousness and become sons and daughters of God.
Mosiah 27:28–29	Alma the younger suffered everlasting burning and eternal punishment, the punishment of God, but did not suffer never-ending punishment or torment.
Mosiah 27:31	Every knee shall bow and every tongue confess that God is God.
Mosiah 27:35–36	Making restitution is a part of the process of repentance.

General Authority Quotations

President Spencer W. Kimball • Mosiah 26:29–31

The confession of sin is an important element in repentance. Many offenders have seemed to feel that a few prayers to the Lord were sufficient and they have thus justified themselves in hiding their sins. The Provers tells us:

> He that covereth his sins shall not prosper, but whoso confesseth and forsaketh them shall have mercy. [Proverbs 28:13]

> By this ye may know if a man repenteth of his sins—behold, he will confess them and forsake them. [D&C 58:43]

Especially grave errors such as sexual sins shall be confessed to the bishop as well as to the Lord. There are two remissions that one might wish to have: first, the forgiveness from the Lord, and second, the forgiveness of the Lord's church through its leaders. As soon as one has an inner conviction of his sins, he should go to the Lord in 'mighty prayer,' as did Enos, and never cease his supplications until he shall, like Enos, receive the assurance that his sins have been forgiven by the Lord. It is unthinkable that God absolves serious sins upon a few requests. He is likely to wait until there has been long sustained repentance as evidenced by a willingness to comply with all His other requirements. So far as the Church is concerned, no priest nor elder is authorized by virtue of that calling to perform this act for the Church. The Lord has a consistent, orderly plan. Every soul in the organized stakes is given a bishop who, by the very nature of his calling and his ordination, is a 'judge in Israel.' In the missions a branch president fills that responsibility. The bishop is one's best earthly friend. He will hear the problems, judge the seriousness thereof, determine the degree of adjustment, and decide if it warrants an eventual forgiveness. He does this as the earthly representation of God, who is the master physician, the master psychologist, the master psychiatrist. If repentance is sufficient, he may waive penalties, which is tantamount to forgiveness so far as the church organization is concerned. The bishop claims no authority to absolve sins, but he does share the burden, waive penalties, relieve tension and strain, and he may assure a continuation of church activity. He will keep the whole matter most confidential.

Some missionaries have foolishly carried with them their secret, unadjusted guilt into the field and have suffered seriously in the effort to get and retain the spirit of the mission. The conflict in the soul is most frustrating. But he who totally repents, voluntarily confesses, and clears his difficulty so far as possible, triumphs in his work and enjoyed sweet peace.[5]

We read in the scriptures:

> . . .for I, the Lord, forgive sins, and am merciful unto those who confess their sins with humble hearts . . . [D&C 61:2]

---

[5] *Faith Precedes the Miracle*, [1972], 181–182.

> Note: The entire book *The Miracle of Forgiveness* should be read by every member of the Church, and others who are interested. To include pertinent passages here would make the chapter too lengthy.

The Lord says:

By this ye may know that a man repenteth of his sins, behold he will confess them and forsake them. [D&C 58:43]

And Paul:

For with the heart man believeth unto righteousness; and with the mouth confession is made unto salvation. [Romans 10:10]

Challenges to Eternal Life:

1. Choose a principle or teaching of the Church that you do not understand and review it in light of Mosiah 26:3–4. Is it unbelief that is causing you not to understand?

2. Confess to your Bishop or Branch President and to the Lord any unresolved sins or transgressions in your life (Mosiah 26:29).

3. Analyze your feelings towards your fellowman. Have you forgiven others of their trespasses? If not, endeavor to do so (Mosiah 26:31).

4. Make an effort to make restitution as you feel a need to do so, either directly or indirectly (Mosiah 27:35).

5. Choose a challenge or modern message of your own from this reading and incorporate it into your life.

Chapter Fifteen

The Purpose of Government

Mosiah 28–29

*H*istorical Setting: The lives of Alma the elder and King Mosiah, son of Benjamin, were coming to a close. The political leadership of the Nephite lands, under a new form of government, is being passed on to Alma, son of Alma, as well as the leadership of the church. The events of these last two chapters of the book of Mosiah occurred just prior to "the reign of the judges" (Mosiah 29:44). Alma the elder "died being eighty and two years old" and "Mosiah, son of Benjamin, died also, in the thirty and third year of his reign, being sixty and three years old; making in the whole, five hundred and nine years from the time Lehi left Jerusalem" (91 B.C., Mosiah 29:44–45).

Mosiah 28:1–29:4 is Mormon's abridgment of the record from the large plates of Nephi. Mosiah 29:5–32 provides the words of a letter sent by King Mosiah to his people. However, Mormon did not include all of Mosiah's words (see Mosiah 29:33–36). The rest of the king's message was abridged by Mormon.

Precept of this Reading:

26 Now it is not common that the voice of the people desireth anything contrary to that which is right; but it is common for the lesser part of the people to desire that which is not right; therefore this shall ye observe and make it your law—to do your business by the voice of the people.

27 And if the time comes that the voice of the people doth choose iniquity, then is the time that the judgments of God will come upon you; yea, then is the time he will visit you with great destruction even as he has hitherto visited this land. [Mosiah 29:26–27]

We learn from these chapters how we should conduct our business in government, and also how to escape the judgments of God.

An outline of the chapters in this reading follows as a preparation for further study.

OUTLINE • MOSIAH 28–29

➤ Mosiah 28:1–5 The sons of Mosiah and others returned to their father, the king, and pled to go to the land of Nephi to preach and impart the word of God to their Lamanite brethren.

   a. They desired to bring the Lamanites to the knowledge of God and convince them of the iniquity of their fathers (v. 2).

   b. They desired to cure the Lamanites of their hatred towards the Nephites that they might rejoice in the Lord, that there should be no more contention (v. 2).

   c. They desired that salvation be declared to every creature (v. 3).

      1. They could not bear that any human soul should perish.

      2. The thought of endless torment for any soul caused them to quake and tremble.

   d. The Spirit of the Lord worked upon the sons of Mosiah for they were the vilest of sinners (v. 4).

      1. The Lord saw fit in his infinite mercy to spare them.

      2. They suffered much anguish of soul and the fear of being cast off.

➤ 28:6–9 King Mosiah inquired of the Lord, and the Lord said to let them go.

a. The Lord said many shall believe on their words, and they shall have eternal life (v. 7).

b. The Lord would deliver his sons out of the hands of the Lamanites (v. 7).

c. Mosiah granted permission and the sons left (vv. 8–9).

d. An account of their proceedings will be given later (v. 9).

➤ 28:10–20 King Mosiah had no one to confer the kingdom upon. He took the records, the interpreters, and other things and conferred them upon Alma, son of Alma.

a. None of his sons would accept the kingdom (v. 10).

b. The king gave Alma, son of Alma, the plates of brass, the plates of Nephi, other things preserved by the commandments of God, and the plates of gold found by Limhi's people (v. 11).

c. King Mosiah, son of Benjamin, had translated the plates of gold with the two stones fastened to the rims of a bow (vv. 12–16).

   1. The people desired to know of the people who were destroyed.

   2. The two stones were prepared from the beginning and handed down from generation to generation for the purpose of translating languages.

   3. The records had been kept and preserved by the Lord to show those who inhabited the land the iniquities and abominations of these people.

   4. Whoso has these stones is called seer, as in ancient times.

d. The gold plates gave an account of a people who had been destroyed (vv. 17–19).

   1. The record told of the people building the great tower when the Lord confounded the languages of the people and scattered them abroad upon the earth.

2. The record went back from that time to the creation of Adam.

3. The account filled the people of Mosiah the son of Benjamin, with great sorrow, but they gained much knowledge.

4. This account shall be written hereafter that all people should know these things.

e. Alma, son of Alma, was commanded to hand down all these things down from generation to generation as they had been since the time Lehi left Jerusalem (v. 20).

➤ 29:1–3   King Mosiah, son of Benjamin, sent among all the people desiring who should be their king.

a. The voice of the people desired Aaron, his son, to be their king (v. 2).

b. Aaron had gone to the land of Nephi, and he would not take the kingdom, nor would any of the sons of Mosiah (v. 3).

➤ 29:4–36   King Mosiah sent a written message among the people saying:

a. You are desirous to have a king, but he to whom the kingdom belongs has declined (v. 6).

b. If another is appointed in his stead contentions may arise (vv. 7–10).

1. My son may lead part of the people after him and there be much bloodshed and perverting of the way of the Lord.

2. We have no right to destroy my son nor any other who might be appointed.

3. Let us be wise and do the things that will make for peace.

c. King Mosiah, son of Benjamin, said he would be king for the remainder of his days but will appoint wise men to be judges, who will judge the people according to the commandments of God (vv. 11–15).

      1. It is better to be judged of God than of men. God's judgments are always just, but man's judgments are not.

      2. If you could always have just men to be your kings, as was Benjamin, it would be expedient to always have a king.

      3. Mosiah, son of Benjamin, had labored to teach the commandments of God and establish peace.

      4. He had punished those who committed iniquity according to the crime and the law given by the fathers.

  d. It was not expedient to have a king, for a wicked king can cause much iniquity and destruction (vv. 16–20).

      1. King Noah was an example of a wicked king bringing his people into bondage.

      2. Had not the all-wise creator delivered them, they would still be in bondage.

  e. You cannot dethrone an iniquitous king but by contention and bloodshed (vv. 21–24).

      1. The king has friends in iniquity and keeps guards about him.

      2. He tears up laws of those who ruled before and tramples the commandments of God.

      3. He enacts laws following his own wickedness, and destroys those who do not obey them or who rebel against them.

      4. An unrighteous king perverts the ways of all righteousness.

      5. It is not expedient that such abominations come upon you.

  f. Choose judges by the voice of the people that will judge by the laws given by our fathers (v. 25).

      1. Laws which are correct.

      2. Laws which were given them by the hand of the Lord.

g. Observe, and make it your law, to do business by the voice of the people (vv. 26–27).

   1. It is not common that the voice of the people declare anything that is not right.

   2. It is common for the lesser part of the people to desire what is not right.

   3. If the people choose iniquity, the judgments of God will come upon them.

h. Judges who do not judge according to the law can be judged by a higher judge (v. 28).

i. If a higher judge does not judge righteously, they can be judged by a small number of lower judges (v. 29).

j. King Mosiah, son of Benjamin, commanded the people to do these things in the fear of the Lord, and have no kings (vv. 30–31).

   1. The sins shall be answered upon the heads of the people.

   2. Sins caused by an iniquitous king will be answered on the head of the king.

k. King Mosiah, son of Benjamin, desired no more inequality, and to have a land of liberty (v. 32).

   1. Every man would enjoy his rights and privileges.

   2. Their posterity would enjoy the same rights and privileges.

l. King Mosiah, son of Benjamin, wrote many more things to them (v. 33).

   1. He unfolded all the trials of a righteous king.

   2. The burden of government should come upon all people, every man bearing his part.

   3. He unfolded all the disadvantages of an unrighteous king.

   4. All the unnumberable iniquities ought not to be. They are repugnant to the commandments of God.

➤ 29:37–41 The people were convinced of the truth of King Mosiah's words and relinquished their desire for a king. They desired every man to have an equal chance and answer for his own sins.

   a. They assembled throughout the land and chose judges and rejoiced in their liberty (v. 39).

   b. They loved Mosiah, son of Benjamin, and esteemed him more than any other man (v. 40).

      1. He was not a tyrant looking for gain, or for lucre that corrupted the soul, nor did he delight in shedding blood.

      2. He established peace and granted deliverance from all manner of bondage.

   c. They appointed judges throughout the land to judge them according to the law (v. 41).

➤ 29:42–47   Alma, son of Alma, was appointed the first chief judge commencing the reign of the judges.

   a. Alma, son of Alma, was also the high priest (v. 42).

      1. The office was conferred upon him by his father.

      2. He had charge concerning all the affairs of the church.

   b. He did walk in the ways of the Lord, judged righteously, and had continual peace (v. 43).

   c. Alma the elder died at age eighty-two having lived to fulfill the commandments of God and found the church (vv. 44, 47).

   d. King Mosiah, son of Benjamin, died in the thirty-third year of his reign, at age sixty-three, being five hundred years since Lehi left Jerusalem. Thus ended the reign of the kings over the people of Nephi (v. 46–47).

NOTES AND COMMENTARY

Introduction: In A.D. 1835 The Church of Jesus Christ of Latter-day Saints issued "A declaration of belief regarding governments and laws in general" (section heading Doctrine and Covenants 134).

1 We believe that governments were instituted of God for the

benefit of man; and that he holds men accountable for their acts in relation to them, both in making laws and administering them, for the good and safety of society.

2 We believe that no government can exist in peace, except such laws are framed and held inviolate as will secure to each individual the free exercise of conscience, the right and control of property, and the protection of life. [D&C 134:1–2]

King Mosiah's, son of Benjamin, decisions and his written instructions to his people are examples of the three fundamentals that every government should provide for each individual in their society: "The free exercise of conscience, the right and control of property, and the protection of life" (v. 2 above). As King Mosiah's, son of Benjamin, example and words are studied, we should compare them to what the governments of today are providing for their subjects, and see how we can help to support or improve those governments to provide those essential fundamentals.

Mosiah 28:1–9 • The Sons of Mosiah Plead to Go to the Lamanites

1 Now it came to pass that after the sons of Mosiah had done all these things, they took a small number with them and returned to their father, the king, and desired of him that he would grant unto them that they might, with these whom they had selected, go up to the land of Nephi that they might preach the things which they had heard, and that they might impart the word of God to their brethren, the Lamanites—

2 That perhaps they might bring them to the knowledge of the Lord their God, and convince them of the iniquity of their fathers; and that perhaps they might cure them of their hatred towards the Nephites, that they might also be brought to rejoice in the Lord their God, that they might become friendly to one another, and that there should be no more contentions in all the land which the Lord their God had given them.

3 Now they were desirous that salvation should be declared to every creature, for they could not bear that any human soul should perish; yea, even the very thoughts that any soul should endure

endless torment did cause them to quake and tremble.

4 And thus did the Spirit of the Lord work upon them, for they were the very vilest of sinners. And the Lord saw fit in his infinite mercy to spare them; nevertheless they suffered much anguish of soul because of their iniquities, suffering much and fearing that they should be cast off forever.

5 And it came to pass that they did plead with their father many days that they might go up to the land of Nephi.

6 And king Mosiah went and inquired of the Lord if he should let his sons go up among the Lamanites to preach the word.

7 And the Lord said unto Mosiah: Let them go up, for many shall believe on their words, and they shall have eternal life; and I will deliver thy sons out of the hands of the Lamanites.

8 And it came to pass that Mosiah granted that they might go and do according to their request.

9 And they took their journey into the wilderness to go up to preach the word among the Lamanites; and I shall give an account of their proceedings hereafter. [Mosiah 28:1–9]

The sons of Mosiah and their friends went to their father as the king, not for fatherly advice. Their request is another evidence of the separation of church and state. The effect of the missionaries going to the Lamanite nation was a political matter as well as a church matter. We often use the church and the kingdom of God as synonyms, but the kingdom of God is a larger organization of which the church is a part. In the early days of Mosiah, son of Benjamin, and also from the early days of Nephi (see 2 Nephi 5:18–19; Jacob 1:9–11), the church and kingdom were administered through one head, Mosiah being a prophet, seer, and revelator (see Mosiah 8:16). However with the growth of the church, as spoken of in Mosiah chapter 25, Mosiah "had given Alma the authority over the church" (Mosiah 26:8).

The kingdom of God is administered by revelation and through the priesthood. In an earlier discussion, Mosiah, son of Benjamin had "consulted with his priests" regarding the persecution upon the church

(Mosiah 27:1). This was a different body of priests than the "one priest to every fifty of their number" that was ordained by Alma to assist him in the church (Mosiah 18:18). Regarding his sons going on a mission, Mosiah "inquired of the Lord" and not only received a revelation to allow them to go, but was given promises of success and protection (Mosiah 28:6–7).

The kingdom of God established among the children of Israel following the period of the Judges was similar to Mosiah's organization, but it was under a different priesthood and therefore had some differences. Israel's king was Jehovah [Christ] or the God of Israel, but the people wanted "a king to judge us like all the nations" (1 Samuel 8:5). The Lord recognized their agency, and after warning them of the consequences through Samuel "the seer" (1 Samuel 9:19), he harkened to their demand for a king. Through revelation from the Lord, Samuel selected Saul to be the king (see 1 Samuel 9–10). Nathan succeeded Samuel as the prophet and seer. Although the Lord "took Moses out of their midst, and the Holy Priesthood also; . . . the lesser [Aaronic] priesthood continued" with Israel (D&C 84:25–26). However, both Samuel and Nathan held the Melchizedek Priesthood. "All the prophets had the Melchizedek Priesthood and were ordained by God himself" (*TPJS*, 181). Although David, and therefore probably Saul, had the priesthood, "he never did obtain the . . . the fullness of the priesthood" (*TPJS*, 339). Whatever priesthood David and Saul had, Samuel and Nathan had a higher authority. They anointed the kings (see 1 Samuel 16; 2 Samuel 12). The prophet and seer was the highest authority in the kingdom of God.

The millennium reign will have a similar organization to that of the time of Mosiah, son of Benjamin. Christ himself will be the king. A prophet, seer, and revelator will be the earthly servant to administer the Church and political kingdom under Christ. Joseph Smith was given the keys of the kingdom.[1]

---

[1] The Lord revealed to Joseph who the root of Jesse spoken of in Isaiah was:

(continued...)

2 Therefore, thou art blessed from henceforth that bear the keys of the kingdom given unto you; which kingdom is coming forth for the last time.

3 Verily I say unto you, the keys of this kingdom shall never be taken from you, while thou art in the world, neither in the world to come;

4 Nevertheless, through you shall the oracles be given to another, yea, even unto the church. [D&C 90:2–4]

Joseph's successor have and will continue to hold those keys until the kingdom of heaven comes. "Wherefore, may the kingdom of God go forth, that the kingdom of heaven may come, that thou, O God, mayest be glorified in heaven so on earth, that thine enemies may be subdued; for thine is the honor, power and glory, forever and ever" (D&C 65:6). When Christ "reigns whose right it is to reign, and subdues all enemies under his feet" (D&C 58:22), there will still be a separation of church and state, but both will work together as did Mosiah, son of Benjamin, and Alma the elder worked for "the immortality and eternal life of man" (Moses 1:39).

In the millennium mortality, will continue and mortals will still

---

[1] (...continued)

6 Behold, thus saith the Lord, it is a descendant of Jesse, as well as of Joseph, unto whom rightly belongs the priesthood, and the keys of the kingdom, for an ensign, and for the gathering of my people in the last days. [D&C 113:6]

The descendant was obviously Joseph Smith. As a descendant of Joseph (of Egypt) he had the authority to establish the Church. Judah was given the political keys of the kingdom (see Genesis 49:10), thus Joseph Smith also had the authority to establish the political kingdom. This he did on April 7, 1842 and it was called the "Council of Fifty." The Church was established first to prepare a people to be governed by revelation. The Council of Fifty functioned in the territory of Deseret under Brigham Young for a time but was discontinued. The ground work was laid and set for the millennium. [For further information see: Brigham Young University Studies, vol. 20, no. 3, page 253, Andrew F. Ehat, "It Seems Like Heaven on Earth"; Joseph Smith and the Constitution of the Kingdom of God; see also John Taylor, "The meaning of the Kingdom of God," *The Gospel Kingdom*, ed. G. Homer Durham, [1987], chapter XIX, govern. The Prophet Joseph Smith said: "Christ and the resurrected Saints will reign over the earth during the thousand years. They will not probably dwell upon the earth, but will visit it when they please, or when it is necessary to govern it. There will be wicked men on the earth during the thousand years" (*TPJS*, 268–69). The wicked men are not the telestial type of our day, but those among what the Lord calls the "congregations of the wicked" who have not and may not accept the gospel (see D&C 60:13; 61:33; 62:5). They are "under darkness and under the bondage of sin . . . because they come not unto me" (D&C 84:49–50). They will not "come unto [Christ] and be baptized in my name" (3 Nephi 27:20). The millennium mortals will have their agency and by their choices may become terrestrial beings. Isaiah described them: "In those days there shall be no more thence an infant of days, nor an old man that hath not filled his days; for the child shall not die, but shall live to be an hundred years old; but the sinner, living to be an hundred years old, shall be accursed" (JST, Isaiah 65:20). However, the Lord said of the majority of those living in the millennium: "And the earth shall be given unto them for an inheritance; and they shall multiply and wax strong, and their children shall grow up without sin unto salvation. For the Lord shall be in their midst, and his glory shall be upon them, and he will be their king and their lawgiver" (D&C 45:58–59).

Malachi also prophesied of the millennium people: "But unto you that fear my name shall the Sun of righteousness arise with healing in his wings; and ye shall go forth, and grow up as calves of the stall" (Malachi 4:2). Calves growing up in a stall are protected from the elements of the world. The millennial children will be protected from Satan.

> 24 And the time cometh speedily that the righteous must be led up as calves of the stall, and the Holy One of Israel must reign in dominion, and might, and power, and great glory.
>
> 25 And he gathereth his children from the four quarters of the earth; and he numbereth his sheep, and they know him; and there shall be one fold and one shepherd; and he shall feed his sheep, and in him they shall find pasture.

26 And because of the righteousness of his people, Satan has no power; wherefore, he cannot be loosed for the space of many years; for he hath no power over the hearts of the people, for they dwell in righteousness, and the Holy One of Israel reigneth. [1 Nephi 22:24–26]

The sons of Mosiah and their companions had the eternal status of their Lamanite brethren in mind. Having suffered eternal torment themselves, they did not want others to suffer as they had (Mosiah 28:2–3). They were also desirous to maintain their own redeemed state (v. 4). The account of their mission among the Lamanites (v. 9) is recorded in Alma chapters 17 through 29.

Mosiah 28:10–16 • Mosiah Translates the Records of Those Destroyed

10 Now king Mosiah had no one to confer the kingdom upon, for there was not any of his sons who would accept of the kingdom.

11 Therefore he took the records which were engraven on the plates of brass, and also the plates of Nephi, and all the things which he had kept and preserved according to the commandments of God, after having translated and caused to be written the records which were on the plates of gold which had been found by the people of Limhi, which were delivered to him by the hand of Limhi;

12 And this he did because of the great anxiety of his people; for they were desirous beyond measure to know concerning those people who had been destroyed.

13 And now he translated them by the means of those two stones which were fastened into the two rims of a bow.

14 Now these things were prepared from the beginning, and were handed down from generation to generation, for the purpose of interpreting languages;

15 And they have been kept and preserved by the hand of the Lord, that he should discover to every creature who should possess the land the iniquities and abominations of his people;

16 And whosoever has these things is called seer, after the manner of old times.

The account of the men of King Limhi's expedition finding the plates of gold (v. 11) is found in Mosiah 21:25–27 and Mosiah 8:7–12. This incident was previously discussed under those verses.

The two stones set in the bow are not mentioned again in the Book of Mormon until the book of Ether where Moroni tells us "the Lord commanded [the brother of Jared] to seal up the two stones he had received" (Ether 3:28). Moroni does not tell us from whom he had received the two stones. However, Mormon, his father, as he abridges the Nephite record tells us that they were handed down from generation to generation for the purpose of interpreting language (Mosiah 29:14). Apparently there was no further need of them between the time of Mosiah, son of Benjamin, and Moroni. The record was to be a warning to future inhabitants of the Americas (v. 15), and so were delivered to Joseph Smith for the purpose of translating the Book of Mormon record. Moroni, now an angel, described them to Joseph Smith before he was given them.

> 34 He said there was a book deposited, written upon gold plates, giving an account of the former inhabitants of this continent, and the source from whence they sprang. He also said that the fulness of the everlasting Gospel was contained in it, as delivered by the Savior to the ancient inhabitants;
>
> 35 Also, that there were two stones in silver bows—and these stones, fastened to a breastplate, constituted what is called the Urim and Thummin—deposited with the plates; and the possession and use of these stones were what constituted "seers" in ancient or former times; and that God had prepared them for the purpose of translating the book. [Joseph Smith—History 1:34–35]

Joseph describes his obtaining the record and the two stones and calls them the Urim and Thummim, the biblical name (see Exodus 28:30).

> Having removed the earth, I obtained a lever, which I got fixed under the edge of the stone, and with a little exertion raised it up. I looked in, and there indeed did I behold the plates, the Urim and Thummim, and the breastplate, as stated by the messenger. The box in which they lay was formed by laying stones together in some kind

of cement. In the bottom of the box were laid two stones crossways of the box, and on these stones lay the plates and the other things with them. [Joseph Smith—History 1:52]

The three special witnesses of the Book of Mormon were later given a promise of seeing the plates, the Urim and Thummim, and other sacred Nephite items if they were faithful.

1 Behold, I say unto you, that you must rely upon my word, which if you do with full purpose of heart, you shall have a view of the plates, and also of the breastplate, the sword of Laban, the Urim and Thummim, which were given to the brother of Jared upon the mount, when he talked with the Lord face to face, and the miraculous directors which were given to Lehi while in the wilderness, on the borders of the Red Sea.

2 And it is by your faith that you shall obtain a view of them, even by that faith which was had by the prophets of old.

3 And after that you have obtained faith, and have seen them with your eyes, you shall testify of them, by the power of God; [D&C 17:1–3]

The promise was fulfilled and their testimony of that experience is included in the front of every copy of the Book of Mormon.

The possessor of the sacred stones being called a seer (Mosiah 28:16) was again stated by Moroni when he appeared to Joseph Smith (Joseph Smith—History 1:35; quoted above). Apparently a seer may be given the keys, but may not be called upon to translate until or if there is a need. Today, the First Presidency and the Twelve Apostles are sustained as prophets seers and revelators, but none since Joseph Smith have needed to translate ancient records. However, when the time comes for the promised other records to be brought forth the keys are here. Also, the Nephites had prophets who were probably seers after the time of Mosiah, but there is no record of anything they may have translated. Since Alma was given the interpreters (Mosiah 28:20), it would seem that he was given the keys.

Mosiah 28:17–20 • An Account of the Destroyed People

17 Now after Mosiah had finished translating these records, behold, it gave an account of the people who were destroyed, from the time that they were destroyed back to the building of the great tower, at the time the Lord confounded the language of the people and they were scattered abroad upon the face of all the earth, yea, and even from that time back until the creation of Adam.

18 Now this account did cause the people of Mosiah to mourn exceedingly, yea, they were filled with sorrow; nevertheless it gave them much knowledge, in the which they did rejoice.

19 And this account shall be written hereafter; for behold, it is expedient that all people should know the things which are written in this account.

20 And now, as I said unto you, that after king Mosiah had done these things, he took the plates of brass, and all the things which he had kept, and conferred them upon Alma, who was the son of Alma; yea, all the records, and also the interpreters, and conferred them upon him, and commanded him that he should keep and preserve them, and also keep a record of the people, handing them down from one generation to another, even as they had been handed down from the time that Lehi left Jerusalem. [Mosiah 28:17–20]

The people who were destroyed are called the Jaredites. Their account was later abridged and included in the record of the Book of Mormon by Moroni. It is the book of Ether, the next to the last book in the Book of Mormon. The building of the great tower (v. 17) is recorded in the Bible, Genesis 11:1–9. That record verifies what Mormon abridged: "So the LORD scattered them abroad from thence upon the face of all the earth: and they left off to build the city. Therefore is the name of it called Babel; because the LORD did there confound the language of all the earth: and from thence did the LORD scatter them abroad upon the face of all the earth" (Genesis 11:8–9). All people have or will have an opportunity to know of the Jaredites through the book of Ether (Mosiah 28:19). Mormon, abridging the record nearly five hundred years after Mosiah I had translated them, confirms that the records and sacred things had been handed down from generation to generation from the time Lehi left Jerusalem (v. 20).

Mosiah 29:1–4 • None of the Sons Will Take the Kingdom

1 Now when Mosiah had done this he sent out throughout all the land, among all the people, desiring to know their will concerning who should be their king.

2 And it came to pass that the voice of the people came, saying: We are desirous that Aaron thy son should be our king and our ruler.

3 Now Aaron had gone up to the land of Nephi, therefore the king could not confer the kingdom upon him; neither would Aaron take upon him the kingdom; neither were any of the sons of Mosiah willing to take upon them the kingdom.

4 Therefore king Mosiah sent again among the people; yea, even a written word sent he among the people. And these were the words that were written, saying:

The reason for the sons of Mosiah refusing to take the kingdom is not given, but it was implied earlier. Their desire to make restitution for their own sins, and to bring the Lamanites to the truth was their primary goal (Mosiah 28:2–3). They recognized the value of eternal life as much more important than power or position in this life (28:4).

Mosiah 29:5–10 • Do What Will Make Peace For This People

5 Behold, O ye my people, or my brethren, for I esteem you as such, I desire that ye should consider the cause which ye are called to consider—for ye are desirous to have a king.

6 Now I declare unto you that he to whom the kingdom doth rightly belong has declined, and will not take upon him the kingdom.

7 And now if there should be another appointed in his stead, behold I fear there would rise contentions among you. And who

knoweth but what my son, to whom the kingdom doth belong, should turn to be angry and draw away a part of this people after him, which would cause wars and contentions among you, which would be the cause of shedding much blood and perverting the way of the Lord, yea, and destroy the souls of many people.

8 Now I say unto you let us be wise and consider these things, for we have no right to destroy my son, neither should we have any right to destroy another if he should be appointed in his stead.

9 And if my son should turn again to his pride and vain things he would recall the things which he had said, and claim his right to the kingdom, which would cause him and also this people to commit much sin.

10 And now let us be wise and look forward to these things, and do that which will make for the peace of this people.

These words are what Mosiah wrote, not what Mormon abridged. His words continue through verse thirty-three.

The "descendants of Nephi" (Mosiah 25:13) were the ones to whom the kingdom rightly belonged (29:6). There is no record of when or by whom this patriarchal line of kingship was declared, but it originated with the Lord's promise to Nephi that he would "be made a ruler and a teacher over thy brethren" (1 Nephi 2:22). An angel of the Lord later reminded Laman and Lemuel that "the Lord hath chosen him to be a ruler over you" (1 Nephi 3:29). Nephi had no desire to be his people's king but did fill the role because of what the Lord had told him (see 2 Nephi 5:18–19). Those who did "reign in his place and stead were called by the people, second Nephi, third Nephi, and so on according to the reign of the kings" (Jacob 1:11). The record does not say whether his successors were or were not his sons or direct descendants.

Jesus Christ will reign as king in the millennium, and the political right to rule belongs to the tribe of Judah through which he was born. The Lord promised David, king of Israel, through the prophet Nathan: "And thine house and thy kingdom shall be established for ever before thee: and thy throne shall be established for ever" (2 Samuel

7:16). Christ will be the ultimate fulfillment of that prophecy. The Prophet Joseph Smith said: "the throne and kingdom of David" will be "given to another by the name of David in the last days, raised up out of his lineage" (*TPJS*, 339). This often controversial prophecy will also be fulfilled by Jesus Christ in the millennium.[2]

King Mosiah's, son of Benjamin, explanation of why another should not be appointed in his son's stead is well reasoned and self-explanatory. His final statement of these verses gives the basic purpose of government, and correlates well with Doctrine and Covenants 134:2. Mosiah, son of Benjamin, says the system of judges would bring peace to his people (Mosiah 29:10). Paul taught the same concept: "For kings, and *for* all that are in authority; that we may lead a quiet and peaceable life in all godliness and honesty" (1 Timothy 2:2).

Mosiah 29:11–15 • Better to Be Judged of God Than of Man

11 Therefore I will be your king the remainder of my days; nevertheless, let us appoint judges, to judge this people according to our law; and we will newly arrange the affairs of this people, for we will appoint wise men to be judges, that will judge this people according to the commandments of God.

12 Now it is better that a man should be judged of God than of man, for the judgments of God are always just, but the judgments of man are not always just.

13 Therefore, if it were possible that you could have just men to be your kings, who would establish the laws of God, and judge this people according to his commandments, yea, if ye could have men for your kings who would do even as my father Benjamin did for this people—I say unto you, if this could always be the case then it would be expedient that ye should always have kings to rule over you.

---

[2] For extensive scriptural evidence of Christ being the son of David to so rule see chapter 11 in Bruce R. McConkie, "The Lord is Our King," *The Promised Messiah* [1978].

14 And even I myself have labored with all the power and faculties which I have possessed, to teach you the commandments of God, and to establish peace throughout the land, that there should be no wars nor contentions, no stealing, nor plundering, nor murdering, nor any manner of iniquity;

15 And whosoever has committed iniquity, him have I punished according to the crime which he has committed, according to the law which has been given to us by our fathers.

Mosiah's proposal for a government to judge by the standard of the commandments of God rests upon choosing wise men as judges. In a revelation to the Prophet Joseph Smith, the Lord warned of choosing wicked men and then said:

9 Nevertheless, when the wicked rule the people mourn.

10 Wherefore, honest men and wise men should be sought for diligently, and good men and wise men ye should observe to uphold; otherwise whatsoever is less than these cometh of evil.

11 And I give unto you a commandment, that ye shall forsake all evil and cleave unto all good, that ye shall live by every word which proceedeth forth out of the mouth of God. [D&C 98:9–11]

The choosing of wise men must be combined with honest and good men. A man may be honest, but not intellectually capable of understanding the political ramifications of government. A man may be good in his personal standards, but lacking in wisdom to interact with the people. The lack of integrity leads to deceit and corruption. Evil men are influenced by Satan to lead the people astray. Thus, all three attributes; honesty, goodness, and wisdom are required to bring peace among the people.

Justice is a divine attribute of God, but is not always found in man. The guarantee of a just man being king is expedient because a king as leader is much more efficient. While democracy has checks and balances, it takes much longer than a system that operates on revelation and the commandments of God. The Lord has and will continue to reveal the principles for establishing and maintaining peace. Mosiah and his father Benjamin (vv. 13–15) are examples of a peaceful reign under righteous kings.

Mosiah 29:16–23 • Much Iniquity Caused By One Wicked King

16 Now I say unto you, that because all men are not just it is not expedient that ye should have a king or kings to rule over you.

17 For behold, how much iniquity doth one wicked king cause to be committed, yea, and what great destruction!

18 Yea, remember king Noah, his wickedness and his abominations, and also the wickedness and abominations of his people. Behold what great destruction did come upon them; and also because of their iniquities they were brought into bondage.

19 And were it not for the interposition of their all-wise Creator, and this because of their sincere repentance, they must unavoidably remain in bondage until now.

20 But behold, he did deliver them because they did humble themselves before him; and because they cried mightily unto him he did deliver them out of bondage; and thus doth the Lord work with his power in all cases among the children of men, extending the arm of mercy towards them that put their trust in him.

21 And behold, now I say unto you, ye cannot dethrone an iniquitous king save it be through much contention, and the shedding of much blood.

22 For behold, he has his friends in iniquity, and he keepeth his guards about him; and he teareth up the laws of those who have reigned in righteousness before him; and he trampleth under his feet the commandments of God;

23 And he enacteth laws, and sendeth them forth among his people, yea, laws after the manner of his own wickedness; and whosoever doth not obey his laws he causeth to be destroyed; and whosoever doth rebel against him he will send his armies against them to war, and if he can he will destroy them; and thus an unrighteous king doth pervert the ways of all righteousness.

The wickedness of King Noah's reign is well summarized into

two major points. First, his iniquity caused the people to be brought into bondage, and only through the wisdom and mercy of God were they delivered (vv. 18–20 compare 23:23). Second, it is difficult to dethrone a wicked king because of his friends in iniquity and power, and in his replacing the laws of God with Satan's laws that bind people in chains (vv. 21–23 compare 2 Nephi 28:19–22).

Mosiah 29:24–27 • Do Business By the Voice of the People

24 And now behold I say unto you, it is not expedient that such abominations should come upon you.

25 Therefore, choose you by the voice of this people, judges, that ye may be judged according to the laws which have been given you by our fathers, which are correct, and which were given them by the hand of the Lord.

26 Now it is not common that the voice of the people desireth anything contrary to that which is right; but it is common for the lesser part of the people to desire that which is not right; therefore this shall ye observe and make it your law—to do your business by the voice of the people.

27 And if the time comes that the voice of the people doth choose iniquity, then is the time that the judgments of God will come upon you; yea, then is the time he will visit you with great destruction even as he has hitherto visited this land.

The three conditions of the laws that were to govern the people through the judges (v. 25) may be equated with the United States Constitution. The laws to govern the Nephite people were passed from Nephi to his successors (see Jacob 1:9–11). First, the Constitution came down from the Founding Fathers.

4 And now, verily I say unto you concerning the laws of the land, it is my will that my people should observe to do all things whatsoever I command them.

5 And that law of the land which is constitutional, supporting that principle of freedom in maintaining rights and privileges, belongs to all mankind, and is justifiable before me.

> 6 Therefore, I, the Lord, justify you, and your brethren of my church, in befriending that law which is the constitutional law of the land; [D&C 98:4–6]

The laws of the Constitution were given for the moral agency of man.

> 77 According to the laws and constitution of the people, which I have suffered to be established, and should be maintained for the rights and protection of all flesh, according to just and holy principles;
>
> 78 That every man may act in doctrine and principle pertaining to futurity, according to the moral agency which I have given unto him, that every man may be accountable for his own sins in the day of judgment.
>
> 79 Therefore, it is not right that any man should be in bondage one to another. [D&C 101:77–79]

The second condition, the laws enacted by the fathers must be correct (Mosiah 29:25). The laws had been altered by King Noah (v. 23). Likewise, laws interpreting the Constitution (not following it) have changed its meaning since it was established, according to the revelations to Joseph Smith.

"And as pertaining to law of man, whatsoever is more or less than this, cometh of evil" (D&C 98:7), and "And again I say unto you, those who have been scattered by their enemies, it is my will that they should continue to importune for redress, and redemption, by the hands of those who are placed as rulers and are in authority over you" (D&C 101:76). The historical setting of both the above revelations shows they were given in answer to the unjust persecution upon the Saints, another parallel with the Nephites under Noah.

The third condition is that the laws had been given by revelation (Mosiah 29:25). The Nephites were "those who believed in the warnings and the revelation of God" given to Nephi (2 Nephi 5:6). Those who followed Mosiah I, father of King Benjamin, "were as many as would hearken unto the voice of the Lord" (Omni 1:12). King Benjamin, with the help of the prophets, "did once more establish peace in the land" (Words of Mormon 1:18).

Our Constitution came from God. "I, the Lord God, make you free, therefore ye are free indeed; and the law also maketh you free" (D&C 98:8). "And for this purpose have I established the Constitution of this land, by the hands of wise men whom I raised up unto this very purpose, and redeemed the land by the shedding of blood" (D&C 101:80).

To do business by the voice of the people does not necessarily mean by majority vote. As practiced in the Church today, the voice of the people comes through a sustaining vote, for those who have been chosen by revelation, given to those holding the keys of administration for the various units of the Church, and for the directions and admonitions given through both. Negative votes are listened to, and if there are valid reasons for not sustaining the person or the proposed direction, the action may be withdrawn. If the voting against is not for valid reasons, the action continues. Thus, the vote is according to the law "given them by the hand of the Lord" (Mosiah 29:25). "The elders are to receive their licenses from other elders, by vote of the church to which they belong, or from the conferences" (D&C 20:63). "And all things shall be done by common consent in the church, by much prayer and faith, for all things you shall receive by faith" (D&C 26:2).

The majority of the people are usually basically good and desire to follow the right way. "The right way is to believe in Christ, and deny him not" (2 Nephi 25:28–29). Only when the servants of Satan rule will the majority of the people choose iniquity, and then they face the judgments of God that will follow (Mosiah 29:27). The sad part is that many good people suffer because of the iniquity of others, but their reward will come in eternity.

Mosiah 29:28–32 • The System of Judges

28 And now if ye have judges, and they do not judge you according to the law which has been given, ye can cause that they may be judged of a higher judge.

29 If your higher judges do not judge righteous judgments, ye shall cause that a small number of your lower judges should be gathered together, and they shall judge your higher judges, according to the voice of the people.

30 And I command you to do these things in the fear of the Lord; and I command you to do these things, and that ye have no king; that if these people commit sins and iniquities they shall be answered upon their own heads.

31 For behold I say unto you, the sins of many people have been caused by the iniquities of their kings; therefore their iniquities are answered upon the heads of their kings.

32 And now I desire that this inequality should be no more in this land, especially among this my people; but I desire that this land be a land of liberty, and every man may enjoy his rights and privileges alike, so long as the Lord sees fit that we may live and inherit the land, yea, even as long as any of our posterity remains upon the face of the land.

The checks and balances of the higher judges correcting or sustaining the lower judges (v. 28), and a small number of lower judges correcting or sustaining a higher judge (v. 29) is also a part of the U. S. Constitution. The systems of appeals and sustaining or overruling decisions is used at all judicial levels.

In the Book of Mormon, the system of government was given by King Mosiah, son of Benjamin. He received these governing principles by revelation. The people being responsible for their sins and iniquities also suggests that the people were given a voice in sustaining or rejecting the king's commandments. Their casting of votes and rejoicing in their liberty (vv. 37–39) supports this suggestion. The concept of accountability and magnifying of one's office was discussed earlier (see Jacob 1:19 in chapter 1).

Mosiah 29:33–36 •The Rest of Mosiah's Message Summarized

33 And many more things did king Mosiah write unto them, unfolding unto them all the trials and troubles of a righteous king,

yea, all the travails of soul for their people, and also all the murmurings of the people to their king; and he explained it all unto them.

34 And he told them that these things ought not to be; but that the burden should come upon all the people, that every man might bear his part.

35 And he also unfolded unto them all the disadvantages they labored under, by having an unrighteous king to rule over them;

36 Yea, all his iniquities and abominations, and all the wars, and contentions, and bloodshed, and the stealing, and the plundering, and the committing of whoredoms, and all manner of iniquities which cannot be enumerated—telling them that these things ought not to be, that they were expressly repugnant to the commandments of God.

The summary of the rest of King Mosiah's epistle to his people undoubtedly contained many more principles and admonitions, but in Mormon's abridgment there is one principle of great importance. The burden of government should come upon all the people, and every man should bear his part (v. 34). It was to be of the people, by the people, and for the people. Again we are reminded of the Constitution of the United States. The description of the other things written by Mosiah, but not included by Mormon imply they were an extension of what had already been said (vv. 33, `35–36).

Mosiah 29:37–41 • Judges Are Appointed

37 And now it came to pass, after king Mosiah had sent these things forth among the people they were convinced of the truth of his words.

38 Therefore they relinquished their desires for a king, and became exceedingly anxious that every man should have an equal chance throughout all the land; yea, and every man expressed a willingness to answer for his own sins.

39 Therefore, it came to pass that they assembled themselves together in bodies throughout the land, to cast in their voices concerning who should be their judges, to judge them according to the law which had been given them; and they were exceedingly rejoiced

If you do become a victim of identity theft, here are the steps you should immediately take:

- Contact the financial institution immediately where the suspicious activity occurred to let them know of the incident and possible fraudulent activity.
- File a complaint with the Federal Trade Commission. Their Identity Theft Hotline can be reached, toll-free at (877) 438-4338. Any suspicious emails or calls should also be reported to the Federal Trade Commission.
- File a police report with your local police department.
- Notify your major creditors. Contact your credit card companies to check for fraudulent charges and to stop future charges.
- Place a fraud alert on your credit bureau reports and review your reports for any suspicious activity. You only need to contact one of the reporting agencies to place the alert on your report. That agency is required to notify the other agencies. The contact information for the credit bureaus is as follows:

Equifax Credit Information Services, Inc.
P.O. Box 740241
Atlanta, GA 30374
(888) 766-0008

TransUnion Fraud Victim Assistance Department
P.O. Box 6790
Fullerton, CA 92834
(800) 680-7289

Experian
475 Anton Blvd.
Costa Mesa, CA 92626
(714) 830-7000
(888) 397-3742

If you would like more information about identity theft, please contact:

Federal Trade Commission
Consumer Response Center
600 Pennsylvania Avenue NW
Washington, DC 20580
(877) FTC-HELP [877-382-4357]
www.ftc.gov click on Avoid ID Theft

⊔⊓ LPL Financial

Member FINRA/SIPC
DP-03705-0908

Avoiding Identity Theft

Identity theft is a serious crime, one that affects millions of Americans each year according to statistics published by the Federal Trade Commission (FTC).

Identity theft occurs when someone steals your personal information in order to commit fraud or other crimes such as opening credit in your name or using your information to make unauthorized purchases.

Unfortunately, anyone can be victimized and it can cost you hundreds of dollars and many hours of your time to repair the damage that can be done to your credit and your personal reputation. LPL Financial is committed to protect your privacy, but there are specific steps you can take to reduce your risk of identity theft.

- Shred all documents containing personal information before you discard them.
- Protect your Social Security number. Don't carry your Social Security card with you and do not provide it to anyone unless absolutely necessary.
- Keep your personal information in a secure place.
- Never click on unsolicited emails and do not provide passwords or personal information on sites that you do not know or look unfamiliar.
- Monitor your accounts and billing statements for any unusual activity and take immediate action when you spot it.
- Check your credit reports annually from all three major credit bureaus: Equifax, Experian, and TransUnion. Place fraud alerts on your credit report with the credit bureaus if you suspect suspicious activity.
- Close any accounts where suspicious activity has occurred or that are no longer active or being used by you.
- If you become a victim of identity theft, file a police report and report your incident to the Federal Trade Commission.

(Continued on reverse)

⌐┘ LPL Financial

because of the liberty which had been granted unto them.

40 And they did wax strong in love towards Mosiah; yea, they did esteem him more than any other man; for they did not look upon him as a tyrant who was seeking for gain, yea, for that lucre which doth corrupt the soul; for he had not exacted riches of them, neither had he delighted in the shedding of blood; but he had established peace in the land, and he had granted unto his people that they should be delivered from all manner of bondage; therefore they did esteem him, yea, exceedingly, beyond measure.

41 And it came to pass that they did appoint judges to rule over them, or to judge them according to the law; and this they did throughout all the land.

The people were given their agency in accepting King Mosiah's proposed government. It was indeed a government of freedom for the people (v. 39).

The love of the people for Mosiah, son of Benjamin, was well earned. Their esteem for him "more than any man" (v. 40) implies that they esteemed God above all. Mosiah's not seeking for lucre that corrupted the soul (v. 40) reminds us of problems in the biblical world. Samuel the Prophet appointed his sons as judges in Israel; but they "turned aside after lucre, and took bribes, and perverted judgment" (1 Samuel 8:3). Peter warned against "filthy lucre" (1 Peter 5:2), as did Paul who told Timothy that "the love of money is the root of all evil" (1 Timothy 3:3; 6:10).

Mosiah 29:42–47 • Alma, the First Chief Judge

42 And it came to pass that Alma was appointed to be the first chief judge, he being also the high priest, his father having conferred the office upon him, and having given him the charge concerning all the affairs of the church.

43 And now it came to pass that Alma did walk in the ways of the Lord, and he did keep his commandments, and he did judge righteous judgments; and there was continual peace through the land.

44 And thus commenced the reign of the judges throughout all

the land of Zarahemla, among all the people who were called the Nephites; and Alma was the first and chief judge.

45 And now it came to pass that his father died, being eighty and two years old, having lived to fulfil the commandments of God.

46 And it came to pass that Mosiah died also, in the thirty and third year of his reign, being sixty and three years old; making in the whole, five hundred and nine years from the time Lehi left Jerusalem.

47 And thus ended the reign of the kings over the people of Nephi; and thus ended the days of Alma, who was the founder of their church.

The church and state were still separate institutions although Alma was the head officer of both (v. 42). The account of his reign as chief judge and as the high priest of the church is given in the book of Alma. The death of Alma the elder, founder of the church, and of King Mosiah, son of Benjamin, were spoken of in the Historical Setting at the beginning of this chapter. Alma the elder had been the head of the church for about fifty-five years, from 147 to 91 B.C. (Mosiah 18:16–18; 29:45). Mosiah had been king for over thirty-two years, 124 to 91 B.C. (Mosiah 6:4; 29:45).

SACRED WRITING

Preaching (writing) which is sacred:
Mosiah 29:5–36   King Mosiah's epistle about government.

Revelation which is great:
Mosiah 28:2–4   The Spirit of the Lord working upon the sons of Mosiah.

Prophesying:
Mosiah 28:7   The Lord's promise to King Mosiah concerning his sons.

Doctrines Learned:

Mosiah 28:4   The Spirit of the Lord works upon people to accomplish the Lord's purposes.

Mosiah 28:14–15   The two stones (Urim and Thummim) were prepared from the beginning for the purpose of interpreting languages.

Mosiah 28:16   Those who possess the Urim and Thummim are called seers.

Mosiah 29:6   The office of king was hereditary under the Nephites.

Mosiah 29:11   Wise men should be appointed to judge the people by the commandments of God.

Mosiah 29:13   A king is the best system of government if the king is righteous.

Mosiah 29:25   The Lord has revealed laws periodically by which the people should be governed.

Mosiah 29:26–27   Governments should do their business by the voice of the people. When the people choose wrong, the judgments of God follows.

Mosiah 29:34   The burden of government should be upon all of the people.

General Authority Quotes

President Joseph Fielding Smith • Mosiah 28:11–16

We have no record of Lehi bringing with him to America the Urim and Thummim. The Lord did give to Lehi the *Liahona*, which was a ball which directed him the way he should go, and writing appeared on it from time to time, but this was not the Urim and Thummin.

King Mosiah possessed "two stones which were fastened into the two rims of a bow," called by the Nephites *Interpreters*, with which he translated the Jaredite record, and these were handed down from generation to generation for the purposes of interpreting languages. How Mosiah came into possession of these *two stones* or Urim and Thummin the record does not tell us, more than to say that it was a "*gift* from God." Mosiah had this gift or Urim and Thummim *before* the people of Lemhi discovered the record of Ether. They may have been received when the "large stone" was brought to Mosiah with engravings upon it, which he interpreted by the "gift and power of God." They may have been given to him, or to some other prophet before his day, just as the Brother of Jared received them—from the Lord. [*Doctrines of Salvation*, comp. Bruce R. McConkie, 3 vols. (1954–56), 3:223–224]

The Prophet Joseph Smith • Mosiah 29:25

"It is reasonable to suppose that man departed from the first teachings, or instructions which he received from heaven in the first age, and refused by his disobedience to be governed by them. Consequently, he formed such laws as best suited his own mind, or as he supposed, were best adapted to his situation. But that God has influenced man more or less since that time in the formation of law for His benefit we have no hesitancy in believing; for, as before remarked, being the source of all good, every just and equitable law was in a greater or less degree influenced by Him. And though man in his own supposed wisdom would not admit the influence of a power superior to his own, yet for wise and great purposes, for the good and happiness of His creatures, God has instructed man to form wise and wholesome laws, since he had departed from Him and refused to be governed by those laws which God had given by His own voice from on high in the beginning. But notwithstanding the transgression, by which man had cut himself off from an immediate intercourse with his Maker without a Mediator, it appears that the great and glorious plan of His redemption was previously provided; the sacrifice prepared; the atonement wrought out in the mind and purpose of God, even in the person of the Son, through whom man was now to look for acceptance and through whose merits he was now taught that he alone could find redemption, since the word had been pronounced, Unto dust thou shalt return. [*TPJS*, 57–58]

President J. Reuben Clark • Mosiah 29:35

" . . . In this Church, the power of 'nominating' or calling to office, is not in the body of the Church. This power is vested in the General Authorities of the Church, and in final analysis in the President of the Church who comes to his place under the guidance of inspired revelation. As a matter of fact, as our Articles of Faith—more or less the equivalent of the creeds of other Churches—declare:

'We believe that a man must be called of God, by prophecy, and by the laying on of hands, by those who are in authority to preach the Gospel and administer in the ordinances thereof.'

"When the presiding authority has so 'nominated' or chosen, or called any man to office, that man is then presented to the body of the Church to be sustained, in political language 'elected.'

"Thus the body of the Church has no calling or 'nominating' power, but only the sustaining, or politically speaking, the 'electing' power.

"When the presiding authority presents any man to the body of the Church to be sustained, the only power which the assembly has is to vote, by uplifted hand, either to sustain or not to sustain." [CR, Oct. 1940, 35]

The Prophet Joseph Smith • Mosiah 29:25

When Egypt was under the superintendence of Joseph it prospered, because he was taught of God: when they oppressed the Israelites, destruction came upon them. When the children of Israel were chosen with Moses at their head, they were to be a peculiar people, among whom God should place His name; their motto was: "The Lord is our lawgiver; the Lord is our Judge; the Lord is our King; and He shall reign over us." While in this state they might truly say, "Happy is that people, whose God is the Lord." Their government was a theocracy; they had God to make their laws, and men chosen by Him to administer them; He was their God, and they were His people. . . .

. . .The world has had a fair trial for six thousand years; the Lord will try the seventh thousand Himself; [*TPJS*, 252]

Elder Harold B. Lee • Mosiah 29

" . . . Follow scriptural guidelines in deciding whom to vote for. It is no uncommon thing, as we approach an election . . . , to have faithful members who will come and say, just like a sweet sister did down in California, 'Brother lee, who should we vote for in this coming election?' I can't think of more trouble I could get into than by answering as I would feel, but I said, 'I'll tell you who to vote for. You read the 134th section of the Doctrine and

Covenants, where the Lord has said to an inspired prophet, "We believe that all governments necessarily require civil officers and magistrates to enforce the laws of the same; and that such as will administer the law in equity and justice should be sought for and upheld by the voice of the people if a republic, or the will of the sovereign" (D&C 134:3).' I said, 'Now, that's your first guide. Then you turn to Mosiah, the 29th chapter, and read what King Mosiah advised concerning the voice of the majority of the people. The reason why we get into the hands of autocrats in politics is because many of us criticize and stay home and don't go to our district meetings. And we don't allow ourselves to become candidates, or representatives to vote for those who will represent us in the nation, or the county, or the state. 'Well,' I said, 'You read those two and then you pray about it. You'll know who to vote for' " [64–05]. [*Teachings of Harold B. Lee*, 367]

Challenges to Eternal Life

1. Study the issues and the candidates in the coming election and read Mosiah 29 as a preparation to vote (Mosiah 29).
2. Select a law of the land you have previously regarded as unimportant and relate it to the commandments of God to find out its purpose (Mosiah 29:25).
3. Make a commitment to share the burden of government by attending local meetings, voting, and serving as called upon (Mosiah 29:34).
4. Choose a challenge or message of your own from this reading and apply it to your life.

Scripture Index

OLD TESTAMENT

NEW TESTAMENT

BOOK OF MORMON

Jacob	(cont.)	**PAGE**
2:17		26, 41, 45
2:17–19		25, 252
2:18		26
2:19		27, 45
2:20–21		28
2:21		29
2:22–26		29
2:22–33		9
2:23		30
2:24		30
2:25		32, 40
2:27		41
2:27–28		309
2:27–30		32
2:28		41, 43, 45
2:30		31, 33, 41, 45, 309
2:31–35		34
2:34–35		10
2:35		35
3:1		37
3:1–2		6, 10, 45
3:1–4		36
3:3–11		10
3:4		157
3:5–11		38
3:6		41
3:7		45
3:9		41
3:10		41
3:12–14		11, 40
3:13		2
4:1–2		2
4:1–3		56
4:1–12		48
4:3		47
4:3–12		101
4:4		101, 116
4:4–5		58, 97
4:5		59, 60, 101, 217
4:6		101, 114
4:6–10		60
4–6		12, 47, 48
4:7		62
4:8		47, 62, 101, 248
4:9		62, 102

Jacob	(cont.)	**PAGE**
4:10		47, 103
4:11		47
4:11–12		62
4:12		64
4:13		65, 101
4:13–18		49, 64, 101
4:14		66, 103
4:17–18		66
4:19		57
5		47, 67, 99, 101, 102
5:1–2		50, 71
5:3		69
5:3–6		72
5:3–14		50, 72
5:6		73
5:7–14		74
5:15		77
5:15–28		50
5:15, 29		72
5:16–18		78
5:16–28		77
5:19–28		79
5:23		80
5:25		81
5:26		81
5:26–28		81
5:29		81
5:29–69		51
5:30–37		82
5:30–75		81
5:32		83
5:38–50		84
5:39		77
5:43		86
5:44		86
5:47–48		87
5:51–60		87
5:54		77
5:57–60		90
5:61–74		90
5:63		92
5:69		93
5:74		94
5:77		69, 70, 95
5:70–71		93

DOCTRINE AND COVENANTS

PEARL OF GREAT PRICE

Topical Index

Searching the prophets, 61

Second Comforter, 130, 131, 135, 479, 480

Second death, 11, 39, 40

Seed of Christ, 369

Similitude, 58, 60

Sin

definition of, 205

Smith, Joseph, 11, 22, 27, 30, 63, 67, 69, 71, 81, 83, 84, 100–102, 121, 128, 133, 135, 145, 148–150, 155, 157, 164, 170, 174, 192, 225, 230, 245, 247, 248, 258, 288, 300, 338, 353, 356, 371, 382, 384, 387, 399, 401, 417, 456, 481, 483, 487, 493, 510, 511, 514, 515, 523

Lectures on Faith, 245, 247

Teachings of the Prophet Joseph Smith, 33, 57, 62, 67, 69, 93, 102, 116, 117, 132–134, 203, 208, 224, 228, 247, 251, 258, 280, 300, 333, 334, 338, 353, 401, 418, 478, 480, 489, 510, 512, 519, 530, 531

the prophet, 22, 33, 57, 69, 116, 133, 203, 207, 220, 251, 279, 290, 333, 371, 399, 418, 470, 479, 480, 489, 493, 512, 519, 520, 530, 531

Smith, Joseph F., 43, 90, 410

Gospel Doctrine, (book) 43, 90, 410

Smith, Joseph Fielding, 18, 19, 31, 67, 69, 102, 103, 131, 135, 210, 233, 264, 340, 378, 388, 407, 418, 471, 529

Answers to Gospel Questions, (book) 19, 32, 67, 70, 102, 407, 409, 471

Doctrines of Salvation, (book) 19, 136, 234, 341, 378, 530

Successful marriage, 314

—T—

Talmage, James E.

Articles of Faith, The (book), 388

Tame olive tree, 50, 69, 72, 73, 75, 76, 78

The Family, A Proclamation to the World,

309, 314

Traditions of their fathers, 191, 229, 296, 307, 463, 476

True peace, 369

Truth, 27, 45, 49, 64, 66, 67, 108, 134, 192, 218, 279, 280, 334, 339, 376, 393, 397, 399, 401, 416, 467, 470, 490, 506

definition of, 65

Twelve Apostles, 309, 314, 515

—U—

Unpardonable sin, 108, 118, 133, 134, 207

Urim and Thummim, 164, 287, 288, 290, 456, 514, 515, 529

—V—

Voice of the people, 194, 269, 273, 274, 422, 446, 501, 502, 504–506, 517, 522, 524, 525, 529, 532

—W—

West wind, 282

Whitmer, David, 93

Wild olive tree, 50, 69, 70

Works of Ixtlilxochitl, 166

—Y—

Young, Brigham, 45, 71, 234, 314, 401, 417, 511

Discourses of Brigham Young, (book) 45, 235, 417

—Z—

Zarahemla, 142, 174, 178, 197, 269, 271, 274, 286, 287, 294, 298, 427, 446, 448, 456

land of, 142, 143, 156, 157, 164, 167, 168, 173, 177, 187, 195, 196, 210, 267–269, 271–274, 284–286, 293, 299, 409, 419, 425–427, 431, 443,